International Management

We work with leading authors to develop the
strongest educational materials in management, bringing
cutting-edge thinking and best learning practice to a
global market.

Under a range of well-known imprints, including
Financial Times Prentice Hall, we craft high quality print and
electronic publications which help readers to understand
and apply their content, whether studying or at work.

To find out more about the complete range of our
publishing, please visit us on the World Wide Web at:
www.pearsoneduc.com

International Management
Theories and Practices

Edited by Monir Tayeb

 Prentice Hall
FINANCIAL TIMES

An imprint of **Pearson Education**
Harlow, England • London • New York • Boston • San Francisco • Toronto • Sydney • Singapore • Hong Kong
Tokyo • Seoul • Taipei • New Delhi • Cape Town • Madrid • Mexico City • Amsterdam • Munich • Paris • Milan

Pearson Education Limited
Edinburgh Gate
Harlow
Essex CM20 2JE
United Kingdom

and Associated Companies throughout the world

Visit us on the World Wide Web at:
www.pearsoneduc.com

───────────────────────────

First published 2003

© Pearson Education Limited 2003

ISBN 0 273 65127 7

British Library Cataloguing-in-Publication Data
A catalogue record for this book is available from the British Library

Library of Congress Cataloguing-in-Publication Data

10 9 8 7 6 5 4 3 2 1
08 07 06 05 04 03

Typeset by 3 in Stone Sans 9.5/12pt
Printed and bound by Ashford Colour Press Ltd., Gosport

Contents

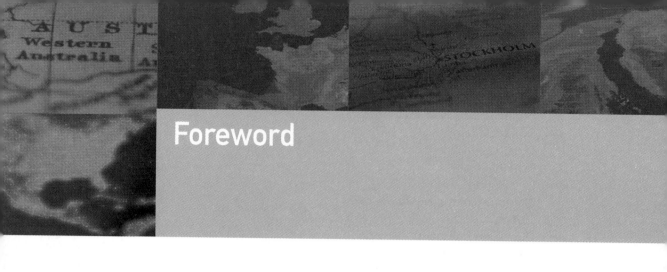

Foreword

We are all internationalists now. We might be employed by multinational corporations, export to any country in the world, or work alongside ethnic minority colleagues. And, of course, we all consume products from all over the world. So we need to understand whether the working practices of people and organisations in one culture are anything like those in another. How far and in what ways are they different? Further, are these differences converging and so becoming less important, or do they remain major barriers which must be understood and coped with continually? (Cf. Hickson and Pugh, 2002, which discusses the distinctive cultures of the seven major cultural groupings around the world with illustrations of their impact on management practices in 21 example countries.)

This present volume, however, focuses specifically on such key topics in international management as strategic planning in a multinational environment, communication and negotiation across borders, selling and marketing in various countries, e-commerce, cross-culturally different and challenging ethical systems and practices, and the effective supervision of expatriate managers. These are all powerful and confronting issues which are among those which must be understood and grappled with by managers in today's internationally shrinking world.

I therefore welcome this important book in which Dr Monir Tayeb has brought together the contributions of a number of scholars who have examined cultural differences and their impact on organisational functioning. They present their findings in an accessible way, well illustrated by contemporary case studies. It makes a distinctive contribution to the literature of the subject, and will be of use to all managers and students of management.

Professor Derek S. Pugh AcSS
Emeritus Professor of International Management
Open University Business School

Reference

Hickson, D. J. and Pugh, D. S. (2002) *Management Worldwide: Distinctive Styles Amid Globalization*, 2nd edn. Harmondsworth: Penguin.

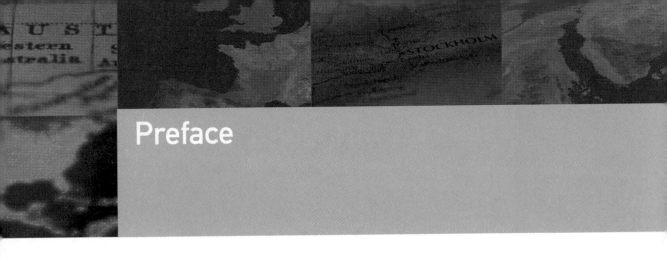

Preface

This book is the outcome of a joint project between a group of academic researchers and teachers and a publishing team. All chapters and long case studies in the book and on its website have been written by invitation specifically for this book by authors who are all experts in their field and have a wide range of teaching, research and professional experiences in various parts of the world. I should like to take this opportunity to express my gratitude to them for their total dedication and commitment.

I am also grateful to the staff at Pearson Education who were involved in the management and production of this book, notably Tina Cadle-Bowman, Stuart Hay, Angela Hawksbee, Sadie McClelland, Liz Sproat, and Martin Sugden for their generous support and advice whenever I needed them. Penelope Allport handled the copy editing with exemplary efficiency and professionalism.

My special thanks go to the panel of reviewers for their constructive comments and helpful suggestions on an earlier draft from which the book has greatly benefited.

Monir Tayeb
Heriot-Watt University
Edinburgh

May 2002

List of contributors

Cordula Barzantny is an Associate Professor in international and cross-cultural management at Groupe ESC Toulouse Business School, France, where she lectures regularly to MBA and executive classes on international and European management. Her main research interests are multicultural teams and workgroup diversity, culture change and the sharing of knowledge in international organisations. With these topics she conceives corporate executive development programmes and works on various consulting, coaching and training assignments with multinational corporations.

Contact address: Groupe ESC Toulouse Business School, 20, bd Lascrosses, BP 7010 F-31068 Toulouse Cedex 7, France. E-mail: c.barzantny@esc-toulouse.fr. Web: www.esc-toulouse.fr

Jaime Bonache is Professor of Human Resource Management at the University of Carlos III of Madrid in Spain. Professor Bonache's research interests are in the areas of international management development, expatriate management and cross-cultural management. His research work has been published in journals such as the *International Journal of Human Resource Management, Human Resource Planning, Human Resource Management Journal,* and *Economia Industrial.* He has participated in a number of European and Spanish research projects in the area of international human resource management.

Contact address: Facultad Ciencias Sociales y Jurídicas, Dept. de Economía de la Empresa, Universidad Carlos III de Madrid, 28903 Getafe (Madrid), Spain. E-mail: bonache@emp.uc3m.es

Pawan S. Budhwar is a Senior Lecturer in OB and HRM at Cardiff Business School, UK. He has been conducting research in IHRM since 1993. His current interests are in the fields of HRM and firm's performance, leadership, HRM in developing countries and transfer of HRM from headquarters of MNCs to subsidiaries located in India. His publications include several articles in academic journals, two books and contributions to edited books.

Contact address: Cardiff Business School, Colum Drive, Cardiff CF10 3EU, UK. E-mail: Budhwar@cardiff.ac.uk

Julio Cerviño is Professor of International Marketing at University Carlos III of Madrid. He has been conducting research in international business and management of Spanish corporations abroad, especially in Latin America. His current interest is in the area of international transfer of best practices and the relationship between country image, company/employees' image and brand management overseas. His publications include several articles in academic journals, books and contributions to edited books. His most recent book, *International Brands: How to Build and Manage Them* (Piramide, Madrid), was published in 2002. He is a visiting professor in several Latin American universities. He has worked in the area of international business in companies such as McDonnell Douglas Corporation (USA), Caterpillar Tractor Co. (USA) and Maritz Ltd (Madrid).

Contact address: Facuttad Ciencias Sociales y Jurídicas, Dept. de Economía de la Empresa, Universidad Carlos III de Madrid, 28903 Getafe (Madrid), Spain. E-mail: jcervino@emp.uc3m.es

Brian M. W. Clements is a Senior Lecturer in strategic and international management at the University of Sunderland. He lectures in international business strategy, logistics strategy and e-commerce. His current research is in the strategic effects of the introduction of e-commerce on international logistics. He is developing an academic career based on 30 years' experience working in logistics, shipping and international trade for several international enterprises, for the last 15 years as managing director/CEO or at board level.

Contact address: University of Sunderland.

Angelica C. Cortes is an Assistant Professor at the University of Texas Pan-American. Her research interest has been in cross-cultural marketing and management from 1989, with an emphasis on the importance of culture and its effects on international business. Her publications include several articles in academic journals, contributions to edited books and conference proceedings.

Contact address: College of Business at University of Texas Pan-American, Edinburgh, Texas 78539, USA. E-mail: Cortesa@panam.edu

Simon Denny is Lead Trainer at Sunley Management Centre, University College Northampton. He has been conducting research into cross-cultural studies of training and development since 1994. His current research is in the training and development practices of foreign-owned heavy truck importers based in the UK.

Contact address: Sunley Management Centre, University College Northampton, Boughton Green Road, Northampton NN2 7AL, UK. E-mail: Simon.Denny@northampton.ac.uk

Anna Marie Dyhr Ulrich is a doctoral researcher at the Department of Marketing, University of Southern Denmark. Her current interest is in international strategic alliances, practices in how to reduce the distance to an alliance partner and cross-cultural issues. Her publications includes articles in edited books and contributions to conferences.

Contact address: University of Southern Denmark, Grundtvigs Alle 150, DK-6400 Sønderborg, Denmark. E-mail: adu@sam.sdu.dk. Web: www.sdu.dk

Alan Feely entered academic life only after retiring in 1999 having accumulated 30 years of experience in international management, often working in culturally and linguistically challenging environments. He is currently undertaking research into the strategic and operational consequences of cultural and linguistic diversity in multinational companies and has authored articles discussing the way in which the language barrier operates and the options open to companies in the way they choose to manage language. He has also collaborated on the second phase development of the linguistic auditing methodology.

Contact address: Aston Business School, Aston University, Birmingham B4 7ET, UK. E-mail: feelyaj@aston.ac.uk

Rajen K. Gupta is a Professor at the Management Development Institute, Gurgaon, India. He has been involved in the research activities related to cross-cultural management and organisation design and development. His publications include books and 40 research papers in various international and Indian academic journals.

Contact address: Human Behaviour and Organisational Development, Management Development Institute, Gurgaon 122 001, India. E-mail: rgupta@mdi.ac.in

Wes Harry has held senior Human Resources Manager positions in airlines and banks in South East Asia and the Middle East, often being the only non-national to hold particular positions in locally owned organisations. Currently he is Head of Human Resources in a major Islamic bank. In addition to his activities as a businessman, he continues to undertake academic research, particularly in the areas of localisation (replacing expatriates with host country nationals) and transnational managers (international managers not tied to a particular employer).

UK contact address: Dr Wes Harry, 23 Red Road, Borehamwood WD6 4SR, UK. E-mail: wesharry@hotmail.com

Svend Hollensen is an Associate Professor in marketing at the University of Southern Denmark. His current research interests are in international marketing and strategic alliances. He has authored two books on marketing and marketing management.

Contact address: University of Southern Denmark, Grundtvigs Alle 150, DK-6400 Sønderborg, Denmark. E-mail: svend@sam.sdu.dk

Lin Lerpold is a doctoral researcher at the Institute of International Business, Stockholm School of Economics, Sweden. She has conducted research in alliance management since 1994 and has taught alliance and strategic management to graduate and executive students in Scandinavia. Her current research deals with linking alliance motivation to organisational identity adaptation. Her writings include articles in business journals, edited books and international academic conferences.

Contact address: Institute of International Business, Stockholm School of Economics, Box 6501, SE-113 83 Stockholm, Sweden. E-mail: Lin.Lerpold@hhs.se. Web: www.iib.edu

Geoff Mallory is a Lecturer in strategy at the Open University Business School, UK. He has recently been a Visiting Professor at Groupe ESSEC in Paris and at the Eric Sprott School of Business, Carleton University Ottawa, Canada. His research interests include strategy for international and multibusiness organisations and the impact of national culture on the role of managers in international organisations. His publications include books, numerous journal articles and contributions to edited books and collections. He is currently working on a new book about global dimensions of culture.

Contact address: School of Business, The Open University, Walton Hall, Milton Keynes MK7 6AA, UK. E-mail: G.R.Mallory@open.ac.uk

Kamel Mellahi is a Lecturer in strategic management at Loughborough University Business School, England, UK. His research interests include global strategic management, business ethics and management in Arab countries.

Contact address: Loughborough University Business School, Loughborough LE11 3TU, UK. E-mail: K.Mellahi@lboro.ac.uk

Abinash Panda is a doctoral researcher at the Management Development Institute in the area of human behaviour and organisational development. His areas of interest are cross-cultural management and organisational culture. Before joining the doctoral programme he worked in the industry for seven years. He has already published several research papers in academic journals.

E-mail: abinash@mdi.ac.in

Monir Tayeb is a Reader at Heriot-Watt University, Edinburgh. She has been teaching and conducting research in cross-cultural studies of organisation since 1976. Her current interest is in the human resource management policies and practices of foreign multinational companies located in Scotland. Her publications include several articles in academic journals, books and contributions to edited books.

Contact address: School of Management, Heriot-Watt University, Edinburgh EH14 4AS, Scotland. E-mail: m.h.tayeb@hw.ac.uk. Web: www.som.hw.ac.uk/busmt

Lena Zander is an Assistant Professor at the Institute of International Business, Stockholm School of Economics, Sweden. She has been teaching and conducting research in cross-cultural management since 1990. Her current research interests include managing post-acquisition integration processes, multicultural teams and developing theory within cross-cultural management. Her publications include contributions to edited books and articles in academic journals.

Contact address: Institute of International Business, Stockholm School of Economics, Box 6501, SE-113 83 Stockholm, Sweden. E-mail: lena.zander@hhs.se. Web: www.iib.edu

Acknowledgements

We are grateful to the following to reproduce copyright material:

Figure 7.4 adapted from 'Making mergers and acquisitions work: strategic and psychological preparation', *Academy of Management Executive* 15(2): 80–92, Academy of Management (Marks, M.L. and Miruis, P.H., 2001). Republished with permission, conveyed through Copyright Clearance Center Inc.

Financial Times: Ch. 1 opening case study, 23 Sep. 2000 in FT CD-ROM, 2000; Ch. 2 opening case study, 09 Oct. 2000 in FT CD-ROM, 2000; Ch. 2 closing case study, 29 Dec. 2000 in FT CD-ROM 2000; Ch. 4 opening case study, 11 May 2000 in FT CD-ROM, 2000; Ch. 5 opening case study, 13 Dec. 2000 in FT CD-ROM, 2000; Ch. 6 opening case study, 21 Oct. 2000 in FT CD-ROM, 2000; Ch. 7 opening case study, 19 Sep. 2000 in FT CD-ROM 2000; Ch. 8 opening case study, 6 Dec. 2000 in FT CD-ROM 2000; Ch. 9 opening case study, 12 Dec. 2000 in FT CD-ROM 2000; Ch. 10 opening case study, 28 Sep. 2000 'Cultural barriers: Sergey Frank analyses the communication and language difficulties when doing business in post-communist Poland'. Sergey Frank is a German trained lawyer, a partner of Kienbaum Executive Consultants and managing director of the London office of the Kienbaum Group. He is an author and speaker on international communication issues. Reproduced by permission of Sergey Frank, appeared in FT CD-ROM 2000; Ch. 11 opening case study, 13 Dec. 2000 in FT CD-ROM 2000; Ch. 12 opening case study in FT CD-ROM 2000; Ch. 13 opening case study 02 Dec. 2000 in FT CD-ROM 2000.

Case studies: Dandy Chewing Gum – development of the Dandy-KGFF relation reprinted with permission from Holger Bagger-Sørensen, Dandy A/S, Dandyvej 19, 7100 Vejle, Denmark; Fenix: European management revisited, reprinted with permission of Philippe Cavalié.

In some instances we have been unable to trace the owners of copyright material, and we would appreciate any information that would enable us to do so.

Website

A supplement download website accompanies *International Management* edited by Monir Tayeb, which can be accessed at www.booksites.net/tayeb.

PART 1

Setting the scene

Introduction

Monir Tayeb

Quelle verité est-ce que ces montaignes bornent mensonge au monde qui se tient au delà?

What truth do these mountains hide that is considered a lie on the other side?

(Essays by Michel de Montaigne, French philosopher, 1533–1592)

Montaigne, the great French philosopher and thinker, here insightfully identifies the principal difficulty facing all students of culture – who is the arbiter of truth about any phenomenon? When a German manager believes that his opinion is best, who is to say that that of a French or Spanish manager is better? As Segalla (1998) would imply, in today's world questions such as these have taken on much more than philosophical implications. Multinational companies operating around the world are faced with integrating many value systems into an organisational framework that not only can survive but also effectively compete in tough markets.

The aim of this book is to provide an introduction to the complexities of international management by examining how socio-cultural differences, and our understanding of these, affect all aspects of management. The influence of culture is examined at all levels of an organisation, from strategic planning to managing expatriate employees, from negotiating with people from different countries to deciding on training programmes in subsidiaries scattered around the world, from selling goods and services on the internet, to dealing with the delicate issue of business ethics.

Culture is often narrowly perceived and defined variously as meaning 'cultured' (educated or well-bred), nationally determined or something that 'others' possess (i.e. what makes them different). Within management the subject has also attracted criticisms of oversimplification and stereotyping. For these reasons this book begins by exploring and defining the notion of culture in its many forms. The book moreover adopts a broad definition of national culture encompassing institutional as well as attitudinal aspects.

However, as you will note throughout the book, international management is more than just management of cultural differences. There are many non-cultural factors that managers of international and global companies have to consider in all their strategic and operative decisions and activities. Consequently, the present book discusses the significant role of these factors as well.

Figure I.1 shows how the 14 chapters of the book present and discuss various issues from the origins of national culture to the world of the international manager who has to deal with a multitude of managerial matters and cope with many challenges within a complex multicultural world.

Plan of the book

The book consists of 5 parts divided into 14 chapters, each of which deals with a major topic of international management. Each chapter starts with a learning objective section and an opening case study, and ends with a summary, followed by a closing case study and an annotated recommended further reading as well as reference list. The cases studies are based on real-life examples of a company or a management-related issue or event and demonstrate the practical implications of theoretical models and arguments under discussion. There is a final long case study, which forms Chapter 14 and integrates the main themes covered throughout the book. There are also discussion questions related to the main text of each chapter and its closing case study. These are intended to encourage you to assess your understanding of various theories covered in the relevant chapters and apply them to real-life management situations.

Part I

Part 1 consists of five chapters and sets the scene by discussing the socio-cultural world within which multinational and global firms operate. Chapter 1 focuses on the ways in which national culture comes about through major primary and secondary institutions, while discussing also other factors which have significant bearings on the cultural make-up of a nation. Chapter 2 explores how major national and international institutions might contribute to the creation of national culture and also influence business activities of companies.

Chapter 3 concentrates on major cultural values, attitudes and other characteristics that people may hold and explores briefly their implications for workplace behaviours. Chapters 4 and 5 will then examine the issue of national culture and workplace behaviours further with a special reference, respectively, to a major European multinational company and a group of emerging countries in the Persian Gulf region.

Part 2

Part 2 consists of Chapters 6, 7 and 8, which discuss some of the main issues involved in going international. This part does not cover such international business topics as theories and modes of internationalisation. These have been extensively covered in another book edited by the present author, *International Business*

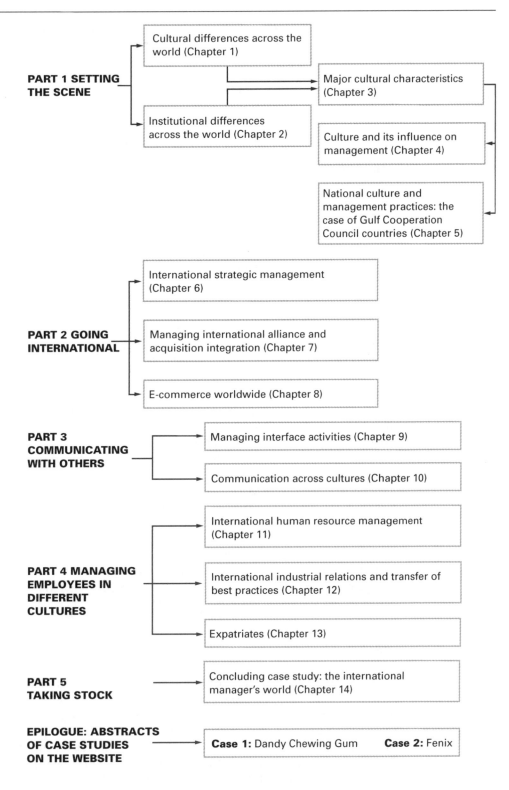

Figure I.1 Plan of the book

– Theories, Policies and Practices (2000, Pearson Education). Instead, it concentrates on three other international management topics which are either not covered at all or not in sufficient depth in textbooks on international management.

Chapter 6 focuses on international strategic management and starts off by defining strategy and exploring how companies devise their strategies. It then discusses the ways in which national culture can impact on strategy. Chapter 7 concerns the management of firms which have made a strategic choice to go international through either buying a company located in a different country or merging with one. The chapter focuses specifically on how such firms effectively manage their cultural integration and what challenges they face in the process.

In recent years the internet has provided enormous opportunities for companies of all sizes and forms, and its strategic and operative significance cannot be overestimated. In particular, firms with international and global interests are ideally placed to take advantage of the internet's potential and actual opportunities. Chapter 8 explores in detail all the major issues involved in e-business from a worldwide perspective.

Part 3

Part 3 continues with the theme of going international and focuses on how companies communicate with people and organisations from different national backgrounds than their own. Chapter 9 presents the interfacing of companies with government, customers, suppliers and the like and discusses the cultural issues that are intertwined in the process. The chapter ends with a discussion of the delicate balance of maintaining an ethical corporate policy across the countries in which a firm has operations.

Chapter 10 moves the discussion to the complexities involved in communication between people whose native languages are different from one another, a process which is prone to misunderstanding and misinterpretation if not handled carefully by the parties concerned. Whereas such misunderstandings would be relatively harmless if one is a tourist visiting someone else's country, in business negotiations they could have disastrous consequences.

Up to this point, the book deals with the *external* environment of the international firm: institutions, organisations and people who are not part of the firm but provide the context of its activities, supply its raw materials, provide the services it needs and buy its products or services.

Part 4

Part 4 takes the flow of the discussion 'into' the firm and focuses on its *internal* activities. At this level, national culture shows its highest influence and impact on the management–employee relationships in general and the management of human resources in particular. Chapter 11 starts with a general discussion of developments in the field of human resource management (HRM) and then moves on to highlight some of the key issues related to the topic of international HRM from the perspective of multinational companies.

Chapter 12 focuses on some of the national contextual elements, notably government legislation and culture, which could help or hinder the successful implementation of the so-called 'best practices' which, some argue, are associated with high performance everywhere regardless of national differences.

For various reasons most multinational and global companies dispatch expatriates from their home base to their subsidiaries located in different parts of the world. The effective management of these expatriates is a major challenge. Chapter 13 focuses specifically on expatriates and the challenges they pose to their employers.

Part 5

Part 5 provides a fitting conclusion to the book with Chapter 14, which brings together all the main issues and topics discussed within the framework of a long case study. The case is 'located' in the Middle East, but similar situations to those described arise in other parts of the world as well.

Finally, the book also has a supplement download website for use by students and their teachers throughout the world which can be accessed at www.booksites.net/tayeb. At the time of writing, the site offers, among other things, two real-life European case studies, one concerning a cross-border alliance and the other a cross-border acquisition. The cases examine different managerial issues but have in common multicultural, multinational settings. The abstracts of these two cases are in the book, in the Epilogue.

Reference

Segalla, M. (1998) 'National cultures, international business', *Financial Times*, 7 March. Survey section.

CHAPTER 1

Cultural differences across the world

Monir Tayeb

Learning objectives

When you finish reading this chapter you should:

■ know what culture is and distinguish between culture as it is popularly understood and the anthropological notion of culture

■ be able to make a distinction between nation state and culture

■ learn about the origins of national culture in major natural phenomena, historical events and societal institutions

■ know about cultural influences on people's values and attitudes

■ learn about non-cultural influences on people's values and attitudes

Opening Case Study:
Good at camping: how the land Down Under grew up

Journalists are among Australia's best exports: Robert Hughes, Clive James, John Pilger, to name a few. Phillip Knightley is a less flashy version of the breed, a reporter who has spent a long career as a spy specialist probing the soft underbellies of states and individuals. Now he turns his forensic scepticism on his native land, and himself as one of its products. He was born, a generation after the six Australian states federated, into a family predominantly English Protestant with an Irish Catholic mix. His 'biography' covers the century of Australian nationhood from 1901, charting the changes wrought on that old, divided Anglo-Celtic world from within and without.

He begins with questions. Is there such a thing as Homo Australiensis? If so, how did he and she come about? Did the land make them? The answer is surprising. Not so much the land itself, but a geographic isolation that brought populations and cultures into unexpected interaction – Aborigines, British and Irish convicts and their overseers, post-war refugees and Asian boat people – creating a society with its own peculiar way of doing things.

Knightley notices, for instance, how Aboriginal behaviour has been borrowed by white Australians, who paint their faces for ceremonial events like cricket matches, go barefoot in business class, and like to sear their meat on the end of a stick. The author offers his thesis lightly, via an anecdote from Ryszard Kapuscinski, the Polish chronicler of Soviet communism. If the twentieth century witnessed an argument between conflicting ideologies in which American-style capitalism won out, was there nowhere that found a middle way? 'Yes,' answers Kapuscinski, 'it's called Australia.'

Knightley analyses Australian history in terms of the continuously redefined relationship between an anxiously independent nation and the Mother Country. He is at his best when he uses new material to revisit controversial landmarks, such as the role of Australians fighting with Britain in the Great War and the fall of Singapore in 1942, which shocked Australia into seeking a new protector in the United States. Domestically he focuses on the tension between progressive nationalists and those whose interests were served by looking after Britain's. There are fascinating chapters on how left-leaning movements were outmanoeuvred by an opaque Anglo-Australian ascendancy – by covert McCarthyite moves against communist sympathisers in the 1950s and in the sacking of the reformist Whitlam government by the Governor-General in 1975.

Knightley lards his account with diverting comments from witnesses, mostly fellow journalists. Why do Australians make such good correspondents, especially in war? An answer comes from one of the best, Murray Sayle: 'It's because Australians are good at camping.' They are adaptable. These nifty, or shifty, qualities extend to other areas of national life – in the way the bodyline bowling dispute in the 1932–33 test series between England and Australia was settled, or the way homophobic New South Wales has come to host the world's biggest gay party, or the way Pauline Hanson has held the present Howard government to ransom with her minority populist agenda. Adaptability is what Australia's leaders need in spades. As former prime minister Paul Keating put it: 'When a small nation has inherited a Garden of Eden, your footwork has got to be exemplary.'

'Who's your best mate?' The question put at an Australian dinner party apparently results in most women naming their husband and most men naming a male friend. Knightley prefers collectivism to mateship as a defining Australian quality, quoting cricket captain Mark Taylor, who could accept playing badly himself as long as the team won: 'I was a loser personally, but the team was winning. What better lesson can you get for living than that?' Such collectivism is probably adapted from the Aborigines too. It's how a wandering tribe survives.

Source: 23 Sep. 2000, *Financial Times* CD-ROM 2000

Introduction

This chapter focuses on the ways in which national culture comes about through major primary and secondary institutions, while discussing also other factors which have significant bearings on the cultural make-up of a nation. These include factors such as geographical location of a country and its climatic conditions, historical events and ups and downs that a nation may collectively experience over centuries. The chapter points out the ways in which values and attitudes of people reflect their national culture. At the same time, it is argued that there are various non-cultural factors which create variations in people's values, attitudes and behaviours at regional, community and personal levels.

Definition of culture

'Culture' is very hard to define because of its woolliness as a concept. What is more, there is no single definition on which most people can agree. There are almost as many definitions of culture as there are writers and researchers, in various disciplines, who have written on the subject. To give a taste of the controversy which has surrounded the issue: some researchers argue that culture is something that a group of people *has*, and others assert that culture is something that a group of people *is*. In addition, there are scholars who define culture in terms of what it *is* and those who define it as what it *is not*. Consequently, culture to some researchers *is* some combination of norms, values, feelings, thinking, roles, rules, behaviour, beliefs, attitudes, expectations, meanings and so on. To others, culture *is not* economics, politics, law, religion, language, education, technology, industrial environment, society or the market.

It is however important to note that the discussion of whether culture is something people *are* (social construction perspective) or *have* (critical variable perspective) – or both – is essentially a paradigmatic one. For example, in a social construction perspective, culture is something organisations *are*. Culture gives greater understanding, culture is supposed to explain behaviour and culture can be useful in generating knowledge. In a critical variable perspective culture is something that organisations *have*. Culture is a management tool and can be used for guiding behaviour. Finally, culture can be used for generating knowledge or for solving problems. However, it might be useful to perceive culture as something that organisations both *are* as well as *have* since you need to have an understanding of what culture is before you can use it as a management tool. You also need to generate knowledge about what cultural problems can arise before you can solve them. This understanding may be useful for example in cross-border acquisitions.

In the present chapter, culture is defined as historically evolved values, attitudes and meanings that are learned and shared by the members of a given community, and which influence their material and non-material way of life. Members of the community learn these shared characteristics through different stages of the socialisation processes within institutions such as family, religion, formal education and society as a whole.

This is not to say that all members of a community think and behave the same way or hold the same values and attitudes. There are, of course, as we shall see later in the chapter, variations among people from the same community or even the same family. However, any given culture constitutes a recognisable whole, a discernible general pattern of values, attitudes and behaviours, which may differ from another recognisable whole in another place or time in significant ways (Tayeb, 1988). In other words, in any culture one can distinguish between individual variations and the dominant general pattern. For instance, although not all

Indians are alike, one can always tell an Indian person from, say, a person from Sweden, not only by their physical differences, but also by the differences in their world views and other invisible attributes.

Defined like this, a 'culture' which is distinguishable from another can be any formal or informal grouping of people: nation, industry, corporation, department, a class of university students attending a course in international management in their final year. In fact, any two or more people who engage in and sustain a relationship over a length of time would develop their own culture with its own unique recognisable features. The focus of this chapter is of course the *national* culture, hereafter referred to simply as culture. There are a few important points about culture and its scope which should be borne in mind.

1. The differences between cultures are in many cases of degree, not of kind. For instance, sexual discrimination against women is a socio-cultural characteristic common to almost all societies. However, the extent of this discrimination varies from one society to another. Another example: there is no culture in the world from which honesty as a trait is totally absent, or another where everybody is honest. However, it is true that some cultures are more (or less) honest than others. For reasons such as these cultural characteristics of a people should really be considered in relative terms, that is in comparison with others: corruption in Country X is far more widespread than in Country Y; in Country Z people have more freedom to express their political and religious views than in Country W.

2. Cultural characteristics, as will be discussed later in this chapter, have their roots in history and are often centuries old and change very slowly, whereas other social characteristics are less deeply rooted and short lived. An example of the former is the individualism of the English, whose origins can be traced at least as far back as the thirteenth century (McFarlane, 1978). Social taboos, such as stigma attached to joblessness, attitudes to homosexuals and cohabitation of unmarried couples, which change with time and are replaced with others, are not considered as deep-rooted cultural characteristics.

3. Cultures are different from one another, but they are not better or worse than one another: the English are more reserved; the Americans are more open; some Middle Eastern people may express their emotions more openly in public; the Japanese are more hard working; the French have a finer taste for clothes and food than many other nations. None of these peoples is either superior or inferior to the others because of these attributes. A word of warning: it is important not to confuse different nations' culture with the stereotypes attributed to them, in many cases without any foundations whatsoever.

Culture versus nation

It is very easy to confuse *nation* with *culture* and equate one with the other. Although in many cases there may be no problems with this, there are also many cases where this equation is problematic. For example, when we talk of Japanese culture we instantly think of people who live in Japan and when we hear of

English culture we may think of all the people who live in Britain. But there is a huge difference between these two cases. For various historical reasons, Japan has been able to isolate itself from the rest of the world in terms of immigration and settlement of non-Japanese people within its geographical and political territory. As a result, only a fraction of the people who permanently live there are of non-Japanese origins. The rest of the population has collectively shared all their centuries-old traditions, religion and all the ups and downs that the history and nature have thrown at them. This has resulted in a homogeneous culture which equates also perfectly with the national political entity called Japan.

Britain, or to give its proper name, the United Kingdom of Great Britain and Northern Ireland (UK), is a distinctive nation, a political entity, which occupies a certain amount of landmass off the mainland of Europe and enters into all sorts of relationships with the rest of the world under that name. But are all the people who live in the UK English? Do they all share the same centuries-old traditions, religions and ups and downs? The UK consists of four distinctive major cultures: Scots, Irish, Welsh and English, who live, broadly, in Scotland, Northern Ireland, Wales and England, but also intermingle in all the four constituent parts of the kingdom. These four cultures, or peoples if you like, have only relatively recently in historical terms got together, either by force or voluntarily, and formed a nation state sharing certain political and economic institutions. For the best part of their existence, they have experienced different religions, history, languages and cultural traditions.

In addition to these four main cultures, since the end of the Second World War and indeed before that time to a lesser extent, many immigrants from around the world have settled in the UK as permanent citizens. These immigrants have come from totally different religious backgrounds and heritage and have preserved many of their distinctive cultural characteristics.

Similar points can be made about many other countries where the 'nation state' does not equate with 'culture': France, Germany, United States, India, China, Russia, Iran, Israel, Iraq and the former Yugoslavia are major examples here.

It follows from the above that national culture is by and large a heterogeneous and diverse entity. The flip-side of this situation is where the same culture straddles the political boundaries of two or more nation states. The Kurds, a distinctive people in cultural terms, currently live in three separate nation states: Turkey, Iraq and Iran. The vast majority of the Chinese live in mainland China, but there are also millions of Chinese who live elsewhere in Asia – notably Hong Kong, Taiwan, Singapore and Malaysia, and many other countries in Europe and north America.

The distinction between culture and nation is of course important because of the different implications for organisations which operate within them or deal with them from the outside. This point will be discussed in detail later in the book, especially Chapter 2, but here is a foretaste.

Arguably, culture in its narrow sense – a set of historically evolved, learned and shared values, attitudes and meanings – influences organisations at the micro-level: workplace behaviour, human resource management, superior–subordinate relationships, and a host of such matters. Nation, by way of contrast, through mainly political economic institutions, has implications for organisations at the macro-level: employment laws, anti-pollution legislation, industrial structure, economic and foreign trade policies, and many other measures. This means that any organisation situated in any part of the world would simultaneously have to consider the implications of these two sets of influences for its activities.

Before we leave the subject of culture and its scope, one further point needs to be made – notably parity of meaning of various social concepts and constructs across different cultures. A simple example can clarify this point. The term 'school leavers' in the UK context refers to 16-year-old pupils who, having completed their secondary school education, wish to seek employment rather than going on to college or university for further studies. In the United States this term might be interpreted as 'drop-outs', i.e. pupils who leave school prematurely not by choice but because, for example, they cannot afford to complete their studies or do not feel intellectually up to it. The issue at hand here is not language but the meaning of a concept in two different nations, both of which speak English as their main language.

Here is another example. What would you understand by the concept of 'coolness' if used, for instance, to qualify something such as in 'cool Britannia'? Would you think it means 'Britain is a country with cold climate'; or 'the British are unfeeling'; or 'Britain is a nice place to live in'; or what? A former British member of parliament with left-leaning political views has recently spoken on this very issue: 'When I hear the words "cool Britannia" I think of old-age pensioners who suffer from hypothermia.' But the internet generation, with its own distinctive culture, might assign a more positive meaning to the word 'cool' in 'cool Britannia'.

Culture layers

As members of a global 'village', we have much in common with other human beings: we all like to be appreciated if we do a good turn for somebody; we all get upset if we lose a loved one; we all enjoy leisure and recreational activities; and we all would like to succeed in life.

But as individuals we are also different from one another in many respects: our mannerisms, political views, likes and dislikes, and so forth which are absolutely unique to us and not shared by anybody, not even our brothers and sisters.

As Figure 1.1 shows, in between these two extremes (global culture and individual characteristics) there are a few other layers which contribute to our 'cultural' make-up, part of which we share with different groups in different places and at different times.

For example, when at school we hold certain views in common with our classmates. At the university we enter into different groupings and pick up new ideas or modify the old ones. Later, at work, we face a different environment and again change some of our views. Yet at the same time a constant thread runs through our lives which makes us distinguishable from others, especially those in other countries: this thread is our national culture.

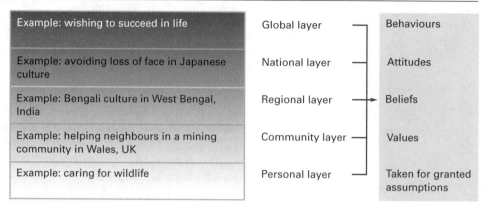

Figure 1.1 Major cultural layers

The origins of national culture

It is difficult to pinpoint the origins of culture accurately; even more so because of the interconnectedness of the various sources and factors which arguably contribute to the distinctive character of a culture. These sources and factors also reinforce the impact of one another, to the point where one does not know which one came first – chicken or egg? To make matters even more complicated, these factors might even in some cases partially cancel out each other's contributions as origins of culture. Figure 1.2 shows some of the major factors which collectively help create national culture.

Climatic and geographical sources of culture

The climatic and other physical conditions of the environment within which a community lives may have some bearing on the way it evolves as a culturally

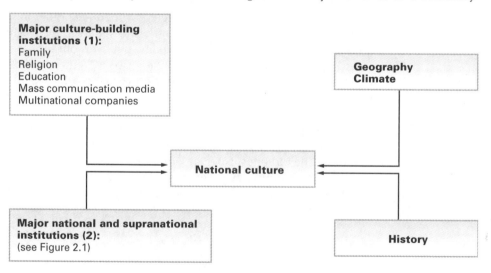

Figure 1.2 Major culture-building factors

coherent group. Imagine a country where the climate is harsh and hostile, with severe cold or hot seasons, and the land is difficult to cultivate and other natural resources are not easily accessible. It is reasonable to expect that the people who live under these conditions would be aggressive, tenacious, hard working and 'fighters'. In contrast, people living in fertile lands, with mild climates and abundant natural resources, might be passive, easygoing and non-violent.

Some of the Arian tribes who, thousands of years ago, migrated from Central Asia and settled in Iran, faced harsh variable seasons, salt deserts and very few rivers. It was not perhaps an accident of history that they became an aggressive nation, fought many nations, conquered their lands and built the Persian empire which ruled over a vast area for centuries.

In this connection Bani-Asadi (1984) makes a similar point. In the past, most Iranians used to make their living through agricultural activities, in some thousands of small villages, depending upon their agricultural output. These villages were scattered throughout the land without connecting roads. They were isolated, self-sufficient, closed systems. Wherever there was a small water source, there was also a small village. The agricultural life was difficult in the relatively dry climate of the Iranian plateau. Bani-Asadi (1984) explains that these conditions gradually brought about patience and acceptance of hardship among Iranians.

Misumi (1994, p. 257), a Japanese scholar, similarly attributes the hard-working character of Japanese people to the fact that historically they 'made a living from farming in their small island country ... have always been condemned to work hard to survive ... Their farmland, if neglected, would be overgrown with weeds and would be ruined.'

Reader (1997) explains some of Africa's cultural heritage by its fragile soils and erratic weather, which make for conservative social and political systems. He argues that the communities which endured were those that directed available energies primarily towards minimising the risk of failure, not maximising returns. This created societies designed for survival, not development. The qualities needed for survival are the opposite of those needed for developing, i.e. making experiments and taking risks.

History and culture

The history of a nation plays a significant part in creating and shaping the values of its members. Austrians, for example, have had a chequered history and the present size and political borders of their country go back only to the aftermath of the Second World War. Since then a national consciousness of their cultural identity has set in and resulted in a strong sense of pride in their culture and nationalism. Their socio-political ideology, based on respect for authority, avoidance of uncertainty, a preference for compromise and social partnership, has evolved out of the desire to maintain their national cohesion and identity.

Australia is another example of the influence of history on people's values and attitudes. The origins of modern Australia can be traced to the eighteenth century, when Britain used to send her convicted political and social offenders there. The convicts carried with them their lack of respect for authority. On the ships that took them there everyone was on an equal footing with their fellow passengers. This combination of low respect for authority and a belief in equality has over time evolved into a democratic political system which is more or less unique within the immediate neighbouring region, excepting New Zealand. Today, Australians are as law abiding as any other nation, but they are sceptical about people in positions of power, such as politicians, police and judges. Their federal system of government reflects their belief in decentralisation and delegation of authority.

North Americans are said to be one of the most individualistic, assertive, entre-preneurial and at the same time successful nations in business terms. One could arguably trace the origins of these characteristics to some of their ancestors' migration from Europe. The white settlers, who make up the vast majority of the population, are descendants of the people who left the 'old world' over five hun-dred years ago, with barely a worldly possession to their names, in search of new horizons and opportunities – a feat not for the faint hearted.

In this connection, Hofstede (1980) explains some of the groupings of the country scores in his study by their common history (see also Chapter 3). The Latin cluster countries, which today speak a Romance language (French, Italian, Spanish, Portuguese), scored high on power distance (unequal power relation-ships). They also scored high on uncertainty avoidance (low tolerance for ambi-guity). Hofstede argues that these countries have inherited at least part of their civilisation from the Roman Empire, which in its day was characterised by the existence of a central authority in Rome and a system of law applicable to all cit-izens throughout the empire. This established in its citizens' minds the value com-plex which we still recognise today: centralisation fostered by large power distance and a stress on laws fostered by strong uncertainty avoidance. By con-trast, the Germanic part of Europe, including Great Britain, never succeeded in establishing an enduring common central authority and the countries which inherited its civilisations show smaller power distance.

As Hofstede argues, assumptions about historical roots of cultural differences always remain speculative, but in certain cases, such as those mentioned above, these assumptions look quite plausible.

Culture-building institutions

Most of us in one way or another go through the socialisation process which binds us culturally to other members of the society in which we live. Figure 1.2 shows major primary and secondary social institutions that contribute to the cre-ation of national culture. See also Chapter 2 for the significant contributions of other national and supranational institutions.

Family

The societal, national cultural characteristics are learned in the wider environ-ment and most members of the society share them to a large extent. Family is the basic unit of society in which a person encounters the outside world and takes his or her first steps on a lifelong journey of socialisation and acculturation, and of learning from and contributing to a living environment. Family could arguably be described as the cradle of culture. It is here where most people start learning how to relate to others: attitudes toward powerful and experienced seniors, hierarchical relationships, attitudes towards the other sex, moral standards, expected behaviours in various situations, and many more.

Our parents, who have learned their values and modes of behaviour from theirs, teach us these values and behaviours. They employ various forms of reward and punishment to ensure that we behave in a manner acceptable to the society in which we live. As children, we learn in our homes whether or not to respect or even fear our seniors; to consider ourselves as equal regardless of our gender and our position in the family; to live together as a coherent group or to go our separate ways; to trust outsiders, and so forth. For example, a little boy in India is told to respect his father's wish and not to challenge him when he issues an order; the young in Iran have been taught by their parents that sitting with their backs to the people who are their seniors is rude; British children of tender age learn to have their own private territory (a separate bed in a room shared with their siblings, or even a separate room) and keep an emotional as well as spatial distance between themselves and others.

What we learn at home on our parents' knees could have a lasting effect on our lives, in terms of basic values and attitudes, even though our later experiences might make us modify some of our views. But most of us remain fundamentally loyal to the deep-rooted values that we learnt at home as children.

The present author conducted a comparative study of English and Indian cultures and organisations a few years ago. At the same time as I was collecting my data, a colleague of mine completed her study of English, Asian and West Indian children's play behaviours. Her sample consisted of a group of pre-school children who lived in Birmingham. My sample consisted of English and Indian adults who lived and worked in their respective countries. It was very interesting to note how similar were the attitudes and values that the adult sample expressed in my survey to those observed by my colleague among Indian and English children. In both studies, the English placed a higher value on independence, individual territory and privacy; they were more aggressive, and showed less respect for and fear of people in senior positions than did their Indian counterparts (for details, see Child, 1982; Tayeb, 1988). These similarities demonstrate how early in life basic cultural characteristics are formed and how they persist across generations and even across geographical and national boundaries.

Religion

Religion is an institution which plays a significant role in how we view the world and relate to it and its inhabitants, irrespective of whether or not we are believers. Let us elaborate this argument further. One of the many features that distinguishes us from other animals is the ways in which we bring order to the societies in which we live, through laws and regulations, codes of conduct if you like. And after centuries of experimentation we have now set in place elaborate codes to regulate our behaviour in public and even in private; codes which we shall continue to modify and adjust as we go along. Arguably these codes in the main originated in religion.

Religions range from the tribal rituals and paganism of prehistoric times, to the so-called revealed creeds such as Judaism, Islam and Christianity, to those which were founded by revered individual sages and hermits, such as Confucianism and Buddhism. All have one thing in common: they have set out codes of conduct for people – what is right or wrong, what is good or bad, what to do under what circumstances, etc. These codes govern our lives even if we do not believe in them. They are part of our collective subconscious, and most of us obey them without even being aware of their presence.

As human beings we are part of nature and should really be following the law of nature in all aspects of our lives, but we do not, arguably because of these codes. There is, for instance, nothing inherently or naturally wrong in stealing something which belongs to your nextdoor neighbour; all other animals are doing it all the time. Just take a look out of your sitting room window and see how the bigger birds feeding in your garden steal pieces of bread from the beaks of smaller birds. But most people do not go about killing or stealing or cheating, or whatever, even if they are physically capable of doing so. This is because of their upbringing and their society's values, which are in turn heavily influenced by the precepts and dictates of their religion.

The power relationships that one develops with others in society might also have their roots in religion. For example, in some religions God is the Almighty who commands from on high and whom the believer should obey and fear; God will severely punish in hell those who do not do as they are told. A God–human relationship such as this is characterised by inequality of power between the two sides concerned, an inequality which is justified and legitimated on the basis of the unquestionable power of God over human beings.

In some religions, the believers consider God as a symbol of love and humility, who in fact lives in a human form on earth alongside ordinary men and women. Here the emphasis is on forgiveness, not on fear, on 'I am like you', not on 'I issue orders you obey'. Arguably this sort of God–human relationship could be conducive to a perception of power equality between the two sides.

The powerful–powerless relationship and role patterns which are thus originated in religious teachings may be mirrored in other aspects of social relationship and may permeate society as a whole. In cultures where the first kind of religion is practised one would expect to observe more respect and even fear of authority than in those societies where the second type is prevalent.

Education

Education plays a significant role in modern societies in that, among other things, it determines the quality of their human resources. Formal education, especially in societies where there are well-developed educational institutions, contributes to the formation of culture, both through the value system and the priorities on which it is based (the macro-level) and the teaching practices and styles (the micro-level).

At the macro-level, some nations emphasise the importance of free and universal schooling for their young in order to equip them with a firm foundation to start a vocation or go on to higher education, which may not necessarily be free. In many cases students are expected to find ways of financing their higher education, such as part-time jobs, deferred payment loans, sponsorship, scholarship and parental assistance. Many South East Asian countries, New Zealand and recently the United Kingdom are among the nations which have adopted policies along these lines. The top priority in these countries is to ensure the maximum possible literacy rate for the population as a whole. Policies of this kind mean that, as far as business organisations are concerned, the workforce at all levels has a minimum of standard of education, if not higher for some at least.

There are some countries, like India, which are top heavy: an excellent university-level educational system, but poorly equipped and maintained primary and secondary-level education. Here the literacy rate is rather low and managers are handicapped by a shortage of skilled workers at shop-floor levels. Training these employees to become operators of sophisticated machinery and computerised equipment could be a tall order for many, especially small and medium sized firms.

Then there is the value system which underpins the educational principles of a nation. In the UK, for instance, teaching of applied science and commerce is given a lower status compared to that of pure science and arts subjects. The top two universities, Oxford and Cambridge, dating back a few centuries, which dominate major political and managerial positions in the country, have always prided themselves on being excellent at the arts, literature, philosophy and pure sciences. Courses in business and management, for instance, are relatively new in these establishments and their beginnings go back to the 1960s. For many years it was left to polytechnics (recently reorganised as universities) and the so-called red brick universities with specialist courses in technology and engineering to train the bulk of the university-educated workforce for the manufacturing sector. Most of these establishments were created in the mid-nineteenth and twentieth centuries.

This contrasts sharply with the United States' far better treatment of commerce and business in educational institutions. In Germany there is much emphasis on and prestige for technological courses. Here vocational education, apprenticeship and technical courses are highly valued and employees with engineering degrees are well remunerated. Doing things by hand is as good as, if not better than, doing things by brains.

Another macro-level issue to note is the extent to which the state controls and determines the system, regardless of private or state ownership of schools, colleges, universities and other educational establishments. In some countries the central government sets minimum requirements to ensure that all students are taught certain courses necessary for their future careers. Some countries leave it totally to the schools or local educational authorities to decide their curriculum. Yet in some other nations the schools and other educational establishments are controlled by the political elite to ensure that the 'party line' is followed. In such cases, certain courses which oppose the current political ideology may never be taught, while other courses are monitored closely, censored and even deliberately distorted. The ex-communist countries are examples of these sorts of educational policies, when they were under communist regimes.

At the micro-level, that is learning and teaching practices, we can also note differences among nations. In some countries teaching is student centred, that is students are actively involved in the learning and teaching process, through experimentation, trial and error, participation in class discussions and self-directed small group activities, and practical as well as theoretical learning. Students are generally encouraged to challenge, to explore, to criticise, to analyse, to make mistakes and to learn from mistakes in a constructive manner. In other countries, by contrast, teaching is a one-way activity, performed by the teacher. Learning is a passive activity and students are expected to accept facts as imparted in the lectures and read in the textbooks.

The implications of these two different styles of teaching practices for inter-personal relationships, especially in terms of power, authority and ability to stand on one's own feet in life, are obvious. In the first-type countries, people go through an educational system which prepares them to face and meet unknown challenges, to take risks, to believe in themselves and to be self-confident. In the second-type nations, people are encouraged to rely on their seniors and to ask for advice on major issues, and may as a result suffer from low self-esteem. These two opposite cases are of course hypothetical extreme poles. In practice the situation is less rigid than this. Various nations are in fact located on a continuum ranging from one extreme to the other. Moreover each nation has a complex mixture of various educational practices and priorities at different times and in different places. But what is important to note is that in some countries the overwhelming proportion of educational establishments may be closer to one end and in others closer to the other end of the continuum.

For instance, as Sayigh (1982) points out, education in the Arab countries, at the time of his publication, had little relevance to the needs and problems of society and the economy and was not primarily of the problem-solving type. The system essentially prepared individuals for their successful upgrading in their attempt to climb the economic and social ladder and was minimally oriented to the implanting of the notions of public service in Arab youth. As far as method-ology was concerned, education failed to provide sufficient scope for innovation and intellectual stimulation and concentrated instead on cramming the students' memories with information. Also, there was insufficient practical work and exper-imentation in workshops, classrooms and laboratories. Only a small proportion of secondary education was actually in technical training (see also Chapter 5).

Both macro- and micro-level educational policies determine to a large extent the level of technological advancement as well as the quality of a country's work-force. A quick look at the composition of the world shows a wide range from highly advanced nations, such as Japan, Germany and France, to middle-of-the-road countries, such as Brazil and Turkey, to certain destitute African nations whom most of the advances of the twentieth and twenty-first centuries have passed by. The discussion regarding the complex causes of these variations is beyond the scope of this chapter, but the implications of such variations for busi-ness organisations are obvious.

Mass communication media

The birth of a truly mass communication media can perhaps be traced to the invention of printing which made it possible for people to disseminate infor-mation through the written medium to a much wider audience than had hith-erto been possible. Centuries later, the latter part of the nineteenth and then the whole of the twentieth century saw the advent of telegraph, telephone, radio, television, telex, fax, e-mail and, of course, the internet. These media have trans-formed the world in which we live, not only in terms of bringing people closer together irrespective of their geographical locations, but also in terms of spread-ing values, attitudes, tastes, meanings and vocabulary – in short, culture. The electronic communications media have perhaps done more than any other invention to break down cultural barriers between people in different parts of the world.

This is not to say that distinctive cultural characteristics of different nations have disappeared – far from it. Rather, there is now a new common ground, a new cultural layer if you like, which we can all share if we wish or are given the opportunity to do so. Cultural layers of this kind, created by mass media, are not of course new or unique to our own time, but the magnitude, depth and geographical reach of the electronic media make the creation and maintenance of cultural layers far quicker and more effective. In the eighteenth and nineteenth centuries, if you wanted to hear your favourite composer's music, you would either have to hear it in a piano reduction in someone's private 'salon', or travel to where the music was performed in a concert hall. In the twentieth century you could buy a vinyl and later a compact disk and listen to it at home or in your car as well as being able to hear it in a live concert. Now you download your favourite 'song' from a remote location and play it on your computer within minutes of its being placed on the internet. The same speed and reach apply of course to news, political, cultural and economic events. You can now buy anything, find information about any subject, express your views on any issue, within the time needed to type a few words and click a button.

Having said all this, it is worth noting the limitations that exist on the use and reach of all forms of the mass communication media, for technical, political and many other reasons (see also Chapter 8). There are, for instance, many countries where the mass media are either owned or their editorial policies heavily controlled by the state. There are those in which people can broadcast and publish anything they like so long as they do not libel others or infringe people's privacy. In modern times, where satellites can beam any radio or television programmes into any home, the state's ability to control such media is being challenged, but it has not been eliminated. Recently, a media firm that provides satellite television services to, among other nations, an Asian country, cancelled its contract with a world-class broadcasting corporation. The reason, it was alleged, was that the corporation's news programmes, which followed its tradition of impartiality and telling the truth, were not welcomed by the officials of the host country.

Multinational companies (MNCs)

MNCs are very much a part of our lives these days, as they have been for decades. They are set to continue their worldwide presence and, as Perlmutter (1997) points out, they are and will be irreversibly committed to technological innovation and world-class standards and to creating markets in all parts of the planet. Some will fail, others will take their place, but they will not go home. After all, what is 'home' in a world where there is no place to hide? The most sanguine prospects are for a golden age in which all nations share in a global boom.

Multinational companies can also be considered, to some extent, as culture-building institutions. They play a significant part in the movement of goods and services and of people around the world. In the process they also change our lifestyles as well as accommodate them. McDonald's, for instance, has introduced clean lavatories to Hong Kong and Coca-Cola won the Olympics for its home town of Atlanta.

In recent years there has been a lot of academic and professional interest in the socio-cultural as well as technical and economic sides of multinational companies in relation to their host countries. Some major household companies have come under close scrutiny and sometimes even criticisms. Coca-Cola and McDonald's are particularly favourite targets for those (usually French-speaking) Europeans who worry about Cocacolonisation, McWorld, and so on. Even voices that are more friendly to US commerce tend to treat the brands as monolithic creations, whose success is as uniform as it is inevitable (*The Economist*, 16 May 1998).

However, the change and influence process is a two-way one. Companies such as these are also personal, local affairs whose images, uses and tastes are changed by the people who lead them and also by the people who produce and consume their products.

Non-cultural influences on people's values and attitudes

As was discussed earlier, family and religion are two powerful primary sources of culture which shape a person's values and general outlook on life, certainly in the formative years. However, as a person grows up and goes through life experiences he or she picks up different influences, some of which come from other culture-building institutions while others are more or less unique to that person.

The debate on nature versus nurture is beyond the scope of this chapter, but suffice it to say that some of the predispositions that people have will influence the way in which they interact with their society and their environment. They pick up things from it in a personal way. This is why brothers and sisters, even though exposed to the same family and religious traditions, grow up to be different people and may even hold different values and attitudes from one another. Major non-cultural factors which contribute to our personally held values, attitudes and personal characteristics are level of education, age and profession. National culture, as the present author has argued elsewhere, should not therefore be considered as an overarching concept which would determine our thoughts and actions all the time and in all circumstances. As Tayeb (2001) points out, it is true that our behaviours and actions are informed by our values and taken for granted assumptions, but these are not purely based in the national culture. Our education, age, occupation and life experience in general exert powerful influences on our values and taken for granted assumptions. That is why, for instance, an older person might be more tactful in encounters with others, a well-travelled person might be more tolerant of other nationalities, a senior manager might be more time conscious than a junior office clerk, a well-educated person might have a more intellectually developed mind and sharper problem-solving faculties, than their opposite numbers within the same culture.

It goes without saying that within the context of work, organisational culture and indeed professional culture (managers, shop-floor workers, accountants, etc.) are some additional factors which influence our behaviours in the workplace – more on this in later chapters. Figure 1.3 shows the cultural and non-cultural influences on organisations.

As discussed earlier and shown in Figure 1.2, national and supranational institutions are some of the building blocks of national culture and therefore have significant implications for organisations. These institutions and their influences will be discussed in detail in Chapter 2.

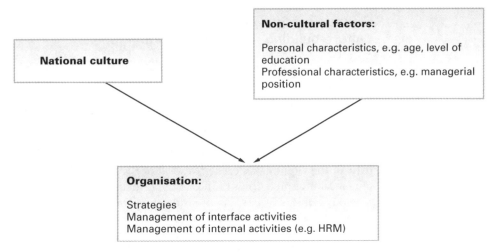

Figure 1.3 Cultural and non-cultural influences on organisations

Summary

This chapter pointed out the difficulties in defining unambiguously national culture and made an attempt in that direction. The scope of national culture was also explored. The chapter then focused on major primary social institutions, notably family, religion and education, and examined the ways in which they create and sustain people's cultural values and attitudes. Geographical and ecological factors and their roles were also discussed. The chapter argued, however, that values and attitudes could be formed and/or influenced by non-cultural factors as well. Among these are level of education, profession, and life experience as a whole. It can be argued, for instance, that a highly educated 50-year-old senior executive could hold values and views totally different from those of his or her 20-year-old compatriot who has only primary school-level education and has not yet had an opportunity to hold a senior position in a company.

Discussion questions

1. What is the difference between 'nation' and 'culture', and why is it important to make a distinction between these two concepts?

2. In what ways does education contribute to the formation of national culture?

3. What are the major factors which could bring closer together the otherwise culturally diverse peoples around the world?

4. What are the major factors which could distance people from one another in terms of values and attitudes even if they live together in the same community?

Closing Case Study:
Culture-building institutions in Iran

Religion

At the heart of Iranian culture lies its main religion, Islam, to which over 98 per cent of the population subscribe.

Before going any further, it is important to note that Islam, although it has certain precepts and principles which are followed by the believers living in different parts of the world, takes on a great deal of the local 'colour', partly because of genuine local interpretation of some of the principles and partly for political and non-religious considerations. As a result there are differences in both secular and religious aspects of social lives among Muslim nations. Saudi Arabia, for instance, adheres strictly to the Sacred Law (Sharia) in many spheres of life, while Turkey has turned to secular laws for the administration of its economic and social affairs. A few years ago in Turkey, a newly elected member of parliament was barred from taking up her seat because she wished to wear Islamic head cover – her action was considered politically undesirable.

For Muslims, Islam is not a man-made institution: the Koran contains the words of God, revealed syllable by syllable to Mohammed some 1,400 years ago. The deeds of its adherents are therefore inseparable from divine commandments. Islam is generally viewed by some non-Muslims as being a fatalist religion. But the Koran specifically asserts that humans are able to choose and to intervene in their destiny, and that they are held responsible for the consequences of their deeds. However, they are not left alone to run their lives. God has equipped them with the Koran and the traditions of Prophet Mohammed, which in Islamic view are two of the most important sources of guidance that humans can use to steer their actions and beliefs.

Islam permeates people's taken for granted values and assumptions as well. Ultimate fear of and trust in God alone, piety and abstinence, decency, truthfulness, helping the poor and weak, respect for age and seniority, hospitality, loyalty, obedience to leaders and looking up to seniors for direction, family orientation, uncertainty avoidance and fatalism yet acceptance of responsibility for one's actions are among the Islamic roots of Iranian culture. Islam also asserts that the nature of relationships among people should be egalitarian, and urges leaders to consult their followers in the running of their affairs.

History

Throughout its long history, the nation has experienced many unpleasant and hard times as well as happy episodes: authoritarian regimes, repression, wars, domination and invasion by foreign powers and loss of territory. Some of these events have created a deep scepticism and distrust in the national psyche and a need to take refuge in the security offered by religion and in the comfort of home and family, which alone alongside God can be trusted.

The way that Iranian people coped with internal dictators and external enemies and occupiers was through either resistance and struggle or 'false adaptation' (Bazargan, 1958). This peculiar adaptability has for centuries enabled the Iranians to live with the autocracy and corruption of their kings and rulers or oppressions. The people have also become distrustful to governors and careless to obey the rules and laws made by lawmakers. In fact, disobedience of the ruler and their rules or commands was a value. Those who did it were perceived as heroes fighting against cruelty and injustice. All this, one can argue, could lead to a culture of unwillingness to carry out orders.

Encounter with the west

Iran's cultural, economic and military contacts with the west go back to the Persian empire and its wars with the Greeks (under the Achaemenid Persians) and the Romans (under the Sassanian Persians), if not before. In more recent times, France, especially since the time of Napoleon I, has been a major source of western ideas and practices. In the twentieth century, the Shah's father, the founder of the Pahlavi dynasty, was instrumental in modelling certain civic institutions, such as the legal system, education, the civil service, and the armed forces after those of France. Modernisation was invariably equated with westernisation (or to be precise, Europeanisation, initially at least). Western engineers and advisers were brought in to build and modernise the country's infrastructure such as railway networks and suspension bridges. Men and women were forced, sometimes brutally by the armed forces and the police, to change their traditional costumes and wear contemporary western clothes, as part of the process of secularisation as well as westernisation of society: women had to abandon their traditional chador (veil) and men had to wear ties. Western arts, from theatre to cinema and classical music and later its pop variety, which had been introduced to the country in a limited way before the Pahlavi dynasty, permeated cultural life, especially in cities and other urban areas, alongside the traditional arts. The 'swinging 60s' were as much alive in Tehran as they were in London and Paris. During the Shah's own reign, American influence in the country's affairs increased and to some extent replaced that of Europe.

This long-term exposure to western culture, notwithstanding cultural differences between various western countries, arguably introduced the Iranians to certain secular industrial values and ideas such as economic and material growth, security, individualism, democracy, and comfort and enjoyment. However, what the Shah and his father did not encourage were the west's long fought-for and won democratic practices and respect for individual liberty and human rights.

A final point to make here is that the above major sources of culture have had varying degrees of influence on the cultural make-up of the Iranians over time and at different levels of society. Whereas, for example, one might observe individualistic attitudes and behaviours among employees in relation to their workplace, similar to those the present author found in British and certain Indian companies (Tayeb, 1988), at the family and other in-group levels collectivism prevails. As for the time dimension, across its long history the nation has gone through both ups and downs and changes of collective mind: from being proud and powerful empire builders to being humiliated, for a short period, during the Second World War by being occupied and carved out by the Allied forces; from taking on board many western values and fashions to rejecting outright anything which came from the west; from being the closest that one can get to secularism to being completely engulfed in religious teachings and practices.

Closing case study questions

1. What are the main values of Islam and in what ways have they contributed to the Iranian culture?

2. What other major factors have helped to create this culture?

3. If you were to set up a company in Iran as a foreign investor, which aspects of that country's culture would be relevant to you and your business, and how would you handle them?

Annotated further reading

Hofstede, G. (1980) *Culture's Consequences*. Thousand Oaks CA: Sage.
A seminal study which has had a profound impact on the debate on national culture and organisations at both theoretical and practical levels.

Reader, J. (1997) *Africa: A Biography of a Continent*. London: Hamish Hamilton.
An in-depth analysis of cultural and historical roots of the state in which African countries find themselves in our time.

Tayeb, M. H. (2000) *The Management of International Enterprises: A Socio-Political View*. Basingstoke: Macmillan.
It discusses major economic, social, political and historical causes of successes and failures of some nations and their enterprises in international markets.

References

Bani-Asadi, H. (1984) 'Interactive planning on the eve of the Iranian Revolution'. PhD dissertation, University of Pennsylvania.

Bazargan, M. (1958) *Sazgari Irani* [Iranians' adaptation]. Tehran: Yad (in Farsi).

Child, E. (1982) 'Individual and social factors associated with the behaviour of children in a play setting'. PhD thesis, Aston University.

Hofstede, G. (1980) *Culture's Consequences*. Thousand Oaks CA: Sage.

McFarlane, A. (1978) *The Origins of English Individualism*. Oxford: Blackwell.

Misumi, J. (1994) 'The Japanese meaning of work and small-group activities in Japanese industrial organizations', in H. S. R. Kao, D. Sinha and S.-H. Ng, *Effective Organizations and Social Values*. New Delhi: Sage. pp. 256–68.

Perlmutter, H. (1997) 'Rocky roads to the emerging global civilisation', *Financial Times* web site.

Reader, J. (1997) *Africa: A Biography of a Continent*. London: Hamish Hamilton.

Sayigh, Y. A. (1982) *The Arab Economy: Past Performance & Future Prospects.* New York: Oxford University Press.

Tayeb, M. H. (1988) *Organizations and National Culture: A Comparative Analysis.* London: Sage.

Tayeb, M. H. (2001) 'Conducting research across cultures – overcoming drawbacks and obstacles', *International Journal of Cross-Cultural Management* 1(1): 113–29.

CHAPTER 2

Institutional differences across the world

Monir Tayeb

Learning objectives

When you finish reading this chapter you should:

■ be familiar with major national institutions and their role in creating a nation's character

■ have a broad knowledge of institutional differences between various nations around the world

■ be familiar with the impacts that these national institutions could have on domestic and foreign firms

■ learn how regional and international institutions could also influence some of the policies and practices of domestic and foreign firms

---

Opening Case Study: The new battlegrounds for capitalism

The conflict between capitalism and socialism came to an end a decade ago, only to see a new one rising from its ashes. Business and academia alike began to argue that capitalism was in fact many capitalisms, each with its own economies, social systems, cultural values and management styles.

Anglo-Saxon capitalism, which had evolved in the UK and US, was distinct from the version found in Japan and Germany, occasionally referred to as the Rhenish model. Indeed, the former was frequently viewed as inferior. In the 1980s and early 1990s, Japan was admired for its management styles and operational practices. Many US and UK manufacturers tried to emulate Japanese methods such as just-in-time inventory control and employee involvement.

Today, however, something new is happening. After a decade in which Rhenish capitalism, to varying degrees, has been struggling, both Japanese and German corporations are restructuring and reforming along the lines of their US and UK counterparts. The argument that Japan and continental Europe have to catch up in areas such as shareholder value and corporate governance, not to mention information technology, has been won. Moreover, Japanese business is coming to terms with the fact that US corporations and others have beaten them at their own game.

By designing and building in customer-facing processes to all aspects of their business, US companies have extended Japanese management styles beyond the shop floor.

Although there is scope for disagreement over the depth of reform taking place, it is significant that multinationals everywhere champion similar objectives. Increasingly, shareholder value is the measure of corporate performance and corporations are willing to use similar tools, such as downsizing, to reach performance goals. Overall, it is hard to dispute that management styles around the world are locked in to a similar trajectory and, in the process, are becoming more homogeneous.

It is useful to place change in a wider context. The starting point is that the dominant framework in which business operates has changed dramatically in the past two decades. Post-war 'corporatist' relationships between the state, business and labour, always weak in the US, were dismantled during the 1980s in the Anglo-Saxon world. Reforming labour relations led to industrial and corporate restructuring in the 1980s. In the 1990s, the corporatist framework continued to erode, allowing organisational freedom, efficiency and flexibility. Gradually, another framework was built around corporate governance. Here, the focus shifted to shareholder value, management accountability and transparency. Japan and continental Europe are still faced with the tensions of both frameworks, while Anglo-Saxon nations have made the change.

Source: 09 Oct. 2000, *Financial Times* CD-ROM 2000

Introduction

The previous chapter discussed the origins of national culture. The present chapter explores the ways in which major national and international institutions might influence business activities of companies. A distinction is also made between 'national culture' and 'national institutions' in terms of the mechanisms by which they exert influence. National cultural norms and 'way of doing things' tend to be internalised, but national institutions make their presence felt through externally generated and imposed rules and regulations.

It will be argued that both internal matters of a company, such as human resource management, and its relationships with the environment can be affected by these institutions. Foreign firms operating within the jurisdiction of a nation can at times also be subject to further rules and regulations. The extent and scope of these will be shown to be different from one country to another.

Institutional influences on organisations

Does institutional environment matter?

A series of studies conducted by Liberman and Torbiörn (2000) in eight European subsidiaries of a global firm found that many aspects of management practices, including employee management, are influenced by both national culture and national institutions. Liberman and Zander's (2000) research conducted in four subsidiaries of a multinational company in the United States, United Kingdom, Germany and Sweden shows interesting patterns of management policies and practices which reflect some of the institutional characters of their respective host countries. The host nations were divided into two institutional settings: the United States and United Kingdom were identified as flexible labour market institutional environments, while Germany and Sweden were defined as restrictive labour market institutional environments. The study found that both strategic (e.g. wide purpose routines such as human resources) and tactical (e.g. short range routines, such as conflict management) practices differed across the two institutional settings. These differences were related to the differences in their respective labour market conditions.

For example, the researchers found that in Germany and Sweden it was significantly more common that the *strategic management practices* involved more quantification and that the control exercised by the company was intense. Formality when describing activities and stress on seniority when deciding on promotions were more common, as was the preference for tangible rather than intangible rewards than in the more regulated institutional environments. In addition, the subsidiaries in the Germany and Sweden group indicated that informal promotion procedures existed to a larger extent than in the United States and United Kingdom. Regarding UK and US *tactical management practices*, more demands of compliance and rigour in decision making from managers were identified, as well as more formality in communication, more compliance rewarding and more direct interventions in crises and special problems than in the other two countries. At the same time, managers were reported to use the consensus approach more frequently. Moreover, the subsidiaries that were categorised as working in restrictive settings regarding labour practices were found to have more informality in progression practices.

Other studies in different parts of the world also found various national institutions do exert pressures of all kind on organisations to which they have to respond (Brewster, 1995; Budhwar and Sparrow, 1998; Ferner and Hyman, 1999; Tayeb, 1988).

It is important to note that cultural norms are internalised, through a long-drawn socialisation process (see Chapter 1). By contrast, national institutions influence people's actions and behaviours through externally imposed rules and regulations, enforceable by the law of the land in most cases. For instance, if in a culture it is generally considered impolite to address an older person by his or her first name, no legal action is taken against someone who does not obey this cultural norm. But if someone wilfully damages another person's property, he or she will be judged in a court of law and punished accordingly.

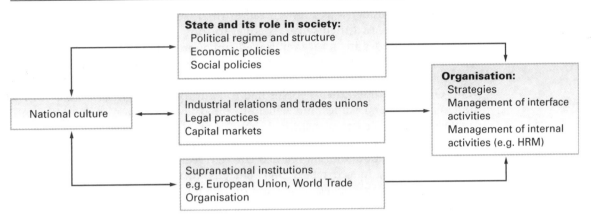

Figure 2.1 Major national and supranational institutions and their influences on organisations

So what are these influential institutions and in what other ways do they impact on society and the management of organisations operating within it? Figure 2.1 shows some of the most significant among these institutions. It should be borne in mind that the relationship between national culture and its institutions is two-way. A nation's character is created largely by its institutions, which are in turn created and influenced by it. The main consequence of this self-renewing process is the perpetuation of national culture across generations. The two-headed arrows in Figure 2.1 indicate the two-way relationship between a national culture and its institutions.

State and its role in society

Political regime and structure

A country's political system is normally an organically grown, integral part of its very fabric, an outcome of its historical and cultural evolution. It is compatible with the local culture and therefore survives and indeed flourishes. Sometimes, however, the history tells us, a military coup d'état, an ideologically driven revolution or interference by foreign powers might impose an 'alien' political structure on a nation. This alien system could well be incompatible with the local culture and time-honoured traditions, and as a result might eventually either collapse or lose much of its initial character. Here are some examples: Franco's dictatorship in Spain gave way to the country's current democracy and constitutional monarchy; the short-lived Greek military government was replaced after a few years by a democratic parliamentary regime in the 1970s; the 1989 popular revolutions in central and eastern European countries swept away over forty years of communist rule, which had been imposed by the former Soviet Union.

In the same vein, one could argue that a democratic political system usually develops and flourishes in cultures where people believe in sharing power and responsibility. In these cultures consultation and respect for other people's opinions are considered as strength rather than weakness. People demand to be consulted and regard themselves as equal to those in positions of power. These values and attitudes are in turn reinforced and perpetuated by the political climate that they have helped to create. This is not, however, to say that modern democracies in various parts of the world were always democracies as we know them now. On the contrary, their peoples had to fight for their right to vote, but their underlying cultural values and beliefs inspired and sustained their fights until they won and their rights enshrined them in their political system.

By contrast, in many parts of the world autocratic regimes, if they are not imposed on a nation and maintained through fear of persecution or other coercive means, may indeed reflect their citizens' own preferences, based on their long-held values and beliefs. There are quite a few nations scattered around the globe where benevolent and paternal absolute monarchies or centralised almost dynastic republican systems are in place and which are judged by their own people as right for them.

The above argument is not intended to offer support for or rejection of democracy and authoritarianism, but to draw attention to the cultural origins of political institutions which have been sustained with no major challenge over decades if not centuries.

Management policies and practices of companies reflect, to a large extent, the general political culture of a country. Take human resources management, for example. In a democracy, employees are more likely to have a larger say in the decisions which affect their jobs than in non-democratic societies. The political ideology of the government of the day, however, also has a great influence on the process. For instance, in democratic Britain, under a left-of-centre government workers enjoy far more protection and rights than under a right-of-centre government. In communist countries and the pre-1989 revolution eastern and central European societies, workers, in theory at least, have had the greatest amount of protection and rights among the citizens – these countries were supposed to be worker states. In India and many other socialist-oriented countries, workers are far more protected than in market-oriented economies such as the United States. In a comparative study involving a sample of Indian manufacturing firms, Tayeb (1988) found a reflection of the government policies in the human resource management practices pursued by these firms. In all the participating organisations, the punishment strategies adopted for manual workers were generally mild and of a non-financial kind, such as shortening annual holidays and failure to promote. Because the government's regulations aimed at maintaining employment and minimum living standards for this group of employees, the managers would not be allowed, for instance, to fire manual workers or reduce their wages under any circumstances, even if they committed gross misconduct and a breach of contract.

Economic policies

Since the early 1980s, everywhere, with a few notable exceptions, the general trend of economic and trade policies has been towards liberalisation, deregulation, privatisation and 'small government', a trend which is set to continue in the twenty-first century. In the international sphere the liberalising trend has also accelerated, with initiatives such as Europe's single market, North Atlantic Free

Trade Association (NAFTA) and above all the Uruguay round of the General Agreement on Tariffs and Trade (GATT) talks that gave birth to the World Trade Organisation (WTO). The picture is not of course in every case as clear cut as this.

The extent to which state controls trade and other economic and business activities varies from one country to another. For instance, in most countries some parts of the economy (notably education, health service, pensions and labour markets) are still dominated by public provision and/or heavy regulations, and in quite a few nations these services are performed by a mixture of public and private sectors. In general, under capitalist and market-oriented economies the type of activities performed by the government is of necessity limited, whereas this is not the case under socialist and other non-market-oriented economies. In the latter, the formal political apparatus is responsible to a much wider extent in determining who gets 'what, when and how'. In other words, the political process decides the distribution of resources between various social groups and interests.

In most developing countries the government, of whatever political persuasion, plays an all-pervasive and crucial role in the management of the economy as well as in politics. Almost all of them pursue protectionist industrial and economic policies, and a vast majority of them have centralised non-democratic governments.

There are however some variations here. For instance, India, for long a protectionist centralised economy, has recently opened up its market and allowed some degree of trade liberalisation. A few years ago, Mexico and Chile, having suffered from the consequences of their debt crises, adopted a decentralised and liberal economic and trade policy, largely as a condition to receive loans from the International Monetary Fund (IMF) and the World Bank.

In advanced, industrialised countries the picture is patchy too. In the United States and United Kingdom, especially when conservative parties are in power, governments usually adopt a relatively hands-off policy, certainly with regard to manufacturing sector, compared to their liberal and socialist counterparts. In Japan, France and the newly industrialised countries of South East Asia, governments play a more active role in the management of the economy.

The ex-socialist countries of eastern and central Europe are currently in the process of moving from a centrally planned economy to a more decentralised one, with varying degrees of success. In China a process of decentralisation and privatisation of economic activities has been taking place for over two decades. Also, there are coastal regions which are practically run on a capitalistic model. But the political regime of the country as a whole is still highly centralised and based on a communist model, with the state in full control. A handful of nations, notably North Korea, Cuba, Vietnam and Laos, are still communist both in their political and economic policies and practices.

Social policies

Similarly, in the social sphere there are varying degrees of governmental intervention across the world. In some countries, the state plays a minimum role, usually confined to law and order, education and health. In many countries, especially in the developing world, the state takes a more active and direct role well beyond those mentioned above – to encompass a wide range of social policies, religion and cultural education of their people and how they might behave publicly or in private. Some of these policies are relevant to the workplace behaviour as well.

In Iran, for instance, women have to follow a strict Islamic dress code at work, and indeed elsewhere. A policy of segregation of sexes is observed in prayers, wedding ceremonies, public transport, queues at shops, and so forth.

In Saudi Arabia women are not allowed to drive their cars (those who are rich enough to own a car usually hire a chauffeur). As far as work is concerned, women are barred from public office. As a result, they have turned to business and the professions, but here too they work under certain constraints. According to *The Economist* (4 February 1995), most women active in private businesses (as owners) are in the retail trade: in a shopping mall in Jeddah, 8 out of 20 shops are owned and run by women (notices forbid men to enter the shops women run). Teaching posts are among the professions open to women but it is rather difficult for them to apply for positions which are located outside their home towns. In this patriarchal society, women must have written permission from their husbands or fathers before they can travel. Women generally operate under difficulties: they have to be discreet and the places where they work are segregated.

Social policies devised and implemented by the state are prevalent in various forms in developed nations as well. For example, in Scandinavian countries 6 to 12 months' paid maternity leave is the norm. There are also stringent laws with regard to firing pregnant women and women on maternity leave.

Industrial relations and trades unions

Another way in which nations vary from one another is in their use of trades unions, which are a form of pressure group. Free and independent trades unions are institutions which are encouraged and flourish in many democratic nations (e.g. Germany, United States, France, Scandinavian countries). In some societies the unions are rubber-stamping puppets of the regime (e.g. the pre-1989 eastern and central European countries, China). In yet others they are either non-existent or repressed (e.g. some countries in the Middle East).

The nature of the ideology and activities that unions might adopt also differs from one society to another. For instance, in France unions are highly political and tend to engage in class struggles. The Polish trades union, Solidarność, and the Siberian miners of the Republic of Russia in the former Soviet Union are other examples of highly politicised labour movements. In Britain, trades unions are more pragmatic and have no intention of overthrowing or challenging the authority of the management or government. They fight for their jobs and for better working conditions. Trades unions in the United States are even less militant and more pragmatic than those in Britain.

There are differences, too, in the nature of industrial relations in different countries. In Britain, for instance, the management–workers relationship in many companies is hostile and characterised by a 'them and us' division. In Japan the character of unions and management is moulded by the company culture and the relationship between the two sides, if they can be separated as two sides, is based on cooperation and harmony.

Forms of unionisation are also different among nations. Trades unions in Japan, for instance, are company based: Toyota, Nissan and Hitachi have their own unions. Compare this with Britain, where unions are craft based: that is, transport workers have their own union (Transport & General Workers Union); coal miners theirs (National Union of Mineworkers); teachers theirs (National Union of Teachers), and so on. As a result, in a Japanese company there is only one union, but in a typical British manufacturing company the workers are represented by a number of unions, depending on the number of crafts or jobs that the workers and other employees perform.

Trades unions enjoy differing degrees of power depending on where they are situated and under what economic and political conditions they function at any given point in time. As mentioned earlier, free and independent trades unions did not exist in most of the European communist countries before the 1989 revolutions, and still do not exist in China and other communist countries. The workers who organised themselves as such were quickly suppressed and dispersed by the ruling party.

In some countries, such as India, which has traditionally had socialist-oriented policies, the organised sector is relatively very small compared to the total workforce, but industrial relations laws are 'pro' workers and the unions have more power compared to their counterparts elsewhere.

The overall industrial relations culture of a country has implications for its companies, including their employee management. In the former and current communist/socialist countries, workers' participation in management decision making is legitimised and practised much more widely than in the capitalist countries, in theory at least. The former Yugoslavia's self-management with worker directors was the most extensive form of workers' participation. The future of self-management, like so much else in that country, is uncertain if not already destroyed. The country has virtually disintegrated. Four of its constituent republics, Slovenia, Croatia, Bosnia-Hercegovina and Macedonia, declared their independence in the 1990s. Almost all the former constituent republics were either directly involved in a bloody civil war between major ethnic groups or indirectly affected by it for most of the last decade of the twentieth century. The civil war destroyed, among other things, much of the economic infrastructure and many of the businesses of the former Yugoslavia and its unique model of self-management.

In capitalist economies, especially those with 'right-of-centre' policies, market conditions determine to a large extent what rights employees will have. At times of economic boom and low unemployment, workers are sought after and could have a great deal of power and influence over their choice of working conditions, pay and other employment rights. At times of recession and high unemployment, managers have more power to impose working conditions and other employment contracts on their employees, such as no strike deals. Some governments may also take sides with managers and, through various legislation, increase management prerogatives and erode workers' power and influence. In Britain, for instance, since 1979 trades unions have lost much of their power in large part because of anti-union legislation.

In some capitalist countries such as Germany, where there is a great emphasis on social market ideology, workers' rights are enshrined in law. Codetermination and workers' councils are examples of the ways in which the participation of employees in the management of their workplace is legally ensured.

In most developing countries protection of workers is part and parcel of a larger design based on the principle of social welfare through industrial policies. In India, for instance, labour-intensive technologies are encouraged in order to increase the level of employment. Quotas are set for the companies to recruit workers from among lower castes and migrants from rural areas. There are minimum wages regulations and measures which make it almost impossible for managers to sack their manual workers or deduct from their wages, even if they do not carry out their tasks properly. This is because, given the tradition of extended family in India, the livelihood of so many depends on the head of the household's earnings that to sack him may mean starvation for several people. The picture is slowly changing but there is still a long way to go before industrial and welfare policies are separated from one another.

This kind of situation exists mainly because almost all developing nations lack an extensive and well-developed national welfare state. People depend largely on their families and other relatives for help when they get old, sick or are without a job. They also expect the organisations for which they work to look after them. Social issues such as poverty, unemployment and even ethnic problems are therefore tackled through economic plans via business organisations.

Legal practices

All nations regulate business activities to some degree and companies like individuals are subject to the laws of the country in which they operate. However, some nations have relatively hands-off policies as far as business laws are concerned. The limits beyond which firms, domestic and foreign alike, cannot venture are specified and within those limits the firms are free to pursue their legitimate commercial interests. By contrast, there are other countries where detailed rules and laws cover anything from permission and licence to operate, to social responsibility and specific internal organisation activities. Health and safety, maternity and paternity leave, statutory minimum wage, physical working conditions, protection of employees against dust and noise pollution, pension and medical provisions and childcare facilities are examples of workplace activities which are governed by laws and regulations in many countries.

In France many companies, especially the large ones, are required to spend a certain percentage of their annual turnover on employee training. In the United Kingdom the management has to recognise trades unions as representatives of their employees if a majority of them demands it. In some countries like Germany and Norway, regulations regarding environmental considerations, such as preservation and sustainable use of forests and permissible emission levels, are far more stringent than in their fellow European countries such as Spain, Portugal and Greece, and many developing nations elsewhere.

Sometimes rules and regulations are used as tools to implement governments' trade and industrial policies. For instance, if a country wishes to encourage inward investment it will make it easier for foreign firms and individuals to bring in their capital and to start up a business either on their own or in partnership with local firms. By contrast, if the government wishes to curtail and deter foreign investment, without appearing overtly to do so, it could create a web of red tape and bureaucratic procedures, the unravelling of which might take months if not years before permission to operate is granted to a foreign firm.

The laws regulating HRM practices can also be tied in with other government policies and programmes. In some developing countries HRM must be in line with the national development plans prepared by central planning authorities. In Japan HRM practices are scrutinised in terms of their ability to generate long-term comparative advantage. In France HRM practices reinforce protectionism or neo-mercantilism. In Sweden and the Netherlands they enhance social welfare, and in the United States they comply with market regulations (Johnson, 1985).

Business and employment laws cover both domestic and foreign firms. In the case of foreign companies, in addition to those mentioned above, there could be further rules and regulations with regard to such matters as the amount of assets and shares they may own and the proportion of the profit which they would be allowed to repatriate.

In general, different governments have different regulations regarding the international firms which operate within their territories. Some regulate closely the day-to-day business operations of the firms; some only control the larger scale movements and operations of the foreign enterprise which could have a direct effect upon its domestic economy.

The Canadian government, for instance reserves powers over certain aspects of the operations of international companies, such as when an existing foreign-controlled firm wishes to diversify into new and unrelated industries within Canada. The expansion of already established firms into 'related' businesses, is, however, left unhindered.

Some developing countries, especially those which are suspicious of the activities of the western multinationals, would monitor every single movement of the firms within their country and subject them to various rules and regulations.

The governments of most industrialised countries generally tend to exert rather less control over the operational activities of multinational companies, for example, initial capital inflows, local borrowing, intercorporate debt, transfer pricing, capital transfers among affiliates, and profit allocations. The reason may be because not only are these countries 'host' to the majority of multinationals, they are also 'home' to a large number of them. Therefore unreasonable actions and unnecessary interference with the legal business operations of their 'guest' companies might provoke retaliation by other fellow industrialised countries which host theirs.

Business laws and regulations can sometimes create confusion and difficulties, particularly for multinational firms. For instance, the Japanese practice of forcing older managers into 'voluntary' retirement by withholding their work assignments (Namiki and Sethi, 1988) would violate the Age Discrimination in Employment Act if done in the United States. Quality circles, a well-known vehicle for participatory decision making in Japan, would be illegal in the unionised US settings if the bargaining agent objected to their implementation (Sockell, 1984).

Capital markets

Raising funds for investment can be a complex affair for firms, especially those with operations in different nations. Capital markets around the world have different structures and the companies which would like to raise capital locally need to adjust to these differences, which have their roots in some cases in their respective national ways of doing things.

Advanced industrialised nations, such as those in North America, western and northern Europe, South East Asia, have well-developed capital markets and stock exchanges. The impact of significant fluctuations in interest rates and share prices in some of these markets, such as London, Tokyo and New York, go well beyond their national territories and send powerful 'ripples' around the world.

In many developing countries and some of the ex-socialist economies, capital markets are either non-existent or at early stages of their formation and development. An issue directly related to the capital market is of course companies' fundraising strategies. In some countries such as the United Kingdom and United States, public share ownership is widespread and many companies sell shares to the general public as well as various institutions to raise substantial funds for their investment plans. A consequence of this is that companies' primary obligation is to their shareholders which they have to fulfil by making profits on an annual basis and paying out part of it as dividends. By implication, this shortens planning time horizons to a few years at the most. Long-term planning requires sacrificing short-term gains – something that will not be tolerated by shareholders who might find a more promising outlet elsewhere for their funds.

In some countries, such as Germany and Japan, public share ownership is less prevalent, and shares in many companies are owned by a handful of big institutions. Sometimes, certainly in major Japanese companies, these institutions are represented on the board of directors. Although these companies also have to make profits and satisfy their shareholders, the nature of the ownership pattern makes it easier for them to plough back a large part of their profits into investment. As a result they can afford to take riskier decisions and have long-term planning horizons which might even span over a decade or more.

In many developing countries and emerging economies, local banks rather than shareholders are the primary source of funds. Banks are of course a source of capital in advanced countries as well, but for the system to work properly certain conditions must be in place. For instance, detailed and reliable information on the financial health of the borrowing company and its future plans must be readily available before any funds can change hands. In addition, a strong legal and insurance infrastructure must be in place to recover any likely bad debts.

All advanced countries and many others do have all this, but there are many which do not. In the latter cases, banks lend money to local companies not on the basis of information about their performances, which can be sketchy, out of date and often unreliable, but on the basis of informal connections and networks. Financial institutions which lend money to business enterprises, instead of relying on less than dependable financial reports, take other factors such as the reputation of the borrower, the lender's personal knowledge about the borrower's financial creditability and substantial security pledged in the form of personal property into consideration when evaluating the creditworthiness of the borrowing companies. Such practices could be so firmly embedded in the national financial culture that it might not allow for exceptions to be made for foreign firms with creditable documents about their performance as a security for loans.

Supranational institutions

Global and regional institutions such as the World Trade Organisation (WTO), International Monetary Fund (IMF), International Labour Organisation (ILO) and European Union (EU), have over decades introduced and implemented certain principles and practices in their member states which have significant implications for their economies and the companies which operate within them. In consequence, there is a fair amount of similarities of actions and cultural affinity among these nations.

The WTO agreements, for instance, set out legal ground rules for international commerce and trade policy. They intend to help trade flow as freely as possible, to achieve further liberalisation gradually through negotiation and to set up an impartial means of settling disputes.

The IMF sets out strict conditions for dispensing loans to countries which are temporarily in need of outside help. These conditions usually entail extensive restructuring of the economy, the rolling back of state intervention and subsidies and privatisation of the industry.

The ILO is another global institution with over 170 members. It was set up in 1919 after the Russian revolution to show workers elsewhere that capitalism cared. Its core standards are freedom to form trades unions and bargain collectively, a ban on forced labour and child labour and non-discrimination in the workplace. These are the subject of ILO conventions and implicitly accepted by countries when they join the organisation.

The EU has gone further and deeper than any of the above institutions and devised a whole series of directives which have significant impacts on many economic and social aspects of lives of people and companies within its jurisdiction. These range from the mundane and day-to-day issues, such as traffic signs and road signposts, to economic policies, such as competition laws, and to political strategies, such as foreign affairs and global environment initiatives. The Single Market, which removes any impediment to the free movement of people, capital and goods, the euro, which has so far been adopted by 12 out of 15 member states as their common currency, the establishment of a European rapid reaction force to deal with regional conflicts, the harmonisation of many business laws and employment practices are some of the means by which the member states are coming closer.

None of the above institutions has escaped criticism but nevertheless they do bring some pressure to bear on companies operating within their member states to follow certain standards and conventions. See also Burmester (2000) and Tsogas (2000) for detailed discussions of the aims, structures and directives of the above and other major global and regional institutions and their implications for organisations.

Summary

This chapter explored the role of national and supranational institutions in the formation of what one might also call national identity or national character of a country. The chapter specifically focused on the role of state and its political, social and economic structure and policies, trades unions and legal systems. Examples were also given of major global and regional institutions to demonstrate how supranational institutions can influence companies operating within their member states.

Discussion questions

1. In what ways can the state 'manage' a country's economy and other major affairs? Give a few examples.

2. To what extent does your government participate in the management of your own country's economy and other business-related matters?

3. Are there any trades unions in your country? If yes, how do they compare, for instance, with the British or Japanese models? If not, what mechanisms are there for employees to express their views to senior management?

4. Why should domestic and foreign companies bother at all about legal systems in the countries in which they operate?

Closing Case Study:
GM facing legal action over closing Luton

British union leaders are threatening legal action against the world's largest car-maker over plans to end car assembly at its Luton plant. Unions representing more than 8,000 workers at Vauxhall, General Motors' subsidary, have taken legal advice on whether the proposals breach a 1998 wage agreement. They hope to raise the issue in a meeting with Rick Wagoner, GM's chief executive, in Detroit, from where the Luton closure was announced earlier this month.

GM has arranged a meeting next month between union officials and Mike Burns, president of GM's European arm, but union leaders want to take their case directly to Mr Wagoner. 'We do not believe the GM chief executive was aware of the commitments made in the wage agreement,' said one union leader. 'And we understand that he overrode the advice of his European management in opting to close Luton.'

GM said yesterday that its European strategy board had fully endorsed plans to shed more than 2,200 jobs by ending car production at the Bedfordshire plant. In all, the carmaker is shedding 5,000 jobs across Europe and reducing production capacity by 400,000 cars. After production of the Vectra car ends in 2002, the Luton plant will assemble only vans and off-road vehicles.

Under Vauxhall's 1998 wage agreement, the US carmaker pledged to maintain car assembly with a Vectra replacement at Luton. It also promised new investment to increase output from about 30 to 45 cars an hour. In return, unions agreed to new working patterns and conditions. Yesterday, GM declined to comment directly on the latest legal threat to the Luton plan.

It is already facing possible action over an alleged breach of European law in failing to consult unions about the proposals. Officials nevertheless indicated that the company would fight any legal challenge over the 1998 wage agreement. They pointed to a clause enabling GM to reconsider its commitments following 'adverse changes to the economic environment'. GM lost $181 million (£121 million) in Europe in the third quarter and some analysts fear that its fourth-quarter losses in the region could exceed $500 million.

The US group's handling of Vauxhall and the closure announcement are being investigated by the British parliament's trade and industry select committee. The committee is to hold open hearings in Luton next month about the GM restructuring. Union leaders want the committee and government ministers to condemn GM's plans. So far, ministers have expressed disappointment at the move and offered assistance for workers threatened with redundancy.

Source: 29 Dec. 2000, *Financial Times* CD-ROM 2000

Closing case study questions

1. What were the main causes of the unions' grievance and decision to take legal action against General Motors?

2. How did GM managers justify their strategy which was opposed by the unions?

3. How did GM management react to the unions' threat of legal action?

4. If a situation such as this occurred in your country, how would it be handled by the two sides (employees and management)?

Annotated further reading

Budhwar, P. S. and **Debrah, Y. (eds)** (2001) *HRM in Developing Countries*. London: Routledge.
The book covers a large number of developing countries and discusses HRM within their specific societal context.

Lane, C. (1995) *Industry and Society in Europe: Stability and Change in Britain, Germany and France*. Aldershot: Edward Elgar.
An analysis of the influences of a country's major societal institutions on the management of organisations operating within that country.

Warner, M. (ed.) (1999) *Management in Emerging Countries*. London: International Thomson.
This book differs from the above in two ways: First, it covers countries which have come through the developing status and are now fully on their way to industrialisation. Second, the management issues discussed go well beyond HRM.

References

Brewster, C. (1995) 'Towards a European model of human resource management', *Journal of International Business Studies* 26(1): 1–22.

Budhwar, P. and Sparrow, P. (1998) 'National factors determining Indian and British HRM practices: an empirical study', *Management International Review* 38: 105–21.

Burmester, B. (2000) 'Global and regional institutions: the international governance of international business', in M. H. Tayeb, *International Business*. London: Pearson Education. Chapter 3.

Ferner, A. and Hyman, R. (1999) *Changing Industrial Relations in Europe,* 2nd edn. Oxford: Blackwell.

Johnson, C. (1985) 'The institutional foundations of Japanese industrial policies', *California Management Review* 27: 59–69.

Liberman, L. and Torbiörn, I. (2000) 'Variances in staff-related management practices in eight European country subsidiaries of a global firm', *International Journal of Human Resource Management* 11(2): 37–59.

Liberman, L. and Zander, L. (2000) 'Does institutional environment matter? – management practices across four subsidiaries of a multinational company'. Paper presented at the Academy of International Business conference, Phoenix, Arizona, November.

Namiki, N. and Sethi, S. P. (1988) 'Japan', in R. Nath (ed.) *Comparative Management: A Regional View*. Cambridge MA: Ballinger. pp. 1–22.

Sockell, D. (1984) 'The legality of employee-participation programs in unionised firms', *Industrial and Labour Relations Review* 19: 357–94.

Tayeb, M. H. (1988) *Organizations and National Culture: A Comparative Analysis*. London: Sage.

Tsogas, G. (2000) 'Labour standards, corporate codes of conduct and labour regulation in international trade', in M. H. Tayeb, *International Business*. London: Pearson Education. Chapter 4.

CHAPTER 3

Major cultural characteristics

Rajen K. Gupta and Abinash Panda

Learning objectives

When you finish reading this chapter you should:

- understand both holistic and analytical approaches to the study of culture
- understand how major researchers have defined cultural characteristics
- understand how cultural values are linked to work values
- understand how nations could be clustered on the basis of cultural characteristics

Opening Case Study:

A Japanese–American Conversation

Have you ever observed a Japanese and an American conversing? The Japanese person places himself at a distance that is uncomfortably far for an American. The American responds by unconsciously inching toward the Japanese. The Japanese responds to the American's advance by moving slightly back.

Concern for accuracy

Recently, a friend of ours had gone to Mumbai, a city in western India, from Delhi, the capital city located in the north. One night, he was roaming with his cousin along the street. He wanted to know the time. He saw a stranger coming from the opposite side.

Our friend: Excuse me, what is the time now?

The stranger: It is 12 minutes past 11.

Cousin of our friend [as he could not hear]: What?

Our friend: Around 11:15.

The stranger overheard their conversation. To the surprise of our friend, the stranger came back and said, 'It is not 11:15, it is only 11:12.'

Introduction

Let us analyse these two examples given above. The first example is about what Edward Hall terms 'proxemics'. It signifies the distance people keep between themselves in various social situations. The second example is about how attitude and behaviour vary within a country. It is about the difference in attitude toward 'precision' between the Mumbaites and the Delhites, within India. If one keeps on observing the behaviours and attitudes of people, there is no dearth of instances such as described above. These indicate that culture differs at various levels. It could vary between nations or between regions within a country.

The previous two chapters discussed the origins and scope of national culture. Here we study major cultural values, attitudes and other characteristics that people may hold and we explore briefly their implications for workplace behaviours. Chapters 4 and 5 will then examine the issue of national culture and workplace behaviours further with special reference to a major European multinational company and a group of emerging countries in the Persian Gulf region.

Cultural characteristics

The cultural characteristics of a society are manifested in terms of the values, behaviour and attitudes displayed by its members. Culture and its normative characteristics are crystallised in the values that they hold about life and the world around them. These values in turn affect their attitudes about the form of behaviour considered more appropriate and effective in any given situation. What are the differences between values, attitudes and behaviour?

Values

A value is that which is explicitly or implicitly desirable to an individual or group and which influences the selection from available modes, means and ends of actions. Values can be both consciously and unconsciously held. Values, therefore, reflect general beliefs that either define what is right and wrong or specify general preferences.

Research has shown that personal values of top level managers affect corporate strategy and that managerial values affect all forms of organisational behaviour, including selection and reward systems and supervisor–subordinate relationships. They also influence group behaviour, communication, leadership, and conflict management modes. For example, American managers strongly believe in individual achievement, whereas Indian managers strive for the enhancement of family status.

Attitudes

An attitude expresses values and disposes a person to act or react in a certain way towards something. Attitudes are the basis for the kind of relationship between a person and an object. For example, market research has shown that French Canadians have a positive attitude towards pleasant and sweet smells, whereas English Canadians prefer smells with efficient or clean connotations. Advertisements for Irish Spring soap directed at French Canadians therefore stress pleasant smell, whereas the advertisement for English Canadians stresses the inclusion of effective deodorants. Attitudes are people's beliefs about specific objects or situations. Attitudes can be positive or negative, whereas values are always positive preferences.

Behaviour

Behaviour is any form of human action, which can always be observed. The example of the conversation between a Japanese and an American in the opening case study shows that the Japanese stand farther apart than the Americans. This is so because the Japanese culture is different from the North American culture. Culture guides the behaviour of people living in that cultural system.

How to understand a culture

There are several ways to study and understand national culture such as by exploring the way a nation has evolved, reviewing the literature and art, or through rigorous study of various aspects (or dimensions) of the culture. In this section we examine two major approaches to understanding national culture.

Holistic approach

The most common-sense approach to understanding a culture is to see it as a 'way of life' of its people. Different elements or aspects of a way of life are connected with each other. There is a natural consistency among them. In this sense, culture is a holistic idea, which cannot be easily broken into its elements. Culture can also be seen as a holographic phenomenon, in which every part contains the essence of the whole. This is because all parts must be guided by the same set of values. Hence one way of understanding culture may be to understand a characteristic object, event or ritual with a salient position in that culture. Gannon (1994) has used such a holistic approach to understand cultures across the world. He has adopted the concept of cultural metaphor for quickly understanding the cultural mindset of a nation. The method involves identifying some phenomenon or activity of a nation's culture that all or most of its members consider very important and with which they identify closely. The characteristics of the metaphor become the basis for understanding the common characteristics of the culture.

Table 3.1 Cultural metaphors used by Gannon to describe countries

Country	Metaphor	Country	Metaphor
Italy	Italian opera	Britain	Traditional British house
Germany	Symphony	France	Wine
Sweden	Stuga	Belgium	Lace
Spain	Bullfight	Ireland	Conversation
Israel	Kibbutzim	Nigeria	Marketplace
Japan	Japanese garden	India	The Dance of Shiva
USA	American football	China	Family altar

Source: Adapted from Gannon (1994)

It was Geertz (1973) who authored the pioneering study of using metaphors as conceptual systems. He studied 500 Balinese cockfights, both ethnographically and statistically, and demonstrated that Balinese cockfights represent the hidden culture of Bali, particularly the male culture.

Gannon (1994) uses cultural metaphors to describe countries and, as can be seen in Table 3.1, he proposes various metaphors for a number of countries around the world.

As an example we discuss here Gannon's (1994, p. 301) choice of 'The Dance of Shiva' (Coomaraswamy, 1969) as the cultural metaphor for India. He explains his choice thus:

> It is not always possible to identify a nicely logical and easily understandable basis for many of the contradictions that exist in Indian society . . . In India, the philosophy of life and the mental structure of the people come not from a study of books but from tradition. However much foreign civilisation and new aspirations might have affected the people of India, the spiritual nutrient of Hindu philosophy has not dried up or decayed; within this tradition, the role of the Dance of Shiva, described below are accepted by all Hindus:
>
> Shiva rises from his rapture and, dancing, sends through inert matter pulsing waves of awakening sound. Suddenly, matter also dances, appearing as brilliance around him. Dancing, Shiva sustains the world's diverse phenomena, its creation and existence. And in the fullness of time, still dancing, he destroys all forms – everything disintegrates, apparently into nothingness, and is given new rest. Then out of thin vapour, matter and life are created again. Shiva's dance scatters the darkness of illusion (*lila*), burns the thread of causality (*karma*), stamps out evil (*avidya*), showers grace, and lovingly plunges the soul into the ocean of bliss (*ananda*). (Gannon, 1994, p. 301)

Religious diversities and contradictions coexist in Indian society. The majority of Indians are tradition oriented. The idea of cycles is a common thread in traditional Indian philosophy and is manifest in every aspect of life in India: Cyclical Hindu Philosophy (a journey toward salvation), the Cycle of Life (student – family – retirement – *sannyasin*), the Family Cycle (continuation of generation), the Cycle of Social Interaction (a sense of *dharma*), the Work and Recreation Cycle (progress toward salvation through unselfish performance of work) are well represented by the Dancing Shiva.

The Dance of Shiva portrays the world's endless cycle of creation, existence and recreation, and Hindu philosophy depicts the endless cycle of soul through birth, life, death and reincarnation. India's history reflects the cycle of chaos and harmony epitomised by the Dance of Shiva. The Dancing Shiva has been used to describe India and the Indian mindset. In that sense, cultural metaphor is a guide, map or beacon that helps an outsider understand and relate to a particular culture. This approach takes a 'holistic' view of culture. In an holistic approach, one takes a general overview of the cultural characteristics. In the process, the diversities and contradictions to the general patterns of behaviour are ignored as 'deviations'. Such a holistic approach is useful in getting a quick insight into a culture, but it does not make it easy to compare two or more cultures. For such a purpose a more analytical approach is used.

Analytical approach

In an analytical approach, every culture is characterised by a set of dimensions. Cultures are compared along these dimensions. Cross-cultural psychologists and cultural anthropologists emphasise a small number of factors or dimensions while comparing societies and cultures. This approach is also known as a dimensional approach. (Useful ideas based on such an approach are described later in the chapter.)

Comparing both approaches

When we compare both holistic (cultural metaphor) and analytical approaches, we find the following:

- Metaphors are readily understandable to both researchers and laypersons because they are anchored to easily recognised phenomena.
- The cultural metaphor method is open to new perspectives and viewpoints and new metaphors for a particular nation are welcome if they increase our understanding.
- Cultural metaphor method is grounded, whereas analytical method is based upon abstraction.
- An analytical approach is useful to study various micro-aspects of a culture.
- An analytical approach is useful for cross-cultural studies, hence, has been used in many cross-cultural studies.

Kluckhohn and Strodtbeck's value orientation model

Two anthropologists, Florence Kluckhohn and Fred Strodtbeck (1961), used dimensional approach to characterise cultures. In their efforts to compare the cultures of Native Americans, Anglos and Hispanics in the American Southwest, they

Table 3.2   Kluckhohn and Strodtbeck's value orientations

Attitude toward (problem areas)	Coping mechanisms		
	1	2	3
Nature	Subjugation	Harmony	Mastery
Time	Past	Present	Future
Human nature	Basically evil	Basically good	Mixture of good and evil
Activity orientation	Being	Containing and controlling	Doing
Human relationship	By rank and class	By entire group	By individual
Space	Private	Public	Mixed

Source: Adapted from Kluckhohn and Strodtbeck (1961)

developed six dimensions related to six basic problem areas which all human societies face and have found solutions for in their own various ways. As Table 3.2 shows, these dimensions are: (1) Relationship to nature; (2) Time orientation; (3) Basic human nature; (4) Activity orientation; (5) Human relationship; (6) Attitude towards space. According to Kluckhohn and Strodtbeck, societies could be compared with one another on the basis of these dimensions, and a number of cross-cultural researchers have done just that in order to assess various national cultures in their studies.

Relationship to nature: subjugation, harmony and mastery

Societies that view themselves as subjugated to nature consider life as essentially ordained. People in these societies are not masters of their own destinies. They believe that any attempt to change the inevitable is futile. Societies that view themselves as living in harmony with nature believe that people must alter their behaviour to accommodate nature. Societies that view themselves as able to master nature think in terms of supremacy of the human race, and harnessing the forces of nature.

The NASA expedition of the United States was clearly an attempt to dominate the natural world, whereas the Japanese and Chinese believe in living in harmony with nature. The Japanese refer to Mount Fuji as Fujiyama San. In the Japanese language, 'San' is an honorific adjective, similar to Mr or Mrs in English. Feng Shui is popular in China and literally means that 'wind water' are earth forces. The goal of Feng Shui is to be in harmony with nature. The layout and position of offices or rooms in houses are guided by Feng Shui.

Compared to Japanese and Chinese, the Arab culture is fatalistic towards attempts to change the world. In 1990, when a tunnel collapsed in the holy city of Mecca in Saudi Arabia, during the annual pilgrimage, King Fahd told Saudi security officials that it was God's will, which is above everything. Had the people not died there, they would have died elsewhere and at the same predestined moment (*The Independent*, 4 July 1990).

Time orientation: past, present, and future

Societies that are oriented towards the past look for solutions there: what would our forefathers have done? Societies that are present oriented consider the immediate effects of their actions: what will happen if I do this? Societies that are future oriented look to the long-term results of today's events: what will happen to future generations if we do these things today?

Generally, Hollywood box office hits are based on sci-fi and space odysseys, which are futuristic, while historical drama dictates box office collection in the past-oriented Japanese society. Samurai movies are usually the most popular in Japan. The weather forecasting system in China uses techniques that are long-term past oriented. Their forecasting is based on data which are 3,000 years old.

Basic human nature: evil, good and mixed

Societies that believe people are primarily evil focus on controlling behaviour through specified codes of conduct and sanctions for wrongdoing. Societies that believe people are essentially good exhibit trust and rely on verbal agreements. Societies that see people as mixed probably also see people as changeable and would focus on means to modify behaviour, to encourage desired behaviour and discourage behaviours that are not desirable.

During a two-year stay in Japan, an Indian recounted an interesting experience. He had to order some books from PHP Inc, a Japanese publishing company. In his words:

I was quite taken aback when my Japanese friends advised me to send money to the publisher in an envelope. Back in India we are not used to sending money in an envelope. I put the money including some coins in an envelope and sent through ordinary post. To my surprise, I received all the books I had ordered within four days.[1]

The Japanese see the individual as good and inherently trustworthy, whereas the Indians have a different view about individual. The number of legal litigations is much higher in India than in Japan. The police in Japan have the primary duty of showing directions, whereas for the Indian police it is crime control.

Activity orientation: being, containing and controlling, and doing

Societies that are primarily 'being' oriented are emotional. People react spontaneously based on what they feel at that time. Hindu and Buddhist cultures are being oriented. They believe in reincarnation, which means that individuals are born into their present status and circumstances by virtue of their behaviour in a

1 As experienced by Abinash Panda, co-author of this chapter, from his stay in Japan from 1992 to 1994.

previous life. Achievement is of marginal importance to them. They accept life as it is without much struggle for material gain.

Societies that are 'doing' oriented are constantly striving to achieve. Self-identification is achieved through action, performance and achievements. People are driven by a need to accomplish challenging tasks. Those concerned with containing and controlling focus on moderation and orderliness. People seek to achieve a balance in life and in society. For instance, Canadians working in Malaysia found that workers were more interested in spending extra time with their families and friends than in earning an overtime pay bonus (Adler, 1997).

Human relationship: individual, lineal, and co-lineal

Societies that are primarily individual oriented believe that individuals should be independent and take responsibility for their own actions. Those that are lineal are concerned with the family line and the power structure that underlies a hierarchy. Those that are co-lineal are group oriented and emphasise group interactions and actions.

American culture values individualism and perceives fulfilment as gained through personal achievement. When Tiger Woods was winning the 1997 Masters by a record 12 strokes, one American spectator commented: 'What this young man is doing out here is phenomenal. ... I like him for his demeanour, how he handles himself so well for such a young kid' (*International Herald Tribune*, 7 November 1997). In contrast, even at informal dinners, a Japanese talks about himself by saying 'we Japanese' rather than 'I' (Sullivan, 1992).

Family members of Indian political leaders find it easier to enter into politics compared to family members of American politicians. The late Rajiv Gandhi was accepted by Indians as the prime minister after the death of Mrs Indira Gandhi, whereas President George W. Bush (Jr) had to prove his credentials before he was nominated as presidential candidate for his party. These differences exist because American society is individualistic, whereas Indian society is lineal and Japanese society is co-lineal.

Conception of space: private, public and mixed

Societies that conceive space as private respect private ownership, value privacy and maintain social distance. Those that conceive space as public are suspicious of activities conducted in secret. Social proximity is taken for granted. Public meetings are valued. Finally, societies that have 'mixed' attitudes distinguish private and public activities. Americans are inhibited about entering the office of a colleague when the door is closed. It is usual to knock on the door. Germans dislike open offices and prefer to work with their doors closed. In Japan, space is mostly public and activities conducted in private are suspect.

Cultural context: Edward T. Hall

The well-known anthropologist Edward T. Hall (1976) has carried out many studies using the analytical approach. He focuses primarily on the communication pattern found within cultures and emphasises three dimensions along which societies can be compared:

1. *Context*, or amount of information that must be explicitly stated if a message or communication is to be successful.
2. *Space*, or the ways of communicating through specific handling of personal space.
3. *Time*, which is either monochronic (scheduling or completing one activity at a time) or polychronic (not distinguishing between activities and completing them simultaneously).

Let us explore these dimensions further.

High context and low context cultures

Hall places societies in a continuum of high context through low context on the 'context' dimension, as shown in Table 3.3, although no culture exists exclusively at either extreme. In general, a high context culture is homogeneous to the point that meaning is communicated as much through the context of the communication as through the content. By contrast, low context cultures are usually heterogeneous. Meaning must be communicated principally through the content because context is an unreliable indicator of what somebody else, who is in a different group, means. Groups could be on the basis of caste, religion, educational achievement, and so forth.

Communication in high context cultures such as Japan, China, and the Arab countries uses far more expressions than are usual in low context cultures, such as Germany, Scandinavia and the United States. Many Japanese communicate with each other without words at all, called *haragei* or 'belly language'. They speak with great reserve and expect listeners to pick up implied messages. In a simple gesture or in the tone of the speaker, the Japanese listener gleans the whole meaning. The Japanese learn from an early age how to understand one another without verbal communication.

Table 3.3   Hall's dichotomy of high context and low context cultures

Aspects	High context culture	Low context culture
Human relationship	Long lasting	Shorter duration
Communication	Implicit (through shared code)	Explicit
Authority	Centralised at the top	Diffused
Agreement	Verbal	Written
Insider–outsider	Distinguished	Less distinguished
Cultural patterns	Ingrained, slow to change	Change relatively easily

Personal space

'Proxemics' is a word coined by Hall to describe the personal space dimension. It signifies the distance people keep between themselves in various social situations. People operating within the same culture know, without giving the matter any thought, how far apart to stand during first meeting, whether it is appropriate to shake hands or hug, or how close to stand at a cocktail reception. Moving closer than the situation calls for will be interpreted, depending upon the specific circumstance, either as aggressive, presuming an unwarranted degree of friendship, or as sexual advance. Placing oneself too far away from another person in a given situation will be interpreted as standoffishness, a lack of interest, enmity or disgust.

As a general rule, given the same circumstances, the Japanese tend to keep a greater physical distance than Americans. In a study of touching behaviours in the United States, Puerto Rico, France and Britain, researchers observed people seated in outdoor cafés in each of the four countries and counted the number of touches during one hour of conversation. The results were: San Juan, 180 touches per hour; Paris, 110 per hour; Florida, 1 per hour; London, 0 per hour (Munter, 1993).

P-time and M-time

Hall (1983) distinguished two patterns of time that govern the individualistic and collectivistic cultures: monochronic time schedule (M-time) and polychronic time schedule (P-time). According to Hall, P-time stresses the involvement of people and completion of transactions rather than adherence to pre-set schedules. Appointments are not taken seriously and, as a consequence, are frequently broken.

M-time patterns appear to predominate in individualistic, low context cultures, while P-time patterns appear to predominate in group-based, high context cultures. M-time cultures tend to have a linear and compartmentalised view of time, while P-time cultures are generally more flexible. In P-time cultures, time is seen as contextually based and relationally oriented.

In sum, in a high context society time tends to be polychronic. There is a heavy investment in socialising members so that information does not need to be explicitly stated to be understood. Members of such a culture would have known one another for long periods of time and there is a strong agreement as to what is and is not expected. In the high context Japanese society there is even an aphorism that expressly addresses this issue: 'He who knows does not speak; he who speaks does not know.' Hence, verbal communication is frequently not needed and may well impede the transmission of the message. Members of the high context societies tend to have less physical space between them when communicating than do those in low context societies.

Culture and workplace

Basic social values get expressed in various settings, including the workplace. Social values relevant for a work setting are accepted as work values. Work values are beliefs pertaining to a desirable end state (e.g. high pay) or behaviour (e.g. working with people). As work values refer only to goals in the work setting, they are more specific than social values.

Chapter 4 will critique in detail major work-related values and attitudes and their implications for management styles and other workplace behaviours, using an empirical study conducted in Britain, France and Sweden. Here we mention general issues, principles and models and describe some useful ways of looking at work values.

Hofstede's cultural dimensions

Hofstede's (1980) research compares work-related values across a range of cultures. He investigated the attitudes held by 116,000 employees in branches and affiliates of IBM in around 40 countries. His findings show that:

- Work-related values are not universal.
- Underlying values persist when a multinational company tries to impose the same norms on all its foreign ventures.
- Local values determine how headquarters' rules and policies are interpreted.
- A multinational that insists on uniformity across its ventures is in danger of creating morale problems and inefficiencies.

Further, Hofstede proposes four dimensions of national culture: individualism/collectivism, uncertainty avoidance, power distance and masculinity/femininity.

Individualism is the degree to which individual decision making and action are accepted and encouraged by the society. *Collectivism* is the opposite. Where individualism is high, the society emphasises the role of the individual; where collectivism is high, the society emphasises the role of the group. Some societies view individualism positively and see it as the basis for creativity and achievement. Others view it with disapproval and see it as disruptive to group harmony and cooperation.

Uncertainty avoidance is the degree to which people feel threatened by ambiguous situations and try to avoid them. Where uncertainty avoidance is high, the society is concerned with certainty and security and seeks to avoid uncertainty. Where uncertainty avoidance is low, the society is comfortable with a high degree of uncertainty and open to ambiguities. Some societies view certainty as necessary, so that people can function without worrying about the consequences of uncertainty. Others view uncertainty as providing excitement and opportunities for innovation and change.

Power distance is the degree to which power differences are accepted and sanctioned by society. Where power distance is high, the society believes that there should be a well-defined order of inequality in which everyone has a rightful place. Where power distance is low, the prevalent belief is that all people should have equal rights and the opportunity to change their position in the society.

Some societies view a well-ordered distribution of power as contributing to a well-managed society because each person knows what their position is. Others view power as corrupting and believe that those with less power will inevitably suffer at the hands of those with more.

Masculinity is the degree to which traditional masculine values are important to a society. Traditional masculine values include assertiveness, performance, ambition, achievement and material possessions, while traditional feminine values focus on the quality of life, the environment, nurturing and concern for the less fortunate. In societies that are high on masculinity, sex roles are clearly differentiated and men are dominant. If *femininity* is high sex roles are more fluid and feminine values predominate throughout. Some societies see the traditional male values as being necessary for survival; that is men must be aggressive and women must be protected. Others view both sexes as equal contributors to society and they believe that dominance by traditional male values is destructive. Most countries are not at the extreme, but moderately high or moderately low.

Later on, based on research by Michael Bond among students of 22 countries, Hofstede added a fifth dimension: *time orientation* (long-term versus short-term). This is also known as Confucian dynamism (Hofstede and Bond, 1988). This measures employees' devotion to the work ethic and their respect for tradition. Long-term oriented societies (or nations) value thrift and have greater degree of perseverance. Many observers attribute the rapid economic growth of Asia's 'Four Tigers' – Hong Kong, Singapore, South Korea and Taiwan – to their extremely strong work ethic and commitment to traditional Confucian values.

André Laurent's study of management styles

Besides work values, another aspect of organisational life that is equally important is managerial style. André Laurent (1983) has studied the diversity in managerial style across nations.

Every manager has his own set of preferences that in some way guide his behaviour in organisations. It is critical for managers to identify and understand these preferences. Laurent argued that these preferences guide managers to develop their own management theories. These management theories are implicit to the manager himself. These implicit management theories get expressed in the form of attitudes towards managing. As the preferences of managers vary across cultures and nations, so do the implicit management theories.

Laurent focused primarily on the attitudes towards power and relationship. In his study he included nine European countries (Switzerland, Germany, Denmark, Sweden, United Kingdom, Netherlands, Belgium, Italy, France) and the United States. He used four parameters: perceptions of organisation as political systems authority systems, role formulation systems, and hierarchical relationship systems. This study treated management as a process by which managers expressed their cultural values. The major finding, as discussed in the following sections, is that the national origin of European managers significantly affects their views of what proper management should be.

Organisations as political systems

This aspect deals with (a) political role played by managers in society; (b) manager's perception of power motivation within the organisation; (c) assessment of the degree to which organisational structures are clearly defined in the minds of managers. The French and Italian managers have stronger perceptions of their political role and emphasise the importance of power motivation within the organisation. They also report a fairly hazy notion of organisation structure. The opposite is true for the Danish and the British. These results may provide some insight into the extent to which managers from different countries tend to interpret their organisational experience in power terms.

Organisations as authority systems

This aspect deals with the conception of hierarchical structure in the organisation. It examines if managers agree to (a) the belief that the reason for having a hierarchical structure is to know who has authority over whom; (b) if there is a perception of authority crisis in the organisation; (c) the image of a manager as a negotiator. The study revealed three country clusters: Latin countries (Belgium, Italy and France) at the upper end of the continuum, the United States, Switzerland and Germany at the lower end and the rest of the countries in the middle. Organisations are seen more frequently as authority systems by French managers than by American managers.

The French, Italian and Belgian managers reported a more personal and social concept of authority, which is based on personal traits and relationships, that regulates relationships among individuals in organisations. The American, Swiss and German managers seem to report a more rational view of authority, which is based on the attributes of the role or function, that regulates interaction among tasks and functions.

Organisations as role formalisation systems

This aspect focuses on the relative importance of defining the functions and roles of organisational members, with emphasis on detailed job descriptions, well-defined functions and precisely defined roles. The study found that there is a lower insistence on the need for role formalisation in Sweden, the United States and the Netherlands than in the remaining seven countries.

Organisations as hierarchical relationship systems

This aspect deals with managers' attitudes toward organisational relationships. It was found that there are sharp differences in management attitudes towards organisational relationships as one moves from northern Europe and the United States at the lower end of the continuum to the Latin countries of Europe at the higher end. These differences in attitudes help one to understand managers' preferences for traditional hierarchical structures, which are primarily characterised by unity of command or matrix structure which involves reporting to more than one boss. Managers who accept organisational relationships as hierarchical are uncomfortable with the matrix structure. In this respect, the score of the Swedish managers is the lowest and Italian managers the highest. Consequently, matrix-type organisational structure should have better prospects in Sweden than in Italy. The phenomenal success of matrix-type structures in ABB, a Swedish organisation, validates the finding.

Schwartz's study of cultural values and meanings of work

Building on previous research on the meaning of work, Schwartz (1999) examined the association and influence of values on the ways in which people in various cultures attribute meanings to work. His study was based on data collected on cultural values from 49 countries, and his samples were teachers and students in those countries. He explored types of values by which societies or nations can be compared and identified seven values: conservatism; intellectual autonomy; affective autonomy; hierarchy; egalitarianism; mastery; harmony. He structured these seven values in three dimensions: (a) conservatism versus autonomy (includes both intellectual and affective aspects); (b) hierarchy versus egalitarianism; (c) mastery versus harmony. Table 3.4 summarises the seven types of values and what each of these value types emphasises.

Schwartz further explored how these values are associated with and influence individual work values and focused on three aspects of work: work centrality; societal norm about work; work goal.

Work centrality

Work centrality is the importance and significance of work in a person's total life. Schwartz found that work is more likely to be experienced as central to life in societies where mastery and hierarchy values are important and less in societies where affective autonomy, egalitarianism, harmony and conservatism are valued. Work was found to be central to the lives of the Japanese, Germans and Americans.

Table 3.4   Schwartz's seven value types

Types of values	Cultural emphasis on
Conservatism	Maintenance of status quo, propriety, solidarity of the group or traditional order
Intellectual autonomy	Desirability of individuals independently pursuing their own ideas and intellectual directions
Affective autonomy	Desirability of individuals independently pursuing affectively positive experience
Hierarchy	Legitimacy of an unequal distribution of power, roles, and resources
Egalitarianism	Equality, social justice, freedom of individual members
Mastery	Self-assertion, ambition, success, competence
Harmony	Living in harmony with nature

Source: Adapted from Schwartz (1999)

Societal norm about work

The societal norm about work concerns whether society accepts an individual's right to meaningful and interesting work versus whether society forces individuals to accept work as a duty or obligation that everyone owes to that society, even if the work is not interesting or satisfying for the individual. In societies where egalitarianism and intellectual autonomy are important, it is more likely that the individual's right to meaningful and interesting work is accepted by the society. In societies where conservatism and hierarchy values are important, the societal norm is more likely to make people accept work as a duty or obligation that one owes to society, even if the work is not interesting or satisfying for the person. In Germany it is accepted that each individual is entitled to interesting and meaningful work. The extent of social acceptance of this view of work is lower in Japan and the United States.

Work goal

The rewards that people generally seek or try to achieve through work are their work goals. In societies where hierarchy and mastery values are emphasised (e.g. China and the United States), people are more likely to work for prestige, authority and power than in societies where egalitarianism and harmony are valued (e.g. Sweden and Finland). In societies where autonomy values are emphasised, people are more likely to view work as a medium to fulfil their urge for personal growth, autonomy and creativity than in societies where conservatism is valued. In societies where conservatism and hierarchy are valued, people work for pay and security.

Let us consider two countries – Zimbabwe and Switzerland (the French-speaking part). The findings of the study indicated that the Zimbabweans give strong emphasis to conservatism and hierarchy values and weak emphasis to intellectual autonomy values, whereas the French-speaking Swiss emphasise just the opposite. It follows that a Zimbabwean is more likely to work for pay and security than a Swiss. Naturally higher pay and a guaranteed job can be successfully used as motivators for the Zimbabwean. One can successfully explore cultural characteristics in relation to work on the basis of the cultural groupings of nations and positions in the above-mentioned three dimensions.

Trompenaars's study of business cultures

Another study of how cultures differ by Fons Trompenaars (1993) is receiving increasing attention. He administered a research questionnaire to over 15,000 managers from 28 countries. He developed his seven dimensions on the bases of Talcott Parsons value and relationship dimensions (the ways in which people deal with each other) besides dimensions related to attitudes towards both time and environment taken from other studies. The results of his research offer a wealth of information that helps to explain how cultures differ and offer practical ways in which multinational corporations can do business in various countries. The following discussion examines each of the seven dimensions developed by Trompenaars.

Universalism versus particularism (relationships and rules)

Universalism is the belief that ideas and practices can be applied everywhere without modification. Particularism is the belief that circumstances dictate how ideas and practices should be applied. For instance, rules penalising sales staff who do not fulfil their quotas apply whether or not the individual claims extenuating circumstances. The particularist emphasises the obligations of relationship. A salesman who failed to fill quota because of his concern for a sick son can be excused. Trompenaars found that in countries such as the United States, Australia, Germany, Sweden and United Kingdom there was high universalism, while countries such as Venezuela, former Soviet Union, Indonesia and China were high on particularism.

Collectivism versus individualism (group and individual)

Individualism refers to people regarding themselves as individuals, whereas collectivism refers to people regarding themselves as part of a group. Do we relate to others by discovering what each one of us wants individually and then try to negotiate differences or do we place ahead some shared concept of the public and collective good? The United States, Czechoslovakia, Argentina, former Soviet Union and Mexico have high individualism, whereas Nepal and Kuwait have lowest individualism.

Neutral versus affective (feelings and relationships)

A neutral culture is one in which emotions are held in check. Both Japan and the United Kingdom are high neutral cultures. People in these countries try not to show their feelings; they act stoically and maintain their composure. An affective culture is one in which emotions are openly and naturally expressed. People in affective cultures often smile a great deal, talk loudly when they are excited and greet each other with a great deal of enthusiasm. Mexico, the Netherlands and Switzerland are examples of high affective cultures.

Specific versus diffuse (how far we get involved)

A specific culture is one in which individuals have a large public space they readily let others enter and share and a small private space they guard closely and share with only close friends and associates. A diffuse culture is one in which both public and private space are similar in size and individuals guard their public space carefully, because entry into public space affords entry into the private space as well. For instance, if the marketing manager met his or her salesperson in the club, their encounter would be minimally influenced by their work relationship. In diffuse cultures, the superior–subordinate work relationship pervades all other dealings. Austria, the United Kingdom, United States and Switzerland are all specific cultures, while Venezuela, China and Spain are diffuse cultures.

Achievement versus ascription (how we accord status)

An achievement culture is one in which people are accorded status based on how well they perform their functions. An ascription culture is one in which status is attributed based on who and what a person is. Australia, the United States, United Kingdom and Switzerland are achievement cultures, while Venezuela, Indonesia and China are ascription cultures.

How we manage time

Besides the five dimensions related to relationships, Trompenaars identified two other dimensions. One of these is related to the way in which people deal with the time. He has identified two different approaches: sequential and synchronous. In cultures where the sequential approach is prevalent, people tend to do one activity at a time, keep appointments strictly and show strong preference for following plans as they are laid out and not deviating from them. In cultures where the synchronous approach is common, people tend to do more than one activity at a time, appointments are approximate and may be changed at a moment's notice and schedules generally carry less importance than relationships.

In the United States, people tend to be guided by sequential time orientation and thus set a schedule and stick to it. Mexicans operate under more of a synchronous time orientation and tend to be much more flexible, often building slack into their schedules to allow for interruptions. The French are similar to Mexicans and when making plans often determine the objectives they want to accomplish but leave open the timing and other factors that are beyond their control.

Another interesting time-related contrast is the degree to which cultures are past or present oriented as opposed to future oriented. In countries such as the United States, Italy and Germany, the future is more important than the past or present. In countries such as Venezuela, Indonesia and Spain, the present is the most important. In France and Belgium all three time periods are of approximately equal importance.

How we relate to nature

Trompenaars also examined the ways in which people deal with their environment. Specific attention should be given to whether they believe in controlling outcomes (inner directed) or letting things take their own course (outer directed). One of the statements in Trompenaars's questionnaire was: 'What happens to me is my doing.' Managers who believe in controlling their environment would agree with it. In the United States, managers feel strongly that they are masters of their own fate. This helps to account for their dominant attitude towards the environment and discomfort when things seem to get out of control. Many Asian cultures do not share this view. Managers from Asian societies agree with the statement: 'Sometimes, I feel that I do not have enough control over the directions my life is taking.'

Trompenaars's system meets practical more than academic needs. It draws together and applies ideas contributed by a range of scholars: Kluckhohn and Strodtbeck (particularism versus universalism; the way we relate to time and nature); Hofstede (universalism versus particularism; collectivism versus individualism; how we accord status) Laurent (specific and diffuse; how we accord status); Hall (how we manage time). It may be worth mentioning here that Trompenaars derives practical tips on the basis of value categories discussed above from interactions with managers from different cultures.

Clustering nations

As can be observed from earlier discussions, people across a group of nations have similar attitudes toward various aspects of life, which are different from those in another group. A cluster is a group of nations that has similar characteristics. The use of national units of clustering is logical because national boundaries delineate the legal, political and social environments within which organisations and workers operate. Yet, to understand why certain countries cluster, one should look across national boundaries for the dimensions underlying the clusters, which primarily could be geography, language or religion.

Geography precedes other variables, such as language and religion, because a culture spreads first to those areas nearest its 'birthplace'. A language contains meanings and values that are likely to influence individuals' work values. Language and geography are highly interdependent. The spread of language and culture is associated primarily with physical elements. Religion also affects how countries cluster. Religious beliefs are associated with certain values and norms. Ajiferuke and Boddewyn (1970) have established empirically a high correlation between religious norms and work goals.

Ronen and Shenkar (1985) reviewed eight studies to synthesise their findings and assign countries to different clusters, as shown in Table 3.5. Although this clustering is debatable it gives a fair idea of which groups of countries behave in a similar way.

Schwartz (1999) has identified seven values with which to compare nations, which has been discussed earlier in the chapter. On the basis of the scores on these seven values, Schwartz assigned the sampled countries to six clusters: English-speaking, Latin American, East Europe, West Europe, Far East and Islamic countries.

Table 3.5 Ronen and Shenkar's clustering of nations

Name of the clusters	Nations
Far Eastern	Malaysia, Singapore, Hong Kong, Philippines, South Vietnam, Indonesia, Taiwan, Thailand
Latin American	Argentina, Venezuela, Chile, Mexico, Peru, Colombia
Latin European	France, Belgium, Spain, Italy, Portugal
Anglo	USA, Australia, Canada, New Zealand, UK, Ireland, South Africa
Germanic	Switzerland, Germany, Austria
Nordic	Finland, Norway, Denmark, Sweden
Near Eastern	Turkey, Iran, Greece
Arab	Abu Dhabi, Bahrain, UAE, Kuwait, Oman, Saudi Arabia
Independent	India, Brazil, Israel, Japan

Source: Adapted from Ronen and Shenkar (1985)

The English-speaking nations tend to emphasise mastery and affective autonomy at the expense of conservatism and harmony, whereas the east European nations show the opposite emphasis. Countries in the Far East emphasise hierarchy and conservatism, whereas west European countries emphasise egalitarianism, intellectual autonomy and harmony.

The practical implications of country clustering can be illustrated in the following hypothetical case. A multinational company is establishing a venture in Switzerland. The corporation's directors must determine whether management skills will be imported from its subsidiaries in France, Germany and Italy (all three languages are spoken in Switzerland, albeit in different areas). The country clustering suggests that managers should be brought in from Germany, because Switzerland and Germany belong to the same cluster of work values. German managers can therefore be expected to be closer to and more familiar with workers' attitudes in Switzerland.

Summary

This chapter argued that culture is the 'way of life' of a people. Different elements or aspects of a way of life are connected with each other. There is a natural consistency among them. In this sense, culture is a holistic idea, which cannot easily be reduced to its elements. Hence one way of understanding culture may be to understand a characteristic object, event or ritual having a salient position in that culture. Gannon (1994) has used this holistic approach to understand cultures across the world. He has adopted the concept of cultural metaphor for quickly understanding the cultural mindset of a nation. The second approach is the analytical one. Every culture is characterised by a set of dimensions and cultures are compared along these dimensions. The chapter discussed major studies undertaken following this approach and examined the cultural dimensions that they have identified.

The chapter then focused on work-related values and showed how societies might differ from one another on the extent to which they subscribe to these values. Finally we discussed some recent studies which have attempted to cluster countries into similar cultural groupings to study similarities and differences.

Discussion questions

1. What are the two approaches used by various scholars for understanding culture? Distinguish and discuss the two.

2. In what way is Trompenaars's study a synthesis of more than one of the earlier studies?

3. Relate each of the following managerial decisions/behaviours to appropriate cultural characteristics (use Kluckhohn and Strodtbeck's value orientations).
   (a) Emphasis on the training and development of the employees.

(b) Policy decisions made to build dams and roads.

(c) Employees only work as much as needed to be able to live.

(d) Employees work hard to achieve goals.

(e) Executive holds important meetings in a moderate sized office in an open area, with open doors and many interruptions from employees and visitors.

Closing Case Study:
Ashis

I found Ashis, an Indian creative writer by profession, very depressed when I met him for the first time one evening in March 1971 in New York. He explained that he was desperately caught between extreme westernisation in his upbringing as a child and youth by a highly dominating father and a 180-degree turn to Hinduism in his early twenties when he had rejected much of his westernised upbringing. Now, however, at the age of 36, he felt semi-paralysed in his work. He was feeling deeply inhibited and despairing of developing a career in India, in spite of being extremely well connected socially and with ample financial resources.

While Ashis expressed considerable despair over his current situation and state of mind in a whining voice, he also conveyed that he had a real ray of hope. Just the previous year his wife had gone to Brighu, a temple in Punjab, for an astrological reading on Ashis from one of the Brighu shastras (ancient books). His horoscope predicted that at around this time – the time that Ashis was beginning to see me – his career would turn around and take a sharp turn for the better. He explained to me that the Brighu shastras are horoscopes written on palm leaves by a sage several hundred years ago at this temple in Punjab. One goes there with the exact time of one's birth and the temple priests will fetch the relevant horoscope, which will reveal not only one's future but one's past as well.

Ashis belongs to Kshatriya caste. A dominant father who completely identified with the British and their lifestyle had raised Ashis with overwhelming western values. At one period he sent Ashis to an English boarding school in India attended primarily by English children to prepare him for the available careers in the civil service. At all these kinds of schools, Indian boys such as Ashis were exposed only to western learning and anything Indian was denigrated to varying degrees.

Ashis's father came from an extended family with some illustrious men, including a family member who had been one of the leaders of a major Hindu reform movement. He used to espouse the value of Hinduism and Indian nationalism that calls for a simple, almost ascetic lifestyle. But what led his father to break with this tradition and opt for a westernised identity I never learned.

During our conversations, many times I observed Ashis becoming angry while discussing how his father had foisted upon him a westernised upbringing and values. Ashis described his father as being authoritarian in the sense of being domineering, bullying, critical and inconsiderate to anyone under him. Unfortunately, he had died when Ashis was 19 years old. He always carried with him notes or books of three great Indian figures he profoundly revered – Tagore, Coomaraswamy and Gandhi – and discussed his thoughts about certain of their passages whenever he got the chance.

When I arrived in Bombay in the summer of 1977, six years after our first meeting in New York, Ashis occupied a rather significant position in an important organisation connected with the film industry and communications. While he was in New York, some of his writings had come to the attention of an Indian man of international stature and nationwide respect who was then at the United Nations. He gave Ashis an important position in his organisation in India after he completed his graduate work in the summer of 1971. Ashis worked for him in a highly productive and creative manner. This man died suddenly and tragically a few years later. Further journal and newspaper articles brought Ashis to the attention of another eminent man, who then hired him for his current position. By the time of my arrival, Ashis was about to publish a novel.

Even though his career had skyrocketed and he had become recognised as a writer, Ashis was quite depressed and seemed once again semi-paralysed in his work. He was therefore eager to discuss his problems with me. His depression seemed immediately related to the resignation of the head of his agency a few months ago because of changes in the political climate. The former director was apparently a man greatly revered by all and deeply respected by Ashis, who spoke of his abilities and high level of creativity and strong spiritual presence. He sounded quite similar to Ashis's previous benefactor. Both men had taken a personal interest in Ashis, recognising his rather special combination of literary, technological and organisational skills, together with his strong commitment to Indian culture and his spiritual inclinations. Both had given Ashis a free hand in his work while being responsive to his ideas and initiatives.

Ashis complained that he no longer had anyone to look up to and had thus lost interest in his work. The new director was far too bureaucratic, quantitative and unimaginative for Ashis to be involved with in any way comparable to his former relationships with superiors at work. Moreover, although the new director was apparently aware that Ashis is a highly creative person, he showed him little appreciation, considering him something of an oddball for writing office memos in verse, and immature because he openly expressed and asserted himself at meetings. This is simply not done in hierarchical relationships.

During one of our conversations, I suggested that he should join a new organisation with an appreciative boss. He elaborated on how difficult it was to be creative in India without a superior who really appreciated you. He said that he might go abroad temporarily to write until another such superior turned up, or perhaps set up his own organisation with international support to assist Indian creative artists.

When I next saw Ashis, in July of 1980, I learned that he had stayed on in his current position, waiting for a promotion in the organisation. He was continuing with his writing, particularly on films, art, literature and other traditional modes of communication in India. His thesis was that development was based far too much on western models and did not sufficiently take into account the Indian modes and models. In his view, the wholesale adherence to western models held by many westernised Indians was in various ways highly inappropriate to Indian development.

Source: Adapted from Roland (1992)

Closing case study questions

1. Is Ashis right in highlighting the difference between the east and west?

2. What could be the underlying cultural reasons for Ashis to be angry with his father?

3. What kind of relationship do subordinates in India desire from their superiors?

4. What are the work values that seem to prevail in Indian society?

Annotated further reading

Gannon, Martin J. and **associates** (2001) *Understanding Global Cultures: Metaphorical Journeys Through 23 Countries*. Thousand Oaks CA: Sage.
Gannon views cultures through metaphors. He elaborates the national culture of 23 countries.

Hofstede, Geert (1991) *Cultures and Organizations: Software of the Mind*. New York: McGraw-Hill. This book elaborates Hofstede's study of national culture and its impacts on work values.

Trompenaars, Fons and **Hampden-Turner, C.** (1998) *Riding the Waves of Culture: Understanding Cultural Diversity in Business*, 2nd edn. New York: McGraw-Hill.
This book elaborates Trompenaars's study on diversity in cultural characteristics across nations and its impacts on the business world. It contains practical tips on how to do business in various countries.

References

Adler, N. J. (1997), *International Dimensions of Organizational Behavior*, 3rd edn. Ohio: International Thomson.

Ajiferuke, B. and **Boddewyn, J.** (1970) 'Culture and other explanatory variables in comparative management studies', *Academy of Management Journal*, 13(1): 53–165.

Coomaraswamy, A. (1969) *The Dance of Shiva*. New York: Sunwise Turn.

Gannon, M. J. (1994) *Understanding Global Cultures: Metaphorical Journeys Through 17 Countries*. London: Sage.

Geertz, C. (1973) *The Interpretation of Culture*. New York: Basic Books.

Hall, E. T. (1976) *Beyond Culture*. New York: Doubleday.

Hall, E. T. (1983) *The Dance of Life*. New York: Doubleday.

Hofstede, G. (1980) *Culture's Consequences*. London: Sage.

Hofstede, G. and Bond, M. H. (1988) 'The Confucius connection: from cultural roots to economic growth', *Organizational Dynamics* 16(4): 4–21.

Kluckhohn, F. and Strodtbeck, F. (1961) *Variations in Value Orientations*. Evanston IL: Row Peterson.

Laurent, A. (1983) 'The cultural diversity in western conception of management', *International Studies of Management and Organization* 13(1–2): 75–96.

Munter, M. (1993) 'Cross-cultural communications for managers', *Business Horizon* 36: 69–78.

Roland, A. (1992) *In Search of Self in India and Japan: Toward a Cross-cultural Psychology*. New Delhi: Ajanta.

Ronen, S. and Shenkar, O. (1985) 'Clustering countries on attitudinal dimensions: a review and synthesis', *Academy of Management Review* 10(3): 435–54.

Schwartz, S. H, (1999) 'A theory of cultural values and some implications for work', *Applied Psychology: An International Review* 48(1): 23–47.

Sullivan, J. (1992) *Invasion of the Salarymen: The Japanese Business Presence in America*. Westport CT: Praeger.

Trompenaars, F. (1993) *Riding the Waves of Culture*. London: The Economist Books.

CHAPTER 4

Culture and its influence on management:
A critique and an empirical test

Simon Denny

Learning objectives

When you finish reading this chapter you should:

- be familiar with the strengths and weaknesses of major research into the differences between national cultures (nationalities)

- understand some of the influences that culture has on management practices, through a three-country empirical study

- realise the limitations of national culture as a predictive or explanatory variable or tool

Opening Case Study:
Making Britons love business

Today a clutch of Britain's foremost entrepreneurs, business leaders and politicians will gather in Downing Street to help the Prime Minister launch a high-powered attempt to make the British love entrepreneurs. Enterprise Insight, jointly led by the British Chamber of Commerce, the Confederation of British Industry (CBI) and the Institute of Directors, has the lofty aim of achieving a measurable increase in entrepreneurial activity.

It is also intended to improve the image of enterprise by explaining what business people do, and demonstrating the existence of a link between business activity and welfare and social services. 'Business has got to make sure that the next generation of skilled people are business-attuned,' says the director-general of the CBI. 'They might not choose a career in business, but at least they will understand it and what it can do for the wealth-creation process.' If it succeeds, the campaign could have a substantial impact on national prosperity. A study of ten countries published last year by the London Business School and Babson College, in Boston, Massachusetts, which specialises in entrepreneurial issues, concluded that entrepreneurial activity accounted for up to a third of variations in economic growth.

But it will not be easy. The same study, the 1999 Global Entrepreneurship Monitor, found that although the UK was more entrepreneurial than most European countries, it scored less than half as well as the US and Canada, and way behind Israel as well. In a graphic illustration of the differences, the research found that one adult in 12 was trying to start a business in the US, compared with one in 30 in the UK. Only 16 per cent of Britons thought there were good opportunities for a start-up in the short term, compared with 57 per cent in the US.

Perhaps surprisingly, government figures show that the UK has a higher proportion of sole traders than the European Union average. But many of these are lifestyle businesses, which do not grow into entrepreneurial companies. As a result, a smaller proportion of business turnover in the UK is produced by companies employing 10 to 250 workers – the range most likely to include fast-growing entrepreneurial businesses.

The reasons are complex, probably including access to finance and regulation. Entrepreneurs themselves, surveyed for the Enterpriser Survey 2000, published last month by Ernst & Young, said their biggest problem was red tape. But there is widespread agreement that social attitudes are a key issue: most Britons would rather work for someone else, and many of those who do strike out on their own do not want to employ other people. As the LBS/Babson study puts it: 'The most pressing issues for the UK entrepreneurial sector are cultural and social norms, which tend to be anti-enterprise, and the education system, where entrepreneurship is not encouraged.'

Source: 11 May 2000, *Financial Times* CD-ROM 2000

Introduction

National culture has repeatedly been shown to influence the attitudes and behaviours of managers. This is not a new observation; as long ago as 1774 the German philosopher Herder, in *Another Philosophy of History*, argued that it was a mistake to suggest that intellectual harmony would one day be achieved without regard to local differences in culture and custom. Because of these local differences, Herder suggested, human nature expressed itself in widely differing systems of values.

Chapter 3 described major studies that have been conducted into national cultures. The present chapter will critique these and discuss their strengths and weaknesses. Those management practices that seem to be particularly influenced by national culture will then be examined, with specific reference to three European countries. The limitations of national culture as a predictive or explanatory variable or tool will be highlighted. Finally, other non-cultural influences upon managers will be suggested.

Research into national culture and management

Culture is very widely accepted by academics as a variable acting upon organisational behaviour. Brief examples will serve to illustrate this point. Bournois and Metcalfe (1991), in their study of human resource management (HRM) structures and policies and techniques in Europe, conclude that only nationality proved a significant factor in how organisations made their choices. Adler and Bartholomew (1992) argue that the overwhelming consensus, both inside and outside North America as well in both the academic and professional communities, is that culture is important and does make a difference. Hickson (1993) states that first and foremost each manager is a person in a society (or societies) and so the processes of managing and organising are not separate from societies and their cultures. Clark and Mallory (1996) suggest that differences in national cultures lead to different ways of thinking about management and organisations. Sparrow and Hiltrop (1995) in a literature review observe there were six 'obvious' links between national culture and HRM in Europe, including: the attitudes and definitions of what makes an effective manager and their implications for the qualities recruited, trained and developed; the expectations of the manager–subordinate relationship and its implications for performance management and motivation; and the mindsets used to think about organisational structuring or strategic dynamics.

Finally, Hall (1976, p. 14) perhaps goes further than other writers in asserting the impact and influence of culture upon behaviour when he wrote:

> Culture is man's medium; there is not one aspect of human life that is not touched and altered by culture. This means personality; how people express themselves, the way they think, how they move, how problems are solved, how their cities are planned and laid out, how transportation systems function and are organised, as well as how economic and government systems are put together and function. (Hall, 1976, p. 14)

However, as we saw in Chapter 1, culture is a 'problematic' concept as it is difficult to define, the units of analysis are difficult to identify and the identification of some variables as reflecting culture is not simple. The fact there are so many definitions of 'culture' (a famous 1952 review lists 164 separate meanings of the word) led Roberts and Boyacigiller (1984) to suggest that the lack of agreement as to how to define culture and the consequent lack of a currency within which to conduct studies is a most fundamental problem for cultural theorists.

In addition, there are three main dangers inherent in any discussion of culture and cultural differences. First, culture can be used as a 'dustbin category' – there's a difference, I don't know why, it must be culture. Second, speculation and vague generalities of terminology are always a danger in the social sciences. Third, in talking about national cultures there is a potential danger of slipping into thought patterns and language that could be described by some as racist. Finally, Tayeb (1988) and Pugh (1995) point out that national boundaries do not necessarily enclose homogeneous cultures, and Pugh (1995) also notes that all cultures are continually changing.

Despite these potential problems, it is clear that culture is different between nations. A nation's culture or national character is shaped by historical, geographical and philosophical factors. As each country has a different (view of) history, geography and philosophy, so they have different cultures. Culture can be said to exist as a research variable because researchers have been able to compare it at two levels: observation of behaviour and questioning of values and attitudes.

This chapter will use the term culture in the way defined by Hickson and Pugh (1995, p. 17), that is, culture means 'the shared values that typify a society and lie beneath its characteristic arts and architecture, clothes, food, ways of greeting and meeting, ways of working together, ways of communicating and so on'. This definition is similar to Hofstede's (1980, p. 19) 'collective programming of the mind' based on values, defined as 'a broad tendency to prefer certain states of affairs over others'.

A critical analysis of comparative research on work-related attitudes and values

As we saw earlier in Chapter 3, most cultural researchers, such as Hall, Hofstede, Laurent and Trompenaars, have based their research on trying to identify the values and attitudes that make up culture and which can be used to distinguish between one nation and another. Further, some researchers have highlighted the ways in which national culture can influence work-related attitudes and values, and by implication management style. This section critically assesses the influential contributions made by major studies in this field.

Mead (1994) suggests that managers have six behaviours to look for to compare other cultures to their own: how members of the culture greet each other; how they behave in the presence of superiors and subordinates; how decisions are taken and how they are communicated; how conflicts erupt and how they are resolved; how much importance is given to starting work on time and being on time for meetings; what factors motivate performance. Although Mead does not go on to use these behaviours to identify similarities and differences between countries, and does not attempt to suggest they can be used to explain differences, he does highlight the important point that differences in culture can only be overtly noted by focusing on observable behaviour.

We saw in Chapter 3 that Hall (1976) distinguishes between high context and low context cultures. In *high context cultures*, the external environment, situation and non-verbal behaviour are crucial in creating and interpreting communications and meaning is often communicated implicitly. Relationships are relatively long lasting, people in authority are personally responsible for the actions of subordinates and agreements tend to be spoken rather than written. 'Insiders' and 'outsiders' are closely distinguished from each other and cultural patterns are ingrained and slow to change.

In *low context cultures*, by contrast, the environment, situation and non-verbal behaviour are relatively less important, and more explicit communication is necessary. Relationships between individuals tend to be shorter in duration, authority is diffused throughout a bureaucratic system and agreements tend to be written rather than spoken. 'Insiders' and 'outsiders' are less closely distinguished and cultural patterns are faster to change.

This model seems to hold promise for distinguishing between countries but, although it is conceptually neat, it is based on qualitative insights rather than quantitative data and Hall does not attempt precisely to locate countries on a low–high context scale. In fact it is possible to see aspects of both high and low context cultures in all countries. However, the model does provide insights into the values that determine how a range of management functions are performed across countries.

Hofstede's research

Unlike Hall, Hofstede (1980) makes a distinction between values and culture. Values are defined as 'a broad tendency to prefer certain states of affairs over other' (1980, p. 19), while culture is a broader concept, 'the collective programming of the mind which distinguishes the members of one human group from another' (1980, p. 25). Hofstede admits that this is not meant to be a complete definition but it covers what he was able to measure. Culture, for Hofstede, includes systems of values, and values are among the building blocks of culture. He makes one further distinction: culture is used to describe entire societies (nations); for groups within societies the term 'subculture' is used. The other outstanding difference between Hofstede and earlier cultural theorists is that he used extensive quantitative data to develop his model.

Chapter 3 pointed out that Hofstede's (1980) mammoth study enabled him to identify four dimensions along which variation between countries was found to occur. He names these dimensions *power distance, individualism, uncertainty avoidance* and *masculinity*. In later studies Hofstede and his colleague (Hofstede and Bond, 1984, 1988) identified a fifth dimension, which they first termed Confucian dynamism and then renamed as *time orientation*.

Hofstede clearly demonstrates that work-related values are not universal. He found, for instance, in his study of IBM that underlying national values appear to persist when a multinational company tries to impose the same norms on all its foreign interests. Indeed, local values seem to determine how parent company rules and regulations are interpreted.

Criticism of Hofstede

Hofstede's work however has not been without its critics. First, as Sondergaard (1994) points out, all Hofstede's original respondents came from the marketing and service departments of IBM, a company assumed to have had a highly distinctive organisational culture, and we do not know what effect this had on his results.

Second, Pugh (1995) notes that Hofstede's data represent values, i.e. the attitudes of the IBM employees. Values certainly affect behaviour, but they are an internal factor and other external factors also affect behaviour. The concentration on values is, of course, a major problem of much of the work in the cultural field; studies often survey what people say rather than do.

Third, Jaeger (1983), Tayeb (1988) and Pugh (1995) argue that Hofstede's analysis inevitably compresses and simplifies. It characterises national work cultures by taking the average for the respondents of each nation. This is a gross oversimplification since there will be a range of differences in people's attitudes in all cultures. It also leads to dangers of stereotyping.

Fourth, Pugh (1995) also argued that Hofstede overcomplicates his cultural map. Looking at power distance and individualism, they conclude that with a few exceptions there is basically one dimension. At one end are the hot, poor, collectivist, large power distance cultures; at the other the cold, rich, individualist, small power distance cultures; with many cultures middling along the way in between.

Fifth, Sondergaard (1994) and Smith *et al.* (1996) point out that the IBM data were collected between 1968 and 1973. They question whether the dimensions developed from these data could be artifacts of this period of analysis and whether increasing modernity has reduced or changed the types of cultural difference which were apparant at that time. Smith also asks whether international businesses could have created transnational cultures.

Sixth, Sondergaard (1994) and Smith *et al.* (1996) note that the four dimensions were identified by Hofstede from analysis of attitude-survey questionnaires, originally designed by IBM staff for quite other purposes. As Hofstede himself acknowledges, the formulation of these questions may have left other dimensions of cultural variation undetected. He also admits (Hofstede, 1991) that his research was inevitably culture bound, as is all research, especially that carried out by individuals or teams from a single country.

Finally, Mead (1994) claimed that some connotations overlap or even paraphrase each other, e.g. 'independent' non-conformism with group norms can be explained either in terms of low power distance or high masculinity.

Contribution of Hofstede

However, the importance and value of Hofstede's work cannot be overstated. Mead (1998) claims that the criticisms levelled at him are dwarfed by the strengths of Hofstede's work in comparing cultures and applying cultural analysis to practical management problems. Certainly, having a controlled informant population enables real comparisons to be made. The four dimensions tap into deep cultural values and allow significant comparisons to be made across national cultures. Finally, Mead observes, Hofstede has carried out the biggest and almost certainly the best study of cultures that there is. To ignore his findings would be inexcusable.

This last rather bold statement is given extra weight when the results of replicate studies of Hofstede's work are examined. Shackleton and Ali (1990) reported that their study testing power distance and uncertainty avoidance on Sudanese, British and Pakistani managers produced results very close to those reported by Hofstede. Sondergaard (1994) reports 61 replications either trying to find support for the cultural differences in other populations, or to validate the dimensions by interpreting the differences according to the same cultural dimensions. Some of these studies used Hofstede's questionnaire while others used different research designs and instruments. He concluded that the analysis of the replications showed that the differences predicted by Hofstede's dimensions were largely confirmed and that there are remarkably few non-confirmations. Interestingly, he also cites Tayeb's (1988) study carried out in a number of Indian and British organisations where both the IBM questions and new questions were used, with the results showing the same dimensions. Smith (1994) observed that there are no indications that the cultural diversity mapped by Hofstede is in process of disappearing. Recent studies show just as much diversity as those done earlier. Winch *et al.* (1997) produced results largely replicating Hofstede's findings regarding cultural values in their study of the British and French workers of Transmanche-Link.

Laurent's research

Laurent (1983, 1986) suggests that the nationality of managers significantly affects their view of the organisation: its role, functions and operation. Between

1977 and 1979 he administered a 56-item questionnaire to 817 participants in executive development programmes at INSEAD. The participants were from nine European countries and the United States. From his analysis of these questionnaires, he identified four indices or dimensions that represent attempts to capture a structure of collective managerial ideologies that meaningfully differentiates national culture (1983). The *organisations as political systems* dimension looks at the political role played by managers in society, their perception of power motivation within the organisation and the degree to which organisation structures are clearly defined in the minds of the individuals involved.

The *organisations as authority systems* dimension indicates the way managers regard the purpose of a hierarchy, whether it is to allocate power or to enable the organisation to run effectively. The third dimension, the *organisation as role formalisation system*, focuses on the relative importance different cultures attach to defining and specifying the roles and functions of organisational members. The questions that make up this dimension stress the values of clarity and efficiency that can be obtained by implementing such organisational devices as detailed job descriptions, well-defined functions and precisely detailed roles.

The final dimension, *organisations as hierarchical relationships systems*, looks at the desirability of eliminating conflict from organisations, whether a manager should know more than his or her subordinates and whether managers can cope with bypassing the hierarchy or having two bosses.

Laurent (1986) reported the results of a new study where matched national groups of managers working in the affiliated companies of a large US multinational firm were surveyed with his INSEAD questionnaire. He later replicated this study with smaller matched national samples of managers in several American and European multinational corporations. The overall results gave no indication of convergence between national groups and led to the conclusion that deep-seated managerial assumptions are strongly shaped by national cultures and appear quite insensitive to the more transient cultures of organisations.

Laurent's results contrast Latin and northern European and North American management style. He suggests that individual managers hold their own set of beliefs about good and bad management behaviour which are moulded from their own national cultures. His findings cast serious doubt on the universality of management and organisational knowledge and practice. Together with the work of Hofstede, Mead (1994) and Randlesome *et al.* (1993), his contribution stresses the importance of understanding social and cultural aspects of a society.

Trompenaars's research

Trompenaars (1994), like Hofstede, based his cultural model upon extensive quantitative data gathered from questionnaire responses given by 15,000 informants on training courses. Respondents represented a range of companies and were from some 50 countries. His model meets practical business rather than academic needs, although this is hardly surprising as Trompenaars is a management consultant.

As we saw in Chapter 3, Trompenaars develops seven parameters against which countries can be measured: *universalism vs particularism, collectivism vs individualism, neutral vs emotional, diffuse vs specific, achievement vs ascription, sequential vs synchronic* and *inner directed vs outer directed*.

The practical approach of Trompenaars (his book is full of advice for managers working or about to work in an unfamiliar culture) has the advantage that in deriving his questionnaire and cultural parameters he draws together and applies ideas contributed by earlier cultural theorists. Hofstede's individualism dimension has influenced the collectivism vs individualism parameter and his power distance dimension can be related to the idea that status can be ascribed. Laurent's work influences the specific vs diffuse and achievement vs ascription parameters. Finally, Hall's ideas on how high and low context cultures view time is at least echoed in the sequential vs sychronic parameter.

However, this synergistic, holistic approach to culture theory does not mean that the manager looking for the way to compare national cultures can simply turn to Trompenaars for the answer. His research is in some ways problematic, lacking the focus and clarity of Hofstede (Mead, 1998). The pool of informants is vaguely defined and, consisting as it does of both managers and administrative staff, lacks homogeneity. The neutral vs emotional parameter is based on responses from only 11 countries. The development of the sequential vs synchronic parameter is based not on quantitative or qualitative data but on other writers' work. In addition, somewhat frustratingly from the point of view of anybody trying to compare Trompenaars's ranking of countries with Hofstede's, cultures are only ordered in terms of their responses to case study questions and not on the basis of parameters.

The influence of culture on management: evidence from Britain, France and Sweden

Hickson (1993) makes the valuable point that culture, whether national, regional, occupational or organisational, represents the crystallisation of history in the thinking, feeling and acting of the present generation. It is transferred to future generations through education and socialisation. This is helpful as it highlights the need to look at the historical development of countries and their national characteristics if we are to understand culture and its influence on management.

To try and identify some of the influences of national culture upon management, the history of three European countries – Britain, France and Sweden – will be examined briefly and compared with the findings of the cultural researchers described above.

The evolution of the state

Britain is a nation that has evolved, based on an insular security (Almond and Verba, 1963). The development of the civic culture can be seen as a series of clashes between modernisation and traditionalism, which were sufficient to result in significant change but not so violent that they resulted in disintegration or polarisation. Britain, largely unified since the eleventh century, has been able to tolerate a greater measure of local and individual autonomy and non-conformity than could much of continental Europe. The separation from the Church of Rome dramatically marked the British journey towards a secularisation of society and the development of an individual, entrepreneurial and relatively mobile culture based on a thriving and self-confident merchant, later middle, class that had been apparent since the thirteenth century (Tayeb, 1993). Consequently, Britain entered the industrial revolution with a political culture that made it possible to assimilate the large-scale and rapid changes in the eighteenth and nineteenth centuries without overthrow of the system.

What evolved in Britain was a pluralistic culture based on communication and persuasion, a culture of consensus and diversity; change was permitted (rationalism and radicalism) but moderated (traditionalism). Thus this gradualist culture enabled the model of British parliamentary democracy to develop: 'parliamentarism and representation, the aggregative political party and the responsible and neutral bureaucracy, the associational and bargaining interest groups, and the autonomous and neutral media of communication' (Almond and Verba, 1963, p. 8). The modern manifestations of the historical evolution of the British (English) culture that are most likely to have a bearing on the business climate and the approach to management include individualism, deference and acceptance of inequality, self-control and reserve, conservatism, xenophobia (although there is also a greater liberalism towards foreign companies than in most of western Europe, Calori and De Woot, 1994), honesty and trust, regard for liberty, and class consciousness (Tayeb, 1993).

France is a nation that was created by the state. Until the seventeenth century France was still a heterogeneous collection of regions, with different languages and loyalties. From this period onwards a series of centralising monarchs (l'état c'est moi – Louis XIV the most obvious example) influenced by the interventionist philosophy of Colbert (1619–83) used their powers, in particular over the education system (Garrison and Rees, 1994), to create a highly centralised state that played an omnipresent role in the economy. French heroes have always been authoritarian centralisers (Lawrence, 1992). The French revolution and subsequent royalist and republican governments continued this centralising, bureaucratic tradition until 1982 when Mitterrand's devolution of power from central government to the regions and departments attempted to redress the balance somewhat.

Centralisation has, not surprisingly, reinforced the French 'predilection for hierarchies' (Barsoux and Lawrence, 1990). The Age of Reason and the revolution may have sensitised the French to questions of personal freedom but, as Graves (1972) points out, they have not eliminated their concepts of absolutism and authority. He quotes a senior French manager to sum up this paradox: 'the Frenchman is not an industrial animal: he is an artisan, an individualist. The problem is that they not only need to be shown what to do, but they also want to be cared for, and loved. They want to touch the hem of your garment' (p. 52). Johnson (1996) suggests that French managers often assume the workers are 'blameless children'. Many are considered unmotivated and possibly untrustworthy. In France there is a constant tension between the demand for strong authority, and individualistic assertion against it (Sorge, 1993). Those aspects of French culture that are most likely to have a bearing on the business climate and the approach to management include a quite individualistic national temperament, a style of management which is fairly authoritarian and intuitive, preferably cultivating hierarchy and a pyramid-shaped organisation (Rojot, 1993).

Sweden, historically dominant in Scandinavia, was unified in the thirteenth century with a common language and one ruler. Although possessing both a monarchy and aristocracy, Sweden avoided the feudal system with the majority of the population being free-holding peasants with representation. The strong central government managed a political system based until the mid-nineteenth century upon four estates; nobles, clergy, burghers and peasants. Late and rapid industrialisation between 1860 and 1900 replaced these four estates by a political system representing two classes: labour and capital. Thus a strong central government has been combined with a tradition of mass participation. This has resulted in a strong sense of egalitarianism in Sweden which has permeated every aspect of institutional and economic life (Lawrence, 1992).

The Swedes have developed codetermination, not hierarchies (it should be noted that the Vikings had no hereditary monarchy). A strong sense of the value of equality has led to consensual decision making characterising governmental and economic institutions. Although the government is highly interventionist in the planning and distribution of the fruits of the market economy, all political parties share a 'managerial mentality' and accept this role (albeit to different degrees). Indeed, Sweden has been described as 'one big firm' (Guillet de Monthoux, 1991). Industrial relations are characterised by an ability to find agreement in even the most difficult of situations, before stoppages occur (Lawrence and Spybey, 1986). Swedish managers are very professional and do not admit to amateurism: punctuality, rigour, the work ethic and good citizenship are the norm (Tixier, 1996).

Religion and philosophy

The contrasting British, French and Swedish ways of organising society can be derived from their different religious and philosophical experiences. British Protestantism is essentially individualistic (Tayeb, 1994) and imbued with the spirit of capitalism. Work is a means of fulfilment (the Protestant work ethic). An empirical, pragmatist philosophy (Lessem and Neubauer, 1994), reliant on experience and experiment and not on theory, has led to a distrust of great ideas or 'fictions masquerading as sacred truths' (Passmore, 1966).

By contrast, French Catholicism is strongly hierarchical and traditionally anti-capital. Work was considered a simple necessity, rather than a focus for personal and collective fulfilment. Cartesian reasoning, with its desire to arrive at the residue of certainty (Passmore, 1966), encouraged and reinforced the development of rules and hierarchies to enforce them. Thus we can explain the elitist tradition that has existed, until recently, against a background of widely felt antipathy to industry and the notion of profit (Trouve, 1994).

In Sweden the religious heritage is Lutheran, nationalistic and historically anti-Catholic and the philosophy of rationalism and pragmatism is founded on fundamental Protestant values. It is exhibited by a strong sense of individual responsibility and a belief in the virtues of equality combined with a dislike of flamboyance and swank and a feeling of responsibility for the welfare of others (Tixier, 1996). Swedes find it embarrassing to set themselves above others, according to Lawrence and Spybey (1986). The spirit of social solidarity is very developed and there is a national propensity to reasonableness and compromise and a strong

Protestant work ethic. Problems are solved through politeness and consideration for people (Tixier, 1996).

Form of economic organisation

Historical and philosophical factors have inevitably affected the way work organisations are managed. In Britain, despite the end of laissez-faire capitalism after the end of the First World War and increased nationalisation after the Second World War, there is still a widespread distrust of central planning and an acceptance of the primacy of market forces. This is demonstrated clearly by the policies of the New Labour government that took power in 1997 and both continued with many of the economic policies of the previous Conservative administration and failed to re-nationalise privatised industries. Although the British economy cannot be described as pure capitalism (Tayeb, 1993), it functions as a decentralised, market-driven entity with strong international links and large amounts of foreign ownership of 'British' firms. Companies are commodities – they can be bought and sold, and hostile takeovers are frequent.

One clear consequence of this system of economic 'management' is that of short termism (Grinyer et al., 1998; Tayeb, 1993). Short termism is manifested in a fascination with 'financial engineers in the City rather than the real thing in the country's manufacturing industries; in the preference for asset holders rather than product makers; in the exposure of the country's leading industrial companies to hostile take-overs by financial manipulators' (Randlesome et al., 1993, p. 203). Companies have to concentrate on profit in the short term rather than investment for the future. However, the UK business culture is receptive to new ideas, innovative and outstandingly adaptable.

In France, the tradition of centralisation has been maintained since the end of the Second World War with the government taking an active role in industry, directing investment, maintaining and increasing state ownership in key sectors and until recently even fixing the prices of some commodities. Charles de Gaulle defined the French style of central planning as 'a pressing obligation' (Garrison and Rees, 1994) and France has developed, for a western European economy, an unusually high dependence upon the state. The propensity to central planning, with its Cartesian reliance upon reason and the seductive attraction of the idea, when combined with financial traditions, capital structures and a protective state that means companies have not (until very recently) been bought and sold as commodities but have a relatively stable existence, has meant that French managers tend to have a long-range view of the business cycle. Coale (1994) reports this as resulting in objective and thorough (even voluminous) analysis and discussion before decisions are made and action taken.

In Sweden, despite primarily socialist administrations since the 1930s, there has been a tradition of strong privately owned companies. Although the government often intervenes in corporate affairs, according to Axelsson et al. (1991) relatively few Swedish firms are government owned or dominated. Indeed, the Swedish industrial economy is dominated by two business groups (the Wallenberg group and the Handelsbank group that together control 52 per cent of the stock value of all the corporations listed on the Stockholm stock exchange); each consisting of industrial and financial corporations connected through relations of ownership, interlocking directorates and financial service (Collin, 1998). In contrast to French-style central planning with its clear linking of national and industrial interests, Swedish government intervention is almost totally devoted to measures to enhance social protection, a linking of social and industrial interests. Even companies sometimes take decisions for reasons of social responsibility rather than economics (Segelod, 1995). In Sweden, as Lawrence and Spybey (1986) point out, taxes are high, income distribution is narrow, management salaries are low by international standards and fringe benefits are virtually non-existent. Associated with social protection is a strong (almost aggressive) sense of informality and egalitarianism. There is deep public resentment of large pre-tax salaries. In 1994 a 100 per cent pay rise for the head of Sweden's profitable and competitive post office was greeted with such public fury that the prime minister was forced to step in and quash it.

Is the history supported by research?

These brief reviews of British, French and Swedish history indicate that there are differences between their national cultures. Are these differences also shown in the results of the research?

As noted above, Hofstede stands out from the researcher crowd both because of his use of extensive quantitative data and the number of confirming replicates of his work that have been carried out. It is interesting to compare the scores for Britain, France and Sweden against four of his dimensions (see Table 4.1).

The raw numbers clearly indicate differences between the three countries. Britain and Sweden are more similar to each other in power distance and uncertainty avoidance than either is to France. Britain has a higher masculinity score than both France and the very low scoring Sweden. Sweden and France have a lower individualism score than Britain. The key question is whether these scores can be related to the differences in national history reviewed above and to discernible influences upon managers, remembering that the descriptions of Hofstede's first four dimensions are as follows:

- *Power distance* – the extent to which members of a society accept that power is distributed unequally.

- *Uncertainty avoidance* – the degree to which people feel threatened by ambiguous situations and create beliefs and institutions which try to avoid the uncertainty.

Table 4.1 British, French and Swedish scores against four of Hofstede's dimensions

	Power distance	Uncertainty avoidance	Individualism	Masculinity
Britain	35 (low)	35 (low)	89 (v. high)	66 (high)
France	68 (high)	86 (v. high)	71 (high)	43 (medium)
Sweden	31 (low)	29 (low)	71 (high)	5 (v. low)

Source: Adapted from Hofstede (1980)

- *Individualism* – distinguishes between countries in which individuals see their identity as determined by their own continuing individual choices as how to act, and countries where identity is collectively defined.

- *Masculinity* – the extent to which achievement through such values as visible success, money and possessions is given priority over more 'caring' values such as nurturing and sharing.

It is highly recommended that readers should re-read the section on the historical development of Britain, France and Sweden, looking for ways in which Hofstede's dimensions are manifested. It should be noted that it is normally easier to identify manifestations of power distance and uncertainty avoidance than the other two dimensions. Table 4.2 gives a list of suggested manifestations.

Table 4.2 Suggested manifestations of Hofstede's dimensions in the historical development of Britain, France and Sweden

Dimension	Britain	France	Sweden
Power distance	Relatively mobile, pluralistic culture. Culture of consensus and diversity. Autonomous and neutral media.	Centralising state. Heroes 'authoritarian centralisers'. Concept of absolutism and authority. Hierarchical. Catholicism.	Tradition of mass participation. Consensual decision making. 'Aggressive egalitarianism'.
Uncertainty avoidance	Toleration of local and individual autonomy and non-conformism. Change gradual and permitted. Empirical, pragmatic philosophy. Distrust of great ideas. Distrust of central planning. Short termism.	Bureaucratic tradition. Change often violent. Desire for 'residue of certainty'. Long-range view of business cycle.	Change gradual and permitted. Rational, pragmatic philosophy.
Individualism	Individual, entrepreneurial merchant/middle class. Individualistic Protestantism.	Individualistic assertion against authority.	Individualistic Protestantism.
Masculinity	Keen on profit. Acceptance of primacy of market forces.	Antipathy to notion of profit.	Strong sense of egalitarianism. Dislike of swank. Consideration for others. Government concerned with social protection. High taxes. Narrow income distribution.

A review of Table 4.2 and hopefully the reader's own conclusions strongly suggest that Hofstede's dimensions (based remember on IBM samples) are correlated with the more observational, qualitative conclusions about the national cultures of Britain, France and Sweden derived from a review of their history. The authoritarian, centralising French have a higher power distance score than the more pluralistic, consensual British and Swedes. The French intellectual tradition of Cartesian reasoning, with its 'residue of certainty', is shown in a very high uncertainty avoidance score, whereas the more pragmatic, empirical British and Swedes have a lower uncertainty avoidance score. And so on. These results have clear implications for management behaviour. Table 4.3 suggests how culture influences four vital management functions in Britain, France and Sweden.

Table 4.3   The influence of culture on vital management functions

Management function	Britain	France	Sweden
Leadership	Control based on reciprocal, personal trust. People ranked, not roles. Manager may defer to experts. Subordinates expect to be consulted. Dislike of strict rules. Ideal boss = resourceful democrat.	Control based on authority. Roles ranked, not people. Manager knows best. Subordinates expect to be told what to do. Emotional need for rules. Ideal boss = benevolent dictator.	Exercise of authority by reference to formal 'rules' is suspect. People ranked, not roles. Subordinates expect to be consulted. Informal egalitarianism. Consensual ethos.
Communication	Oral communication valued. Premium placed on face-to-face relationships. Communication is pragmatic and non-didactic.	Written communication preferred. Verbal communication often formal. Communication is abstract and didactic. Communication rituals reinforce authority relationships.	Communication verbal, informal and very clear. A norm of accessibility and openness. Communication is concise and focused on the business in hand.
Problem solving and decision making	Individual and group based. Ideas count, not roles. Subordinates may be experts. Manager's role to facilitate the solution. Limited reference to models and precedent.	Individual based. Roles count. Subordinates expect to be given the answer. Manager's role is to know answer and make decision. Extensive reference to models and precedent.	Group based. Ideas count, not roles. Subordinates may be experts. Manager's role is to facilitate the solution. Limited reference to models and precedent.
Strategy and planning	Often short term. Short written documents. Business focus a management function.	Often long term. Long and formal written documents. Business focus a management function.	Often short term. Short written documents. Business, society and environment focus a joint function.

However, while culture clearly has a significant influence on management, it is obvious that it does not operate as a nationally homogenising force. People are different. In addition, it is not the only influence on management behaviour. Indeed, reliance upon solely national culture as a predictor of behaviour would be both foolish and dangerous.

The limitations of culture as a predictive or explanatory tool

Single explanations such as national culture are insufficient as explanations for organisational structures and managerial attitudes and behaviours (Tayeb, 1988). Institutional factors, while often having a large part of their origins in culture, also exert their influence. As there was no single universally accepted definition of culture, so there is no agreed list of institutional factors. However, a synthesised list (Denny 1999, pp. 78–9) suggests that a nation's institutional context can be seen as consisting of the following elements:

- social stratification
- government policy towards the economy
- the legal environment
- trades unions
- the orientation of the economic system
- the quality and quantity of the workforce
- the competitive environment.

As was also discussed in Chapter 2, individually or collectively these institutional factors can influence management behaviour in ways that may mean managers do not demonstrate in culturally typically behaviour. This is particularly well demonstrated in the closing case study at the end of this chapter.

Summary

The points made by this chapter can be summarised as follows :

- National cultural differences exist and have been mapped by researchers.
- Hofstede's study of national cultures dwarfs all others in its extensive use of cultural data and its many replications.
- Culture must be seen as a product of the historical development of a nation.
- The behaviour of managers is influenced by their national culture.
- National culture does not have a homogenising effect; wide variations in behaviour exist within any national population.
- In organisations, culture is a good predictor of certain types of behaviour (e.g. how delegates react towards their trainers).
- Non-cultural factors can influence managers so they act in ways that are culturally atypical to those expected.
- The amount of competition in a market, and the market share currently

enjoyed and desired in the future, are factors that can significantly influence management action, especially in areas of competitive advantage such as customer service and training and development.

Discussion questions

1. What are the advantages of understanding the influences that national cultures can have on management behaviour?

2. What could some of the disadvantages be?

3. Which of the institutional factors listed above are least affected by national culture?

4. What development would you recommend for a manager going to work abroad for a two-year secondment?

Closing Case Study:
Planning, organising and conducting training and development in Scania Great Britain and Scania France

Background

The French market for heavy trucks had been traditionally dominated by Renault (who in 1996 had 42 per cent of the total market and 70 per cent of the fleet market), which was heavily subsidised by the French government who owned most of the company (53 per cent in 1995, declining to 44 per cent in 1999). Renault was vital to the French economy; it was the third biggest French firm in terms of turnover in 1993 and the thirtieth biggest company in the world in terms of sales in the same year. The French state had provided Renault with FF13 billion in the years 1984 to 1995 to save it from bankruptcy. Massive state support gave Renault, as the only domestic producer, an enormous advantage over the foreign truck manufacturers who were also represented in the French market. This advantage was greatly increased when the buying habits of the French customers were taken into account. As Barsoux and Lawrence (1990, p. 215) observe: 'There is a strong nationalistic element in French life. French people buy French cars, eat French food, go on holiday in France.' According to the managing director of Scania France, this nationalistic element also influenced truck purchases: 'Trying to get somebody away from Renault which we must do to get the market share we desire is very difficult. Once people have a connection they never review their offering and buy from somebody else.' The effect of these factors was that foreign truck manufacturers faced a strong loyalty to the Renault marque and were essentially competing for less than 60 per cent of the total market and only 30 per cent of the fleet market. Although large haulage companies were capturing a growing share of the transport market, about 30 per cent of hauliers were still one-vehicle firms in 1997.

By contrast, in Britain there was no dominant domestic manufacturer (indeed by 1998 there was no wholly owned UK manufacturer) and the UK truck market was held, by the trade press, to be the most open in Europe. The market was dominated by eight major manufacturers who were all competing intensely for market share and all of whom had made a public commitment to be among the top four manufacturers in terms of sales by 2001. The UK haulage industry was largely composed of fleet operators who bought repair and maintenance contracts, as well as (and sometimes instead of) the truck. The fleet market was vital to manufacturers' market share, but there was an increasing emphasis on niche markets, e.g. dustcarts, petroleum transporters, where significant added value in terms of specialist bodywork existed. There was no national loyalty to a particular marque and many operators deliberately maintained mixed fleets of different manufacturers trucks. This allowed them to both compare the merits of different makes and play one manufacturer off against another.

The case companies

Scania France had its own dealer/distributor networks. The network was mainly composed of small/medium companies with an exclusive geographical trading area who kept traditional opening hours. Family firms were common. Network companies had to make a high level of investment in repair, maintenance and spares facilities. Most managers in the dealer networks were ex-mechanics or hauliers although in some of the larger companies graduates could be found. Network staff generally had long service (and family connections) in the truck industry, low levels of entry qualifications, low levels of professional training and only limited technical training. Managers in Scania France were normally graduates with long service in the industry, although some professional finance and computer staff had been brought in from other industries. Market share in 1992 was 9 per cent.

In Britain the Scania dealer networks consisted mainly of medium sized companies with long, often all day, every day, opening hours. Each dealer had an exclusive geographical trading area. Dealers had made a high level of investment in repair and maintenance and spares facilities. Network managers were almost exclusively non-graduates who had spent years in the industry. Family firms were common. Network staff, like those in France, generally had long service in the industry, but only low levels of entry qualifications and professional training. Limited technical training was provided. Competition for trained and competent mechanics was fierce and skill shortages were experienced by some dealers. Managers in Scania Great Britain usually had long service in the industry, but less than 20 per cent were graduates. Accountants held professional qualifications, but few other managers held qualifications. Some computer staff were brought in from other industries. Market share in 1992 was 9 per cent.

Key issue

In 1995, Scania AB (the Swedish parent company) set both its British and French subsidiaries the target of gaining 20 per cent market share by 2000. How would the subsidiaries *plan, organise* and *conduct* the training and development necessary to help achieve this goal?

If management behaviour were influenced by national culture, Scania France could be expected to develop detailed *plans*, integrated with commercial strategy (high uncertainty avoidance). The *organisation and control* of training and development could be expected to be highly centralised and directive (high power distance). Training would be *conducted* on a more formal, tutor-centred basis (high power distance). By contrast, Scania Great Britain could be expected to have more short-term, even ad hoc, training *plans*, possibly weakly linked to commercial strategy (low uncertainty avoidance). *Organisation and control* could be expected to be more diffuse and consensual (low power distance). Training would be *conducted* in a more informal, learner-centred way.

What happened?

Research (Denny, 1999) clearly showed that, as expected, training was *conducted* in typically French or British ways. However, the *planning* and *organisation* of training was completely at variance with what national culture predicted. In Scania Britain, *planning* of training was long term, detailed and totally integrated with commercial strategy. *Organisation* of training was centralised and heavily directive. In Scania France, the opposite applied.

Closing case study questions

1. Why was culture a poor predictor of the ways in which managers in the subsidiaries planned and organised training and development?

2. Why was culture a good predictor of the way in which training was conducted in the subsidiaries?

3. Was it appropriate for the parent company to set the subsidiaries the same market share targets?

Annotated further reading

Hickson, D. J. and **Pugh D. S.** (1995) *Management Worldwide*. Harmondsworth: Penguin.
A wide-ranging book with many mini-case studies examining national culture and its influence on behaviour. Very good at integrating the historical development of national cultures with research findings.

Joynt, P. and **Warner, M.** (1996) *Managing Across Cultures*. London: Thomson.
Twenty-two chapters on culture and management from experts in the field – good coverage of Asia.

Schneider, S. C. and **Barsoux, J.-L.** (1997) *Managing Across Cultures*. London: Prentice Hall.

A very useful book, with a European focus and lots of examples, showing how culture influences management and giving tips on how to cope.

References

Adler, N. J. and Bartholomew, S. (1992) 'Academic and professional communities of discourse: generating knowledge on transnational human resource management', *Journal of International Business Studies* third quarter: 551–69.

Almond, G. and Verba, S. (1963) *The Civic Culture: Political Attitudes and Democracy in Five Nations*. Princeton: Princeton University Press.

Axelsson, R., Cray, D., Mallory, G. and Wilson, D. (1991) 'Decision style in British and Swedish organisations: a comparative examination of strategic decision making', *British Journal of Management* 2: 67–79.

Barsoux, J.-L. and Lawrence, P. A. (1990) *Management in France*. London: Cassell.

Bournois, F. and Metcalfe, P. (1991) 'Human resource management of executives in Europe: structures, policies and techniques', in C. Brewster and S. Tyson (eds) *International Comparisons in Human Resource Management*. London: Pitman.

Calori, R. and De Woot, P. (eds) (1994) *A European Management Model: Beyond Diversity*. Hemel Hempstead: Prentice Hall.

Clark, T. and Mallory, G. (1996) 'The cultural relativity of human resource management: is there a universal model?', in T. Clark (ed.) *European Human Resource Management*. Oxford: Blackwell. pp. 1–33.

Coale, D. J. (1994) 'International barriers to progress', *Journal of Management Development* 13(2): 55–8.

Collin, S.-O. (1998) 'Why are these islands of conscious power found in the ocean of ownership? Institutional governance hypotheses explaining the existence of business groups in Sweden', *Journal of Management Studies* 35(6): 719–39.

Denny, S. (1999) 'The effects of cultural, institutional and parent company influences upon training and development in MNC subsidiaries'. Unpublished PhD thesis, Open University.

Garrison, T. and Rees, D. (eds) (1994) *Managing People Across Europe*. Oxford: Butterworth-Heinemann.

Graves, D. (1972) 'The impact of culture upon managerial attitudes, beliefs and behaviour in England and France', *Journal of Management Studies* February: 40–56.

Grinyer, J., Russell, A. and Collison, D. (1998) 'Evidence of managerial short-termism in the UK', *British Journal of Management* 9: 13–22.

Guillet de Monthoux, P. (1991) 'Modernism and the dominating firm – on the managerial mentality of the Swedish model', *Scandinavian Journal of Management* 7(1): 27–40.

Hall, E. (1976) *Beyond Culture*. New York: Doubleday.

Hickson, D. J. (ed.) (1993) *Management in Western Europe: Society, Culture and Organisation in Twelve Nations*. Berlin: De Gruyter.

Hickson, D. J. and Pugh, D. S. (1995) *Management Worldwide*. Harmondsworth: Penguin.

Hofstede, G. (1980) *Culture's Consequences*. Beverly Hills: Sage.

Hofstede, G. (1991) *Culture and Organisation: Software of the Mind*. New York: McGraw-Hill.

Hofstede, G. and Bond, M. H. (1984) 'Hofstede's culture dimensions: an independent validation using Rockreach's value survey', *Journal of Cross-Cultural Psychology* 15: 417–33.

Hofstede, G. and Bond, M. H. (1988) 'Confucius and economic growth: new trends in culture's consequences', *Organisational Dynamics* 16: 4–21.

Jaeger, A. M. (1983) 'The transfer of organisational culture overseas: an approach to control in the multinational corporation', *Journal of International Business Studies* fall: 91–114.

Johnson, M. (1996) *French Resistance*. London: Cassell.

Laurent, A. (1983) 'The cultural diversity of western conceptions of management', *International Studies of Management and Organisation* 8(1–2): 75–96.

Laurent, A. (1986) 'The cross-cultural puzzle of international human resource management', *Human Resource Management* 25(1): 91–102.

Lawrence, P. (1992) 'Management development in Europe: a study in cultural contrast', *Human Resource Management Journal* 3(1): 11–23.

Lawrence, P. A. and Spybey, A. (1986) *Management and Society in Sweden*. London: Routledge and Kegan Paul.

Lessem, R. and Neubauer, F. (1994) *European Management Systems*. Maidenhead: McGraw-Hill.

Mead, R. (1994) *International Management: Cross-Cultural Dimensions*. Cambridge MA: Blackwell.

Mead, R. (1998) *International Management*, 2nd edn. Oxford: Blackwell.

Passmore, J. (1966) *A Hundred Years of Philosophy*. Harmondsworth: Penguin.

Pugh, D. S. (ed.) (1995) Block 5 Open University Course, *International Enterprise* (B890). Milton Keynes: Open University.

Randlesome, C., Brierley, W., Bruton, K., Gordon, C. and King, P. (1993) *Business Cultures in Europe*. Oxford: Butterworth-Heinemann.

Roberts, K. H. and Boyacigiller, N. A. (1984) 'A survey of cross-national organisational researchers: their views and opinions', *Organisation Studies* 4: 375–86.

Rojot, J. (1993) 'France', in R. B. Peterson (ed.) *Managers and National Culture: A Global Perspective*. Connecticut: Quorum Books. pp. 69–91.

Segelod, E. (1995) 'New ventures – the Swedish experience', *Long Range Planning* 28(4): 45–53.

Shackleton, V. and Ali, A. (1990) 'Work-related values of managers: a test of the Hofstede model', *Journal of Cross-Cultural Psychology* 21(1) 109–18.

Smith, P. B. (1994) 'National cultures and the values of organisational employees: time for another look', *Workshop of the European Institute for the Advanced Study of Management*, Henley Management College.

Smith. P. B., Dugan, S. and Trompenaars, F. (1996) 'National culture and the values of organisational employees: a dimensional analysis across 43 nations', *Journal of Cross-National Psychology* 27: 231–64.

Sondergaard, M. (1994) 'Research note: Hofstede's consequences: a study of reviews, citations and replications', *Organisation Studies* 15(3) 447–56.

Sorge, A. (1993) 'Management in France', in D. J. Hickson (ed.) *Management in Western Europe: Society, Culture and Organisation in Twelve Nations*. Berlin: De Gruyter.

Sparrow, P. R. and Hiltrop, J. M. (1995) 'Redefining the field of European human resource management: a battle between national mindsets and forces of business transition'. Resubmission to *Human Resource Management Journal*.

Tayeb, M. (1988) *Organisations and National Culture: A Comparative Analysis*. London: Sage.

Tayeb, M. (1993) 'English culture and business organisations', in D. J. Hickson (ed.) *Management in Western Europe: Society, Culture and Organisation in Twelve Nations*. Berlin: De Gruyter. pp. 47–64.

Tayeb, M. (1994) 'Japanese managers and British culture: a comparative case study', *International Journal of Human Resource Management* 5(1) 145–66.

Tixier, M. (1996) 'Cultural adjustments required by expatriate managers working in the Nordic countries', *International Journal of Manpower* 17(6–6): 19–43.

Trompenaars, F. (1993) *Riding the Waves of Culture*. London: Economist Books.

Trouve, P. (1994) 'Managing people in France', in T. Garrison and D. Rees (eds) *Managing People Across Europe*. Oxford: Butterworth-Heinemann. pp. 63–91.

Winch, G., Millar, C. and Clifton, N. (1997) 'Culture and organisation: the case of Transmanche-Link', *British Journal of Management* 8: 237–49.

CHAPTER 5

National culture and management practices:
The case of Gulf Cooperation Council countries

Kamel Mellahi

Learning objectives

When you finish reading this chapter you should:

■ be familiar with key institutions that shape management practices in Gulf Cooperation Council (GCC) countries

■ be aware of the management culture in GCC countries

■ understand management practices and work-related values in GCC countries

Opening Case Study:
Seeking the right kind of traffic

An aviation hub, a communications hub and a regional trading centre are the roles which define Dubai's position as the main regional centre for the Gulf. Incentives such as the one allowing 100 per cent ownership of companies in the free zones at Jebel Ali and Dubai Internet City are in sharp contrast to laws which forbid a majority stake for foreigners elsewhere. These have strengthened Dubai's image as the main entrepôt for the region. Dubai's plans to promote trade relations with the central Asian former Soviet republics through increased air traffic has opened up a new link that creates the prospect of future ties beyond the countries surrounding the Gulf region.

Many in the business community hope that in the next few years, with Iran and Iraq reopening links to the Arab world, there will be opportunities for business ties which would increase Dubai's importance as a regional base. Yet, there have been other less positive signs of late. A recent fall in real estate values and rents as part of a general economic slowdown has prompted many to consider the long-term future of a once thriving real estate market. Some analysts argue that a large-scale construction boom since the early 1990s has resulted in an oversupply of properties.

In the long run, one crucial factor will be how much Dubai is prepared to relax its stringent laws barring property ownership by foreign nationals. The change would be an important step forward in attracting not just foreign capital, but also in offering an added measure of reassurance to those who consider their investments are insecure in an environment where they can never qualify for citizenship.

Ayman Al Nabhan of Net Real Estate, a property brokerage, says: 'There has to be more security for foreigners. Strict regulations are enforced which means that no non-national can buy property.' However, there are some signs of relaxation for foreign nationals. Emaar Properties, owned 32 per cent by the Dubai government and listed on the Dubai Financial Market, in early 1999 announced that citizens of the Gulf Cooperation Council (GCC) member countries could buy property at its Emirates Hills villa development. This was the first time that nationals of GCC member countries were allowed to buy property in the United Arab Emirates (UAE). Businessmen say that the privilege may be selectively extended to wealthy non-GCC nationals, though it would be done without a formal relaxation in existing laws.

Another sign of relaxation in the property laws has been an announcement earlier this year from Union Properties, a subsidiary of Emirates Bank International, that it would offer 30-year leases on selected development to foreigners. Officials say that leasing properties to foreign nationals may become an increasing practice. One result of the increasing traffic along Dubai's roads has been the application of increasingly stringent standards for issuing new driving licences. Businessmen say that Dubai will need to tackle its traffic problems in coming years, especially if there is a surge of foreigners coming to the city state, as a result of official incentives. Although that is hardly an issue which is central to the decision for establishing regional offices, businessmen expect rents and property prices in areas with relatively more parking space to rise faster than properties close to congested roads.

Source: 13 Dec. 2000, *Financial Times* CD-ROM 2000

Introduction

The previous four chapters discussed the cultural and institutional factors which contribute to the creation of work-related values and attitudes which would in turn influence organisations and their management styles. Some of these discussions and arguments were empirically tested at the company level in Chapter 4. The present chapter examines their validity at the country level, choosing as location a group of countries in the thriving region of the Persian Gulf in the Middle East. The choice of the region is particularly apposite because of the growing interest in management in the Arab world and Islamic cultures. The region is also strategically very important because it produces the bulk of the world's crude oil, the life-blood of modern economies. In addition, because of the enormous actual and potential business opportunities of its emerging economies, the region has attracted the attention and presence of a large number of multinational companies.

Although Gulf Cooperation Council (GCC) countries, which include the Kingdom of Saudi Arabia (KSA), Oman, Bahrain, Qatar, Kuwait and United Arab Emirates (UAE), differ in terms of population, surface and GDP, their economic structure, political system, national culture and labour market structure are similar. The GCC region is rich in oil, has a population of over 28 million and extends almost over 2.7 million sq km. On average, GCC countries enjoy a very high per capita income.

This chapter describes and assesses the major features of GCC countries' managerial practices. The first part looks at the key factors that are shaping management practices in GCC countries. The second part discusses the cultural values which underlie management behaviour and unique managerial practices in GCC countries.

Key institutions in GCC countries and management

Management in GCC countries is shaped by four factors: political, economic and labour market structures, and the status of women in the workplace. In this section I delineate the fundamental institutional changes taking place in GCC countries and how these changes impact the behaviour of firms and managers.

The political system

The political systems in GCC countries have unique institutional characteristics. They are theocratic, traditional monarchies, based on a tribal system with large royal families. The government heavily regulates most social and political activities and preserves an active involvement in business affairs. The political system lends distinct character to the GCC countries' business environment. Schlumberger (2000) reported that in GCC countries the private sector is dependent on the benevolence of state institutions to operate successfully. For a long time, private and public firms and governments in GCC countries were welded together into a close system of networked relationships through ties of state ownership, tribal structure and reciprocal patronage. This multilevel, networked system preserved many market imperfections and sustained a fragmented economy with few dominant firms, few dominant families and tribes, and little competition. Although, as will be discussed later, recent privatisation programmes signal the diminution of GCC governmental involvement in business governance and ownership, governments still have a strong grip on the running of economic affairs of the country.

The managerial consequence of the state being the most powerful economic actor is obvious: relationship with government bodies and officials have strong importance. Business deals are secured on the base of who you know more than any other factor. In such a context, laws are applied inequitably, perfect competition is manipulated and 'monopolies or de facto monopolies are granted like gifts to a loyal clientele through direct or indirect state intervention' (Schlumberger, 2000, p. 250). In this context nepotism, known locally as wasta, is widespread and plays a central role in daily social and business life. Wasta, the Arab term for 'intermediation', means 'personalistic networks' with the purpose of mutual benefits. It is the social mechanism which determines the allocation of resources in society and economy. Rather than merit, it is personal contact with decision makers, who are able to allocate resources and take decisions, which secures social status and material well-being for the individual (Schlumberger, 2000). While in the west relationships follow successful deals, in GCC countries successful deals follow wasta-based relationships.

The instrumental value of wasta is the reciprocal obligations of the parties involved with respect to the acquisition of resources (Cunningham and Sarayrah, 1993). Once a manager is embroiled in a network of wasta, through the so-called *Diwaniyah,* he maintains face by reciprocating favour for favour. Face is a key element in the development and maintenance of wasta. With the loss of face, the possibility of any future exchange within the wasta network is threatened. Therefore, managers and entrepreneurs must not only establish a wasta network, but also maintain their membership by continuously reciprocating favours.

The economic context

The economy of GCC countries is dominated by the oil sector. The industrial sector's development is based on the ample availability of hydrocarbon resources and strongly influenced by developments in the oil industry. The oil price explosion of the 1970s encouraged GCC governments to channel their massive oil windfalls to finance ambitious infrastructural, industrial and agricultural programmes. It also enabled GCC governments to establish and develop modern health and education and training sectors. From the mid-1980s, however, lower oil prices put increasing pressure on governments' finances, resulting in rising domestic debt and other financial commitments. The sharp fall in oil prices triggered GCC governments to acknowledge the need for reforms and reduce dependency on oil. Prior to the fall in oil prices, GCC nationals enjoyed high income, were guaranteed nearly universal health care at the government's expense and free education. The fall of oil prices was an awakening alarm for GCC governments that they could not rely only on oil and its derivatives. As a result, GCC governments and companies, since the late 1990s, have become more enthusiastic about diversifying their economy and building more contact with the rest of the world. Optimism and the desire to compete successfully with companies in other countries which have not had the experience of being shielded from global competitions for decades coexist with apprehension and anxiety about the consequences of free, unfettered trading (see for instance, Mellahi and Wood, 2001).

While the impact of the global economy is disputed by few in this part of the world, how to react to it however is debated by many. For instance, the way governments in GCC countries have been restructuring their economies has not been a straightforward process. Institutional change in GCC countries has proved to be highly complex because in these formerly closed, tribal-dominated systems, institutions have developed into massive, interdependent networks whose logic of operations depends as much on political influence and personal relationship – wasta – as on concern for efficiency. Due to the sensitivity of political and social considerations, institutional reforms have been non-linear, displaying a mixture of progress and regress simultaneously. Generally, GCC countries have followed the principle of 'pragmatism' with the aim of balancing the pace of reform with social and political stability. Put differently, GCC governments' risk-aversion strategy seems to value stability above radical economic reforms. This principle has enabled them, so far, to implement fairly continuous economic reforms without open conflict between the countries' political and social powers. It has, however, created uncertainties for both foreign and local firms as to the exact speed and direction of reforms.

The most obvious milestone in the development of GCC business environment is its new legal business framework. Since the late 1990s, there have been continuous legal reforms, including regulations governing the status of foreign firms, commercial laws and laws to protect intellectual property rights. In addition, GCC countries have liberalised greatly their foreign direct investment (FDI) policies during the 1990s. The new legal environment has become favourable to foreign investors and only few restrictions remain. Favourable changes include more liberal entry, fewer performance requirements, more incentives and more guarantees and protection for investors (see Table 5.1). The number of activities in which FDI

Table 5.1   Main policies governing FDI in GCC countries

Regulations	Bahrain	Kuwait	Oman	Qatar	KSA	UAE
Limitations on the share of foreign investor.	Nationals have majority share in selected industries. Offshore banks can have 100% share.	Nationals have to hold 51% in selected activities. Foreigners can have more than 51% with special approval.	Foreigners can have up to 100% only in selected projects.	Nationals have to hold 51% of the shares in JVs. Foreign investors can have up to 100% in selected sectors.	Foreign investors can have up to 100% share in many sectors; a negative list will include sectors prohibited for FDI.	In free zones foreigners can have 100% shares as well as in some projects. Generally nationals should hold 51% or more of the shares.
Management	No government regulations.	No government regulations.	No government regulations.	No government regulations.	The general manager must be national.	No government regulations.
Local content	No regulations but local value-added should not be less than 40% to enjoy 100% tax exemption.					
Repatriation	Foreign investors in all GCC countries can remit abroad all profits as well as all funds received.					
Foreign investment law	Legislative Decree No. 13 of 1991	Law No.15 of 1990 and No. 68 of 1980	Royal Decree No. 104/94 Foreign Investment Law	Foreign Investment Law No.13 of 2000	Foreign Investment Law of April 2000	Commercial Companies Law, Federal Law 8, 1984 and amendments JAFZA Dubai Law 9, 1992
Legal system	In all the GCC states, the Sharia (Islamic law) constitutes the prime law. However, most of the laws relevant to foreign investment are contained in legislation enacted by the legislative authority. Most of this legislation is based on the European models, often French, patterned after the Egyptian legislation. Sharia principles are generally applied only in matters affecting the personal status of Muslims. The GCC states introduced judicial and legal system to deal with business disputes outside the Sharia court system.					

Source: Adapted from: Gulf Organisation for Industrial Consulting (GOIC) (2001) *Study on Investment Climate in the GCC Countries for Attracting Foreign Direct Investment*, Doha, Qatar.

is barred or restricted has been considerably reduced, especially in the manufacturing sector but also increasingly in natural resources and services (Mellahi and Al-Hinai, 2000).

The overriding goal of this globalisation policy has been the promotion of increased efficiency through competition, both domestically and internationally, with a view to providing a sounder basis for sustainable and real employment creating economic growth. The prospect of global competition requires firms in GCC countries to utilise all of their available resources in order to survive and succeed in the global economy.

Officials and managers in GCC countries often report that multinational firms will raise productivity levels among locally owned firms in the industries which they enter by improving the allocation of resources and managing them more efficiently than local firms. This is expected for three main reasons. First, it is argued that because FDI and other forms of foreign investment tend to occur in industries with relatively high entry barriers, it will help reduce monopolistic distortions and their associated inefficiencies. Second, through either the multinational's competitive force or demonstration effect, locally owned firms operating in imperfect markets such as GCC countries may be induced to a higher level of efficiency. Finally, the presence of multinational subsidiaries in an industry may speed the process or lower the cost of technology and knowledge transfer. Imitation effects and the movement of personnel trained by multinational subsidiaries also enhance the transfer of knowledge to locally owned firms. This will be done, it is hoped, through the so-called positive contagion effect – where the diffusion of knowledge can be seen by analogy with the spread of a contagious disease.

Management practices are most effectively copied when there is personal contact between those who already have the knowledge and those who eventually adopt it. For instance, based on an interview with Prince Abdullah of KSA, *Business Week* (31 July 2000) noted that GCC countries 'hope to encourage a more open economy where companies compete on their merit rather than by connections. They want foreign investors to bring not just capital but management know-how and technology'. The spill-over of knowledge from multinationals to local firms is not a straightforward process. Research in other countries found that the majority of spill-overs do not arise automatically from the presence of foreign firms. Instead, for benefit to occur, indigenous firms need to invest in 'learning activities'. The ability of indigenous firms to 'catch up' depends on their level of commitment to learning new ways and unlearning old ways of managing.

Despite these changes in the business environment, business in the GCC countries has not adopted the attitudes, values and norms that the new business culture requires. In fact, it could be argued that the new developments in the business environment, with all the problems and challenges entailed, have obliged managers to 'stick to the knitting' and the old ways of doing things. This is happening for three main reasons. First, as will be discussed later, because management practices in GCC countries are believed to be embedded in Islamic and tribal values, managers tend to idealise their practices. They tend to overvalue them and are in most cases emotionally aggrandised and stripped of any negative features. Second, most managers in GGC countries are not equipped with modern management tools to deal with the new business environment. Therefore, when confronted with such a strong force as global competition, they tend to negate or disown its impact. Third, many managers in GCC countries are blinded by the belief in 'old ways of doing things'. They find it so painful to admit that they are obsolete. Denial, rationalisation and idealisation of current practices are expected to stand as an obstacle towards unlearning some current management practices.

Labour market

Within GCC countries, the challenge was and remains to provide ongoing employment security and a relatively high standard of living for nationals. Politicians and observers in GCC countries refer to the current state of the labour market as the 'ticking bomb' that is reshaping GCC countries. Much of the inflow of oil revenues in the 1970s and 1980s accrued directly to the public sector (Shaban et al., 1995). As a result, it was able to offer well-paid employment to locals with generous reward packages and good quality of working life. This has led to a situation where wages in the public sector, with the exception of top management, continue to exceed private sector wages by many times (Gulf Business, 2001). As Shaban et al. (1995) reported, it also resulted in the state sector becoming the only option that indigenous entrants to the national labour force would consider; a government job was and is perceived as a citizen's right.

Since the 1990s, however, the GCC model has been under increasing strain. For instance, the Saudi economy has been growing with an average rate of 2 to 0 per cent while the population growth rate has been closer to 4 per cent since the 'oil boom baby boom' began in the early 1970s. The Economist (22 April 2000) estimated that the economy should grow by 6 per cent annually to generate enough jobs for young male Saudis entering the labour market. This disparity in economic growth and population growth has pushed the issue of unemployment to the forefront as baby boomers are now entering the labour market.

Unemployment is not officially measured in most GCC countries. In Saudi Arabia, using demographic data and private sector employment, Saudi American Bank (2000) estimated unemployment of male Saudis in the 20 to 29 age group to be around 15 to 20 per cent. Gavin (2000) reported that more than 100,000 Saudi males enter the workforce every year, yet the non-oil private sector is only creating enough new jobs to absorb about one in three job seekers. Given the persistent birth rates of around 4 per cent per annum in GCC countries, with more than half of the national population under the age of 15 years, job creation for locals is expected to become more crucial in the future.

Given the breakdown of the official job machine in the public sector in the face of high birth rates and unstable oil prices, the need for 'localisation' of employment in the private sector became increasingly pressing. In an attempt to force firms to fill these jobs with locals, GCC governments introduced laws and regulations to force the private sector to employ a minimum number of locals. However, despite this, and calls by the popular media for greater localisation, the percentage of employment of locals in the private sector has not changed significantly. The legislation and concomitant political pressure have largely been ignored. Most firms have chosen to obfuscate rather than implement the law letter for letter (The Economist, 12 April 1997). There are four interrelated reasons for private sector's resistance to localisation: labour cost; social and cultural factors; management control; multicultural integration.

Labour cost

The influx of cheap foreign labour during the past three decades has resulted in the private sector being reliant on cheap manual labour, deployed in labour-intensive occupations. Indeed, continued profitability hinges on being given a free hand in the utilisation of expatriates. Although, since the mid-1990s, GCC countries have raised the costs of hiring foreigners by introducing compulsory health care for expatriates and increasing the cost of issuing and renewing work visas, local workers still are very much more expensive to hire than are expatriates (Montagu, 1995).

Socialised into an environment where lucrative employment in the public sector was seen as a birthright, there is considerable evidence to suggest that most GCC nationals remain reluctant to accept relatively poorly paid and insecure work in the private sector. It has been argued that more than 85 per cent of jobs in Saudi are paid less than what a Saudi would accept as a minimum (Cooper, 1996). This situation has been exacerbated by deeply entrenched managerial stereotypes: it is commonly alleged that locals will generally demand about six times the salary a skilled foreign worker would be prepared to accept and 'will not work as hard' (*The Economist*, 12 April 1997). Certainly, expatriates are more willing to accept low salaries because they still earn more than they could earn in their home countries, such as India, Pakistan, the Philippines and Bangladesh (Al-Najjar, 1983; Atiyyah, 1996; Owen, 1986). The majority of expatriate workers are young male bachelors and therefore do not have a family to support in GCC countries, even if they remit a significant proportion of their salary to their extended family back home. For local workers however, the high cost of living in GCC countries makes the level of wages offered by the private sector for non-managerial jobs incapable of providing what is seen as an acceptable living standard for local workers and their dependants (Atiyya, 1996; Lumsden, 1993).

Social and cultural factors

Social and cultural perceptions towards work in the private sector greatly influence companies' ability to recruit and retain qualified local workers. Within GCC countries the type of work, sector of employment and social interactions at work determine the social status of the worker and his family (Mellahi, 2000). Most of the jobs in the private sector are manual jobs, which are viewed in a particularly negative light. *Gulf Business* (2001, p. 34) quoted a manager in UAE as saying: 'If I advertise for a secretary I will get 100 applicants; if I need to recruit a national who is a technical manager, I am lucky to get one applicant.'

Management control

It is generally held that expatriates in GCC countries are easier to control and more disciplined than local workers (Atiyyah, 1994, 1996; Lumsden, 1993). Work permits in GCC countries are generally only valid for one year. Foreign workers do not qualify for permanent residency or naturalisation, regardless of the length of their stay. Employers have few legal obligations towards expatriates, who can readily be laid off and sent home at short notice. In addition, expatriate workers hold work permits for a specific occupation with a specific employer. They are prohibited from changing jobs without the consent of their employer or sponsor. Hence, labour turnover and job-hopping among expatriates simply does not exist. Bhuian *et al.* (2001, p. 22) note that expatriates in GCC countries 'have no hopes of expressing any grievances pertaining to their employment because such instances are handled very swiftly and harshly, i.e. termination and deportation from the country'.

Multicultural integration

The fourth and perhaps most important factor is the lack of social integration in multicultural work environments, despite workforce diversity. There is considerable evidence to suggest that a large proportion of indigenous workers are reluctant fully to integrate into a multicultural work environment for fear that it might degrade their existing status (Atiyyah, 1996; Mellahi and Al-Hinai, 2000; Parry, 1997). Mellahi and Wood (2001) argue that social integration, group cohesiveness and the ability to work together in GCC countries requires workers to get to know one another and replace stereotypes, which can result in reduced prejudice and conflict and greater group cohesiveness. They add that failure to understand and capitalise on diversity can lead to misguided assumptions, poor working conditions, underperformance and discrimination.

Women and work

Even though over the past few decades women's roles have certainly been enhanced in GCC countries, women continue to be confronted with tough choices between family, social acceptability and career. Their participation in the formal economic and social sectors is still modest compared to other developing economies. The percentage of native women in employment is reported to be no more than 14 per cent in Qatar and 30 per cent in Kuwait of the total native workforce (Ikhlas, 1996). In Saudi Arabia female (un)employment is not included in most national statistics. This is due to the belief among the vast majority of people in GCC countries that child bearing remain life's principal objective for women (Doumato, 1999) and that the Bedouin values consider family honour dependent on women's chastity (Ikhlas, 1996). Other factors that exacerbate the situation of women in GCC countries include: the high fertility rates which impede women's ability to work (Al-Qudsi, 1998) and an extreme degree of occupational segregation that limits women's chances to obtain work. Even the increasing minority of young women who want to work have their options limited to home economics or the over-bloated sectors of education and nursing. The latter sectors are reported to be employing more than ten times their need to absorb the number of women seeking employment (Ikhlas, 1996).

It is not only the local women who suffer from work inequality in GGC countries. Expatriate women are reported to suffer from both 'within-job discrimination' and 'allocative discrimination'. Within-job discrimination means that women are paid less than men in a given job. Hosni and Al-Qudsi (1988) found that 31.8 per cent of the wage gap between Kuwaiti men and women is due to discriminatory factors. Asked whether men and women are paid equally in GCC countries, a consultant is quoted as saying 'absolutely, definitely, unequivocally, without a shadow of a doubt, no' (*Gulf Business*, 2001, p. 44). The same magazine alleges that not only do local firms discriminate against expatriate women, but 'some international companies are guilty of these practices'. The study found that 'many Arabic and Asian women have been made offers which they felt were considerably below average, simply because they were married'.

Allocative discrimination, which pertains to women facing limited access to attractive and important positions within a firm either at the time of entry or in terms of career advancement, is often rationalised by the inability of women to travel and conduct business activities in some GCC countries. *Gulf Business* (2001) reported that many companies, which have a regional base, prefer not to hire women in sales and marketing as they will be unable to travel to Saudi Arabia; or even if they do hire them, they are on considerably lower salaries.

National culture, work-related values and management practices

Islamic work values

The concepts of Islamic work ethic (IWE) and Islamic work values (IWV) have their origin in the Quran, the sayings and practices of the Prophet Mohammad, who preached that hard work caused sins to be 'absolved' and that 'no one eats better food than that who eats out of his work' (Darwish, 2000). Alhabshi and Ghazali (1994) have suggested a list of core Islamic values and Ali (1988) has developed a list of Islamic work values, as shown in Tables 5.2 and 5.3.

Darwish (2000) argued that in a nutshell the IWE advocates that life without work has no meaning and engagement in economic activities is an obligation. He further notes that IWE views dedication to work as a virtue and puts emphasis on cooperation in work and consultation as a way of overcoming obstacles and minimising the risk of mistakes. Social relations at work are encouraged in order to

---

Table 5.2   Core Islamic values

1. Every act should be accompanied by intention (*niyat*).
2. Conscientiousness and knowledgeable in all endeavours (*itqan*).
3. Proficiency and efficiency (*ihsan*).
4. Sincerity (*ikhlas*).
5. Passion for excellence (*al falah*).
6. Continuous self-assessment (*mohasabet al nafs*).
7. Forever mindful of the almighty – piety (*taqwa*).
8. Justice (*'adl*).
9. Truthfulness (*amanah*).
10. Patience (*sabar*).
11. Moderation, promise keeping, accountability, dedication, gratefulness, cleanliness, consistency, discipline and cooperation.

Source: Adapted from Alhabshi and Ghazali (1994)

Table 5.3   Islamic work values

1. Laziness is a vice.
2. Dedication to work is a virtue.
3. Good work benefits both oneself and others.
4. Justice and generosity in the workplace are necessary conditions for society's welfare.
5. Producing more than enough to meet one's personal needs contributes to the prosperity of society as whole.
6. One should carry out work to the best of one's ability.
7. Work is not an end in itself but a means to foster personal growth and social relations.
8. Life has no meaning without work.
9. More leisure is not good for society.
10. Human relations in organisations should be emphasised and encouraged.
11. Work enables man to control nature.
12. Creative work is a source of happiness and accomplishment.
13. A man who works is more likely to get ahead in life.
14. Work gives one the chance to be independent.
15. A successful man is the one who meets deadlines at work.
16. One should constantly work hard to meet responsibilities.
17. The value of work is derived from the accompanying intention rather than its result.

Source: Adapted from Ali (1988)

achieve a balance between individual and social life. In addition, work is considered to be a source of independence and a means of fostering personal growth, self-respect, satisfaction and self-fulfilment.

As Ali (1988) points out, the value of work in the IWE is derived from the accompanying intentions (*niyat*) rather than from the results of work. Besides constant hard work to meet one's responsibilities, competition is encouraged in order to improve quality. Ahmad (1976) asserts that the IWE stands not for life denial but for life fulfilment and holds business motives in the highest regard.

Management practices

Islamic and Bedouin values and traditions guide management practices in GCC countries. Cultural values and social attitudes to management and work in GCC countries are very different from those found in the rest of the world. Ali (1996) stresses that Islam is one of the most influential forces in the Arab world, moulding and regulating individual and group behaviour and outlooks. Quranic principles and prophetic prescriptions serve as guides for managers in conducting their business affairs.

Islamic values and teaching put strong emphasis on obedience to leaders. Beekun and Badawi (1999) note that in Islam at all times the leader must be obeyed and that Islam considers obedience to the leader so important that it views any kind of insubordination to be abhorrent unless in very specific circumstances. The authority of the leader or manager is thus accepted as right and proper and subordinates are expected to show respect and obedience to superiors. The majority of Muslim scholars advocate what it is called 'dynamic followership'.

Beekun and Badawi (1999) further add that although Islam emphasises that followers should comply with the directives of their leader, it does not condone blind subservience. That is, although the typical Muslim worker does respect his leader, the onus in most cases is on the leader to convince subordinates that his orders are worth obeying rather than impose his will on others by administrative fiat. This is why, according to Sharia, Muslim leaders are asked to consult their subordinates before a decision is made. In addition, Islamic teachings put heavy emphasis on forgiveness, kind-heartedness and compassion. Also, according to Atiyyah (1999), Arab and Islamic values emphasise harmony, cooperation and brotherly relationships. Conflicts should be avoided or suppressed. The business leaders are also expected to show responsibility for the quality of working life of employees and concern for their families and surrounding society.

In addition to Islamic teachings, tribal and family traditions have a strong impact on management practices in GCC countries. The Arab culture is traditional, socio-centric male dominated and encourages dependence on relatives and friends. While the tribal traditions promote consultation in decision making within the same tribe or extended family, *Asabiyah* (intense loyalty to their own tribe or regional group) encourages authoritarianism with non-kin (out-group), such as other tribes and expatriate workers. Several researchers report that the consultative and participative styles are predominantly preferred by GCC managers. Ali (1993) however found that managers tend to adopt an authoritarian management style. He reported that these conflicting results reflect the fact that managers in GCC countries do not tend to create a situation of real consultation, but rather a feeling of consultation. Muna (1980) argues that in Arab culture, while subordinates expect to be consulted about decisions, they do not expect participation in the decision-making process. Bhuian *et al.* (2001, p. 29) note that 'in general a Saudi manager would expect employees to do whatever they are told to do, and an employee's being left on his or her own may be viewed as an indication of the management's dissatisfaction towards the employees'. They also describe management style in GCC countries as 'bureaucratic, group oriented, informal, and tribe or clan oriented'.

The authoritarian management style is a result of the process of socialising outside the family's and tribe's environment which does little to prepare individuals to work within groups outside the family and the tribe (Ali, 1989). Organisations in GCC countries are run much like traditional entities such as clans or tribes in which paternalistic authoritarian managers rely heavily on their social leadership skills to get work done (Atiyyah, 1999).

Using Hofstede's (1980) typology, as discussed in Chapter 4, GCC states could be described as high in power distance and high in uncertainty avoidance. High power distance could be attributed to Muslim belief about respect of authority in Islamic societies as well as Bedouin traditions (Bjerke and Al-Meer, 1993). Ali (1993) argues that Arab tribal values reinforce the concept of absolute right and wrong and 'do not rock the boat' attitudes and any approach that does not conform to acceptable norms is considered a threat to established authority and organisation stability. High power distance and uncertainty avoidance have resulted in lower tolerance for new ideas, low degree of initiative for bringing about change, fatalism, unquestioning acceptance of conventional wisdom and obedience of justified authority (Mellahi and Wood, 2001).

According to Mellahi and Wood (2001), GCC countries are highly collectivist within the in-group (tribe or extended family) and highly individualist with the out-group (non-kin and guest workers). With the out-group ties between individuals are very loose; interactions are limited and the emphasis is on an individual's accomplishment. When dealing with the out-group, managers apply the same standards to all employees and put strong emphasis on tasks rather than relationships. Within the in-group, however, from birth onwards people are integrated into strong, cohesive groups that protect them in exchange for unquestioning loyalty. Individuals subordinate their personal interests to the goals of their collective or in-group. Behaviour within the in-group emphasises cooperation, group welfare, duty, security and stable social relationships. In short, the employer–employee relationship within the in-group is 'moral' and the corresponding managerial style can be best described as directive but welfare oriented or paternalistic (Mellahi and Wood, 2001). Bhuian *et al.* (2001, p. 29) report that 'typical Saudi management style focuses on the group rather than on individuals resulting in less importance being attributed to task identity'. They note that employees in GCC countries regard not being included in the inner circle as a sign of management dissatisfaction which could end up with a non-renewal of the job contract.

The tribal system has reinforced the practice of wasta in GCC countries. As discussed earlier, wasta reflects the delicate fibre woven into most business activities in these countries. It is deeply embedded in their business and social interactions. Informal relationships take place in the evenings outside the formal environment of meetings – often in someone's house – where individuals can talk more freely about what concerns them without a rigid agenda to constrain them. These meetings are valuable, as they are the primary decision-making forums. Informal relationships operate in concentric circles and are often limited to the inner group – with family and tribal members at the core and other acquaintances arranged on the periphery according to the distance of the relationship and trust. Trust-based cultural values and norms underpin behaviour and attitudes. There are strong sanctions for rule breakers who stand to lose their reputation within the network. The strength of the relationship varies but in most cases loyalty to follow members of the *Diwaniyah* network takes precedence over loyalty to the firm.

Therefore, for an employee or manager operating in a system where productivity is largely disconnected from gains, it might just be more efficient to invest socially in personal contacts with decision makers than to strive for improving his performance in the company. Investing time and/or other resources in establishing the right connections is crucial and in many cases more vital to climb the firm hierarchy than enhance work-related performance. For those without or with too weakly established relations, the frustrating struggles for promotion or threats of a co-worker who is better positioned in the firm are demotivating.

Summary

GCC countries' increased involvement in the world market demands that more attention be given to the unique aspects of conducting business in this part of the world. This chapter highlights the peculiarities of the business environment in GCC countries. Managers in GCC face a complex matrix of choices and constraints. In GCC countries, firms and states are closely intertwined actors and the pivotal power points are very contingent on the wider, wasta-based relationship. In addition, distortions in the labour market will continue to play a crucial role in shaping the business environment in GCC countries.

One specific aspect that has been discussed in this chapter is the practice of wasta. In short, wasta involves cultivating personal relationships through the exchange of favours for the purpose of obtaining preferential treatment, developing networks of mutual dependence and creating a sense of obligation and indebtedness. Due to their deep embeddedness, practices such as wasta will not diminish despite the move to a more global market-based economy. Wasta has and will continue to give individuals and firms an imperfectly immutable resource that provides a distinct competitive advantage over others' competitors.

National culture has a strong impact on management practices. In GCC countries, the cultural values and social attitudes to management and work are remarkably different from those found in the rest of the world. They are influenced by Islamic teaching and tribal values. Using Hofstede's typology, GCC countries could be described as high in power distance, high in uncertainty avoidance and collectivist within the in-group and individualist with the out-group. The authority of the leader or manager is accepted as right and proper and subordinates are expected to show respect and obedience to superiors. However, although the typical worker in a GCC country is expected to obey and respect his leader, the onus in most cases is on the leader to convince subordinates that his orders are worth obeying rather than impose his will on others by administrative fiat.

Discussion questions

1. Despite changes in the business environment, managers in GCC countries have not begun to eschew the attitudes, values and norms that the new business culture requires. Why?

2. Discuss the key factors that shape management practices in GCC countries.

3. Nepotism – wasta – has provided and will continue to provide individuals and firms with an imperfectly immutable resource that gives a distinct competitive advantage over others competitors in GCC countries. Discuss the ethical implications of such practices.

Closing Case Study:
Batelco – weathering global competition

The State of Bahrain is an island city-state in the Persian Gulf off the east coast of Saudi Arabia. Although oil was and still is the foundation for its economy, Bahrain has developed into an international banking and business centre. Along with the United Arab Emirates (UAE), it is one of the principal locations for the regional business offices of international companies. In order to maintain this status, Bahrain is seeking to become the principal connection point for regional telecommunications with the rest of the world. Its telecommunication system has given it an edge over its neighbours in attracting foreign investment during the last decades. Bahrain Telecommunications Company (Batelco) has enjoyed monopoly over the last two decades. However, the government in Bahrain realised that in order to maintain its regional dominance status in the telecommunication sector, it had to deregulate the industry and open it for foreign companies.

Batelco was established in 1981 as a Bahraini shareholding company. Over the years, Batelco has been the sole telecommunication provider in Bahrain and enjoyed good reputation for providing world-class telecommunications and information services to customers in Bahrain and other Gulf Cooperation Council (GCC) states. Batelco's shareholders include the government of Bahrain, quasi-government institutions, leading financial and commercial organisations and Bahraini and GCC citizens. Between them, they own 80 per cent of the shares with Cable & Wireless (UK) owning the remaining 20 per cent. The company enjoys a strong association with Cable & Wireless which provides appropriate support, advice and assistance as requested by Batelco.

Because of the small population size of the country (690,000) Batelco has sought to go beyond the local Bahraini market to participate in key investment initiatives for developing regional and international telecommunications between GCC states and other countries. An internal document states that the company is 'well-positioned to extend our expertise beyond the local markets and we will continue to pursue opportunities for growth by investing and expanding, locally, regionally and internationally'. The company aims to establish itself as a the number one telecommunication company in the GCC region. By mid-2001, Batelco had successful joint ventures in Bahrain, Kuwait, Saudi Arabia, Jordan and Egypt.

Batelco has been an exemplar telecommunications company in the GCC region. The company's approach to service delivery was rewarded in October 1996 when it became the first telecommunications company in GCC states to receive the ISO9002 Certificate of Quality from the British Standards Institute. The company's vision is: 'We strive to be a world-class, customer-driven provider of integrated communications solutions.' The company's five corporate objectives are to attain: enhanced customer satisfaction; sustained revenue growth; improved efficiency; enhanced employee satisfaction; an excellent corporate image; in order to achieve a world-class company. The company's vision and corporate objectives are displayed, in both English and Arabic, throughout the organisation and employees use them as screensavers.

The company is highly committed to developing and updating its human resource skills. It invests on average over BD2 million (BD1 = £2) a year on human resource development in a large training centre owned and managed by the company. It conducts various training workshops and seminars to help staff enhance their managerial and technical skills. The company claims that over 95 per cent of its staff are Bahrainis, making it one of the leading companies in the country to offer the highest number of employment opportunities to the local community. Furthermore, during the last decades, Bahraini nationals have been given jobs for life at Batelco. A Batelco employee is perceived to get a better than average salary, training and social facilities. A job at Batelco has been most Bahrainis' dream, but all this is set to change.

In 2001 the Emir of Bahrain announced the end of Batelco's monopoly and opened the Bahraini telecommunications market for global competition. Similar moves were made by other GCC governments. The opening up of the Bahraini telecommunications market for foreign competition is forcing the company to revisit its welfarist management style and long-established policies and practices. Batelco's management claims that they have been preparing for this competition for several years by investing heavily in updating employees' technical and managerial skills; building up state of the art facilities; and creating a trusted brand name in Bahrain and other GCC states. Management often reiterate that its key strengths will insulate it from the storm of open global competition. It argues that GCC countries are different from other markets and local market expertise is a prerequisite. The company lists as its main strengths:

- a very good rapport with the local community established over several decades
- in-depth economic, political and cultural knowledge of the GCC market and customers' needs and behaviours
- a highly qualified, committed and loyal staff
- a highly recognised and trusted brand name
- close association with Cable & Wireless.

Nevertheless, the company recognises that for Batelco to be able to compete with global telecommunications companies, it has to restructure its management system and cut its labour cost. As a result, around 300 people out of just over 2,000 may have to go. Job (in)security is becoming a primary worry among staff in a country with comparatively higher unemployment rates than other GCC states. Furthermore, the new innovative schemes introduced by the company such as a voluntary retirement policy are putting an end to the 'job for life' for Bahraini nationals. For the first time, people at Batelco are worried about their jobs. Job insecurity is affecting employees' morale and could make them more ready to join other foreign companies when they enter Bahrain in the near future. In addition, highly skilled employees believe that competition will give them a better bargaining position for higher salaries. There is a possibility that they would leave if Batelco does not match offers made by global companies. Furthermore, will the company be able to sustain its relatively expensive 90 per cent Bahraini national employment policy if foreign companies opted for cheaper labour costs from the Indian subcontinent and Asia Pacific? Recent statements made by Batelco's management revealed the company's strategy to face up to global competition. No public statement, however, has been made about the crucial issue of changing the labour management policy. Two key issues need to be addressed. Should Batelco retain its paternalistic strategy, keep employees happy and risk being uncompetitive vis-à-vis foreign companies; or should it adopt a lean and mean strategy and risk losing the long-cherished employees satisfaction, loyalty and its social image?

Sources: The case study is based on Batelco's news releases and numerous articles published in the *Bahrain Tribune* newspaper

Closing case study questions

1. What are the key motives for deregulating the telecommunications market in Bahrain?

2. Are Batelco's strengths sustainable?

3. What are the likely consequences of staff reduction and policies such as early voluntary retirement on Batelco's future competitiveness?

4. Should the company continue with its 'employing nationals' policy?

Annotated further reading

Ali, A. and **Al-Shakhis**, M. (1985) 'Managerial value systems for working in Saudi Arabia: an empirical investigation', *Group and Organization Studies* 10: 135–51.
   This article is one of a series of empirical studies by Abbas Ali on managerial attitudes and value systems in several GCC countries.

Bhuian, N. S., **Al-Shammari**, S. E. and **Jefri**, A. O. (2001) 'Work-related attitudes and job characteristics of expatriates in Saudi Arabia', *Thunderbird International Business Review*, 43: 21–31.
   This article examines the management of expatriates in Saudi Arabia.

Muna, F. A. (1980) *The Arab Executive*. London: Macmillan.
   An original study based on a relatively small sample of Arab executives identifying major aspects of attitude to work, use of time and decision-making styles.

Schlumberger, O. (2000) 'Arab political economy and the European Union's Mediterranean policy: what prospects for development?', *New Political Economy* 5(2): 1469–9932.
   A useful general account of the political and economic institutions in GCC countries, encompassing a range of pressing current issues such as the practice of wasta.

References

Ahmad, K. (1976) *Islam: Its Meaning and Message*. London: Islamic Council of Europe.

Alhabshi, S. O. and **Ghazali**, A. H. (1994) *Islamic Values and Management*. Kuala Lumpur: Institute of Islamic Understanding Malaysia (IKIM).

Ali, A. (1988) 'Scaling an Islamic work ethic', *Journal of Social Psychology* 128(5): 575–3.

Ali, A. (1989) 'A comparative study of managerial belief about work in Arab states', *Advances in International Comparative Management* 4: 96–112.

Ali, A. (1993) 'Decision-making style, individualism, and attitudes toward risk of Arab executives', *International Studies of Management & Organisation* 23 (3): 53–73.

Ali, A. (1996) 'Organizational development in the Arab world', *Journal of Management Development* 15(5): 4–21.

Al-Najjar, B. (1983) 'Working and living conditions of foreign workers: foreign labor in Arab Gulf countries'. Proceeding of a seminar organised by the Centre for Arab Unity Studies, Centre for Arab Unity Studies, Beirut. pp.169–81.

Al-Qudsi, S. (1998) 'Labour participation of Arab women: estimates of the fertility to labour supply link', *Applied Economics* 30(7): 931–42.

Atiyyah, H. S. (1994) *Working in the Gulf: An Expatriate Guide to the Employment Laws of the Gulf Arab States.* Plymouth: International Venture Handbooks.

Atiyyah, H. S. (1996) 'Expatriate acculturation in Arab Gulf countries', *Journal of Management Development* 15(5): 37–47.

Atiyyah, H. S. (1999) 'Public organisation's effectiveness and its determinants in a developing country', *Cross Cultural Management* 6(2): 8–21.

Beekun, R. and Badawi, J. (1999) *Leadership: An Islamic Perspective.* Beltsville: Amana Publications.

Bhuian, N. S., Al-Shammari, S. E. and Jefri, A. O. (2001) 'Work-related attitudes and job characteristics of expatriates in Saudi Arabia', *Thunderbird International Business Review* 43(1): 21-31.

Bjerke, B. and Al-Meer, A. (1993) 'Culture's consequences: management in Saudi Arabia', *Leadership & Organisational Development Journal* 14(2): 30–35.

Cooper, J. (1996) 'Putting the kingdom to work', *Middle East Economic Digest* 40(14): 55–9.

Cunningham, R. and Sarayrah, Y. (1993) *Wasta: The Hidden Force in Middle Eastern Society.* Westport CT: Praeger.

Darwish, A. Y. (2000) 'Organizational commitment as a mediator of the relationship between Islamic work ethic and attitudes toward organizational change', *Human Relations* 45(4): 513–37.

Doumato, E. A. (1999) 'Women and work in Saudi Arabia: how flexible are Islamic margins?', *Middle Eastern Journal* 53(4): 568–83.

Gavin, J. (2000) 'Saudi Arabia – the walls come down', *Middle East Economic Digest* 44(19): 4–5.

Gulf Business (2001) 'Are you getting enough? 2001 salary survey', 5(9): 29–44.

Hofstede, G. (1980) *Culture's Consequences.* London: Sage.

Hosni, D. and Al-Qudsi, S. S. (1988) 'Sex discrimination in the labor market of Kuwait', *International Journal of Manpower* 9(3): 10–22.

Ikhlas, A. (1996) 'Attitudes towards women in the Arabian Gulf region', *Women in Management Review* 11(1): 29–39.

Lumsden, P. (1993) 'Dealing with the problem of localisation', *Middle East Economic Digest* 37(10): 46–8.

Mellahi, K. (2000) 'Human resource development through vocational education in Gulf Cooperation Countries: the case of Saudi Arabia', *Journal of Vocational Education and Training* 52(2): 331–47.

Mellahi, K. and Al-Hinai, S. (2000) 'Local workers in Gulf Cooperation Countries: assets or liabilities?', *Middle Eastern Studies* 26(3): 177–91.

Mellahi, K. and Wood, G. (2001) 'HRM in Saudi Arabia', in P. S. Budhwar and Y. A. Debrah *Human Resource Management in Developing Countries*. London: Routledge. Chapter 9.

Mellahi, K., Parker, G., Bortmani, H. and Guermat, C. (2000) 'Motives for FDI in Gulf Cooperation Council State: the Case of Oman'. Twenty-Seventh Annual Conference UK Chapter – Academy of International Business, University of Strathclyde, Glasgow, Scotland, vol. 2, pp. 243–58.

Montagu, C. (1995) 'Making more of national manpower', *Middle East Economic Digest* 39(10): 40–41.

Muna, F. A. (1980) *The Arab Executive*. London: Macmillan.

Owen, R. (1986) 'Migrant workers in the Gulf', *Middle East Review* spring: 24–7.

Parry, C. (1997) 'Saudization', *Al-Iktissad Wa-Amal* year 18: 39–41.

Schlumberger, O. (2000) 'Arab political economy and the European Union's Mediterranean policy: what prospects for development?', *New Political Economy* 5(2): 1469–9932.

Shaban, A. R., Assad, R. and Al-Qudsi, S. (1995) 'The challenge of employment in the Arab region', *International Labour Review* 134: 56–82.

PART 2

Going international

CHAPTER 6

International strategic management

Geoff Mallory

Learning objectives

When you finish reading this chapter you should:

- be aware of the need for clarity of organisational goals in formulating strategy

- understand the role of resources and capabilities in formulating strategy

- understand the logic that drives firms towards internationalising

- be able to extend the role of resource and capabilities into considering internationalisation issues

Opening Case Study:
Starbucks steams into Italy

'Starbucks? Never heard of it,' says the veteran barman at Café Bindi, a large and bustling Milan coffee bar opposite the Cadorna railway station, where thousands of commuters rush in for a quick espresso and a bun on their way to the office and a more leisurely *amaro* on their way home. 'Yes,' admits the barman, mixing a Bellini [fresh peaches, Italian sparkling wine, a dash of rum and Grand Marnier], 'American coffee is becoming quite popular.' But by that, he means an *espresso allungato*, a watered down imitation of the real Italian thing.

Seventeen years ago, an ambitious young American marketing man named Howard Schultz visited a string of Milanese coffee bars, such as the Café Bindi. Inspired by the conviviality and theatricality of the Italian *baristas*, Mr Schultz returned home to Seattle and transformed the small chain of Starbucks coffee shops into an American cultural icon and an international retailing phenomenon. Now Mr Schultz is back in Europe as the chairman of a 3,000 outlet company, determined to sell his own versions of espresso (or tall, skinny, triple decaf with hazelnut) to the Italians. Starbucks has just launched an ambitious expansion drive into continental Europe that will eventually include every sizeable market, including Italy.

Tanned and smartly suited like a Wall Street banker, Mr Schultz is convinced he can succeed with his latest European foray. 'We have opened in 18 countries and every single market has worked,' he says. 'We can elevate the coffee experience. We have very high quality coffee and great service and a relationship with our customers that has defined us.' Yet Starbucks has not yet blown the froth off the cappuccinos of the Milanese *baristas* – and seems unlikely to, according to some Italians familiar with the US chain. In his weekly magazine column, Umberto Eco, the author, once described his experience in a New York Starbucks. It was dreadful. He had to queue for his espresso, the fellow making it hadn't a clue, and by the time he took his cup to the table it was cold: a travesty of Italian culture.

Milan has about one café for every 2,000 inhabitants: some 600 cafés in a city of 1.2 million. The café is part of Italian everyday life, the equivalent of an Englishman's pub, acting like a private club with its own regular clientele. It is not just a place where you drink coffee. In many cafés you can buy cigarettes, lottery tickets, light lunches and sticky pastries while playing the football pools. But it is life in a hurry, because Italian coffee must be gulped down hot and fast. In the fashionable Via della Spiga, Giancarlo Codegoni, owner of the wood-panelled Cigno Nero [Black Swan] café, says he is not worried by Starbucks' arrival. 'Most Italians want real espresso and I don't think the Americans will change their tastes,' he said. Giacomo, one of his customers, adds that he visited New York once and tried Starbucks on Broadway, where the espresso was too bitter. 'One thing we don't need is to be told by the Americans how to make good coffee,' he says.

Starbucks says it faced similar scepticism when it moved into Japan. 'Before we opened they said that no one in Japan would ever walk in the street with a cup of coffee. They would lose face,' Mr Schultz says. 'But we have opened more than 150 stores and have in a sense transformed the culture. You cannot walk down a street in Tokyo today without seeing someone holding a cup of Starbucks.' He adds that Starbucks will approach the Italian market with great humility. 'The respect and admiration I have for the heritage of coffee in Italy is at the highest possible level,' he says. 'But we believe we can still provide something unique to the marketplace, and the customer will be the judge.'

Source: 21 Oct. 2000, *Financial Times* CD-ROM 2000

Introduction

To be successful, firms must make superior returns to their stakeholders, otherwise they will seek other recipients for their investment largesse in whatever form that might take. At an economic level firms who do not return more than the average cost of capital are not making this kind of return. For organisations that operate in a more social enterprise mode this notion of superior return also has important implications as donors or suppliers of resource are increasingly requiring that performance be measured, reported and benchmarked against other organisations.

To be successful, to make superior returns in the long term, do organisations necessarily need a strategy? In beginning to answer this question I am indebted to my former colleague, Professor Susan Segal-Horn, who first drew my attention to Brier's first law. Neither she nor Professor John Constable, who introduced it to her, were ever sure who Brier actually was or if he or she had any subsequent laws. However, the first law gives a raison d'être for all strategists in that it states: 'At some time in the life cycle of virtually every organisation, its ability to succeed in spite of itself runs out' (Segal-Horn 1998, p. 12). Thus while short-term gains may accrue to those without a strategy, longer term success might be more elusive.

Strategy gives a purpose and intent to an organisation. It defines targets for where an organisation might want to be at some future point in time. It is about making choices that affect outcomes, choices that mobilise resources to realise those targets. It sets the aspirations of the company and thus identifies any mismatch between the current and future states of the firm and provokes thinking about the actions that will be necessary to bridge any gap.

An intentional strategy has other consequences. By setting out targets, it clarifies the criteria upon which choices are made. It simplifies things and reduces ambiguity. Decision makers know what it is they are trying to achieve, what they want the organisation to be and, perhaps more importantly, what they don't want it to be. It is also an important way of communicating these intentions across departments and other sub-units, thus giving consistency over both time and space. It provides a vehicle for the dialogue between managers of different units and managers at different levels in the organisation.

What is strategy?

If strategy is to be all of the above then strategic management should be about developing tools to ensure success. Grant (1998) suggests that there are four factors which are conducive to this.

The first is goals that are simple, consistent and long term. We have already discussed this aspect of strategy. The second success factor is rooted in a profound understanding of the competitive environment. What does it take to be a success in this field of endeavour? Who are the significant competitors and what are their strengths and weaknesses? What are their strategies and how will they react to the actions of others? What are the industry conditions? Is the industry attractive or hostile? Third, what are the organisation's strengths and weaknesses? What resources can it mobilise? What gaps or areas of weakness should be protected?

Fourth, and critical to success, is effective implementation. Plans and strategies may be well thought through but if they are not carried out with an effective organisation being built to deliver them they will fail. One of the early students of business strategy, Alfred Chandler (1962), noticed repeatedly the link between the failure of managers to realise the benefits from a strategy and the need to make structural changes to their organisations. Thus he established the linkage that structure follows strategy.

So strategic management is about clarifying goals, analysing the organisation and environment, developing and choosing options and implementing the chosen option. While these labels might differ from text to text, the underlying meaning remains pretty similar.

Clarifying goals

In answering the question as to whether or not organisations have goals, most students, at least in my experience, answer either yes or no, both of which are, of course, incorrect: the correct answer being yes and no. How can organisations have goals when they are not people and yet they must have them, as we said above, to focus and constrain decision making? If goals are the property of individuals or groups of individuals, how do they become transformed into organisational goals? The thread that links the two is the idea of groups and/or individuals being stakeholders in an organisation. They have reasons to participate in the work of an organisation in the expectation that their goals will be reached as the organisation reaches its goals. If, for example, we are employees, one goal we may have is for a high level of remuneration. This will, we expect, be provided by our employer reaching a level of profit due to our (and everyone else's) efforts and is thus in the form of a balanced transaction. That this balance may be disturbed is due to either party feeling that their pay-off does not equate to their effort. Another example is the value of a positive public image to some not-for-profit organisations. To produce that the media may need access to and comment from the organisation's personnel on a wide range of issues. This also begs the question as to whether or not the stakeholders are certain (clear) or somewhat vague about their goals. Can we be precise as to what is an adequate return for our labours?

So if there are multiple stakeholders who produce diverse and maybe vague goals, how can goals that an organisation's managers choose to work with be simple, consistent and long term? In practice of course they are not and they don't. Managers have to cope with the diversity and uncertainties surrounding stakeholders' goals. How to do so with cognitive capacities which have finite limits and goals of their own to satisfy?

Much academic research into decision making over the last 40 years or so has focused on this problem. This effort has not been in vain. The idea that managers do have such limits represents one strand of thinking and is exemplified by the work of Cyert and March (1963). Second, any idea that organisations have a goal (singular) around which everyone is united has been challenged by writers from a political science tradition. Key exemplars of this approach would be Allison's (1971) analysis of the Cuban missile crisis and the application of a political perspective to organisations by such authors as Pfeffer and Salancick (1974) who studied the budgeting process at a university. They found that the power which a university department possessed explained its budget allocation rather than a ranking on such 'rational criteria' as number of students taught. This finding was replicated in several other studies.

Taken together these findings suggest some tactics and devices for managers to use to adjust for their cognitive limits when coping with conflicting preferences. They recognise that people do in fact engage in political activity to enhance their power and thus get what they want. Almost in passing it raises the question as to whether or not political behaviour is positive, in that it is the only way in which issues get resolved, or dysfunctional in that it might paralyse decision making. Certainly coalition building, getting a view on the preferences and expectations of those in powerful positions, is a way of reducing diversity and ambiguity. As Eisenhardt and Zbaraki (1992) succinctly sum this research: 'Power wins the battle of choice.' Goals may need to be clear but we should also be clear as to whose goals they are.

Analysing the environment

All the approaches to the strategic management of organisations have put a greater or lesser amount of stress on the process and tools for analysis of the organisation's environment. In the early days of research into management, when successful strategy was thought of as the outcome of a planning process, analysis was essentially limited to estimating demand for products and the revenues that could be gleaned from particular products in particular markets. Strategy was a plan, which was agreed upon at a certain point in time and implemented or monitored by budgetary systems of varying sophistication. However, as the economic environment for most firms became less predictable, the usual milestone for this being the oil price shocks of the early and mid-1970s, planning and forecasting became less viable as a means of ensuring performance and survival. Instead, researchers began to concentrate more on the characteristics of industries, whether or not they were 'attractive' in that they allowed superior returns to be made. Analysis and decision making became focused on economic factors such as entry barriers, intensity of competition, availability of substitute products and on the power of suppliers of products and services to firms and the power of customers.

The analysis of all these forces (Porter, 1985) could determine attractiveness or indicate ways in which firms might make it attractive. But the focus on the actions and expectations of other organisations and the power that they possess to constrain or deter a potential entrant was given a very different emphasis than that of the earlier planning-oriented approaches. Research into strategic management continued to be focused by what has become known as the market positioning view. Analysis of industries gave important messages to managers as to how firms might successfully compete in any given industry. The idea that firms employ one of a series of 'generic' strategies to compete gained immediate currency. Essentially, in this view (Porter, 1985) firms can compete by employing a low-cost or differentiation strategy over a narrow or wide market focus. As this last sentence encapsulates a lot of important concepts it probably needs a little illustration.

The basic argument revolves around variations in the price and cost of goods or services. Firms who succeed by making superior returns (i.e. returns which are more than any other firm) can do so in one of two ways. The first is by taking the market price for a product or service and making superior margins (profits) by being more cost efficient than the competition. It is logical to conclude that to make the best return a firm would have to be the cost leader in an industry (Porter, 1985). The second way to make superior returns is to add perceived value to the product or service so that the consumer will pay a premium over the market price for this. That is to differentiate your offering from the competition. The other dimension, focus, indicates the breadth of consumers targeted. Is the firm targeting all consumers of their product or service or just a very small sub-set of the total market? For example, an insurance company might target as clients for their policies all automobile drivers or only those over 50 years old. The former is a broad focus; the latter, perhaps obviously, is narrow.

To illustrate the conjunction of these ideas, we can look at the approach of successful airlines such as Southwest Air in the United States, and Ryan Air, EasyJet and Buzz in Europe that offer a low-cost, no frills service targeted more at non-business flyers. They are narrow cost focused. These can be contrasted with larger full service airlines such as American and British Airways that offer a broadly focused, differentiated product. This strategy relies on their ability to communicate the advantages of having connecting flights through partners and being located at major hubs of international air travel such as London's Heathrow airport and JFK in New York. Other airlines such as SAS and Virgin Atlantic seek to differentiate their product to attract more of the full fare, business class passengers who are prepared to pay a premium price for the levels of service they offer. These can range from express check-in, to a limousine service, from multi-channel entertainment to in-flight massages. These can be thought of as more narrowly focused differentiators.

The market positioning view of strategy and the focus of decisions being on desirability of entry, how to compete and/or change the nature of the competitive forces way, held sway for several years. This was until accumulating empirical evidence (Rumelt, 1991) began to suggest that the nature of the industry did not have such a major impact on performance as the characteristics of the firm. Performance was seen as being related to the resources available to the firm and how these were accessed, renewed and deployed to gain sustainable competitive advantage over competitors and thus produce superior performance. This, the resource-based view of strategy, adds into the analytic frame for consideration the internal characteristics of the firm, and completes the environment to firm linkage. Thus managers are faced with decisions about their resource base, what it is, how to sustain and/or renew it and how to deploy it to the best advantage. To do this is not to deny environmental analysis or its importance. Instead the stress is placed on the factors that are key or crucial to the success of the firm. This view thus emphasises the firm as well as the environmental context and looks at those characteristics that can give competitive advantage and thus generate superior performance for one firm over another.

Key or critical success factors

Identifying these factors seems pretty straightforward really. Robert Grant (1998, p. 76) suggests that 'to survive and prosper in an industry, a firm must meet two criteria: first, it must supply what customers want to buy, second, it must survive competition'. This provokes two key questions. First, what do customers or clients want? Second, what does the company need to do to survive competition?

Customers and clients are in some way the industry. They supply the basic rationale for its existence. Even successful companies such as KPMG that succeeded by largely creating an industry around professional accounting and consulting services needed a client base which had need of such services. Otherwise there would have been no rationale for its existence. Thus companies, after identifying who the customers are, should analyse their needs and work out how they select the product or service of one competitor over that of another; what criteria they use to make the purchase decision. There is, for instance, some evidence to suggest that in the United Kingdom at least people are more likely to get divorced from their partner than they are to change their bank. A bank entering into retail banking would need to know why this is. If the answer is related to the cost and hassles of switching over standing orders or direct debit payments and not rate of interest on current accounts, then to induce consumers to change would need attention to reducing these hassles and not necessarily offering better interest rates.

In answering the second question on competition, the firm needs to analyse the basis of competition. How intense is competition and what dimensions are the firms competing on? Are banks out there actually competing for new business or are they making good returns from offering a wider range of products to the same customer base? While good understanding of these facets will not alone be enough to ensure success, it is an essential component in the process of formulating a successful strategy.

Analysing the organisation

The idea discussed above, that industry did not account for the variance found in performance of firms, has led to a focus on key components of the firm rather than characteristics of the industry as being responsible for competitive advantage. Competitive advantage results from exploiting differences between firms in an industry and not by pursuing a particular generic strategy – be it cost focus or broad differentiation. This way of thinking about strategy, called the resource-based view (RBV) has developed over the last ten years or so. It identifies the two key elements as the resources that firms use as inputs to the transformation process and the capabilities it uses to integrate, deploy and renew those resources to obtain competitive advantage.

Resources

This kind of analysis can prove remarkably difficult, as invariably documentary evidence of resources just does not exist. The balance sheet, for example, provides at best a partial and at worst a distorted view of a firm's total assets. It does give clues as to the nature of the firm's tangible resources and the financial and physical assets it uses in the transformation process. What it may do, however, is to obscure the strategically relevant value of such an asset. In valuing the assets of a Canadian carton supplier, successive groups of my students looked to the book value of the much depreciated plant and equipment rather than the more strategically relevant discounted value of the cash flows that the assets were capable of generating. So the focus for analysis should be directed to the firm's borrowing capacity, its ability to generate cash, alternative uses for plant and buildings, raw material reserves, and so on.

What is invisible and not just obscured on most balance sheets is the firm's intangible assets. True, in some parts of the world items such as goodwill, capitalised research and development expenditure are shown. However, this predominant invisibility accounts in some part for the sometimes huge variances between a firm's book value, represented by the balance sheet and its stock market valuation which should reflect the future value of its income stream. These 'missing assets' are usually described as being intangible and such items as reputation and technology fall into this category.

For some firms their reputation can be a significant asset. For service providers whose quality of service is only usually experienced at the point of use, how does a consumer know in advance that they will get value for their money? The reputation that a firm has in the market can be an important decision-making criterion for some would-be consumers. When I moved to Canada in the mid-1980s, I asked friends and colleagues whose judgement I trusted (reputation again) about which dentist, doctor and tax accountant I should consider using. In a similar way consumers may choose which restaurant to eat in, movie to see, book to read, and so on – so it may be for firms who employ consultants, auditors and lawyers, etc.

Brand names and trademarks also have a value, the value in the premium prices that they can generate over unbranded goods. For example, the Harley-Davidson brand allows the company not only to obtain a premium price for its motorcycles, but also allows it to license the name to the manufacturers of clothing, toiletries and other consumer items.

Technology is another important intangible asset. Property rights to knowledge, as opposed to the hardware referred to in our discussion of tangible assets, can be and are expressed in such things as patents, copyrights (who owns the rights to the present book?) and trade secrets. These can be significant resources in establishing competitive advantage. For example, Pilkington, the UK-based glassmaker, developed, protected and subsequently licensed its flat glass technology to enormous advantage over the years.

Human resources are another significant asset in the search for sources of competitive advantage. Although actually taking stock in a financial sense might be difficult (unless you are a sports team that paid a transfer fee for a player), humans offer skills that can be developed and utilised by the firm through further education and training. For some firms, particularly in what we now call 'knowledge-intensive industries', humans are a key source of advantage. McDonald's, the fast food restaurant chain firm, invests heavily in recruiting and training new personnel through its Hamburger University situated in Canada. It also inculcates them carefully into the Andersen way of doing things, working practices and expected behaviours. This ability to recruit, develop and integrate human skills is a facet of an organisation's culture which can in this sense be seen as a resource. In another sense, as a way of deploying teams of assets, it can be seen as a capability.

Capabilities

The possession of assets such as a cadre of trained accountants, health professionals or even academics does not alone assure that competitive advantage accrues to the employing organisation. It is also how the organisation develops and deploys them that may be the source of advantage. For advantage to be gained, the organisation has to do something distinctive in this respect, which is why the literature sometimes uses terms such as distinctive or core competencies to refer to them. This is a useful adjective to apply as it focuses attention on advantage relative to other firms. As an example, while many firms can and do produce personal computers at low cost, it is Dell's radical departure from the usual distribution routes by using first the telephone and then the internet to take customer orders that gave it competitive advantage. This distribution capability, allied later to a flexible assembly capability such as in its Limerick plant, sustains that advantage. Organisations such as Dell, EasyJet, KFC and so on have recognised what it is that they do well. They have then used this as a basis for their strategy.

How do capabilities or competencies get expressed in practice? Mainly by codifying knowledge into routines or rules. It is neither feasible nor economic to require the manager of a fast food outlet to have a detailed understanding of every facet of the expertise that contributes to the product and to the processes used. Instead such information is codified into manuals and procedures which can be used to guide operations. Grant (1998, p. 126) gives us a useful analogy by making the point that 'routines are to organisations what skills are to the individual'. They are more often than not carried out without conscious thought and may be based more on tacit than explicit knowledge, hence culture as a capability.

The origins or rules and routines may lie in the historical development of the organisation; as it faced situations it may well have developed ways of dealing with them. Can they be consciously designed, modified or replicated? Probably, but how to recognise a redundant or inappropriate routine raises other more serious questions which are really beyond the scope of our discussion. However, replication is not and we should consider if and how this can be done in markets for different products and more particularly in different geographic regions.

For a fast food chain, due to the extensive codification of its knowledge system, replication should be fairly straightforward. In other industries and for other firms whose routines depend more on tacit than explicit knowledge and skills, transfer becomes more problematic and may require secondment of key personnel for training and/or mentoring activities.

Our discussion of this aspect of strategy should conclude that in some sense capabilities, particularly those that are either distinctive to or at the core of competitive advantage, are a resource to be leveraged or deployed as much as finance is. The key is in deriving advantage, which is gained through deployment or implementation – hence the need in successful strategy for good implementation.

Going international

Why do firms need to consider adding an international dimension to their strategic thinking? The essence of the answer is that the world is changing. The conclusion of successive General Agreement of Tariffs and Trade (GATT) agreements and the establishment of the World Trade Organisation (WTO) have been major forces for change. Agreements, which result in the reduction of barriers to foreign capital investment and ownership and the reduction or elimination of barriers to the free passage of goods, have now been made. When these are taken together with the mobility of goods and labour made possible by the establishment of customs unions such as the European Union they have had a significant impact on the growth and intensity of international competition.

Robert Grant (1998), discussing the impact of internationalisation on industry structures, suggested that it was possible to identify four types of industry according to the extent of and mechanisms for internationalisation. These were the extent of trade and international investment in that industry. At the higher levels of these two dimensions, global industries such as automobiles and semiconductors exist. At lower levels he identifies a cluster of 'sheltered industries' from which banking, telecommunications and insurance had emerged in the late 1980s and early 1990s. Left was a group made up of fragmented service industries such as drycleaning, hairdressing and small-scale manufacturing such as housebuilding, furniture making and industries which produced no tradeable products, together with areas such as grocery retailing and domestic services.

If we cursorily examine this cluster we can see that some of them have become increasingly exposed to both international investment and trade. While as yet we can see no evidence for the internationalisation of hairdressing salons (as opposed to hair care products), the foundations underpinning industries such as grocery retailing, furniture manufacture and ice cream manufacture are beginning to shift under pressures of internationalisation. Take as an example the US-based Wal-Mart chain, which has been aggressively internationalising over the last decade. When Wal-Mart bought the UK retail chain Asda and the UK supermarket group Tesco began overseas expansion, then the writing was probably on the wall for the sheltered status of the grocery retailing industry. A crucial aspect of this is that not only do industries become exposed to one or two new competitors in their own market, but that these competing firms may have sources of competitive advantage which are unavailable to 'domestic' and 'local' enterprises. The size and purchasing power of an organisation like Wal-Mart may have severe consequences for 'local' business.

In response to these shifts in the framework of competition, most firms have had to face a series of difficult issues and decisions, which have undoubtedly impacted on their performance and thus survivability. In this section we focus on this kind of decision and how firms formulate their response to the perceived threat or opportunity. The nature of these threats was drawn out by Yip (1989) who built a framework of the drivers for globalisation within particular industries; in short when industry conditions provided firms with the opportunity to globalise. Yip suggests that there are four groups of drivers.

The first is a group of market-oriented drivers which essentially depend on customer behaviour and the structure of available distribution channels. So when customer needs are homogeneous or basically the same (or can be made to be the same) or have little variation, e.g. hamburgers, soft drinks, fashion goods and music, conditions are favourable. When customers are global such as the major automobile manufacturers that search the world for suppliers of products and services, conditions are favouring global suppliers over purely domestic companies. Allied with this is the existence of global distribution channels which, to be frank, are very rare. Finally, the marketing effort can be easily transferred across borders. The use of TV advertising that does not use language (or can be overdubbed) or other cultural symbols would be an example of this.

The next group of drivers involves cost and thus depends on the basic economics of the product and its production. To reap benefits from economies of scale and scope and to experience benefits may require firms to seek alternative markets for products. In addition, globalisation may be driven by the quest for sourcing efficiencies, for low-cost production sites, logistic factors such as perishability of goods and tradability of the product. Product development costs attributable to products can also be reduced if global or at least regional products can be developed. Automobile model development is now centred upon global models rather than region or country as in the past.

Government action, a third driver, can also create favourable conditions for globalisation of industries. Their trade policies, expressed through import tariffs or their removal, the imposition of technical standards and marketing regulation via media restrictions are key elements in the globalisation equation for industries.

The final group, competitive drivers, is really related to the actions of firms within a particular industry. Their actions can raise the potential to globalise. If they do it then they could reap benefits to the detriment of other participants unless they too expand the scope of their operations.

When conditions within an industry begin to become favourable, then the managers of participating firms are faced with decisions on how to sustain their competitive advantage; how to secure resources and deploy them to best advantage. Basically they are faced with two key decisions: the first is where to locate production and the second how to enter a market. These two decisions may in some instances be quite closely related, but for the moment we will discuss them as separate issues.

Location

There are three sets of factors which need considering: national resource conditions; firm specific advantage; tradability.

National resource conditions

If a firm is heavily dependent on a resource for competitive advantage, then it must make sense to locate where resource conditions are favourable. So, for instance, firms for whom labour costs are a key source of advantage will tend to locate their production facilities in countries where such costs are low. For example, companies such as Nike, the athletic shoe manufacturer, and Levi-Strauss, the clothing manufacturer, tend to have production facilities in the Far East, China, Vietnam, Thailand and the Philippines. Similarly, most telecommunications and computing companies have a research presence in Silicon Valley to tap into and exploit the basic microelectronics developments that occur in and around that particular geographic location.

Firm specific advantage

If competitive advantage is based on internal resources, then location should depend on where those can best be deployed. It could be argued that a source of competitive advantage of the Japanese auto manufacturers Toyota, Nissan and Honda was their technical, manufacturing and product development capabilities and not access to an external resource base. This latter source is the case of another auto maker, Hyundai, which favours location in a low labour cost environment to realise its strategy. While originally these companies concentrated production in Japan, they clearly demonstrated their capability to transfer those skills to overseas locations.

Tradability

The final consideration relates to transportability. High transport costs associated with the finished product may necessitate local production or assembly. As Yip

(1989) implied, government policies may also have an artificial impact on tradability as the imposition of import restrictions may force manufacturers to locate production in a market they wish to penetrate with their product, even if such production is uneconomic.

Location decision should also take into account the fact that any product is made up of many other products and sub-assemblies whose input requirements in terms of resource or capability can vary considerably. Thus, different locations are likely to offer different sources of advantage at each stage of the final output. International trade patterns are showing a clear trend towards specialisation (Grant, 1998). For example, in textiles fibre production is concentrated in those countries with advantage in agricultural production (natural fibres) or chemical production (synthetics). Turning the fibre into cloth through spinning and weaving tends to be capital intensive and garment manufacture is labour intensive. Hence these different activities may well take place in different countries. Optimum location involves considering the best location for each activity.

However, these considerations should be tempered by the management costs involved in establishing and controlling the linkages that multiple locations incur. Transport costs as well as transaction costs could be significant, as might such things as higher inventory costs and shipping time costs.

Foreign entry decisions

This decision issue is posed as a 'how' question, rather than the 'why and where' questions posed for locating the production function. Strategic thinking here being based around an assumption of attractiveness suggests that firms would only seek to establish a presence in a market where they could make a superior return and by the firm establishing some competitive advantage over local producers.

There are a series of models or frameworks that have been put forward to guide decision makers in this task (see for example, Johanson and Vahlne, 1977). All tend towards the conclusion that there is some sort of chain of escalation of commitment by the firm to the market related to the development of knowledge about and the depth of market penetration; the major distinctions between them being by means of engaging in transactions or by direct investment. This has been thought to be a simple and sequential set of stages related to commitment.

The first and lowest level of commitment can be where the firm has no regular export activity into a territory and just exports to fill one-off orders for its product without really establishing a commitment to or presence in the market. This is essentially a reactive stance.

A more proactive mode of operation and one that develops commitment to a market would involve the firm continuing to export, but doing this via one or possibly a network of agents in the host country. These may or may not exclusively represent the firm.

The next level of commitment is for the firm to establish an overseas sales subsidiary. It continues to manufacture elsewhere but might establish, for example, a warehousing facility together with a sales presence. The UK-based Laura Ashley company chose to penetrate overseas markets in this way.

The next level of commitment sees the fusion of production and sales with the establishment of a fully fledged subsidiary which not only sells via export but also manufactures product in the market. This was the classic establishment pattern of the multinational corporation of the late 1940s and 1950s when major European and American companies in particular established their international presence. The products they produced were geared to that market. Ford of Europe, for example, designed and produced their own models completely independently of Ford America and their Australian subsidiary. There was no concept of the 'world' or even 'European' car then.

Firms have also discovered other ways to penetrate overseas markets by the use of joint ventures or alliances and licensing agreements. The first involves a commitment of some assets, which may be either tangible in the form of investment, or intangible in the form of expertise and knowledge together with those of a partner or partners. The second involves the transfer of rights and knowledge of a product and the manufacturing process to another firm with a presence in the market in return for some form of payment or royalty.

If these are the basic ways of establishing and developing an international presence, then what considerations determine the choice of form? Some are very similar to the considerations involved in locating production. The first of these is whether competitive advantage is based on firm or nation specific resources. If advantage is country based, then exporting becomes the key to exploiting an overseas market. Hyundai, which has a strategy based around market penetration via low-cost product, can really only manufacture in locations with low labour costs. To exploit attractive markets in North America and Europe, the export of cars together with some sort of dealership infrastructure is the only viable route. They have the capabilities to turn a resource advantage into a competitive advantage.

Tradability of the product is the second key consideration. If transport costs are too high or there are import or other restrictions, then accessing new overseas markets needs investment in production facilities or the establishment of some sort of joint venture or alliance. In this way many companies, for example Suzuki, overcame restrictions imposed by the Indian government. The market for motorcycles – a major product in Suzuki's portfolio – in India is enormous, but the only way they could access this was via a joint venture with local partners TVS.

Many companies may also locate sales and/or production facilities to follow a major customer. This is particularly true of service industries such as accounting and consulting, but it also occurs with component suppliers to manufacturers; hence the growth of industry clustered around a major manufacturing facility such as has occurred around the Ford facility in Tamil Nadu, just south of Chennai in India.

The third consideration is whether or not the firm possesses the full range of resource and capabilities to establish advantage in a market. Marketing and distribution are two key considerations here, as Yip's analysis suggests. The key to their success was distribution and they sought to forge alliances and joint ventures to get the product to their target segment within that market.

The form of the relationship might very well depend on the nature of the resource or capability required. If more than marketing is required then the product might well be licensed to a local manufacturer. The accompanying case of the brewing industry has examples of this kind of arrangement.

Yet another consideration is the degree to which resources are appropriable. How well are the rights of the owner protected? Can developers lock in the benefits or can someone else gain the benefits? Some mechanisms offer strong protection to the firm sharing knowledge. In the example we used earlier of Pilkington licensing its flat glass technology, they were strongly protected by patents. Other means for exerting strong control are copyright and trademarks. A few years ago, in an interview I did with the then CEO of Cadbury Schweppes, he commented to the effect that maintaining vigilance over the name Cadbury, the style, the printing font and the colours used on packaging by the various subsidiaries and licensees overseas was a major corporate issue.

A final consideration is the transaction costs of licensing the trademarks, processes, etc. This is the cost of negotiating and monitoring the terms of any agreement as opposed to internalising the transaction within a fully owned subsidiary. This issue is central to considering choices between modes of internationalisation. Transaction costs exist in the form of entry barriers and transport costs. These must be taken into account with other more direct costs such as exchange rate risk and information costs.

The impact of culture on strategy

National culture can impact on strategy in three main areas. First, it can impact on the nature of goods and services that consumers demand and through them on the key success factors in a particular industry or market. In one of the examples used earlier in the chapter to illustrate the discussion of consumer needs, the case of the UK consumer's propensity to change banks was introduced. This recognises, perhaps implicitly, that things might well be different in other countries.

Second, and following on from the nature of products, national differences can impact on market structures through the institutional structure of societies. But perhaps more important from our perspective is the fact that differences can impact on the ways in which managers analyse such structures and their own organisations' resources and capabilities. It may also have an impact on how they respond to the challenges in their environment through the choices that they make.

Finally, national culture has an impact on the way that a chosen strategy is effectively realised. This can happen through a mixture or combination of organisation design, resource allocation decisions or leadership styles.

Culture and consumer tastes

Companies who do business overseas have a tendency explicitly to take different consumer tastes and preferences into account when designing their organisational arrangements overseas. The logical extension of escalating commitment to overseas markets by establishing subsidiaries that we discussed earlier resulted in the multinational corporation – a form of organisation essentially born out of a need to concentrate on and emphasise 'local' preferences and needs. Thus goods and services became tailored to those demands and culture enters the arena as a major source of variation.

However, a convergence in consumer taste and thus a globalisation of markets has long been predicted. The increasing reach and sophistication of communication technologies and the rapid spread of technological developments has led to the emergence of what we now call 'global markets' for standardised products and the concomitant rise of the global corporation. As a key analyst puts it: 'Almost everyone everywhere wants all the things they have heard about, seen or experienced via the new technologies' (Levitt, 1983, p. 92).

According to Levitt, increasing globalisation has actually made the world a simpler and not a more complicated place in which to compete. From the globalisation perspective, a multinational view of the world and the associated multinational structure is decidedly passé. This form of organisation operating in a number of countries, adjusting product, prices and practices in each with the attendant high cost of control, will be or is being replaced by the global corporation selling worldwide product lines. There appear to be plenty of examples of firms operating in this way. Perhaps the most visible are of American origin: the two soft drinks giants, Coca-Cola and Pepsi, the fast food chains and apparel companies.

This global view, while accepting that some differences in markets will persist, postulates that the majority will disappear due to the convergence of consumer preferences. According to Levitt (1983, p. 93), this leads inevitably to 'the standardisation of products, manufacturing and the institutions of trade and commerce'. The fact that Coca-Cola uses a slightly different product formulation for different markets and that it is possible to buy beer in McDonald's outlets in Paris does not invalidate the general trend. The underlying product is basically the same and any distinction is really only marginal.

The basic assumptions behind these ideas have been challenged, for example, by Douglas and Wind (1987) who provided an early critique of the standardised global product view and suggested that it was in fact overly simplistic. They view product standardisation as being only one option among a range of possible product/market strategies that may be successful in global markets and suggest that standardisation may only be appropriate in markets which fit specific underlying assumptions or environmental conditions. They further conclude that a firm's international portfolio of products might contain a mix of both international and regional brands/products.

It seems as though the proponents of convergence would have companies eschew market analysis based on cultural differences and proceed on the assumption that most regional differences are trivial or irrelevant. The question for strategy makers is whether or not to proceed on that basis and assume that the strength of similarities is more significant than any differences which may exist.

Culture and analysis

Considering culture as shaping preferences raises concerns as to how the culture of the strategy makers themselves has an impact on strategy formulation. In our discussion thus far and the introduction to this section, the ways in which strategy makers analyse the industry environment and the nature of their own organisation has also been treated as a culture-free set of activities. Industry and market structures may well vary, but another source of variation must be the national culture of top level managers.

That there is a 'cultural view' of strategy formulation stems in part from the realisation that the manager as strategist is faced with uncertainties and a lack of information when he or she is required to work through and evaluate all possible alternative courses of action in making decisions. These gaps in knowledge are invariably filled by the experience that managers have had with similar issues. These experiences also tend to bias the way in which new events are framed and dealt with. These biases are directly related to and constructed by the manager's views of the environment, which includes their stakeholders, and the interdependence of these environmental components (Calori *et al.*, 1992). In effect, these set up their world view, the rules that they make and the assumptions that they use. This world view may be at once both an individual view and a collective view; individual in the sense that participants have their own views which, through some socio-political processes, become the view of the ruling or dominant coalition of the company. This view of the world has a pervasive or more probably ubiquitous influence on strategy and the outcomes of the decisions taken to realise that strategy. This is what Johnson (1988) has called the organisation's paradigm; the set of assumptions that are more or less held in common and taken for granted within an organisation.

This is the key idea of the cultural view of strategy, which takes in not only the learning and prior experiences of individual decision makers, but also their collective experiences and the routines and procedures that have been developed within the organisation over time. The idea that these assumptions, rules, etc. are also taken for granted is critically important. The paradigm can be likened to a glass cage that reflects or refracts outside events in a peculiar distorted way to the decision makers inside, but cannot be seen directly. It is a cage, but it is of the managers' own individual and collective construction.

The paradigm, at whatever level, stems from the different frames of reference each level uses. The individual manager's frame can be thought of as being a product of national or regional cultures: education and socialisation. In addition, professional orientation – values and training – or a functional specialisation – marketing or finance – add to the mix together with the values of a particular organisation and its ways of doing things. To this we might also add a particular industry and an industry orientation. This can thus be an extremely complex construction.

If national culture helps to shape not only the individual manager's views of the world but also how the collective views at both the organisation and industry level emerge, what impact does it have on strategy and decision making? While there have been several studies on the impact of national culture on decision-making processes (see Cray and Mallory, 1998 for a discussion), there is a paucity of relevant empirical work directly linking culture and strategy. The most notable contribution comes from Susan Schneider (1989) and Schneider and De Mayer (1991).

Schneider (1989, p. 149) reinforces our argument that the steps in the strategy process are likely to be influenced by national culture: 'Assessments of the environment and the organisation are not necessarily "objective" but are a function of perceptions and interpretations which will, in turn, affect strategic behaviour.' The approach taken to scanning the environment, for example, depends on what the strategist expects to encounter. While perceptions may be influenced by factors such as the history of the firm and the structure of the industry, the general tendencies of the surrounding culture are sure to condition the way an individual regards the environment. If the local culture embraces a proactive stance towards the environment, one that assumes the possibility of controlling it, the scanning may be more focused. More reactive cultures will take a wider, less specific view.

Schneider distinguishes between two general culturally influenced types of strategy. The first is a directive strategy. It is controlled by a small group at the top of the organisation and utilises formal techniques for planning and evaluation. This approach is based on the conviction that the environment can be manipulated to accommodate the organisation's strategy. The reactive approach involves more people throughout the organisation and relies to a greater extent on qualitative information and informal evaluation procedures. For organisations embracing a reactive approach, strategic adjustment is more an ongoing task which links forward to the future and back to the past. Between these two general types there is room for an almost infinite variety of approaches.

While Schneider argues for the influence of culture on strategy formation, she makes it clear that it is but one of many factors that shape strategic choice. However, it should be said that the point at which culture is likely to have the greatest impact is, as we have suggested, precisely where the strategy process is most fluid, during the scanning, selection and interpretation stages. While the threats and opportunities for the organisation are still being formulated, the influence of culture on perception and cognition, on the process of recognising and categorising the issues that are likely to impact on the organisation, have the most sway. Once the data have been gathered and evaluated then existing structures channel the process along more predictable lines, although local values and practices will also have shaped them.

In a more empirical piece, Schneider and De Mayer (1991) found that while there were differences among country clusters in interpretation and response, the cultural reasons for these differences remain elusive. They found that national culture did influence crisis and threat interpretations, although these were not related to avoiding uncertainty (Hofstede, 1980), but both countries in their study did rank low on uncertainty avoidance. There are clearly some other institutional forces at work here.

Culture and realisation

Finally if, as we are led to believe, structural change follows a change in strategy, then the design of organisation structure, together with resource allocation decisions and leadership, become critical activities in successfully implementing strategy. While a full consideration of these would require at least another chapter to work through fully we can highlight a couple of key concerns.

First, is there a cultural influence on the designers of structure? In a similar vein to our discussion of the impact of culture on analysis, the views of designers as to what would be an appropriate structure seem to be inevitably coloured by their perception of what organisation is and how it works in terms of authority relationships. The work of Laurent (1983), which cited Hofstede (1991) and Trompenaars (1993), supports this view. Imagine a situation in which structural design is based on a view of the world as seen from, for example, Detroit, Eindhoven or Hong Kong which celebrates or espouses as it were home country values. Would these provoke different reactions from employees from a different culture? What would be the reaction of the structured? Will their national culture influence how they experience and react to structuring?

Second, in a similar vein decision making and leadership can be thought to be culturally influenced. Decision making, as Axelsson and colleagues (1991) demonstrated, can and does vary across national cultures. For example, Swedish managers take longer than their UK counterparts to reach a decision, with the implication that processes involve more intense interactions and more experts and use more criteria than similar decisions in the United Kingdom. There is also an interesting body of research into leadership (see Cray and Mallory, 1998 for a review) which concludes that if effective leadership is situation specific, then the leaders must have an understanding of the situation. This understanding must be driven by cultural forces.

Summary

This chapter has developed the view of the importance and centrality of a firm's resources and capabilities for strategy formation without ignoring the importance of fit with the environment. It should also be noted that resources and capabilities can be stretched to realise the aspirations of its stakeholders. The changing and dynamic nature of the environment has been examined, particularly the forces or drivers for considering the globe and not just a country or region as possible areas to deploy competitive advantage in the pursuit of superior returns. The rationale for and the substance of the key decisions that managers face have also been outlined and discussed.

Discussion questions

1. How can managers cope with diverse goals among their stakeholders?

2. What are the major forces that have shaped the international environment for organisations? What impact have they had on the nature of competition?

3. How useful is the notion of generic strategies for international strategy formation?

4. Critically assess the utility of joint ventures or alliances as ways of going international.

Closing Case Study:
Beer or brands, brewing or marketing?

Is there really an international brewing industry?

The news that Guinness, the manufacturer of the famous Irish stout, was opening a pub in Novosibirsk in Siberia might have passed you by. However, if you have sought out thirst quenching opportunities in almost any of Europe's major cities over the past decade or so, then the chances are that you will have been offered a variety of choices of venue with which to accomplish your goal. Among these, the 'Irish pub' or bar has become an almost ubiquitous feature. There is, for example, a competitive league for the pub game darts for the patrons of the numerous Irish bars in Paris. The story does not end there, however, and the same *Economist* article highlighting the Novosibirsk development reports that in Italy there has been an explosion in the numbers of pubs. Bass, based in Burton-on-Trent in England, was launching 'English' pubs and Scottish & Newcastle (based in Newcastle) 'Scottish' pubs. This trend is not confined to Europe as within a ten-block radius or walking distance of where this case is being written in Ottawa, the federal capital of Canada, one can drink in a 'British pub', one of a number of similar establishments around the city. One could also meander along to a 'Scottish pub' and then an 'Irish bar'. This trend is, however, not that new in Ottawa as quite steadily over the last ten to fifteen years or so the numbers of bars with British-style 'pub' names have been increasing and operating in addition to or as well as more Canadian sounding hostelries. Yet for all the name and super-ficial ambience of such establishments, whatever their location, there is the very real sense that one is still in Milton Keynes, Brussels, Paris, Toronto, or wherever. This is because the systems and operating modes of such establishments have a distinctive cultural overtone in the way one is served, pays for the drinks, and so on. Are the consumers thus buying the experience or just going in to drink beer? Is it beer or brands?

It is when we begin to look at the products offered by these variously named and themed bars, particularly at the beer, that we can begin to answer these questions as in such places we see another pattern or similarity, except that the symbols are more subtle. The beers that we can drink much less than the places we choose to drink them (other than at home) are seemingly becoming more similar and familiar throughout the world. As an example Heineken, a beer brewed by perhaps the world's second largest brewer, a Dutch company, is drunk in 170 countries. It is arguably (*Economist*, 2001) the most international beer, yet it has only 1.6 per cent share of the world market. Budweiser, made by the American brewer Anheuser-Busch, has the largest market share at around 3.6 per cent. Hardly dominant pos-itions for these companies and it would seem, despite the endeavours of the various participants in the industry, that beer is really one of the least global products. Ninety per cent of Budweiser is still drunk in America and around 60 per cent of Heineken and Carslberg (the Danish lager) is drunk within the EU. So while there is a strange mix of sameness and 'local' flavour in both the product, production and final delivery to the consumer, there may be something overwhelmingly 'local' about this industry. There is evidence that Anheuser-Busch's 1989 share of the US market was around 44 per cent (*Economist*, 1990); that Molson had a 45 per cent share of the Canadian market in 2000; and that Bass has 22 per cent of the UK market.

It appears that the major brewers now talk of brands and not beers, for example, in the annual report Scottish & Newcastle, one of the UK's major brewers, talks of generating 74 per cent of sales through 5 'key' brands. What are they selling us, beer or brands or both?

The economics of the industry appear straightforward enough. Beer is mainly comprised of water and is a relatively cheap product both to manufacture and purchase, but not to transport. Traditionally this meant that towns had their local brewers supplying relatively small geographic areas. Transportability was not really an issue. Transporting beer across borders was unheard of. Even today when taxation may add to the difficulties, it is only premium priced beers which make this kind of transaction economic. The German beer produced by Beck and Co., which is exported all over the world, is a notable example of this. So what are consumers buying, if not premium beers and international brands, and how can brewers get the product to consumers in economic ways?

One conclusion from the market share data presented above suggests that they are buying local or regional beers more than the international brands. Second, it appears that the brewers themselves are buying local breweries and products or producing their own brands under some sort of alliance arrangement. According to *The Economist*, most national beer markets are now dominated by at most three major brewers. This has caused some concern as in the UK the acquisition of Bass by Interbrew, the Belgian firm, was blocked by the UK government but looks to have been sanctioned by the European Union. The market in Canada is concentrated in the hands of Molson and Labbatts, the latter being another Interbrew subsidiary. In South Africa, South African Breweries (SAB) is a virtual monopoly, having successfully fought off domestic competition and forged a distribution network that any foreign predator would find difficult to duplicate. Yet SAB is forging alliances and joint ventures throughout Africa and the rest of the world.

So the world of brewing looks to be one populated by a few very large companies such as Anheuser-Busch, Interbrew, SAB, etc. on the one hand producing and distributing international and local brews, and smaller more 'domestic' breweries and very small companies, sometimes called 'craft breweries', on the other. Both exist in a network of alliances to overcome distribution and marketing problems.

A recent example occurred in Canada when one of the smaller breweries, Sleeman, announced deals with Strohs, an American brewer, to produce their beers under licence in Canada and distribution deals with Becks, the German brewer, SAB and the US Boston Beer Company. In return Sleeman will more effectively utilise its brewing capacity and its distribution network and it has found a market for its own beer in the United States via Boston's network (*Globe and Mail*, 2001).

If distribution and production are the key to the economics of this market, what is the role of marketing and brand-building capabilities? Do they add value to the companies competing in this mature, slow-growing industry?

Sources: 'Sleeman brews balance of risk and caution', *Globe and Mail*, 20 June 2001. www.globeandmail.com
'The trend trade', *The Economist*, 27 September 1997. www.economist.com

'Innocent abroad', *The Economist*, 17 March 1990: 102.
'The big pitcher', *The Economist*, 20 January 2001. www.economist.com
'Big lion, small cage', *The Economist*, 12 August 2000. www.economist.com
www.interbrew.com
www.sleeman.ca
www.carlsberg.com
www.scottish-newcastle.com

Closing case study questions

1. Assess the attractiveness of the brewing industry first from the point of view of a large international brewer and second from the point of view of a small to medium sized player.

2. What are the key capabilities needed to compete in the industry in 2001?

3. What actions could the very large global players such as Anheuser-Busch or Interbrew now take to consolidate their position?

Annotated further reading

Bartlett, C. A. and **Ghoshal**, S. (2000) *Transnational Management: Text, Cases, and Readings in Cross-Border Management.*
The latest version of one of the standard texts in this area. There is an exhaustive series of cases allied to a collection of some key articles in the field.

Cray, D. and **Mallory**, G. (1998) *Making Sense of Managing Culture.* London: International Thomson Business Press.
An academic treatment of the impact of national cultures on the management of areas such as strategy, HR, leadership and technology transfer.

Grant, R. (1998) *Contemporary Strategy Analysis.* Oxford: Blackwell.
A seeming paradox as it is both a concise and detailed exposition of the fundamentals of strategy analysis.

Segal-Horn, S. and **Faulkner**, D. (1999) *The Dynamics of International Strategy.* London: International Thomson Business Press.
A thorough and very readable account giving more depth to issues such as the growth of trade, the role of multinationals and organisation design.

References

Allison, G. T. (1971) *Essence of Decision: Explaining the Cuban Missile Crisis*. Boston: Little Brown.

Axelsson, R., Cray, D., Mallory, G. R. and Wilson, D. C. (1991) 'Decision style in British and Swedish organizations: a comparative examination of strategic decision making', *British Journal of Management* 2: 67–79.

Calori, R., Johnson, G. and Sarnin, P. (1992) 'French and British top managers' understanding of the structure and dynamics of their industries: a cognitive analysis and comparison', *British Journal of Management* 3: 61–78.

Chandler, A. D. (1962) *Strategy and Structure: Chapters in the History of American Enterprise*. Cambridge MA: MIT Press.

Cray, D. and Mallory, G. R. (1998) *Making Sense of Managing Culture*. London: International Thomson Business Press.

Cyert, R. M. and March, J. G. (1963) *A Behavioral Theory of the Firm*. New York: Prentice Hall.

Douglas, S. P. and Wind, Y. (1987) 'The myth of globalization', *Columbia Journal of World Business* 22(4): 19–29.

Eisenhardt, K. M. and Zbaraki, M. J. (1992) 'Strategic decision making', *Strategic Management Journal* 13: 17–37.

Grant, R. (1998) *Contemporary Strategy Analysis*, 3rd edn. Oxford: Blackwell.

Hofstede, G. (1980) *Culture's Consequences: International Differences in Work-related Values*. Beverly Hills: Sage.

Hofstede, G. (1991) *Culture and Organization: Software of the Mind*. Maidenhead: McGraw-Hill.

Johanson, J. and Vahlne, J.-E. (1977) 'The internationalization process of the firm – a model of knowledge development and increasing foreign market commitment', *Journal of International Business Studies* 8: 23–32.

Johnson, G. (1988) 'Rethinking incrementalism', *Strategic Management Journal* 9(1): 75–91.

Laurent, A. (1983) 'The cultural diversity of western conception of management', *International Studies of Management and Organization* 13: 75–96.

Levitt, T. (1983) 'The globalization of markets', *Harvard Business Review* 61(3) 92–102.

Pfeffer, J. and Salancick, G. R. (1974) 'Organizational decision making as a political process: the case of a university budget', *Administrative Science Quarterly* 19: 135–51.

Porter, M. E. (1985) *Competitive Advantage*. New York: Free Press.

Rumelt, R. P. (1991) 'How much does industry matter?', *Strategic Management Journal* 12: 167–85.

Schneider, S. C. (1989) 'Strategy formulation: the impact of national culture', *Organization Studies* 10: 347-74.

Schneider, S. C. and De Mayer, A. (1991) 'Interpreting and responding to strategic issues: the impact of national culture', *Strategic Management Journal* 12: 307–20.

Segal-Horn, **S.** (1998) *The Strategy Reader*. Oxford: Blackwell.

Trompenaars, F. (1993) *Riding the Waves of Culture: Understanding Cultural Diversity in Business*. London: Nicholas Brealey.

Yip, G. (1989) 'Global Strategy in a world of nations', *Sloan Management Review* 31: 29–41.

CHAPTER 7

Managing international alliance and acquisition integration

Lena Zander and Lin Lerpold

Learning objectives

When you finish reading this chapter you should:

■ be familiar with why cross-border alliances and international acquisitions exist and why they fail or succeed

■ have an understanding of the dynamics of alliance and post-acquisition integration processes

■ have an awareness of the cultural challenges of managing cross-border alliances and acquisition integration

Opening Case Study: Avoid merger most horrid

When a brash, aggressive US group bought a 180-year-old, family-owned Mittelstand company with a strong culture and well-known brand, it did not take long for the deal to turn sour. Within weeks, senior management at the German company had left and the second-line managers were dashing for the exits. The Americans used first names with everybody, spoke English and closed the canteen in the belief that staff could eat sandwiches on the run. They did not. Germans like hot lunches. The last straw was a morning 'cheerleader' session, when German staff were expected to take part in a rousing two-minute 'we are the best' call to arms.

This is just one example of a recent merger involving a Mittelstand company that failed. 'It was a cross-border catastrophe,' says Valerie Lachman of M&A International, a consultancy that specialises in advising the Mittelstand – Germany's thousands of small and medium sized companies. 'The Americans were not aware of the big cultural differences and they didn't want to spend time trying to understand the German company and integrating it into their operations,' says Ms Lachman. 'The whole deal quickly unravelled. If buyers don't do their home-work properly there will be more [failed mergers].'

The gulf in understanding between a typical Anglo-American concern used to the cut-throat instincts of a competitive capitalist marketplace and a Mittelstand company with 65 employees is problematic for potential partners. The Anglo-

American buyer is financially oriented, looking to 'get bigger' in Europe and has targeted Germany, the largest and most technically sophisticated market in Europe. It needs a high return on investment – probably close to 20 per cent – and the lowest possible purchase price. Above all, it wants figures from the target company. But Mittelstand owners find it hard to part with figures. 'They have a strong desire for financial privacy,' says Ms Lachman. 'Very often it is because the owner does not really understand financial matters.' These owner-managers, often engineers, usually have a detailed knowledge of the technical side of a business they may have built from scratch over 40 years. They are proud of their companies and probably control most aspects of the firm's running. But when it comes to the accounting, this has usually been in the hands of their tax advisers. 'People have been known to keep their mistresses and their boats on the books,' says Ms Lachman. 'You have to understand that they usually don't want to be seen to be making too much money because it gets taxed heavily,' she adds.

Problems with the figures are symptomatic of the chasm that divides the two corporate cultures. 'Imagine a proud, paternalistic Mittelstand owner in his sixties meeting a 50-year-old, Oxbridge-educated finance director of a well-established UK company,' says Ms Lachman. The meeting will be conducted in English. The British director will be informal, whereas the German owner – used to *Sie* (polite form) rather than *du* (informal) – will be the opposite until trust is established. The finance director talks discounted cash flows, Ebitda and due diligence. The Mittelstand owner is keen to talk widgets. The deal may be agreed, but then the buyer decides to shed staff in order to realise cost synergies.

The Mittelstand owner, kept on in a managerial capacity because he understands the business, is outraged. These are trusted staff who have been with him for years. Moreover, he finds himself answering to a British manager half his age, whereas he has been used to dealing with the top people. 'The German company gets swamped by new reporting procedures, morale falls, absenteeism rises, and the best people leave,' says Ms Lachman.

In the end, the acquirer decides the deal has not turned out the way it hoped and re-sells the German company. Researchers at M&A estimate the failure rate for cross-border deals in Germany in the small and medium sized company sector to be more than 50 per cent; and a 1998 PricewaterhouseCoopers study showed a worldwide failure rate of 50 to 75 per cent for mergers involving small and medium sized companies.

Can disasters be avoided? 'Acquiring companies need to plan for post-acquisition phases. They have to think about integrating the German company and value what they are buying, not throttle it with reporting procedures. Above all, they have to respect the language and culture of the company they are buying,' says Ms Lachman. Then deals can go smoothly. Avery, the UK-based labels and office products group, bought Zweckform, a German label-maker, and successfully integrated it into the group. 'They managed that because the CEO for Europe moved from the UK to Munich with his family and personally planned and supervised the integration of the German unit,' says Ms Lachman.

Source: 19 Sep. 2000, *Financial Times* CD-ROM 2000

Introduction

In the previous chapter we noted that firms with international ambitions can choose from a variety of strategies and entry modes. For a variety of reasons discussed below, entering into cross-border alliances and taking over a firm in another country are among the most popular modes of internationalisation. One of the major challenges that cross-border acquisitions and alliances face is how the partner firms manage the process of integrating their business activities and in some cases even their internal organisation. The present chapter focuses specifically on this issue since the success of cross-border partnerships depends heavily on how it is handled.

What are alliances and acquisitions?

Alliances and acquisitions are not the same organisational phenomena since alliance partners are separated by legal boundaries while acquisitions result in a single legal entity. However, the integration and cultural challenges are driven by similar logic and involve many common issues.

Strategic alliances, partnerships, coalitions, joint ventures, franchises, research consortia and network organisations are all different names for the same phenomena: namely, loose or tight cooperations between separate legal entities. The many various forms can all be grouped under a generic label of alliances (see Figure 7.1). A useful way of thinking about alliances is to consider a continuum where inter-firm cooperations perform market-like transactions at one end and transactions within the boundaries of the firm at the other end.

Mergers and acquisitions are included in the single firm end of the continuum since these two types of inter-firm cooperation are conducted within the

Figure 7.1 Alliance and acquisition sphere

Source: Developed by L. Lerpold in 2001 for teaching on the International Organisation and Management course at the Stockholm School of Economics

boundaries of a firm. The word 'merger' is most often used to describe a combination of two equally sized or equally willing companies, while 'acquisition' refers to the takeover of one firm by a larger and/or stronger firm. However, mergers are occasionally discussed as takeovers, or seen as synonymous with acquisitions. Often 'merger' is used as a label for what really is an acquisition, since the more neutral characterisation is hoped to affect the integration process positively. Sometimes it is difficult to define what is going on and people just say 'mergers and acquisitions'.

Motives and strategies for alliance cooperation or acquisition

Companies seek out firms to cooperate with or to acquire due to both external forces or internal motives. Turbulence in world markets along with greater technological and economic uncertainty, economies of scale and scope, globalisation and regionalisation of industries, fast technological change leading to ever-increasing investment requirements and shortening product life cycles are some of the many important external reasons for firms to cooperate or to acquire.

Major internal motives and strategies, which are not mutually exclusive, are: cost minimisation – it is, for instance, more cost efficient to ally with a familiar firm than to buy necessary products or services through the traditional market; profit maximisation – through, for instance, global market capabilities and covering larger geographic areas; organisational learning – through knowledge transfer between partners; cultural access – accessing valuable routines and repertoires embedded in the partner's national cultures.

Why do alliances and acquisitions succeed or fail?

Research evidence shows a high failure rate of mergers or acquisitions and unsatisfactory alliance performances. Researchers and practitioners alike have attributed the difficulties in succeeding with alliances and acquisitions to different reasons. For instance, post-acquisition and alliance integration process and organisational issues, especially the cultural aspects of organisation, management and human behaviour, are increasingly recognised as important for the success of acquisitions and alliances.

Companies venturing into alliance relationships or acquiring new firms within their own country face a series of integration challenges due to, for example, differing organisational cultures, strategies, systems and structures. However, when the alliance partner or the newly acquired firm is of another national origin there is the added complexity of different national cultures. Research findings and practitioner's experience have strongly and clearly demonstrated how national culture influences organisation, management and work values (see Chapters 3 and 4). Furthermore, interpersonal leadership (Zander, 1997), strategy and communication are also related to national culture (see Chapters 6, 9 and 10). The overriding implications of these research results are that international alliances and acquisitions are not just more complex, more problem ridden, more time consuming, but also that they require cross-cultural management skills and awareness in order to succeed.

The numerous studies which have investigated the causes of alliance and acquisition failures highlight the following:

- issues related to decisions made before alliance and acquisition integration e.g. wrong purpose, wrong partner, wrong timing and wrong price

- lack of strategic guidance, management or leadership during the integration process

- cultural differences between the two companies involved, e.g. how things are organised, how people are managed and what values guide decisions.

Factors associated with alliance success include the following:

- commitment from both partners to the alliance, also trust and quality of communication and participation

- compatibility of size and capabilities, existing alliance network, alliance track record, strategy, national and corporate culture, management practices and organisation, manufacturing, marketing, distribution and finance, safety, health and environmental policies, and the like

- capabilities, e.g. contribute complementary strengths and resources to the alliance and whether the alliance falls within a core business or product line of the partners

- management of partner diversity.

The following factors are in particular associated with acquisition success:

- *Clarity*: formulating a clear strategy for the acquisition, not based on ego-strengthening reasons (e.g. becoming the biggest in the industry), with clear criteria for the selection of relevant firms to acquire.

- *Communication*: setting clear expectations, defining the end state of the integration process, in particular the degree of expected cultural change, carrying out psychological preparation including organising courses, using simulations, forming network of experienced managers and finally forming integration teams.

- *Complementarity*: ensuring that routines and repertoires shaped by different cultural contexts are complementary and seen as assets rather than sources of problems, will enhance performance and competitiveness over time.

- *Integrating cultural and human issues* with the strategic and operational criteria in the screening process as well as identifying managerial talent in the acquired firm (both current managers and those next in line).

In summary, there is a strong belief that good management of the alliance and acquisition integration process is the key to success. Issues hampering the integration, in particular cultural differences in organisations and management or other aspects of partner diversity, not only stand out as the main reasons leading to failure but also for enabling success when managed appropriately and thoughtfully. Here we wish to emphasise that although there are cultural differences across companies within a country, the complexity of cultural differences increases dramatically in international alliances and acquisitions, which we will discuss in more detail towards the end of this chapter. There is a need to understand the dynamics of the alliance and acquisition integration process to be able to manage it successfully. In the following sections, we will first introduce the alliance development cycle and its most relevant integration issues and then the acquisition integration process from both the buying company's and the acquired firm's perspectives.

Alliance integration process

Integration developmental phases

It is generally accepted that alliances are dynamic entities with developmental or evolutionary phases. Analogies to the birth and maturation of children and to relationship building in marriages are typical. Researchers have fairly recently become very interested in explaining how alliance relationships emerge, grow and dissolve over time in what many believe are consecutive loops (Doz, 1996; Ring and Van de Ven, 1994). The most common way of describing the evolutionary pattern of alliances is through overlapping phases. As Figure 7.2 shows, four major phases with different logic and important issues are commonly identified: formation, planning, operating and assessing.

1. In the *formation phase*, alliance partners negotiate the terms of the alliance including formal and informal conditions. During this phase, major visions are aligned and equities are decided. The parties develop joint expectations about their motives, possible investments and perceived uncertainties of a business deal that they are exploring to undertake jointly.

2. In the *planning phase*, alliance operations are planned and structured. Organisation of activities and resources is undertaken. This is when the partners reach an agreement on the obligations and rules for future action in the relationship.

3. In the *operating phase*, plans are implemented and the alliance is a fact. The commitments and rules of action are carried into effect.

4. In the *assessing phase*, the workings of the alliance are checked against visions, goals, equities, etc., and either adjustment is made and the alliance continues into a new cycle or the alliance is terminated.

As the alliance progresses through different phases, misunderstandings, conflicts and changing expectations among the partners are inevitable. These issues will probably cause rethinking the terms of the relationship and the subsequent start of a new developmental phase cycle. In these 'renegotiations', new supplemental agreements are typically established to resolve only the contested issues, but all

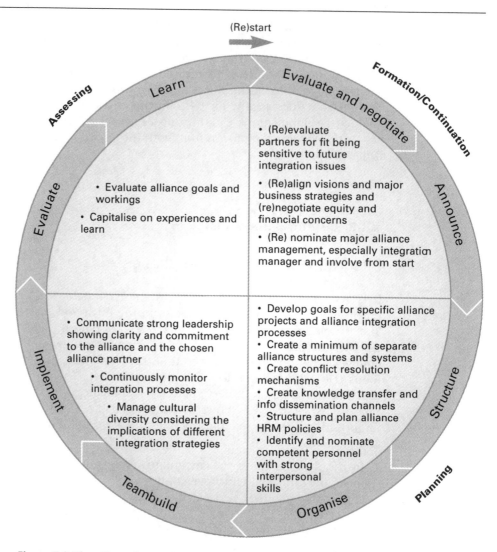

Figure 7.2 The alliance integration wheel

Source: Developed by L. Lerpold in 2001 for teaching on the International Organisation and Management course at the Stockholm School of Economics

other terms and understandings contained in the relational contract remain in effect. In this way, the ongoing relationship is preserved. Figure 7.2 shows the phases and the typical developmental issues usually associated with each phase, which we will discuss in detail below.

Leading alliance teams

As discussed earlier, research has shown that failure rates of alliances are high. Poor leadership has been named as a major factor in alliance failure (Judge and

Ryman, 2001). Strong leadership is naturally important to any organisational change, but especially important in alliance teams because of the very nature of alliances involving at least two partners with diverse strategies, structures and cultures. Partnering with joint project teams usually entails consolidating parallel partner project organisations into sole alliance project organisations. This often entails reducing project personnel numbers, restructuring project responsibilities and career expectations, and geographically relocating personnel to new locations. This initial integration period can be a painful and anxiety producing experience and provides recognition of the importance of integration processes and the need for strong leadership. Three areas are especially important when managing alliance teams: clear and committed leadership; managers with strong interpersonal skills; integration.

Clear and committed leadership

Successful integration of alliance teams requires management who clearly and keenly communicate their commitment to the alliance strategy and the chosen partner. A lack of managerial clarity and commitment to an alliance strategy may otherwise result in confused or disinterested and chaotic management which may undermine the alliance's potential success. To do this it is important that nominated alliance managers are involved at an early stage with forming, planning and implementing alliance strategies and organisation, thus gaining early insight as to the benefits of the alliance as well as understanding the partners' cultures, styles, structures and systems.

Managers with strong interpersonal skills

Dealing with the extraordinary issues associated with integrating alliance teams, such as cross-cultural diversity and the development of trust and conflict resolution, requires managers with special interpersonal skills who can effectively manage the intricacies expected when disparate partner personnel are thrown together. Managing alliance teams requires strong interpersonal skills to create trust and mechanisms for conflict resolution and otherwise solve unavoidable cultural clashes at both the organisational and national level which are inevitable in inter-firm cooperation.

Integration as an important function

Integration activities in an alliance must initially be attributed importance as a vital function on par with other important business functions. Business or operations managers may have difficulties in successfully managing both the business operations and the integration processes at the same time. A business leader will typically not focus adequately on integrating cultures, people and processes, but on the business of normal operations. The practice that alliances are often incorporated among other intra-firm projects compounds the problem. Hence, at least for a time, employing a dedicated alliance integration manager at an equal level with other functions such as control, reporting, or HRM, assisting the business manager should be a natural choice.

Managing cultural diversity

Diversity in national and corporate cultures is an important feature of alliance strategies and integrating alliance teams. A wealth of research gives reasonable conjectures about the intricacies of cross-cultural communication in multinational groups in general and cultural intricacies in alliances in particular. Some potential alliances, such as the failed alliance between the French and Swedish car manufacturers Renault and Volvo, do not even get as far as forming multicultural groups since cultural issues hamper initial negotiation and alliance plans are abandoned. Yet, alliance formation teams often ignore these softer issues when choosing an alliance partner and negotiating the deal. The sensitive areas of differences in values, style, practices, stereotypes, etc. are often difficult to address objectively but are as important as any other alliance consideration. Child and Faulkner (1998) offer a model of two fundamental policy choices at either side of a continuum: first the domination strategy which involves the domination of one partner's culture rather then striving for a balance between cultural contributions from both partners: second, the integration strategy, which attempts to integrate both partners' cultures with the aim of creating synergies from them. The purpose is to combine the best elements in the different cultures to bring about an effective management system and use of resources. The idea is that the whole is greater than the sum of its parts.

These two strategies lead to three possibilities which offer different degrees of cultural fit and a fourth of integration failure ultimately leading to alliance termination:

- The synergy possibility aims at integrating by trying to equally meld the partners' cultures.
- The domination possibility aims at cultural integration through the domination of one partner's culture.
- The segregation possibility aims at a balance between the influence in the alliance of each partner's culture but does not really strive for integrating them.
- The breakdown possibility occurs when one partner seeks cultural domination and the alliance fails securing integration.

Staffing alliances

Partners in national alliances bring different HRM practices to the cooperation. International alliances are further complicated by the presence of diverse cultures and practices conditioned by home country institutions and regulations. From studies we know that carefully considering HRM policies may facilitate integration processes and ultimately the success of the alliance. Communication blockages and conflicts of loyalty are among the most common personnel problems mentioned in international alliances. According to Lorange (1986) there are six critical human resource management issues:

1. Assignment of individuals to cooperative ventures: who should be assigned where?
2. The human resource transferability issue: who 'controls' a particular individual?

3. The trade-off in time spending between operating and strategic tasks among various individuals involved in the alliance.
4. Judgement calls regarding the performance of the human resource in the established alliance: how to avoid biases.
5. Human resource loyalty issues: the alliance versus the parent.
6. Individual career planning issues: how can they achieve career progression through alliance assignments?

Organising alliance structures

Studies have shown that clear organisational arrangements are important for managing alliances (Faulkner, 1995; Lerpold, 2000) and involve structures and systems geared to fulfilling the alliance purpose as well as effectively integrating partner personnel. Three areas are particularly important and have implications for the integration process. A major theme in the three areas is boundary spanning and should be kept in mind when planning organisational arrangements.

Separate alliance structures and systems

Trust, based on empathy and shared values, is a necessary ingredient in any integrated team, and essential for managing multicultural alliance teams (Madhok, 1995). Developing trust in alliance teams entails the creation of a new alliance identity, facilitating the management of diversity across different nationalities and corporate identities. This new supra-identity can be created through a minimum of specific alliance structures and systems giving the necessary bonding mechanisms for the creation of trust.

Conflict resolution mechanisms

The very nature of alliances involving disparate goals, styles, cultures and structures inevitably results in conflicts. Planning for dispute resolution ahead of time eases the integration process and provides quicker solutions. Conflict resolution is probably easier in joint venture-type alliances since they tend to have traditional hierarchies with a sole alliance manager at the top while more loosely coupled strategic alliances may have to solve disputes through partner negotiation.

Knowledge transfer and information dissemination

The transfer of knowledge is specifically important in alliances for organisational learning and information dissemination is also important to facilitate integration in any type of alliance. It is therefore imperative that knowledge and information flows are planned, structured and implemented. The purpose is to stimulate interest and encourage support for the alliance as well as to facilitate knowledge transfer.

Integrating timeliness

Integrating alliance teams involves intricacies beyond those normally associated with integration of intra-firm project organisations. As we have discussed earlier in this chapter, although an alliance might appear strategically and financially sound, badly managed integration may lead to difficulties, diminishing any possible alliance advantages. Alliance teams are faced with issues of cultural diversity at many levels including both differences in national and organisational cultures. They also face the challenge of integrating separate partner structures and systems as well as dealing with new personnel continuously being moved into and out of alliance teams. Timeliness of planning and monitoring alliance integration thus becomes increasingly important for alliance success. Two areas are worth mentioning when dealing with integration processes: planning and monitoring.

Early integration planning

Planning for integration or even the creation of integration strategies already at the alliance formation stage may speed the route to effective and productive alliance teams. It is natural that the strategic and financial aspects initially seem most important when forming alliances, but growing research on alliance performance points to the importance of early inclusion of integration strategies. Creating an integration strategy, connecting major functions involved in alliance operations along with the development of alliance organisations, structures, systems, external and internal communications strategies at an early stage, results in a more cohesive process.

Continuous monitoring

Integration processes require continuous monitoring rather than unique integration activities only at the start. Unlike in mergers and acquisitions where integration has a start with the announcement and an end after a successful merger, integration processes in alliances continues throughout the ad hoc life. When projects last for considerable lengths of time, personnel are exchanged and initial integration processes are either forgotten or have never been experienced. Understanding the need for a continuous monitoring and management of integration processes becomes extremely important.

Let us now turn to the acquisition integration process. We will first present the developmental phases of the acquisition integration process and then highlight a number of important integration issues for management to take into account in order to succeed with their acquisition.

Acquisition integration process

Integration developmental phases

Integrating two companies after an acquisition is a dynamic and emotional process. The acquisition integration process is often seen as consisting of three distinct, but occasionally overlapping phases, which are derived from models of acculturation. These models are originally based on development of cultures and what happens when cultures are challenged, e.g. by invasion, migration of people, or when an area becomes an annexed territory (Berry, 1980a). Applying such a process view of cultural change on acquisitions leads to the inclusion of the following three phases: contact, conflict and adaptation. To this, we add a fourth phase, the pre-acquisition phase, where some of the perceptions and undertakings before the acquisition is carried out play an important part in the integration process following the acquisition.

1. In the *pre-acquisition phase* the knowledge (and rumours) about each other, i.e. 'the historic influence', has an impact both on how buyers formulate the integration approach and on how the acquired firm will view the buyers. The psychological preparation while waiting for the finalisation of the deal is important for future success.

2. In the *contact phase*, the initial reaction from the acquired firm is one of shock and dismay, often followed by feelings of injustice, anger and anxiety. This can be described as the 'acquisition effect', which will influence the integration process and perhaps also spark unexpected problems.

3. In the *conflict phase*, the buying firm has started to implement changes related to the chosen 'integration approach' and the acquired firm feels threatened by the buying firm. The acquired firm's main concern is to survive, and often a we–they attitude is adopted increasing the conflict. Different temporary 'acculturation modes' can describe their reactions during the conflict phase.

4. In the *adaptation phase*, conflict is reduced and the amount of cultural changes decreases. The integration process is moving towards a stabilisation point. One or several 'integration end states' emerge.

Acculturation is often seen as one cultural system dominating another since the cultural flows are usually stronger from one direction, e.g. from the buying company to the acquired firm. This does not mean that the buying company is not influenced by the acquired firm's actions and reactions. Acculturation is 'a culture-producing as well as a culture-receiving process' (Berry, 1980b, p. 217). During the integration process, the two companies will influence each other more or less in a continuous chain of actions and reactions throughout the four phases.

We will introduce a dynamic model of the acquisition integration process (adapted from Janson, 1994), that is depicted along a time line divided into the four phases described above: pre-acquisition, contact, conflict and adaptation. Five integration issues stand out as the most important to take into account when managing the integration process. As shown in Figure 7.3, these five issues are:

1. The *historic influence* in the pre-acquisition phase.
2. The *acquisition effect* in the contact phase.
3. The buying company's *integration approach*.
4. The acquired firm's reaction in the form of *acculturation modes*, which will start in the contact phase and pass through a phase of conflict before reaching the adaptation phase.
5. When there is a reduction of conflict and some type of stabilisation is reached,

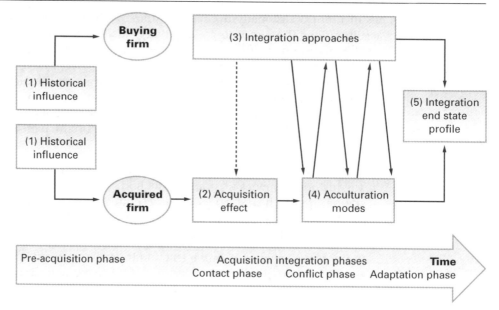

Figure 7.3 The dynamic acquisition integration model

Source: Adapted from Janson (1994)

an *integration end state profile* can be used to describe what cultural changes, if any, have taken place.

Each of these five integration issues is described below in detail.

The historic influence

The past together with the present have an important part in shaping people's perceptions. Obviously, the buyer's knowledge or perceptions about a firm is one of the reasons for making the acquisition. However, both the buying and the acquired firms' histories and perceptions of each other will influence the integration process. The buyer's choice of integration approach is based on the knowledge about the acquired firm at the time of the acquisition. For example, if the buyer 'knows' that the acquired company has a culture which is characterised by informality, it feel that it needs to reorganise the acquired firm to become more formal, in line with their own approach.

The acquired company's reactions to the buyer's ideas and suggestions will in turn depend on how they view the buying company (Veiga *et al.*, 2000). For example, if the buying company is highly admired and respected, the acquired firm could have a positive view on their buyer, in particular if they are dissatisfied with their current owner, the so-called 'white knight' effect. However, if the buying company has a reputation of making acquisitions that involve numerous layoffs and trimming the organisations to become similar to themselves, this will have a negative influence on the acquired company. Attitudes like 'we are going to fight for our way of doing things, we are not going to let them come here and destroy us' will flourish.

The acquired company's own history could also influence its employees' expectations from the buying firm. There could be groups or individuals that for different reasons do not agree with their own management, and they may anticipate new career opportunities and welcome a buying company with promises of change (Veiga *et al.*, 2000). Perhaps these groups see their own culture as dysfunctional and acting as an obstacle rather than a vehicle to success. Consequently, both the buying and the acquired firms' perception of each other's and their own cultures derived from the past and the present will have an impact on the integration process. Consequently, the historic influence is included in the acquisition integration process model (see Figure 7.3).

The acquisition effect

Conflict during the post-acquisition integration process often arises simply because one company has been acquired by another. This is commonly referred to as the 'acquisition effect'. The following reasons for an acquisition effect are often given:

- Acquisitions involve a large power differential between firms. Managers in the acquired firm who once were 'big fish in a small pond' feel powerless, alienated, unappreciated and inferior to the managers in the buying company.

- Acquisitions often involve a unidirectional flow of cultural elements from the dominant firm and are surrounded by 'an aura of conquest' and pressure is placed on managers of the acquired firm to conform to the culture of the buying company.

- Acquisitions often involve anxiety about the future, uncertainty and the feeling of existing in an information vacuum; people are unaware and unprepared for changes in status and organisation structure.

Conflict will arise even if the companies involved are not culturally very different. According to Håkanson (1995), a powerful sense of loss is experienced by employees in the acquired firm after having bought and witnessed how familiar work routines are changed, cherished co-workers leave and teams' spirits disintegrate. Employee resistance due to career concerns as well as cultural differences also influence the acquisition effect and need to be taken into account (Larsson, 1990). The acquisition effect can be expected to place heavy demands on the handling of the integration process and the buyers are often frustrated by strong negative reactions or often outright hostility from the personnel at the acquired firm. Consequently, the acquisition effect has an influence on the integration process and is included in the acquisition integration process model (see Figure 7.3).

The integration approach

How a company chooses to integrate a newly acquired firm, according to Haspeslagh and Jemison (1991), is primarily related to two issues. First is the need for interdependence, which depends on how value is to be created from the acquisition. Financial transfers and knowledge transfers are examples of different types of transfers between the acquired and the buying firm, where the first mentioned type of transfer represents a low need of interdependence between the two firms. Knowledge transfers, by way of contrast, vary in the need for interdependence between the buying company and the acquired company depending on the type of knowledge and vehicles for organisational learning.

Second is the need for organisational autonomy, which could also be expressed as preserving the acquired company's organisational culture, so that the potential for value creation is not destroyed. An example of this is if key capabilities reside in the people who decide to leave because the acquired firm is expected or required to change too much, too fast or in any other way that is perceived as detrimental to the organisational culture by the people working there. This is a particularly difficult issue to handle since there is most often a demand from the acquired firm to remain the same, reinforced by people's general reluctance to change. Consequently, it is important that organisational autonomy should be provided if the survival of the strategic capabilities is dependent upon the organisational culture that they came from (Haspeslagh and Jemison, 1991). This is not a question of how different the cultures of the buying and acquired firms are, but if maintaining the difference is crucial or not. Three integration approaches are briefly described below:

1. The *symbiosis approach* is the most ambitious and perhaps the most difficult in that it requires adaptations from both the buying and the acquired company as well as a will to create something together in order to achieve a successful integration. This strategy will be difficult to implement if the acquired firm is not interested in interacting or in changing their culture together with the buying company.

2. The *absorption approach* involves the more or less total assimilation of the acquired firm and can be exceedingly difficult if the acquired company wishes to retain its cultural autonomy and does not see the value in interacting with the buying company.

3. The *preservation approach* is appropriate when value is generated through nurturing of the acquired firm for which a high autonomy is deemed as necessary while there is a low need for interdependence between the two firms. This strategy could lead to disappointments and difficulties if the acquired firm is expecting to interact with an involved buyer.

Acculturation modes

The acquired firm will react on whatever type of integration approach they are subjected to by the buying firm. Their reactions and actions can be seen as part of the acculturation process, as mentioned earlier. This occurs when two different groups of people (or companies) culturally influence each other, and most often one group is expected to adapt to the other more dominant group of people (or company). Three acculturation modes can be used to describe the reactions that occur in the acquired firm during the integration process: transformation, assimilation and separation.

1. The *transformation mode* characterises the reaction from the acquired firm when they are interested in interacting with the buying company without losing their own culture, on which they place a high value. This mode is often a result of positive historic influence, successful psychological preparation and a carefully and well-managed introduction of the integration approach.

2. The *assimilation mode* is a reaction when the acquired firm is willing to adapt to the buying company's culture and ceases to exist as a distinct cultural entity. This is often the case when the acquired firm perceives its culture as an obstacle and a cause for poor performance and/or when it admires the successful culture of the buying company.

3. The *separation mode* is the acculturation mode that occurs when the acquired firm insists on maintaining its culture and refuses to be assimilated or in any other way integrated. If the buying company intends to integrate the acquired firm, then reasons for this reaction includes negative historic influence, lack of psychological preparation and/or too aggressive and stressful attempts at integration.

Two observations need to be made. First, these three acculturation modes are often temporary and partial during the integration process. In other words, the reaction can vary across different divisions or departments in the acquired firm and the reactions can vary across time during the integration process. Second, the two dimensions used to identify acculturation modes mirror the two dimensions used to identify the integration approaches described earlier in this chapter. In other words, the buying company may identify a high need for interaction and a low need for organisational autonomy for the acquired firm, i.e. an 'absorption' integration approach. The acquired firm, on the other hand, may value its culture highly and have a limited interest in interacting with the buying company, i.e. a 'separation' acculturation mode. 'Absorption' and 'separation' are each other's opposites and when confronted with each other will aggravate the conflict, bringing the integration process to a near halt and placing excessive demands on management. Hence, the acculturation modes will influence the integration process and are included in the model (see Figure 7.3).

The integration end state profile

At some point, the integration process will move into an integration end state. However, this is not an 'end point'. The process of cultural change tends to continue, but when a stabilisation point has been reached, this is often seen as the end state of the intended integration process. According to Marks and Mirvis (2001), it is important to formulate and communicate an intended 'end state' as soon as possible to ensure mutual expectations. They suggest five end states based on the degree of cultural change in the buying company as well as the acquired firm (see Figure 7.4). We have already discussed three of these from both the buying company and the acquired firm's perspective: symbiosis/transformation, absorption/assimilation and preservation/separation. Two new end states are added: 'reverse takeover' and 'best of both'.

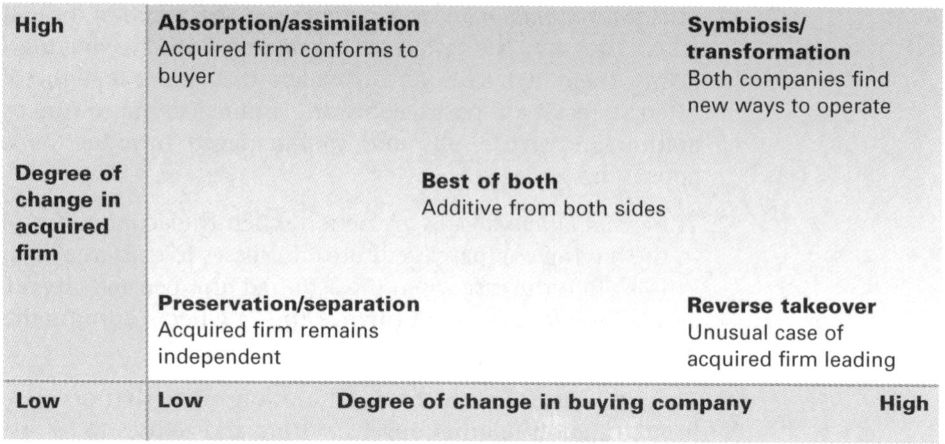

High	**Absorption/assimilation** Acquired firm conforms to buyer		**Symbiosis/ transformation** Both companies find new ways to operate
Degree of change in acquired firm		**Best of both** Additive from both sides	
	Preservation/separation Acquired firm remains independent		**Reverse takeover** Unusual case of acquired firm leading
Low	Low	Degree of change in buying company	High

Figure 7.4 The integration end states

Source: Adapted from Marks and Mirvis (2001)

- *Symbiosis/transformation* has occurred when both companies have fundamentally changed. To reach this stage requires investments in intensive and inventive management. Pfizer Animal Health and SmithKline Beecham's animal pharmaceutical business in Europe underwent serious transformation that managed to change country and culture specific organisations to meet the challenges posed by the European Community (Marks and Mirvis, 2001).

- *Absorption/assimilation* has been carried out when the acquired firm has been assimilated into the buying firm's culture. Brand names disappear and the absorbed company eventually ceases to exist. Usually this has been carried out by changing the acquired firm's management.

- *Preservation/separation* is the end state when the acquired firm has retained its autonomy and culture. This is most common in organisations that are diversified and/or emphasise cultural pluralism.

- *Reverse takeover* is when the acquired firm instead of the buying company has taken the lead and decided the cultural changes that the buying company has carried out. According to Marks and Mirvis (2001), this does not happen often and when it does it is usually isolated to a certain business unit or division.

- *Best of both* is the result of partial to full integration where cultural changes have been made in both organisations. Both firms have experienced difficult times in terms of merging functions, eliminating overlap, reducing forces, etc. Integrations that reach this end state have been the most risky but are often the most successful (Marks and Mirvis, 2001).

Research has shown that to characterise the cultural adaptations which have occurred during the integration process, several integration end states are necessary. For example, an acquired company's management style was retained (preservation), whilst the accounting systems were completely changed (absorption). Consequently, several end states can be used to identify what has happened during the process of cultural change. In other words, what has been absorbed, transformed, preserved, reversed takeover or best of both during the post-acquisition integration. In this way, an integration end state profile consisting of several integration end states can portray the outcome of the integration process.

Cultural fit analysis

The increasing number of cross-border alliances and acquisitions claimed to have failed due to cultural differences has resulted in the recommendation to conduct not only financial and legal due diligence but also a cultural due diligence. A cultural due diligence developed by Garrison and described by Rosenbaum (1999) explores differences in national culture as well as organisational culture, values as well as practices, communication as well as action. Managers and other key employees in the involved companies fill out questionnaires and the scores are used to identify areas of agreement and areas of potential conflict. For example, when Canon was going to establish a subsidiary in Dubai through its Dutch division a cultural due diligence was conducted. The results were surprising in that they identified very similar basic business values but large differences at the communication and behaviour level. It was decided to go ahead with the venture, but to conduct cross-cultural training with both the Dutch and the Arab managers. In another case, the results from the cultural due diligence of an intended British, Italian and German alliance revealed fundamental differences so critical that the venture plans were abandoned. The identified cultural differences in basic business values influenced the partners' expectations from the future alliance. The British were commercially oriented and viewed the alliance as a vehicle for profit generation; the Germans wanted to establish a strong alliance that would operate for a long time; the Italians' concern was that the alliance would have prestige and power (Rosenbaum, 1999). As these two examples show, cultural fit analysis can be helpful in gauging potential areas of cultural problems.

Summary

This chapter has focused on understanding the integration and cultural challenges of international alliances and acquisitions against a backdrop of the motives and strategic intents, as well as reasons for failure and success inherent in these organisational forms. The concept of alliances as evolutionary organisational forms with developmental phases is introduced and integration issues such as leading alliance teams, managing cultural diversity, staffing alliances, organising alliance structures and integrating timeliness are outlined. A model of dynamic acquisition integration processes depicted along a time line with four integration phases is presented. The model includes elements of the historic influence, the acquisition effect, the integration approach, the acculturation modes and an integration end state profile that are discussed in-depth. Finally, an understanding of the importance of performing cultural fit and change analysis is argued along with a discussion of cultural challenges involved in managing international alliance and acquisition integration processes.

Discussion questions

1. What are the similarities and differences between international alliances and acquisitions?

2. What are the critical issues in alliance integration processes?

3. What could be potential areas of conflict, and why, between the buying company and the acquired firm during the integration process?

4. How can a cultural change analysis complement a cultural fit analysis?

Closing Case Study: The BP and Statoil alliance

On the afternoon of 10 March 1997, Ole Eriksen, Vice President of Statoil's International Exploration and Production department, sat in his Stavanger office looking out across the Norwegian fog. He had briefed senior officers in his department about the responsibilities handed down from corporate headquarters six years earlier about making an alliance between Statoil and BP work. Rumours were coming in from alliance management and team members. Everyone seemed to have a different understanding of the Statoil and BP relationship, attitudes towards BP employees were negative, costs were over budget and projects were behind schedule. Ole was to report to Statoil's board on the BP and Statoil alliance and give his recommendations for the future of the alliance. To jog his memory of the alliance development Ole starts browsing through the documents in front of him.

The alliance: aims and expectations

The alliance between BP and Statoil officially started on 28 August 1990 when the two companies' CEOs signed a joint protocol describing the three areas of intended future joint activity between BP Exploration and Statoil. The areas included research and development (R&D), gas transportation and marketing, and international exploration and production (E&P). The intent was to run all activities jointly with personnel seconded from both BP Exploration and Statoil. Oversight of joint activities was to be the responsibility of a joint management committee with equal BP and Statoil representation. The joint activity was intended to be long term. However, each of the individual agreements could be terminated by either part with specified due notice. It was also recognised that there had been, and would continue to be, substantial other joint BP Exploration/Statoil activities outside the three specified areas.

In the international exploration and production leg of the alliance, the parties intended to conduct joint exploration and development in a number of specified areas of mutual interest. Three areas had been targeted: West Africa (Nigeria to

Angola), China Margin (Northern China to Southern Vietnam) and emerging nations in the former Soviet Union (FSU). Initial participation in the joint exploration and production areas would be one-third Statoil and two-thirds BP Exploration. Over time, it was contemplated that Statoil's participation in new licences would increase towards a 50–50 basis. It was also intended that one of the three targeted area programmes (West Africa) would be run out of Norway following an orderly transition period. The other two (China Margin and the former Soviet Union areas) would be UK based. All activities would be jointly staffed. Operatorship decisions in new licences acquired through the joint programme would be made on a case-by-case basis. It was intended that Statoil would participate as an operator and gradually take on a larger operatorship role over time. Table 7.1 shows the estimated expected investments and joint team manning in 1995.

Management and organisation

Joint asset management teams were charged with the task of generating value by drawing on the resources of both companies. They were to be responsible for their respective assets on behalf of the alliance and were to operate within a common framework set by the (executive) alliance management team. Their performance was to be measured against agreed goals and objectives.

Joint asset management teams were to be composed of a manager from the operating company, a deputy from the other non-operating company and other managers drawn, as appropriate, from both companies with the aim of achieving a balanced representation. To facilitate the information flow and provide support to the management of the non-operating company, the function of the focal point was designated as an essential part of the management team. The purpose of these management teams was to provide a 'window' on the skills, experience and technology of their own company, to ensure that the best resources were used from both organisations. Learning was supposed to be encouraged and achievement was to be measured against identified goals in asset performance contracts. The integrated teams were to be staffed, at the discretion of the joint asset management team, with a balance of BP and Statoil personnel in line with the particular skills and experience needed and the availability of expertise. This approach to staffing was supposed to maximise the ability to secure the best people at any time.

In each asset, one of the companies was to be assigned the role of 'lead company'. This company was responsible for leading the activities on behalf of the

Table 7.1 Expected investment expenditures and joint team manning

Project	Expected investments mill. US$ 1995	Joint team at leader headquarters	Joint team at site
Vietnam	145	29	140
Nigeria	815	28	47
AzKaz	778	20	18
Total	1.738	77	205

Source: The BP and Statoil Alliance portfolio analysis and organisational charts from summer 1995. Joint team manning includes only full-time positions

alliance and was to be accountable to the alliance management team. The lead company applied its own systems and procedures, which should also cater for the requirements of the other company to avoid duplication. These systems and procedures were to include business planning and operational management. The two companies were to entrust asset management to each other. It was, however, recognised that each company would retain its own decision-making processes for investment and other major decisions. The lead company's management practices and related procedures were to apply to all members of jointly staffed teams. However, personnel seconded to the lead company would remain employees of their own company and would be administered in accordance with that company's terms and conditions. Figure 7.5 shows the initial alliance organisation. Reporting lines were directly hierarchical.

Technology and corporate culture

The technology of BP and Statoil was to be guided by the alliance technology board which was chaired by the management of both companies. The key purpose of the board was 'to provide the right technology for use in the right place and at the right time'. That technology was to be drawn from the best source within BP or Statoil or acquired externally. Each asset was to have a technology plan that was to be aligned to its business objectives. The technology provision and support were supposed to be directly driven by the commercial challenges faced by the alliance in each area and were to include services, technology transfer and research and development.

In line with this spirit and to gain access to each area and realise value from it,

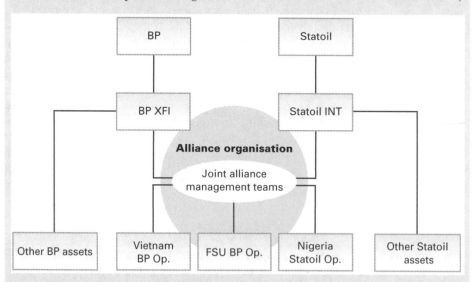

Figure 7.5 Initial alliance organisation

Note: BP XFI stands for the historical strategic business unit in BP called Exploration Frontiers International. The business unit name and organisation has since changed. Statoil INT stands for the strategic business unit responsible for Statoil's international exploration and production operations.

Source: Developed by L. Lerpold in 2001 for teaching on the International Organisation and Management course at the Stockholm School of Economics

the alliance was to exploit the competitive advantages that the synergy of its joint operations provided. At the same time it was to recognise and maintain the strengths of the two major parent companies. These strengths were to arise from the different history, culture and corporate styles of the two companies. The belief was that achieving success over and above the sum of the parts depended on using synergies and individual strengths.

As Ole Eriksen contemplated what to report to Statoil's board, he was also concerned about the fact that BP's business unit manager, responsible for the alliance on BP's side, had recently left the company and was not to be replaced. This seemed to be a great concern among employees in both companies and also left Ole Eriksen without a counterpart and fellow alliance champion. He felt unsure as to how to read the signals about the future and importance of the alliance. Ole decided to sort out his thoughts, and ended up realising that he had to have good answers to the following three questions in order to make the appropriate decision.

Closing case study questions

1. Identify and discuss the integration issues that can be expected in the BP and Statoil alliance.

2. Which integration activities should be proposed to ease the integration processes?

3. How would you recommend that cultural issues in the alliance be managed?

Annotated further reading

Child, J. and **Faulkner, D.** (1998) *Strategies of Co-operation: Managing Alliances, Networks and Joint Ventures.* Oxford: Oxford University Press.
This book gives a good summary of the academic studies on cooperative ventures.

Doz, Y. L. and **Hamel, G.** (1998) *Alliance Advantage: The Art of Creating Value Through Partnering.* Boston: Harvard Business School Press.
This book is a good source for managerial insights to strategic alliance strategies.

Marks, M. L. and **Mirvis, P. H.** (1998) *Joining Forces: Making One Plus One Equal Three in Mergers, Acquisitions, and Alliances.* San Francisco: Jossey-Bass.
In this book the authors present their experience of more than twenty years of studying human, cultural and organisational aspects of over seventy mergers and acquisitions.

Morosini, P. (1998) *Managing Cultural Differences – Effective Strategies and Execution Across Cultures in Global Corporate Alliances.* London: Pergamon.

Regardless of the title the focus of this book is on mergers and acquisitions, and the author presents results from his studies with illustrative business examples against a backdrop of earlier research in the field.

References

Berry, J. W. (1980a) 'Social and cultural change', in H. C. Triandis and R. W. Brislin (eds) *Handbook of Cross-Cultural Psychology*, vol. 5. Boston: Allyn & Bacon. pp. 211–79.

Berry, J. W. (1980b) 'Acculturation as varieties of adaptation', in A. M. Padilla (ed.) *Acculturation.* Boulder CO: Westview Press.

Child, J. and Faulkner, D. (1998) *Strategies of Co-operation: Managing Alliances, Networks and Joint Ventures.* Oxford: Oxford University Press.

Doz, Y. L. (1996) 'The evolution of cooperation in strategic alliances: initial conditions or learning processes?', *Strategic Management Journal* 17: 55-83.

Faulkner, D. (1995) *International Strategic Alliances: Co-operating to Compete.* Maidenhead: McGraw-Hill.

Håkanson, L. (1995) 'Learning through acquisition: management and integration of foreign R&D laboratories', *International Studies of Management and Organization* 25(1–2): 121–57.

Haspeslagh, P. C. and Jemison, D. B. (1991) *Managing Acquisitions.* New York: Free Press.

Janson, L. (1994) 'Towards a dynamic model of post-acquisition cultural integration', in A. Sjögren and L. Janson *Culture and Management in a Changing Europe.* Stockholm: Multicultural Centre and Institute of International Business. pp. 127–52.

Judge, W. Q. and Ryman, J. A. (2001) 'The shared leadership challenge in strategic alliances: lessons from the US healthcare industry', *Academy of Management Executive* 15(2): 71–9.

Larsson, R. (1990) *Coordination of Action in Mergers and Acquisitions: Interpretative and Systems Approaches towards Synergy.* Lund: Lund University Press.

Lerpold, L. (2000) 'Lessons in alliance integration', *European Business Forum* 4: 42–8.

Lorange, P. (1986) 'Human resource management in multinational co-operative ventures', *Human Resource Management* 25(1): 133–48.

Madhok, A. (1995) 'Revisiting multinational firms' intolerance for joint ventures', *Journal of International Business* 26(1): 117–37.

Marks, M. L. and Mirvis, P. H. (2001) 'Making mergers and acquisitions work: strategic and psychological preparation', *Academy of Management Executive* 15(2): 80–92.

Ring, P. S. and Van de Ven, A. H. (1994) 'Developmental processes of cooperative interorganisational relationships', *Academy of Management Review* 19: 90–118.

Rosenbaum, A. (1999) 'Testing cultural waters', *Management Review* July–August: 41–3.

Veiga, J., Lubatkin, M., Calori, R. and Very, P. (2000) 'Measuring organizational culture clashes: a two-nation post-hoc analysis of a cultural compatibility index', *Human Relations* 53(4): 539–57.

Zander, L. (1997) *The Licence to Lead: An 18-country Study of the Relationship between Employees' Preferences Regarding Interpersonal Leadership and National Culture*. Stockholm: Institute of International Business, Stockholm School of Economics.

CHAPTER 8

E-commerce worldwide

Brian M.W. Clements and Monir Tayeb

Learning objectives

When you finish reading this chapter you should:

- know the history, origins and the structure of the internet and world wide web

- understand the way the internet has created channels for commercial transactions

- define and understand the various categories of e-commerce and e-business

- understand the barriers to global e-commerce transactions

- have some knowledge of the problems the industry experienced in 2000 and 2001

Opening Case Study: Father Christmas is just a click away

If ever a business was suited to e-commerce, it must be the one run by Santa Claus. It is hampered by a remote location (Lapland or the North Pole) and logistical problems. It also receives mail from every child in the Christian world and then, within a 24-hour period, delivers gifts to those within that number who have behaved themselves in the last 12 months.

All this, with only a few elves and a reindeer with a bad head cold to help. And so, to streamline the communications side of the business, to create greater efficiencies in logistics and fulfilment, Santa has harnessed the power of the internet to help ease his fourth-quarter bottleneck.

A number of sites have arrived over the past couple of years, with most combinations of Santa and Claus, Father and Christmas, converted into domain names. One such site is Santa-Claus.com. Stephen Bottomley, its managing director, has played a slow, patient game with the site, the only business of the Father Christmas company he runs and part owns. Mr Bottomley has used the last two years attracting customers to the site with the entertainment services on it, which offers 300 products, including toys, decorations and confectionery, that will be available in the United Kingdom this year. But that is only the beginning. 'We have a lot of traffic in the United States and our plan is to go through a learning process this year and then roll it out next year, when we are going to open offices in California,' says Mr Bottomley.

To that end the company has recently secured e-commerce trademark rights to 'Santa Claus' and 'Father Christmas' for e-commerce purposes in the United States, adding to a growing stable of Santa domain names. At the heart of Mr Bottomley's strategy is the good name of Santa himself. 'The difference between us and most dotcom start-ups is they have to build a brand online, which is difficult, whereas we are piggybacking on one of the best known brands in the world: Santa Claus. Unlike dotcoms whose site names may be hard to remember, Santa-Claus.com only has to be heard once.'

Another site trading on the strength of the Santa brand is Santas.net, which is owned by Australian Media, a Sydney-based internet media company. Santas.net contains many of the same entertainment features, including songs, recipes and games. 'It is written from the persona of Santa Claus,' says Andrew Molloy, managing director of Australian Media. 'And judging by e-mails which are sent to Santa, it enjoys enormous credibility with readers, that this in fact could well be the Santa Claus. The domain name helps and sounds authentic.' Unlike Santa-Claus.com, which holds all its own stock, Santas.net sells through affiliates such as Amazon, Disney and Warner Brothers. Santas.net also derives revenue through advertising. Santas.net attracted 3.5 million visitors during November and December last year, its fourth year of trade, and even had around 450,000 in May and June, the year's Christmas low point. Mr Molloy attributes this to the content, which retains interest in the site while Santa spends the Aussie winter in Barbados.

So for Christmas this year, it's Santa down the phone and internet line, rather than the chimney.

Source: 6 Dec. 2000, *Financial Times* CD-ROM 2000

Introduction

E-commerce is globally available, with only language and character sets as barriers to communication. The world wide web is truly global and, provided that physical telecommunication links exist, the same content should be accessible from Manchester or Manchuria.

The major constraint to e-commerce is the physical delivery of products. This is the area that most differentiates national and global e-commerce. The secondary constraints are those created by individual states, which will be examined in detail.

The origins of the internet

During the 1960s, in the search for additional security driven by the Cold War, the US Defense Department decided to devise a method of protecting their communications network in the case of nuclear attack. They considered that the military communications network was vulnerable, so their Advanced Research Projects

Agency (ARPA) funded a project to connect university computer scientists and engineers via their computers and telephone lines across the United States.

The resulting network was named the ARPANET, which allowed sharing of computer power among the participants. A secondary use was soon found, which was the ability to send electronic mail between facilities. This developed into a broadcast communication medium on the same lines as a web board, allowing all parties to read all messages simultaneously. These were created to handle different subject matters for interested groups.

In 1975 Vincent Cerf of Stanford University developed the transmission control protocol (TCP) and an addressing protocol called the internet protocol (IP). TCP breaks down messages into streams of packages that travel via differing routes and are eventually reassembled at their destination. IP controls the direction of travel of these packages through various networks so they reach the destination to which they were addressed.

In 1969 there were just four host computers running the internet. The introduction of the TCP/IP standard caused these to grow to almost 600 by 1983. By this time, TCP/IP had become the industry standard protocol for communications. The US Defense Department then decided to separate out their network and thus ARPANET became MILNET. The internet thus became independent from military influence.

The internet was developed for UNIX computers, which were then the standard in universities and research centres. By the early 1980s, private users had started the development of a communications net that could run on DOS or Apple microcomputers. From this developed a new set of bulletin boards that were available to anyone with a personal computer and a modem. Games and messages could be posted to these boards. By the late 1980s the boards were used for conversations, sharing software and mutual technical assistance. There are still over 30,000 of these bulletin boards in existence in the United States (Courter and Marquis, cited in Frink, 1998).

Also in the late 1970s the first commercial online services were started. These were the Source and CompuServe, both of which provided services charged by the length of time the user was connected to them. These services, the prototype internet service providers (ISPs) permitted communication from large numbers of users simultaneously, by having large numbers of incoming telephone connections. Commercial organisations then began to involve themselves, envisaging the potential of these media for promoting their businesses.

CompuServe was originally an IT data storage enterprise, founded in 1969. It began its online services in 1979, primarily providing business and reference information. It provided local telephone access in 185 countries, giving business travellers a cheap and ready means of contact. During the 1980s CompuServe bought out the Source and were joined by AOL (AmericaOnline) and Prodigy as the major online service providers. The basic services provided by each are:

- electronic mail (e-mail)
- access to the internet
- current news and sports information
- weather reports
- financial and commercial information
- travel and reservations

- reference services
- educational information
- games and entertainment.

Commercially, Prodigy provided what was probably a more important component of the modern ISP. It lowered its charges for connection and supplemented its income by displaying advertising on its pages. If the users were interested in the message flashed up, they could click on it to be connected to the advertiser. Commercial advertising had arrived.

Conversely, AOL originally advertised itself as a service for social users. It provided virtual meeting sites for users and promoted its life, styles and interests pages. However, by the 1990s it had successfully moved into the commercial marketplace as well: 'By the end of 1990 there were over 300,000 hosts connected to the internet, a growth rate of 2000 percent in ten years,' (Courter *et al.*, cited in Frink, 1998, p. 8). Most connections were via universities and businesses and were used mainly for information.

The great advance of the 1990s was made in Switzerland, using the computer services of CERN (Conseil Européen pour la Recherche Nucléaire [The European Organisation for Nuclear Research]) by one of their software engineers, Tim Berners-Lee. He developed a graphical hypertext navigation tool for use on the internet, which he named the world wide web (WWW). This was solely to enable him to access different computer systems at CERN and he was unaware of the impact that this development would cause:

> 'He's someone who thinks very clearly about fundamentals, but besides this, he happened to come upon his idea at the right time,' said Ruth Pordes, Computing Services Division Online Systems Department head. 'His idea was to make distributed information over a network easily accessible to the whole world, and to work out the protocol of how to do that.' (Berger, 1996, p. 1)

Fermilab was one of the first members of the web, which it used for a sky-mapping project. This project needed widespread collaboration, for which the web was particularly beneficial. Pordes attributed the success of the web to its simultaneous development in both Europe and the United States. She said, 'I think it's actually a big success partly because the Europeans felt this was their idea and they could adopt it and support it without thinking this was just something from America coming in and taking over' (Berger, 1996, p. 2).

There seems little doubt that the development of the web will bring great changes to the lifestyles of its ever-increasing circle of users: 'The web lifestyle, like the electricity lifestyle, will be characterised by rapid innovations in applications. Within a decade most Americans and many other people around the world will be living the web lifestyle' (Gates, 1999).

Above all, the internet is about inexpensive, instant communication and it opens up completely new types of interaction within companies and their suppliers, potential employers and their marketplace (Hammond, 1996). It is rapidly becoming an everyday substitute for the telephone and in addition offers many publishing, distribution, transaction and marketing services. It promises to replace static marketing with more interactive relationships between producers and customers. However, the internet has problems: it is at present chaotic and poorly maintained and no match for proprietary networks such as Reuters (Clarke and Clegg, 1998).

What is e-commerce?

E-commerce does not describe one specific activity. It is an abbreviation of electronic commerce and includes a wide variety of applications, including the transmission of data between computer terminals by closed and private methods as well as via the internet. The present authors' definition is that: E-commerce is the transaction of any business with a quantifiable value by the transmission of electronic data between the remote terminals of a communications network.

It should be noted that there does not appear to be any clearly accepted differentiation between e-commerce and e-business. Some practitioners have suggested that e-commerce refers exclusively to business-to-business (B2B) transactions and that e-business covers all categories of transactions. However, in this chapter, e-commerce will be used in its widest possible sense and will include e-business and transactions at any level that fall within the terms of the above definition.

There are several ways of classifying e-commerce and, even though it is likely that these will evolve in the near future, two useful classifications are made on the basis of commercial function or by the type of participants conducting the transaction. In the first of these two classifications, Kalakota and Whinston (1997) suggest that there are four commercial functions or perspectives:

- *Communications*: delivering information, products or services by telecommunication systems or networks.
- *Business processes*: applying technology to automate business processes.
- *Services*: to reduce the cost of services, whilst increasing the quality and speed of service delivery.
- *Online*: enables the purchase and sale of goods via the internet or other online services.

The second classification is that most commonly adopted by the commercial world. A version given in Chen (2001) classifies by participants, or the type of buyer and seller:

- *Business-to-consumer (B2C)*: online stores, travel agencies or airlines.
- *Business-to-business (B2B)*: business procurement and outsourcing.
- *Consumer-to-consumer (C2C)*: classified advertisements and online auctions.
- *Consumer-to-business (C2B)*: individual services offered to businesses, for example, providers of professional services.

The first two are the most commonly used classifications for e-commerce. It would therefore be useful to look at some examples of each in greater detail.

Business-to-consumer (B2C)

Online stores

Online stores are an ideal exploitation of e-commerce. The basic business process of a retail store is retained, but access is possible on a twenty-four hours a day, seven days a week (24/7) basis, i.e. continually. However, the vendor needs to remember several important factors. First, not every visitor to their site, in the same way as not every visitor to their store, knows what they wish to purchase. Therefore it is essential that they are able to browse freely and quickly through the available goods. It is also important that there is a logical progression to this browsing and that the visitor does not have to keep going backwards and forwards to check on specifications, prices and availability.

Some retailers, whilst providing numerous illustrations or photographs of their products, lose business because these are of poor quality. If a potential purchaser cannot handle or see the goods, they need a clearly recognised and detailed photograph plus a comprehensive written description. This tends to be even more important where sales are being offered on an international basis, since there is a greater need to generate confidence in the purchaser. Examples of stores may be found by accessing any search engine and going to the 'shopping' site or instigating a search for a desired product.

It is also necessary that a secure method of payment is available to the purchaser. In B2C business this is normally by credit card, although new payment methods are being introduced to avoid the disenfranchisement of those who do not hold credit cards.

One change in business relationships that has been introduced by the internet has been 'disintermediation'. This is defined by Turban *et al.* (2000) as a new term that refers to the removal of organisations or business process layers responsible for certain intermediary steps in a given value chain. It is becoming increasingly common for manufacturers to offer the products for sale through internet stores. By eliminating the retailer's margin, this allows the producer to sell at a more competitive price, whilst still increasing their own margin. Thus a producer may also be a B2C vendor.

Travel agencies

Travel agencies use global distribution systems such as GALILEO, SABRE and AMADEUS for reservations. As Standing and Vasudavan (2001, p. 123) point out, they may exploit some of the aspects of e-commerce, such as:

- using the internet to build customer relationships – by having customers interact directly with the web site
- gathering information from customers and potential customers to create customer profiles that can be used in marketing and product development
- building information partnerships – cooperation between organisations to provide better service to the customer
- transactions – selling products and services

- building specialised information provision according to the profile of the user
- allowing information and products to be downloaded by the user.

Airlines

Airlines were early adopters of e-commerce, although their original networks were not based on the internet. These were the booking systems developed by travel agencies and were not accessible by the general public. However, these were global systems in two ways. First, the booking and ticketing networks had to be global, otherwise they would not fulfil their function. Second, billing and accounting processes were not carried out in the offices or even home countries of the airlines. India captured much of this work, due to the availability of skilled IT staff at relatively low labour costs. This had the spin-off that employment in the IT sector became even more attractive locally, resulting in more qualified IT personnel and a rapid growth of the industry in the subcontinent.

Some airlines, particularly those offering basic low-cost flights, are cutting out even the travel agents from the value chain. This process is a further example of disintermediation. One such airline is EasyJet.com, which offers a very simple booking system, allowing passengers to check all flight times, pricing and availability online, and then continue to make their firm bookings and payment. The entire process takes about five minutes and the cost is kept low because the airline does not have to pay any commission to a travel agent.

Business-to-business (B2B)

Electronic data interfaces

All B2B transactions are within the value system, as postulated by Porter (1985); that is, they are value-adding transactions, forming part of the value chain of an individual organisation, or group of organisations with a supply chain. This may be raw materials to a primary producer, sub-assemblies to a manufacturer or logistics services to a wholesaler. The earliest B2B transactions were in operation before the expansion of the internet. These networks were known as electronic data interfaces (EDI) and operated under a number of different proprietary IT protocols.

EDI transactions could be between different companies within the same group, or component companies within a supply chain. However, because they created transparent access to both ends of the interface, a high degree of trust was needed before the system could be implemented. According to Metzgen (1990, p.105):

The advantages of EDI are not just from the improved speed and accuracy, but in cost savings such as reductions in transcription of information from one data source to another, better financial and administrative control, improved cashflow, better stock control and better customer service.

EDI networks could be between communities or open-user groups. Examples of early networks were groups such as SHIPNET (freight forwarding and shipping) projects 1985–6, UNIDEX (insurance), LIMNET (insurance clearing houses) and EDICON (construction).

EDI was particularly rapidly adopted by the logistics and shipping industries. One example was the marine cargo processing (MCP) network in Felixstowe. Over 500 freight forwarders and Customs and Excise participated in a network for the customs clearing of cargoes.

The main drawback of EDI was and is the different protocols used for the transmission of data. This has generally been solved by the creation of data translation hubs, such as Descartes.com, that charge for the translation of data from one EDI protocol to another.

B2B on the internet

On the internet, it is still the supply chain that provides a reason for inter-organisational B2B communications. Procurement provides the need on the demand side and marketing on the supply side. Product movements through the whole supply chain are connected by the logistics function, which may be provided by either party or outsourced.

Organisations have internal business and manufacturing processes that are dependent upon this external connectivity. These have traditionally been paper-driven processes, such as ordering, shipment and payment. It is now possible to organise these functions electronically, dispensing with most paperwork and thus creating savings and competitive advantage.

One of the latest developments has been the creation of e-marketplaces for businesses. In these markets, brokers are replaced electronically. It is still possible for the buyer and seller to maintain anonymity in their relationships to each other but, as in the offline world, the broker or electronic market needs the identity of both. Two essential constituents of such markets are:

- a large user base, since otherwise the electronic broker would either be redundant or not generate an adequate revenue stream to survive
- secure means of payment, to ensure the maintenance of trust between anonymous parties.

Consumer-to-consumer (C2C) and consumer-to-business (C2B)

The other two classifications are currently of lesser importance than the first two, but should still be considered. C2C is almost exclusively concerned with online auctions between members of the general public. A good example of this process is eBay.com, which provides a secure online auction site. However, recent analysis shows that even generalised auction sites such as eBay.com are being hijacked by commercial organisations. It is apparent that a number of vendors are either selling on a commercial basis or acting for a commercial organisation.

C2B is included to achieve congruence of the classifications. However, the only individuals likely to have services to sell to 'commerce' are professionals, such as sole-trading lawyers, accountants or business consultants.

Global e-commerce

It is difficult to limit e-commerce within the borders of a single country. The case study at the end of the chapter presents an example of this. If an e-commerce marketplace is created for transportation within a single country or region, some of the carriers will be trading internationally and will not accept geographic limitations.

Similarly, an online store or product outlet may be located anywhere in the world. The vendor would be unreasonably limiting the market were they not to supply to any prospective purchaser.

However, there are problems for the vendor and constrains to the trade. The vendor's main problem is physically fulfilling the order. E-commerce websites are designed with the capacity to accept multiple enquiries and transactions simultaneously. Upwards of a half million a day is technologically straightforward. If the product can be delivered electronically, such as software, information, tickets, reservations or even music, this is not a problem. However, if physical delivery of a 100,000 items a day to 50 countries is needed, logistical problems occur. A classic example of this problem was seen in the early days of Amazon.com, the online booksellers, when they did not have the organisational infrastructure to meet demand and the delays became newsworthy. The other barriers to global e-commerce are created within the destination countries.

Barriers to global e-commerce

According to Turban *et al.* (2000) there are four general barriers to global e-commerce: legal issues; market access issues; financial issues; other issues such as identification of the entity with whom you are trading, trust and security, different cultures, different languages and different currencies. These will be discussed in some detail below.

Legal issues

The internet is available globally, but subject to the laws of each country where it may be accessed. Some of the legal aspects include data protection, taxation (discussed later), intellectual property rights, electronic contracts, harmful content, domain names, electronic payment and consumer protection. The UK has addressed data protection in Part 1, section 4 of the Electronic Communications Act 2000:

Subject to the following provisions of this section, no information which (a) has been obtained under or by virtue of the provisions of this Part, and (b) relates to the private affairs of any individual or to any particular business,

shall, during the lifetime of that individual or so long as that business continues to be carried on, be disclosed without the consent of that individual or
the person for the time being carrying on that business.

Of course, there are the usual exceptions for government and criminal investigations, but it is comforting to see that an effort is being made. However, it
appears that many other states have yet to promulgate similar protection.

At the Organisation for Economic Co-operation and Development (OECD)
workshop on the 'Guidelines for Consumers in the Online Marketplace' held in
March 2001 in Berlin, it was suggested that the international nature of e-commerce required a global approach to consumer protection, to create a transparent
and predictable legal and self-regulatory framework. Responsibility was placed on
every country or jurisdiction to address the issues of e-commerce consumer protection, although it was noted that disparate solutions would effect the growth of
e-commerce. It is hoped that the OECD will be able to oversee a globally coordinated approach to such legislation.

Many of the legal aspects are being addressed and updated on a regular basis.
A useful site for research is that of the Society for Computers and Law
(www.scl.org), which deals specifically with such matters.

Market access issues

The internet is the latest retail outlet but has encountered mixed reception in
many places for technical, cultural and cost-related reasons. American consumers,
for example, have embraced the internet as an alternative mail order shopping
venue with far more enthusiasm than their European counterparts. According to
a report by Jupiter Communications cited in *Time* (30 November 1998), US
shoppers were expected to spend $2.3 billion surfing for products and services
available through retailers' websites on the internet in the run-up to the 1998
Christmas holidays. European consumers were estimated to spend roughly 5 per
cent of that figure. According to the OECD, cited in the same source, 80 per cent
of the $26 billion global e-commerce market is within the United States. Western
Europe's share is just 10 per cent.

The reasons why Europe trails the United States so badly in e-commerce are
myriad, but the cost of going online is a major culprit. The slow pace of telecommunications deregulation and a resulting lack of competition have kept connection costs much higher in Europe than in the United States. Europe's
telecommunications sector can also be blamed for not making up-to-date technology like cable modem access and fibre-optic lines widely available to consumers. Transmission bandwidths across much of Europe are insufficient, which
means that internet connections on the continent are slower than in the United
States, forcing people to remain online longer, further running up phone charges.
The high price of computers in Europe relative to the United States is another
reason why internet usage in Europe is lower.

Financial issues

Sale by mail order is gaining popularity, especially in western Europe and North
America. But such a style of selling may be a long way from being accepted or

adopted in many other countries. Remote sale, apart from a widespread use of credit card and mutual trust between unseen sellers and buyers as a precondition, also presupposes a strong legal and insurance infrastructure to ensure a proper conduct of business transactions by the two sides. This type of financial and legal infrastructure is either inadequate or totally lacking in many countries. There may also be culturally rooted mistrust and misgivings regarding such remote transactions.

The use of credit cards in India, for example, although growing in recent years, involves only a relatively small number of people. In 1998 of an estimated 30 million adults who were eligible, only 3 million had a card (*The Economist*, 5 December 1998). Most Indians prefer cash, partly because it leaves no trace – the government added credit cards to the list of assets whose owners must file a tax return in 1998. Major foreign banks, which issue credit cards, also have the disadvantage of being relatively unknown in the retail business, particularly in smaller Indian cities. But even if the banks win new customers, they will run new risks. For instance, they have no way of checking if a customer has defaulted on a card issued by another bank. The credit information available is inadequate and often wrong. India's legal system also offers little help; some banks hire agents to collect payments from difficult customers. This can prove embarrassing – as one large British bank discovered when a court in Mumbai [formerly Bombay] censured it for 'roughing up' a defaulting customer (*The Economist*, 5 December 1998).

Trust and security

Over the last century, the degree of trust in commercial transactions has decreased. This is probably because of changes in business practices due to global trade. Historically, trade was executed on a strong basis of trust, because the trading community was either limited or closed and the penalty of exclusion was commercially terminal. With widening of access to trade, such penalties become negligible and opportunities for abuse of trust increased. Now most global offline trade is conducted against secure instruments of payment.

Increasing an organisation's capacity to trade electronically can multiply financial risks. Also the lack of geographical identification of many web-based businesses does little to improve confidence. It was suggested by Shapiro *et al.* (1992) cited in Turban *et al.* (2000) that the desired level of trust is determined by the following factors:

- the degree of initial success that each party experienced with e-commerce and with each other
- well-defined roles and procedures for all parties involved
- realistic expectations as to outcomes from e-commerce.

On the other hand, trust can be decreased by:

- any user uncertainty regarding the technology
- lack of initial face-to-face interactions
- lack of enthusiasm among the parties.

Results from marketing surveys discussed in the case study at the end of the chapter (Easy2ship.com) indicate that users of the planned exchange in other EU countries would be unhappy about using the service unless they could identify a local subsidiary or agent to whom they could direct any complaints in person.

European consumer habits do not help the matter either. As the OECD notes, continental shoppers are less fond of buying goods from afar than their American cousins. European mail order sales, on a per capita basis, are less than half those in the United States. Europeans like to see what they are buying and feel the product. Also in many European countries credit cards, useful in mail order transactions, are not popular. For instance, in Germany, where there are legal and other institutional infrastructures to support remote exchanges of goods and money, mail order retailers are still reluctant to accept credit cards. The German Quelle Schickedanz is one of Europe's largest catalogue retailers with a business built on trust. Customers can 'test' a product for 14 days before deciding whether to keep it. If they want it, they are billed and can pay by cheque, cash or as a direct debit to their bank account, but no credit cards or smart cards are allowed (*Time*, 30 November 1998).

Different cultures

Technology development is, as Bartholomew (1997) argues, embedded in a country's history, cultural values and attitudes. As we saw earlier in the book, societal institutions such as education, industry–university relationships, industrial structure and government policies could all create socially embedded capabilities that the firms can in turn exploit. This does not of course mean that all firms operating in a given society can use these capabilities equally well. But the strongest and the more competent ones can take what is on offer and make themselves competitive in the international market (Tayeb, 1995).

Attitude to technology could also have something to do with national culture. Americans, for instance, are future oriented and strongly inclined to believe that present ways of doing things inevitably are to be replaced by even better ways. By contrast, the British are known for their love of past and for them the view of history is essentially to accept the present as a culmination of past developments and, therefore, as representing the highest achievement attainable (Dubin, 1970). The Americans' future-oriented attitude, one could argue, is immensely helpful as a foundation for technological innovation and use of new technologies, while the British past orientation might be unhelpful in this regard, to say the least.

This does not of course mean that the British are less innovative in scientific and technological fields, but it is true that in the implementation of innovative ideas and inventions they lag behind their counterparts in countries such as Germany, the United States and Japan. Many British inventions and product prototypes have in the past been taken up and converted to commercial products by foreign companies. The compact disk (CD) and computer are examples of British inventions that were developed by Japanese and American companies respectively and turned into what they are now.

Government policies

Companies in many developing countries are still years, if not literally centuries, behind their more advanced counterparts with regard to modern technologies, especially of the information processing kind: 'Though astonishing advances have been made in this direction, it is sobering to realise that according to the UN International Telecommunications Union, 80 per cent of the world's population have no access to a telephone, let alone a computer. The race to connect the world up has several decades to run' (Clarke and Clegg, 1998, p. 189).

The reasons for this state of affairs are legion but politics has a great deal to do with it. Information technology, for instance, could pose a serious threat and challenge to the absolute and semi-absolute powers that certain governments have. As a result, many companies are deprived of such facilities purely on political grounds. The use of telephone, fax machines, internet facilities and computers and consequent flow of information are severely limited and controlled. China is an example here. Recently the government has required the owners of cyber cafés in Beijing to register their users and pass the names on to the Public Security Bureau. This move marks the Chinese government's determination to use the net's power as a communications tool while suppressing the ideas it may be used to communicate. Chinese net users are already required to connect to the internet using only official gateways which block access to any websites that might contain criticisms of the regime, views on Taiwan, or other non-conformist topics (*EasyLifeIP*, 1999, issue 5, p. 2). Under such circumstances it is not possible to catch up with latest developments and emulate latest technologies (Tayeb, 2000).

Different languages

According to sources cited in Chen (2001), approximately 50 per cent of the global population are native English speakers. Many non-native English speakers were probably among the early adopters of the internet, since English is widespread among the tertiary educated, who formed a large part of these early adopters. However, as more and more small businesses use the internet, it is probable that many will create local internet marketplaces. If this is the case, it is likely that they will use the local language. In the EU, most employment agencies tend to publish vacancy advertisements in their national languages, often to create a primary filter for linguistic skills.

Some companies that are based in English-speaking countries are prepared to affiliate non-English-speaking websites to broaden their reach. One such is Amazon.com. Also interesting, as Timmers (1999) points out, is that a referral site can be any local site which is maintained in the local language. Therefore, at least for the marketing front end towards the customer, Amazon can get global multilingual reach with minimum investment. However, for the time being it would appear that most of the major commercial sites will continue to be based in English-speaking countries and that, regardless of local preferences, English will be the global language of e-commerce.

Different currencies

Most international e-commerce is conducted either in US dollars or in the currency of the vendor. If payment is being made by credit card, the value will be converted automatically. Currency only poses an intractable problem for non-convertible currencies. Therefore nationals of such countries are unable to conduct e-commerce unless they are able to access convertible funds. Since this is illegal in some countries, it effectively bars access to B2C or C2C trade and may limit B2B transactions.

Taxation

At present taxation does not constitute a barrier to e-commerce. A key element in the report of the OECD Ministerial Conference, 7–9 October 1998 in Ottawa, Canada, is the guidance it provides to tax authorities regarding the taxation of electronic commerce. The document concludes that the OECD tax authorities believe that the existing taxation principles can work for electronic commerce at this stage of development in electronic commerce.

In addition to this foundation setting framework, a number of specific conclusions were reached. For example, consumption taxes should be levied in the country where consumption takes place and that for the purpose of these taxes the supply of digitised products should not be treated as a supply of goods. This is an important first step in the examination of how various types of electronic commerce payments should be characterised for the purpose of the application of the provisions of tax conventions (www.oecd.org, accessed June 2001).

Also in 1998 the EU agreed a set of guidelines, including that there should be no discrimination between online and offline ways of doing business. Therefore no new taxes such as a 'bit tax' should be introduced (Timmers, 1999). This is embodied in the Legal Framework for the development of Electronic Commerce:

> The proposed Directive would ensure that information society services benefit from the Single Market principles of free movement of services and freedom of establishment and could provide their services throughout the European Union (EU) if they comply with the law in their country of origin. (http://europa.eu.int, accessed August 2001)

Online companies and their difficulties

The year 2000 is significant in the short history of e-commerce. This was the year in which the bubble burst for many of the e-commerce entrepreneurs. To understand this phenomenon, one must re-examine the development of e-commerce during the 1990s. It is the present authors' hypothesis that e-commerce has already been subject to four phases of development: bulletin board, process enhancement, banner advertising and dependent process.

Phase 1: Bulletin board

This was a development of the earliest form of internet communication. Bulletin boards were created by an individual or organisation as a place to post messages or information intended to be accessed and shared by remote users. For instance, in the mid-1980s an agricultural merchant in south west UK created and used a bulletin board to display prices of his merchandise for his customers in the agricultural community. Apart from demonstrating an appreciation of the medium as a vehicle for commerce, it is interesting to realise that for this to be worth his while it was obvious that a large portion of his customers, i.e. farmers, were also communicating by this means. However, this was not a viable way to transact business, since there was neither confidentiality nor security for either party.

Phase 2: Process enhancement

Although this may be considered as the second phase of development, it is still continuing as the main aspect of e-commerce. This may be defined as 'the use of e-commerce materially to improve an existing business process'. The preceding examination of the four classifications of e-commerce is based on process enhancement.

Phase 3: Banner advertising

This phase was spawned by the apparent fallacies that advertising on a website would be effective and that advertisers would pay the owners of such regularly visited websites for allowing them to place their advertising banners. The belief was that websites that had content which would attract browsers would generate sufficient revenue to repay investors. This has not been the case. Response rates to banner advertising have dropped from 7 per cent (of all visits to the host site) in 1996 to 0.5 per cent in 2001 (*The Industry Standard*, 27 August 2001).

Phase 4: Dependent processes

These are the business processes that are dependent upon the internet. The internet adds one or more dimensions without which the process would not work. Such dimensions include instantaneous transmission of information and the ability to handle vast quantities of paperless data with a minimal level of staffing. Examples of these are online auctions, commodity or service exchanges and the dissemination of information and media. Another essential component is the ability of the purchaser to effect immediate and secure online payments.

The outcome

During the second half of the 1990s, internet companies spawned at an exponential rate. Apparent success was demonstrated by market flotation on stock exchanges and on the NASDAQ (National Association of Securities Dealers Automated Quotation), a quotation system and associated market for American shares, particularly associated with hi-tech companies. Investors saw their capital increase 50 or 100 times or more. Most of these early investors were venture capitalists or company entrepreneurs. These capital gains attracted the large institutional investors, who visualised rapid gains for their funds without either investigating or understanding the underlying processes of these internet companies.

However, any business still needs to be run according to the best commercial principles. It will not be successful just because it is an internet company. Many companies were formed by technologically competent people who lacked any commercial knowledge or experience. Good ideas foundered under the burden of bad management and bad ideas were doomed from the outset. Some processes, such as reliance on banner advertising, were incapable of producing adequate revenue. Others, such as the creation of exchanges for limited markets, were equally incapable of generating a return.

The spending or 'burn' of investment capital was uncontrolled and companies often folded before they started trading. During the second half of 2000, the retreat of the institutional investors was faster than their arrival. There remains a suspicion of any nascent business that includes 'dotcom' in its trading name or professes a reliance upon the internet.

Some major prerequisites for creation, maintenance and success of e-commerce

Technical

Without going deeply into the technology of the internet, there are certain technical aspects that every commercial manager needs to be aware of:

1. The software and 'engine' that need to be developed to create the website must be robust. If the web site is not reliable, it will not keep customers. Also, as mentioned earlier, it needs to be easy to navigate, understand and use.

2. The site needs to be able to handle the anticipated traffic. If a site is expected to have half a million visitors a day, that is 350 per minute on a 24/7 basis, it also needs a substantial archiving capacity. If only 10 of each 350 enquiries become a transaction, that is still nearly 15,000 transactions a day which must be recorded and safeguarded over several years.

3. The host service of the site needs both spare capacity and a remotely situated back-up site. A localised power failure should not cause an e-commerce operation to fail.

Industrial/economic

1. It is essential that the market size is adequate to support an e-commerce venture. In an oligopoly with relatively few customers, it would be pointless to create an e-commerce exchange. The business could be easily managed by conventional methods, without resorting to electronic intervention.

2. It is also essential that the business process should be capable of generating sufficient revenue to justify its existence and investment. It should be borne in mind that, like any commercial enterprise involving a substantial customer base, there exist opportunities to exploit other marketing channels.

3. It must be possible physically to fulfil the logistical portion of the transaction within the expectations of the customer.

4. Acceptable methods of payment must be proved and conditions to maintain trust between contracting parties must exist.

5. The operation needs sufficient human resources to meet the day-to-day needs of customer service and to create customer confidence. It might not always be sufficient to rely upon outsourced services of a call centre provider.

Political

1. A political initiative to create or maintain an adequate telecommunications network is imperative and access to this network should not be politically restricted.

2. International initiatives on the harmonisation of taxation, intellectual property rights, data protection, harmful content and consumer protection must be agreed.

Cultural

1. The national culture should include a sufficient level of technological education to use a personal computer, although new TV-based systems could be even easier to access.

2. The cultural factors are those that a marketer needs to consider in devising any marketing strategy.

Summary

According to a Nielsen/Net Rating research survey in August 2001 (reported by Cantrell in *The Industry Standard*, 27 August 2001), 58 per cent of all Americans had internet access at home in July 2001, compared with 52 per cent in July 2000 and 39 per cent in July 1999. Even allowing for the apparent decrease in the growth rate, this is still an enormous domestic marketplace. There may be slower adoption rates in other parts of the globe, but it would appear that e-commerce has been established on a global scale. Should the threatened economic downturn transpire, the efficiencies and overhead savings that e-commerce promises might well increase the rate of its global acceptance.

It is hoped that this chapter has provided an overview of the development of e-commerce, the forces driving its global expansion and an indication of the barriers that need to be removed to foster further expansion.

Discussion questions

1. What are the benefits of online e-commerce compared to offline traditional business processes?

2. Explain the classification of e-commerce into B2C, B2B, C2C and C2B.

3. Why is it important to harmonise taxation policies in global e-commerce?

4. How crucial are logistics in fulfilling international e-commerce transactions?

5. What is the value of the internet as a global marketing channel?

Closing Case Study:
Compuship.com/Easy2ship.com – problems developing a global e-commerce concept into a viable business process

The concept

It is acknowledged by the European transport industry that there exists an inefficiency of over 30 per cent in road haulage operations, i.e. either the vehicle is empty for 30 per cent of its journeys or 30 per cent empty on every journey. In reality this is probably a combination of the two states. Thirty per cent is a minimum conservative estimate and in the United States it could be nearer 40 per cent.

Efforts are always made to reduce this inefficiency by ensuring maximum possible loading or finding return loads. Traditionally this has been difficult. Either there are problems of timing and coordination, or financial problems due to the unknown creditworthiness of shippers of return loads.

By using e-commerce internet connectivity, it is possible to bring together potential carriers and shippers in real time to maximise efficiency. The reduced fixed costs of the carrier should offset freight reductions offered as an inducement to the shipper, as well as providing revenue for the service provider. This creates a win/win/win scenario.

Additionally, by factoring the service through a bank/credit agency, the service provider can guarantee payment to the carrier within a fixed timeframe. Further benefits are the provision of cargo insurance as well as creating a new marketing channel within the transport industry.

The history

In 1997 an American computer reseller became unhappy with the level of service his company was receiving from the carriers he used to deliver equipment to his customers. This caused him to analyse the nature of the carriers transport operations to see if he could identify areas where their services could be improved.

During his research, he discovered only one fact that struck him as being a possible area of improvement. He learned from several sources that road transport had one particular inefficiency. This was that many journeys were undertaken unladen and that many others were made with less than a full load. In fact, it appeared that the industry was running at only some 60 per cent of its maximum capacity.

He decided that it would be a simple matter to create an internet exchange to manipulate a win/win situation. His belief was that the carrier would be prepared to cost price for last-minute loads to fill up empty space; that shippers would benefit from lower than standard freight rates; and that he would be able to charge a small margin on each transaction. He registered Compuship.com and commenced development.

A year later, due to the uncontrolled and unanticipated software costs he had incurred, he lost his previously profitable computer business, his Compuship.com and the rights to the business process he had developed. Undeterred, he eventually found an entrepreneur who was developing a small internet incubation company, I-Global.com, which was interested in developing the concept on his behalf. They joined forces and tried to reacquire the rights to the project development already undertaken. However, they were also suffering from a lack of finance.

They in turn sought external finance. Help came in the form of Ci4net.com, a Channel Island and UK incubation company, recently launched on the NASDAQ market, whose shares were priced at over $100 and who was consequently in a buoyant and acquisitive frame of mind. They purchased I-Global.com, renaming it Ci4netNA.com and financed the reacquisition of the freight exchange for $1 million.

But Ci4net.com was still unhappy about two factors in the proposed operation. First, they believed that the United States was too large and amorphous a market for the initial launch. Second, they insisted that the operation needed professional input and control by logistics industry experts. Two were hired – the CEO who was an expert in international logistics and commerce and the other in UK road haulage and marketing. A wholly owned UK company, Easy2ship.com Limited, was created in early summer 2000 to complete the exchange and launch the concept into the European marketplace.

The two new directors then collaborated in the creation of both business and marketing plans for the exploitation of this new exchange process. It became apparent at the same time that other companies were working on parallel developments, so a measure of urgency was necessary. A beta test and trial launch were planned for October with a full launch to follow at the end of November.

The Ci4netNA.com took responsibility for the final development and hosting of the exchange in the United States. They eventually located a software development company, Techspan, based in California's Silicon Valley. Then came the first major setback. After their analysis of the development work originally undertaken by Compuship.com, Techspan advised that the work completed only constituted a sketchy demonstration and lacked the technical flexibility and robustness to be developed into a commercially viable internet exchange.

The UK directors immediately flew to California and spent some weeks respecifying the business processes and redesigning the structure of the exchange. This delay obviously caused the date of the beta test to be postponed for the ten weeks it was now going to take to develop a working prototype. This would time the beta test for the hectic fortnight before the Christmas holiday in the UK. It was then decided that the only option was to further delay the launch until February 2001.

This delay proved fatal. If the exchange were to be launched in February, the earliest that a revenue stream could be generated would be May. The business plan reflected the fact that growth to a financially self-sustaining state would take about 18 months and that the company would require a substantial injection of cash during the first 6 months of operation to finance a pan-European marketing campaign and the expansion of the company structure.

The problems became apparent at the end of the redesign phase of the development. Techspan wanted payment for the work to date before they were prepared to work on the final stage of development. They had contracted to undertake the work with the Ci4netNA.com and expected payment from them. The UK parent organisation, Ci4net.com, the source of all the finance, admitted 'some cashflow problems' but that these were temporary and would soon be resolved.

At the time that Easy2ship.com was formed, the directors were advised that £9 million was available for the UK launch. Following the preparation of the business and marketing plans, this was formally increased to £25 million each for the pan-European and subsequent North American launches. However, one fact was not disclosed by Ci4net.com. This was that they had failed to secure a second round of funding in May, which was crucial to their development plans. They subsequently acknowledged that they had believed this was a temporary setback and that the second-round funding would be secured before it was needed to meet their commitments to their 50-odd subsidiaries. In reality, Ci4net.com had insufficient skilled managers to control the activities of all these subsidiaries. Their efforts to do so apparently distracted their attention from events in the world's financial markets.

Many of the phase three internet companies had 'burned' their investors' money, without having any realistic hope of developing an adequate revenue stream. Institutional investors had leapt onto the bandwagon when they had seen the immense capital gains to be made from the spectacular and much-publicised IPO capitalisation of many 'dot.com' companies, but the bubble had burst.

Ci4net.com's shares, originally valued at over US$100 on the NASDAQ market, had slumped to under US$1 by early 2001. There was no realistic possibility that they would get second-round funding. They divested themselves of over 80 per cent of their subsidiaries, keeping Easy2ship.com among five or six others. However, they were not able to meet either the development costs they had incurred with Techspan or the operational costs of Easy2ship.com, whose staff was laid off in December 2000 and whose UK directors resigned shortly thereafter.

In summary, the business process is viable. The concept was professionally market tested through focus groups and accepted with enthusiasm by both carriers and potential users. However, due to its failure from causes outside its direct control, as well as the current commercial suspicion of investment in e-commerce, funds are not forthcoming.

This scenario has been repeated in many other commercial sectors, most of which are suffering from lack of confidence on the part of institutional investors. They had their fingers burned by investing heavily in e-commerce without having either made prudent checks that the business process was going to work or that there was the likelihood of the generation of an adequate revenue stream in the foreseeable future.

Closing case study questions

1. Was the development time a significant cause for the termination of the project?

2. What would an investor need to know before making a commitment to fund such a venture?

3. Can a win/win/win scenario really exist, or is there a commercial loser?

4. Could the concept be limited to operation within national boundaries?

5. What are the likely difficulties of expansion into:
   (a) Europe?
   (b) Non-European countries?

Annotated further reading

Because of the rapid evolution of e-commerce and information technology in general, it is advisable to keep one's reading as up to date as possible. The following are suggested as useful works on various aspects of e-commerce.

Chen, S. (2001) *Strategic Management of e-Business*. Chichester: Wiley.
This is a very readable book by Stephen Chen of the Manchester Business School. It provides a comprehensive coverage of the technologies and processes that a manager needs to develop an e-business strategy.

Rayport, J. F. and **Jaworski, B. J.** (2001) *e-Commerce*. New York: McGraw-Hill/Irwin.
This book is aimed to provide both students and managers with an in-depth view of e-commerce. It is reinforced with excellent internet illustrations.

Rayport, J. F. and **Jaworski, B. J.** (2002) *Cases in e-Commerce* (international edition). New York: McGraw-Hill/Irwin.
This is a companion volume to the above work, providing relevant up-to-date case studies on the practical applications of e-commerce.

Turban, E., Lee, J., King, D. and **Chung, H. M.** (2000) *Electronic Commerce – A Managerial Perspective*. Upper Saddle River NJ: Prentice Hall.
The blend of academic and commercial authors gives this book a wide appeal to both students and managers. The authors, since they are working in the United States and Asia, give a strong international perspective to the subject.

References

Amor, D. (2000) *The E-business Revolution – Living and Working in an Interconnected World*. Upper Saddle River NJ: Prentice Hall.

Bartholomew, S. (1997) 'The globalization of technology: a socio-cultural perspective', in J. Howells and J. Michie (eds) *Technology, Innovation and Competitiveness*. Cheltenham: Edward Elgar. pp. 37–64.

Berger, E. (1996) *Birthplace of the Web*. FermiNews: Fermi National Accelerator Laboratory, 19(16), 16 August 1966. http://dbhs.wvusd.k12.ca.us/Chem-History/Hist-of-Web

Chen, S. (2001) *Strategic Management of e-Business*. Chichester: Wiley.

Clarke, T. and **Clegg, S.** (1998) *Changing Paradigms: The Transformation of Management Knowledge for the 21st Century*. London: HarperCollins.

Dubin, R., (1970) 'Management in Britain – impressions of a visiting professor', *Journal of Management Studies* 7(2): 183–98.

Europa.eu.int/ISPO/ecommerce/answers/what.html

Frink, B. (compilation ed.) (1998) *Internet Complete*. Alameda CA: Sybex.

Gates, B. (1999) 'Home is where the internet is', *Financial Times*, 20 March 9.

Hammond, R. (1996) *Digital Business, Surviving and Thriving in an On-line World*. London: Hodder & Stoughton.

Kalakota, R. and **Whinston, A. B. (eds)** (1997) *Electronic Commerce: A Manager's Guide*. Reading MA: Addison Wesley.

Metzgen, F. (1990) *Killing the Paper Dragon – Electronic Data Interchange in Business*. Oxford: Heinemann Newnes.

Oecd.org/dsti/sti/it/news/ottrepor.htm

Porter, M. (1985) *Competitive Advantage: Creating and Sustaining Superior Performance*. New York: Free Press.

Standing, C. and **Vasudavan, T.,** 'Re-engineering travel agencies with the world wide web', in S. Barnes and B. Hunt (2001) *E-Commerce and V-Business. Business Models for Global Success*. Oxford: Butterworth-Heinemann.

Tayeb, M. H. (1995) 'The competitive advantage of nations: the role of HRM and its socio-cultural context', *International Journal of Human Resource Management* 6(3): 588–605.

Tayeb, M. H. (2000) *The Management of International Enterprises: A Socio-Political View*. Basingstoke: Macmillan.

The Industry Standard. Various articles. www.thestandard.com

Timmers, P. (1999) *Electronic Commerce – Strategies and Models for Business-to-Business Trading*. Chichester: Wiley.

Turban, E., Lee, J., King, D. and **Chung, H. M.** (2000) *Electronic Commerce – A Managerial Perspective*. Upper Saddle River NJ: Prentice Hall.

PART 3

Communicating with others

CHAPTER 9

Managing interface activities

Angelica C. Cortes

Learning objectives

When you finish reading this chapter you should:

■ know about international advertising and distributions channels as the main avenues to communicate with customers

■ have an understanding of the different models of buyer–supplier relationships

■ be able to understand the different manners in which governments facilitate on the one hand and restrict on the other the functions of international firms

■ have an understanding of the basics of international negotiations process

■ be able to analyse the importance of business ethics and corporate social responsibility in the context of global business

Opening Case Study: Orange in India

On the day Indian lovers were planning to paint the town red, they woke up to find it was Orange. Hutchison-Max Telecom, a subsidiary of Hong Kong based Hutchison Whampoa, brought the Orange brand into the country on St Valentine's Day this year, and almost overnight it was everywhere you looked in Mumbai, the financial capital of India.

Orange's arrival marked one of the most high-profile brand launches the Indian services sector has seen. Billboards all over the city, full-page ads in leading newspapers, banners, you name the medium it was everywhere. India was the eighth market Orange had entered, but this time there was a difference: its arrival represented an overnight rebranding of Hutchison's existing network, MaxTouch.

The name of the game was maximum impact. You could drive down from upscale Bandra in north Mumbai to the business nerve centre Nariman Point, and the message was as loud as it was clear: He speaks Orange or Speak in Orange. If the regional militant Hindu party, the Shiv Sena, was bemused by the way Orange was saffronising the city, arch rival and Nambiar-owned BPL Mobile was caught on the back foot. A few days after the launch, BPL fired its first salvo. It released full-page advertisements in leading Indian newspapers, featuring a small citrus juicer in blue, BPL's predominant brand colour, next to an orange sliced in two. The message was there in small print, right in the middle of the page: Welcome Orange.

Long before the dust had settled at ad agency cocktail parties, BPL fired another and final shot: this time, a full-pager showing a small blackboard with a menu of fruit juices on it. The copy again read: Welcome Orange. Ad pundits may say what they will, but clearly Orange had stirred the market, if not shaken it. Ever since, the international campaign, replete with the faces of foreigners, has slowly gone more local. An Indian look started to make its presence felt and with the recent launch of OrangeWorld, the operators' internet-based services, it is using an out-and-out local campaign. BPL eventually repositioned itself a few weeks later. We speak your language but Orange still speaks only one language: the international language of youth.

Source: 12 Dec. 2000, *Financial Times* CD-ROM 2000

Introduction

Managers domestically interface with several groups who are the stakeholders of the firm. Some of these boundary spanning functions refer to relationships with customers at one end and with suppliers at the other. Another important group of stakeholders is the government. In the case of international management these stakeholders include customers, suppliers from various countries and the organisations that comprise the channel of distributions, transportation firms, financial institutions, home-country government and host-country government.

This chapter presents the interfacing of the international manager with some of these groups, in particular, customers, suppliers and government. Cultural issues are intertwined in these relationships as well as in the process and mechanics of negotiations. The chapter closes with a discussion about the delicate balance of maintaining an ethical corporate policy across the countries in which the firm has operations. This balance is difficult because ethics is a relative concept. A similarly complex issue is a proactive corporate responsiveness to societal problems. Corporate responsibility may refer to human rights, poverty, employment creation, transfer of technology or protection of the environment. How much can a multinational firm get involved in the host-country's policies related to these societal issues? How much can a foreign firm cooperate and contribute to its host economy without imposing its foreign views, philosophies and socio-cultural and economic models? The chapter will address these issues within five main topics:

1. The interface with customers.
2. The interface with suppliers – different models.
3. The interface with government.
4. Negotiation with external groups.
5. Business ethics and social responsibility.

The interface with customers

There are two main avenues in which this interface takes place: one is through communication, that is, *advertising;* the second is at the point of delivering the product or service to the customer, that is, *channels of distribution*. Both factors in domestic marketing are complex due to regulations, existing choices, limitations of media or channels availability and increasing complexity of both media and distribution channels. When expanded to other countries, these levels of complexity increase tremendously due to the different laws and regulations of each country, different levels of economic development, different cultures between and within countries, and the multiple languages.

Interface with customers through international advertising

Facing strategic decisions of how a business firm will advertise its products or services, the firm must decide on two major issues: first, selecting a mode of advertising that is standardised to all or most of the countries where the firm is marketing its products or adapting the advertising message to each individual market; second, selecting the target market, that is, to find out who are the firm's customers or potential customers.

The first strategic decision refers to how the firm will communicate with its potential customers. The approach of standardising the advertising message as much possible to all the countries where the firm operates has a number of advantages. For example, it is easier to control the advertising campaign across countries, maintain a uniform production quality, maintain a consistent corporate image and increase product and brand recognition around the world (Cateora and Graham, 1999). However, when the firm adopts a policy of advertising standardisation some problems arise: for example, the advertising message may lose its meaning; it is not adapted for cultural differences among the countries; the advertising message may not be easily translated into the host languages.

The other end of the spectrum is to customise the message to each country. The advantages of this approach are: the advertising message is sensitive to the needs of the target market; the message recognises the differences in culture and language of the different countries; it adapts better to the differing laws and regulations of each market. However, there are also problems with this approach. Customised advertising is very expensive and requires a number of local agencies working semi or totally independent from each other with the risk that the resulting product varies greatly in production quality. Moreover, with customised advertising it is difficult to achieve a standardised corporate image and build a consistent product and brand recognition. Customers from different countries may be getting completely different information about the firm's products or services.

In addition to the standardisation vs adaptation of the advertising message, international advertising has a number of other issues that an international manager must consider. Among these issues are legal, language and cultural considerations and media availability. Let us briefly examine each of these issues.

Legal considerations

Each country has a set of laws and regulations regarding advertising. Furthermore in a large number of countries the local advertising industry has some form of self-regulation. Some of these legal regulations concern 'vice products' such as tobacco and alcohol. For example, some Muslim countries prohibit any type of advertising of these products (Al-Makaty *et al.*, 1996). The United States prohibits television commercials of liquor but allows commercials for beer. In a large number of countries tobacco advertising has been severely limited in terms of content and media used.

Another highly regulated area is advertising to children. European countries vary in terms of what is accepted. For example, in Finland children cannot verbally mention the name of any type of product in a commercial (Kotabe and Helsen, 1998). Advertisers must be aware of China's cultural values such as respect for elders and discipline (Ha, 1996). Comparative advertising is also subject to regulations. For example, Germany prohibits any usage of comparative language in advertising, such as better than, less than, the greatest, and so on. Belgium and Luxembourg explicitly prohibit comparative advertising. However, it is accepted in the United Kingdom, Ireland, Spain and Portugal. The United States sees comparative advertising as promoting competition and the advertisement is accepted as long as the comparison is meaningful and can be substantiated (Cateora and Graham, 1999).

Language considerations

Language is a major challenge to effective advertising. Issues of language include countries speaking different languages, such as the European Union with its 15 different languages and countries having a number of languages and dialects. For example, India has one national language, Hindi, 14 official languages, and over 200 dialects.

Another challenge faced by international advertising relates to the usage of words. One problem is poor *translation*. Customers in foreign countries may receive an advertising message that makes absolutely no sense for them. For example, Frank Perdue's original message 'It takes a tough man to make a tender chicken' was translated into Spanish as 'It takes a sexually excited man to make a chick affectionate' (Ricks, 1994).

A second problem derives from words that have different meanings across countries which speak the same language, such as Latin America: for example, the word ball in Spanish is *bola*, but in one country *bola* means ball, in another it means a lie, in yet another it means revolution, and finally in another it is an obscenity.

A third problem derives from idiomatic nuances. A good example is an American airline which advertised that it had leather seats on all its planes, even in economy class. The original message was 'Fly with us in leather'. It was translated into Spanish as 'Fly with us naked'. Idiomatically the expression 'in leather' means naked, unless it is qualified to mean 'seated in leather seats' (Ricks, 1994). (See also Chapter 1.)

Cultural considerations

Following the challenges of communicating in different languages with prospective customers, international managers are faced with the difficulties communicating to prospective customers in diverse cultures. This presents tremendous creative challenges in advertising. Cultural factors, as we saw in earlier chapters, determine people's values, what a society judges as acceptable or not, and how people construct and perceive their reality. If the perceptual framework of the receiver is divergent from the sender's, then the meaning of the message will be understood quite differently. Knowledge of cultural differences must encompass not only the total advertising project, but also the complete manner in which the management interface with customers and suppliers in different countries.

It may be argued that it is the country's predominant religion which is the most determinant factor in defining the value system of a culture. The second major factor is the economic development of the country that allows people gradually to change their lifestyles. Existing perceptions based on these factors are hard to change, but they do change with time.

To complicate matters even further, as noted in earlier chapters, countries have a number of subcultures, e.g UK's Scottish, Welsh, Irish and English cultures. These subcultures, which obviously vary from one country to another, require careful consideration as well. Figure 9.1 shows some of the most common subcultures that one can observe in different countries: rural/urban, age, ethnic background, geographical region, colour and religion.

In communicating with one group, it is important not to offend or alienate another group within the country. For example, a person living in a large city has very different needs and lifestyle from a person living in a rural area; a child of 5 years old has very different needs for products and services from those of a teenager, an adult or an elderly person; or many Muslim women prefer different styles of dress to non-Muslim women.

However, it is important to note that economic development and global communication have influenced people of all cultural and subcultural backgrounds, albeit to varying degrees, to adopt products and customs that in the past were either unheard of, undesirable or even unacceptable. A classical case is Japan where tea is an intrinsic aspect of the culture. A decade ago, Nestlé was successful in introducing instant coffee, especially among the younger Japanese audience.

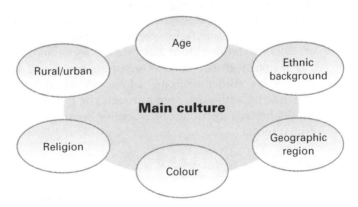

Figure 9.1 Common typology of culture

Media availability

Challenges that an international manager faces in delivering the message to prospective customers varies across countries. Mainly, we can recognise two major problems. The first is the regulations affecting the media, and the second is the availability of the media in the target countries. In the first case, industrialised countries have myriad different broadcast, print, electronic and other types of media, but government regulations place strict limits in terms of the time and manner in which messages are transmitted. The following are examples of time limitations found in some European countries. In Denmark, Norway and Sweden television commercials either don't exist or are very limited. Finland allows only 12 minutes per day to television advertising, whereas Italy limits televisions commercials to 80 minutes and the same commercial cannot be shown less than ten days apart. France permits only 12 minutes per hour per channel. Switzerland, Austria and Germany allow 20 minutes per hour per channel. In Germany advertisers must reserve and pay for the advertising time one year in advance (Keegan and Green, 2000).

The second problem relates to the lack of media availability. In a number of developing countries the broadcast media do not reach populations beyond the main cities. There are also problems with print media. In some countries newspapers reach very few people. In Bangladesh, for example, there is one newspaper for 300 people and in Zaïre there is only one newspaper for every 2,000 people (*Commercial Guide* 2000, US Department of Commerce). Compounding this issue of media availability is the level of illiteracy that limits the usage of print media. Business firms must be very creative in delivering their messages to prospective customers through other less conventional channels. In several developing countries the most reliable means of communication is still personal selling.

Challenges of delivering the firm's products to customers

The second major strategic decision is defining who the firm's customers are and this refers to the firm's market segments. Market segments consist of customers with similar needs and wants for a firm's products or services. Global market segmentation requires the firm to identify those segments with homogeneous needs across country boundaries. These groups may show different cultural and value systems but their lifestyle characteristics share common needs that the firm's product is able to fulfil. In addition, where a market segment in one particular country may be too small to be considered, the business firm may take the region or continent as a whole. In aggregate, these small segments become important in size and develop into profitable markets.

Let us consider a number of issues that an international manager faces when interfacing with customers through the delivery of products and services. These issues include distribution structures, retail patterns, direct marketing and use of the internet.

Distribution structure

The distribution process includes the physical handling of products and their distribution, transference of title and selling negotiations between producers and middlemen, and between middlemen and customers. Each country has its own distribution structure that reflects its traditions and economic development which are replicated in the functions and services provided by middlemen and market characteristics.

Traditional channels in developing countries evolved from economies dependent on imports, creating an import-oriented distribution structure. This is characterised as a seller's market where demand exceeds supply and there is limited market penetration and little mass distribution. The resulting channel structure is limited to the number of middlemen who perform the marketing functions of sorting, assorting, advertising and promotion, financing, warehousing, packaging, etc. Independent middlemen and agencies that provide facilitating functions such as marketing research, advertising and financing are sometimes non-existent or just beginning to emerge. In the developing countries where these agencies are more mature and growing in importance, their functions are still not fully integrated into a distribution system. Typically, developing countries have various parts of their economies at different stages of development.

This situation contrasts with the mass-consumption distribution systems found in industrialised countries. Nations with highly developed economies have a buyer's market where producers try to penetrate the market resulting in a highly developed channel structure that includes an array of intermediaries performing a variety of specialised marketing functions.

Retail patterns

There are extreme variations in retail size found in different countries, going from hypermarkets to one-person stalls and from large international retailers to local producers or farmers selling their products. At one extreme we have the hypermarkets developed in France. Next in size are the supermarkets emerging in one form or another in industrialised and developing countries alike. Discount stores such as Wal-Mart are already in Brazil, Argentina, Thailand, Canada, Hong Kong and China. France's Tati has stores in Lebanon, Turkey, Germany, Belgium, Switzerland and Côte d'Ivoire. In many countries these types of large department stores and discount stores operates side by side with small, fragmented retail structures.

As we saw in Chapter 6, the trend is towards the internationalising of retailing activities, especially American, European and Japanese retailers that can be found all around the world. These retailers perform a large number of marketing functions and services that simplify distribution. Furthermore, the consumer finds conveniences such as self-service, liberal store hours and a broad range of quality product brands at reasonable prices. However, the small, specialised stores continue to be an important factor in the retailing landscape, as are the stalls in the farmers' markets, markets or bazaars.

Direct marketing

Direct marketing refers to selling directly to the consumer, in the form of catalogues, mail, telephone or door to door. This approach to selling has been particularly important in countries with underdeveloped distribution systems. Personal door-to-door selling is still a vital form of distribution in some African,

Asian and Latin American countries where it is very difficult to reach the isolated rural areas or small villages. Catalogues, on the other hand, have experienced a tremendous growth as a distribution channel. However, they require a reliable postal and telephone infrastructure to be in place. The growth of catalogues has been made possible by the changing lifestyle, acceptance of credit cards and improvement of the communication infrastructure to support this type of direct marketing.

Internet as channel of distribution

We saw in Chapter 8 that the internet is becoming an important player in the channel of distributions for international companies as well for domestic companies. Technically e-commerce is a form of direct marketing. It is used to market business-to-business and consumer products and services. In 1996, the worldwide volume of sales through the internet was $500 million. E-commerce grew to an estimated $6.5 billion in 2000 and is expected to continue growing to $6.8 trillion by the year 2004 (*Global Reach Newsletter*, 8 January 2001). In the next five years, Europe will continue experiencing maturity with this new distribution channel. E-commerce will develop faster in northern Europe with Germany and the United Kingdom at the front, followed by France. Southern Europe is still showing some infrastructure and cultural resistance to conducting business online, but these factors may be overcome with the introduction of interactive

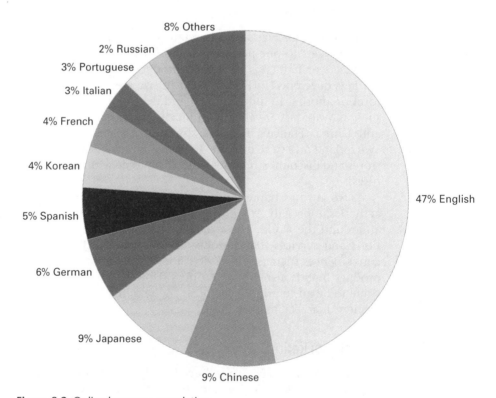

Figure 9.2 Online language population

Source: Adapted from http://glreach.com/globstats

television. Japan has been slow to adopt online shopping, but internet penetration stands at 30.6 per cent or 38.5 million users. The United States continues to be the global leader in online sales, with other continents joining e-commerce at ever-increasing rates.

One interesting development of the internet has been the language used. At the beginning most transmissions were in English, but today fewer than half the people connected to the net use English (see Figure 9.2). The implication of a multilingual net is that the interface with customers and suppliers around the world is no longer only in English. When communication is conducted mainly in one language there is a danger of inferring that cultural differences are greatly minimised. Cultural differences, traditions and business customs continue to exist regardless of whether the transactions are face to face or online.

The interface with suppliers

Over the past decade, there is growing evidence that in order for manufacturers to maintain or increase their global competitiveness they must adopt a different management paradigm. European and American firms are moving from the traditional short-term, adversarial relationship with a large number of suppliers towards a long-term, stable relationship with a few selected suppliers. Suppliers in long-term relationships are forming partnership or strategic alliances with their buyers, forging collaborative relations between manufacturing firms and suppliers.

These new models in the west, known as relationship marketing, resemble the Japanese model of a close-knit relationship among buyers and suppliers, without going as far as forming a *keiretsu*. Long-term relationships allow suppliers to make substantial relationship-specific investments in equipment to customise products, to collaborate in product design, conduct extensive qualification programmes and quality control and be able to function in just-in-time exchanges, where the suppliers produce and deliver products to their customers at the right time, right place and in the right quantity (Lummus *et al.*, 1998). What follows is a brief exploration of the Japanese, European and American models of buyer–supplier relationships and their implications.

Japanese model

Japanese management's interface with suppliers takes place within the context of the *keiretsu* – broadly defined as a bank-centred group of manufactures, services, firms and suppliers. An integral aspect of the *keiretsu* is long-term buyer–supplier relationships, which provide the Japanese manufacturer with a substantial competitive advantage due to the stability of the relationship which allows cooperation, cost reduction and supplier's involvement in the design process for the manufacturer's new products. The stability provided by a long-term relationship has been an important element in just-in-time and zero-defect models of supply chain management. With long-term contracts, it becomes financially feasible to commit large investments in state of the art equipment and quality control to provide the buyer with the right parts at the right time at the right place (Martin *et al.*, 1994). Just-in-time is a model in which neither the buyer nor the supplier keeps extra inventory. For this model to work effectively, there must be perfect coordination between the strategic planning of both supplier and buyer.

European model

In Europe the interface between buyers and suppliers is at a midpoint between the Japanese's long-term orientation and the American's short-term orientation. Europeans tend to have longer relationships with their suppliers, less confrontational relations and more trust than their American counterparts, but without achieving the close-knit alliances of the Japanese. With the integration of Europe, buyer firms have moved towards a common supply and logistic marketplace (Carter and Narasimhan, 1996). This includes a stronger need for cooperation and the use of sourcing teams, strategic sourcing, total quality management and just-in-time exchange. In particular, the European model emphasises the integration of quality management, service marketing concepts and customer relationship economics. Buyer–supplier relationships are moving from being function based to encompassing decisions that are cross-functional in nature, as well as stressing customer retention rather than just customer acquisition.

American model

The interface between buyers and suppliers in the United States has been characterised – and still is in many cases – by a buyer with many suppliers. The buyer seeks price advantage by playing one supplier against another, creating an antagonistic relationship (Kalwani and Narayandas, 1995). These short-term contracts involve instability for the supplier and a disincentive to invest in equipment specific to major buyers. Such an arrangement discourages investment in quality control programmes, making it very difficult to coordinate strategic planning for just-in-time delivery. In the United States this short-term model has been replaced by large manufacturers with a stable, long-term relationship, called the relationship marketing model, in which the buyer has fewer suppliers and creates a stable alliance in which the supplier is brought in as a partner in the buyer's strategic planning. The relationship marketing model allows suppliers to move closer to the Japanese model of stability, cooperation, zero-defect and just-in-time, all key factors for global competitiveness (Sheth and Parvatiyar, 2000).

The interface with government

International business firms are more vulnerable to changes in government policies, government composition and international relations than are firms that operate exclusively in their home countries. Managers must be aware of a number of factors that may influence the host-government's attitude toward the business firm far beyond the control of the expatriate managers. The following are some of the political factors that tend to influence government–business relationships in a positive, neutral or negative manner: business–government relationship, host-government's policies towards foreign trade, host-government and home-government relations, host-government relations towards other countries and regional trade treaties, host-government and home-government membership in international organisations, host-government's economic stability. The types of relationships covered in this section are from the host-government and home-government perspectives, in reference to the business firm and to each other's countries.

Government–business relationship

Government regulations can change rapidly in ways that may affect domestic firms operating in their own country as well as foreign firms' operations. Some of these changes may be negative such as when a government decides to nationalise certain industries, affecting both domestic and foreign firms, or in cases where a government decides to restrict foreign trade, equally affecting both domestic and foreign operations. In situations where the government has a pro-business stance, usually domestic and foreign firms can operate within a more cooperative and stable environment where there are financial incentives, supportive regulations and grants for technology and professional development.

In the particular case of foreign operations, multinationals must abide by the laws and regulations of their home countries and the countries where they have subsidiaries. Sometimes these laws may conflict with each other, placing the international manager in a very delicate position. Foreign firms are guests in the host country. Generally when in doubt or in case of conflicting regulations, the foreign firms must adhere to the host-country's laws first, and communicate this situation to their home countries. Inherent to this issue is the question of political risk. As a rule of thumb, the more volatility exists in the host country about economic decisions, foreign trade policies and political uncertainty, the higher the political risk. Risk is directly related to uncertainty.

Host government and the international firm

The relationship between the host government and the international firm begins sometimes at the point of negotiations or at the point of the foreign firm obtaining authorisation to operate in the sovereign territory of the host country. In some cases the host government grants tax breaks, investments, favourable import/export agreements and other incentives for foreign operations to be located in its territory. These incentives may also include some contractual obligations with the host government such as local content requirements, transfer of technology, employment creation, local procurements, and so on. Embedded in the relationship are the legal constraints and regulatory controls regarding foreign operations.

Changes in government may lead to changes not only in political philosophy but also in trade policies and economic priorities. The degree of political and economic risk to which foreign firms may be exposed by changes in government policies or political sentiment seems to correlate with the type of industry, amount of investment in the host country, degree of visibility and the countries of origin of the foreign firms. Usually, it seems that the two most important factors linking firms to political risk are the country of origin of the foreign operations and the type of industry. For example, the extracting industries, due to the exploitation and exportation of the country's natural resources, seem to be vulnerable to provocation of strong nationalistic feelings in the country's population that can easily be manipulated by some groups for their political gains. Both factors are at the forefront when the government sentiments change into nationalism, which may lead them to apply economic sanctions and conditions of protectionist measures.

Home government and the international firm

This is the other side of the coin: the relationship between the business firm and its home government. The political agenda of the home government may affect the firm through its foreign policies. Sometimes these policies explicitly prohibit firms from doing business with certain countries, such as embargoes and boycotts. In other cases they have trade sanctions limiting the type and amount of trade allowed. Other situations may relate to particular terms in negotiated trade agreements. At the other end of the spectrum the home government may encourage operations in other countries with which they have trade agreements or want to initiate or improve diplomatic and economic relations.

Another way in which the home government affects the business firm is through regulations concerning foreign exchange, mergers and acquisitions, antitrust laws and export/import licensing. These regulations may conflict with the corporation's strategic planning of growth and expansion. However, the firm must abide by its home laws first and the subsidiaries must abide by the host-country laws, placing management in a very difficult balancing act.

Relations between host and home governments

Diplomatic and economic relationships between the two governments are an important factor in the degree of political risk which a foreign firm may face. It is in this context that the country of origin of the foreign operations may place it at risk or protect it from trade sanctions. Multinationals, however, should always survey the political environment in which they operate. Changes may occur slowly over time, or they may come about very fast, and these environmental changes may be positive or negative. Some examples in which foreign firms were expropriated are the American companies operating the largest copper mines in Chile when Allende was elected president in 1970. American and European companies were expropriated in Iran when the Shah was overthrown in 1979. On the other hand, examples of positive changes have been the end of the Cold War, the unification of Germany and the collapse of the Soviet Union. All these events opened opportunities for foreign investments that were not possible before.

Host-country relations with other countries and organisations

Multinationals survey their political environment not only in the context of a specific country, but with a more holistic view concerning the host-country's relationship with other countries, with market trade agreements and with international organisations such as the World Trade Organisation, United Nations, International Monetary Fund, World Bank and the regional developing banks. Membership of these organisations guarantees, to some extent, that the host country will play the trade game by the rules, that is, a government must abide by the agreements prescribed in the charters of these organisations. Furthermore, membership in market trade agreements also provides a degree of stability for foreign operations and opens access to a larger regional market.

Negotiation with external groups

International managers interfacing with the various stakeholders discussed in this chapter are faced with perhaps the most difficult, sometimes elusive, factor of cultural differences. It is easy to assume that business has one language – maximise profit and continue growth – so that it does not matter what national language we speak, because we all understand about market share, profit, growth, effectiveness, etc. One of the most problematic issues in cross-cultural negotiations is the assumption that the other party thinks in basically the same manner as we do. It is comfortable to look for similarities and to ignore the differences. This is a perfect recipe for failure.

It is perhaps in the area of cross-cultural negotiations with prospective customers, suppliers or government officials where the international manager should be most aware of the cultural differences. Knowledge of the cultural factors is very useful to guide the manager through the intricacies of locus of decision making, context of communication, face-saving issues, power distance, relationships oriented or task oriented, group oriented or self-oriented, short-term or long-term oriented, and so on. Probably the most helpful cultural factors to aid international managers to navigate through cultural differences are those developed by Geert Hofstede and Edward T. Hall, as discussed in detail in Chapters 3 and 4.

Negotiations refer to the process of discussion between two or more parties with the aim of reaching a mutually satisfactory agreement. Graham (1985) identified that the process of negotiations usually includes the following steps: (1) preparation; (2) non-task sounding; (3) task-related exchange of information; (4) persuasion; (5) concessions and agreements. These steps may progress in order, or at some point the discussion may regress to previous steps.

Preparation stage

The work for this stage should be done before the parties are seated at the negotiation table. This stage is of utmost importance. Here the managers should learn as much as possible about the individuals with whom they will be negotiating, their cultural framework, their negotiating style, the business protocols of both parties, what both parties much achieve, what both parties hope to achieve, what are the upper and lower limits of each issue, and so on. Knowing the cultural framework makes it easier to understand the negotiation styles of each party. For example, in general, one can expect that when negotiating with Japanese managers they will hide their emotions. Saving face is very important for them; they tend to prefer long-term relationships and use long periods of silence. The American style, on the other hand, is straightforward, tends to go more into litigation rather than conciliation, is more argumentative and not necessarily sensitive to other people's feelings.

Non-task sounding stage

This stage refers to the period of relationship building. Cultures that are monochronic and low context in communication, such as most northern European countries and the United States, are very prone to go right to the business discussions. The problems arise when they are negotiating with polychronic, high context cultures such as most Asian, Latin American and Arabic countries, where it is very important to build a relationship, to get to know each other. This process of relationship building may last several days or even months before the parties involved begin the business discussions. This stage should not be overlooked or hurried. High context cultures do business with people not with businesses. It is with the people that they build the trust and long-term relationships.

Commitment to the relationship is sometimes a more decisive factor in the negotiation than the product, price, warranties, or other issues of the deal. Furthermore, it is important to keep in mind the other culture's business protocols. For example, in some cultures the respect for organisational ranks is very important. This will indicate that the members of the negotiation team should include only high-ranking officials or management at the corporate level. Other cultures that are lower in power distance emphasise the technical composition of the negotiation party rather than organisational ranks. If this stage is not successfully achieved, the negotiations may not continue at all.

Task-related exchange of information stage

This is the negotiation itself, where both parties make their presentation and state their position. The stage is characterised by questions and answers and the discussion of alternatives. American negotiators are most comfortable in this stage. For them it is straightforward, objective and should be efficient. For high context cultures this stage might be more subtle and indirect. For example, the Chinese negotiation style is to ask a lot of questions. They are very specific in the details at hand, but their presentation is usually vague and general. The Russian style is to be very well prepared and knowledgeable in technical details, demanding very specific technical answers to their questions.

Persuasion stage

This stage comes together after both parties know each other's positions and alternatives. They try to persuade the other to give up part of their demands and to accept concessions. This stage takes place not only during the negotiation sessions but also more informally in social settings. However, this stage is very difficult due to cultural differences and misinterpretations of verbal or non-verbal cues may fail the otherwise successful negotiations. It is also at this stage that the negotiating parties try different tactics, some based on threats or making higher demands. Another tactic is to place the other party in stressful situations, such as uncomfortable room temperature, very bright lights, interruptions, rudeness, calculated delays, take-it-or-leave-it attitudes, and so on.

Negotiating parties should also be aware of non-verbal cues, which can be more telling than the 'acting' of the tactics. Humans have little control over the expression and movement of their eyes, but they do have far more control of their facial expressions; the famous Japanese expressionless face is a case in point and very difficult to read. The use of silent periods, facial gazing, body language such as an arm closing across the chest or opening on the table, the body inclining forwards or moving backwards, are all non-verbal communications. For an experienced negotiator these are the most important signs to read and understand, rather than the negotiation tactics used during this stage.

Concessions and agreements stage

This is the final stage in the negotiation process. Some cultures such as Chinese, Russians and Latin Americans tend to start negotiation with extreme positions, demanding far more than they hope to get. Others open negotiations with what they want to get, which is the case with the Swedish. Americans move within a narrow range of what they want to obtain and what they are willing to concede. Furthermore, American style is incremental throughout the negotiation, deciding different points of the deal. Once an agreement is reached they move on to the next point. Asians and Latin Americans are in general more holistic in their approach to negotiation. They tend to decide the whole deal at the end, rather than agreeing about individual issues throughout the process.

The process of reaching agreement may take different forms, not just the signing of a contract. It is useful for international managers to be familiar with four general positions related to the conclusion of the negotiation process, which according to Denfeld and Colosi (1996) include the following:

1. *Formal agreement*: this is the position when the negotiating parties reach a contractual agreement. Terms and conditions are written down in a formal contract in expectation that the parties will carry on their promises.

2. *Informal agreement*: this is the position when the parties reach an implicit agreement. It is bounded in personal trust and the oral agreement is binding. Both parties are committed to long-term relationships and share similar objectives.

3. *Agreement not to agree*: this is the position where the negotiation ends with no agreement. The negotiators find that they do not have common ground; it is

useless to continue with the process. Recognising when to leave the negotiating table on amicable terms is more important than trying to force a deal that will be unworkable. This position allows for relationship building and future cooperation.

4. *Agreement to continue*: this position is particularly important in complex negotiations, where the parties achieve a formal or informal agreement on the basic or most important issues. Then they agree to continue the negotiation process some time in the future. This position is very important in continuing to build a long-lasting relationship, understanding mutual interests and objectives and commitment to mutual cooperation.

Closing a negotiation successfully means more than reaching a narrow list of objectives. Managers involved in negotiations with other management teams, government, potential customers, suppliers, labour union leaders or other stakeholders should consider an ample range of possibilities for agreement. Their objectives should be broad to avoid 'black-and-white' solutions and they should have a clear idea of the ceiling and floor of each issue, when to concede and when to walk away. A winning negotiation does not always end in a contractual agreement. Sometimes the objectives of both parties cannot be reconciled, but if the parties depart with good understanding, leaving the door open for future possibilities or future cooperation, then this is also a successful closure to a negotiation.

Business ethics and social responsibility

Ethics, as prescribed by the business firm and in the countries where it has operations, is another factor that adds complexity and challenge to international managers. The understanding of ethical values also requires an understanding of the cultural values of the host countries in a larger context. The days are long past when a business firm could pursue its economic interests with disregard for ethical concerns. Management must be sensitive to ethical issues and social responsibility. Business behaviours are scrutinised by a number of stakeholders, among them the public, the media, interest groups and government. Internationally, it is very difficult for managers to navigate the different ethical conducts of the various countries where the organisation operates. These ethical conducts sometimes place conflicting expectations on the multinational firm. This is further complicated when international managers interface with a large number of stakeholders across countries. In this section we will examine two separate but overlapping issues, namely ethical behaviour and social responsibility.

Business ethics

Broadly defined, ethics refers to decisions, interactions and behaviours considered right or wrong at the personal level. Business ethics usually refers to the set of standards of conduct accepted as right and moral by the business firm (Boatright, 1988). The framework of what is moral or immoral comes from the country's cultural values. Therefore it is not possible to talk about ethical absolutes. Furthermore, as societies evolve, their value systems and beliefs also change over time.

International managers find that it is not easy to make decisions on issues that are not necessarily black and white because value systems vary across countries. Generally, there are two major tendencies of international firms in their approach to the issues of business ethics in host countries. The first is to follow a policy of ethical ethnocentrism. In this case business firms apply their home-country's moral and values standards regardless of the host-country's ethical values. The second tendency is to follow a policy of ethical relativism where the business firm simply adopt the local value systems of the host country (Deresky, 2000). However, public pressure at home may force multinationals toward a more ethnocentric approach, as in the case of IBM, General Motors, Coca-Cola and other American firms that had to discontinue their operations in South Africa due to the apartheid policies, before the regime was dismantled.

The increasing worldwide socio-economic interdependence has developed an acute awareness of the need for a consensus on what constitutes business ethics. Several writers believe that a consensus is emerging due to the development of global corporate culture, which is gradually lowering country boundaries through the interconnection and interdependence of security markets and communication networks. Furthermore, international organisations are studying corporate policies for ethical conduct and are in the process of developing general guidelines for multinationals. These organisations include the Organisation for Economic Cooperation and Development, the International Chamber of Commerce and the International Labour Organisation, which already have corporate ethical policies for international managers, and the UN Commission on Transnational Corporations, which also is developing a code of ethics (Getz, 1990).

All these codes seek an integration into a common body of ethical conduct as guidance for international managers. Figure 9.3 shows a few examples of these guidelines, most of which are very simple. However, their application is far more complex. For example, most developing countries emphasise the need for job creation. To comply with host-country demands, a multinational may use labour-intensive production, avoiding or delaying transfer of technology that will improve labour skills and productivity. This same multinational may find itself in violation of the international code for improving technology transfer to developing countries. Furthermore, if the host country changes its policy toward technology development, this multinational may be accused of applying labour-intensive production rather than improving labour skills through technology transfer.

Social responsibility

Social responsibility refers to decisions, interactions and behaviours at company and societal level. Specifically, it addresses the organisation's responsibilities toward society and humankind (Manakkalathil and Rudolf, 1995). A policy of corporate social responsibility reflects the duty of the organisation in pursuing its interest by conducting business in a manner that preserves society's welfare. Ultimately, the organisation is judged by its management's responsiveness to expectations placed by society.

Environmental protection
- Multinationals should respect host-country's laws, goal and priorities concerning protection of the environment.
- Multinationals should disclose likely environmental harms and minimise risks of accidents that could cause environmental damage.
- Multinationals should promote the development of environmental standards.

Political payments and involvement
- Multinationals should not pay bribes or make improper payments to public officials.
- Multinationals should avoid improper or illegal involvement or interference in the internal politics of host country.

Employment practices
- Multinationals should not contravene the manpower policies of the host country.
- Multinationals should develop non-discriminatory employment policies and promote equal job opportunities.
- Multinationals should provide favourable work conditions, limited working hours, holidays with pay and protection against unemployment.

Economic and development policies
- Multinationals should cooperate with government regarding local equity participation.
- Multinationals should not dominate the capital markets of the countries in which they operate.
- Multinationals should reinvest some profits in the countries in which they operate.

Laws and regulations
- Multinationals are subject to the laws, regulations and jurisdictions of the countries in which they operate.
- Multinationals should respect the right of every country to exercise control over its natural resources and regulate the activities of entities operating within its territory.
- Multinationals should not request the intervention of their home government in disputes with host governments.

Technology transfer
- Multinationals should develop and adopt technologies to the needs and characteristics of the countries in which they operate.
- Multinationals should conduct research and development activities in the developing countries, using local resources and personnel, to the greatest extent possible.
- Multinationals should grant licences for the use of industrial property rights on reasonable terms and conditions when they do so.

Employment practices
- Multinationals should cooperate with efforts by host government to create employment opportunities in particular localities.
- Multinationals should support representative employers organisations.
- Multinational should contribute to managerial and technical training for nationals of the countries in which they operate, and they should employ qualified nationals in managerial and professional capacities.
- Multinationals should support representative employer's organisations.
- Multinational should contribute to managerial and technical training for nationals of the countries in which they operate, and they should employ qualified nationals in managerial and professional capacities.

Figure 9.3 Some examples of the International Code of Conduct

The issues of social responsibility have been brought to the centre of attention by several tragic accidents in the past; for example, the Union Carbide gas leak in Bhopal, India, in 1984, which killed 2,500 people and injured more than 200,000 others (Bowie, 1987). This incident raised questions about the use of hazardous, sophisticated technology in developing countries. Another tragic accident that greatly affected the environment was the *Exxon Valdez* oil spill in Alaska in 1989 (McCoy, 1991).

International operations are faced with the difficult decision of how much they can be involved in the host-country life. These decisions range from assuming some degree of responsibility for the host-country economic development to taking an active stand in identifying and solving societal problems. The most sensitive issues of social responsibility still centre around poverty and lack of equal opportunity around the world, protection of the environment, consumer concerns and employees' safety and welfare. During the 1960s and 1970s, a number of laws were enacted in North America and Europe to protect workers, the environment and society at large. At the same time, management literature began to discuss models of corporate behaviour. The concept of corporate responsiveness to society's issues implies a proactive approach where the organisation initiates actions to solve potential problems.

An increasing number of multinationals operating in developing countries have taken an active role in their corporate responsiveness to social problems, particularly with regard to human rights, using their economic resources to foster change. Some examples are Phillips-Van Heusen's CEO who requires that all people employed by his company worldwide should enjoy the same constitutional rights as his American personnel, requiring all vendors, suppliers and foreign licensees to comply with the company's code of conduct. He also sets the limits for working hours, prohibits child labour, provides housing and benefits for Asian and Latin American factories and refuses to give any type of bribe, not even incidental 'tips' (Klatsky, 1994). Another example is Levi-Strauss and Co.'s Guidelines for Country Selection, which prohibits the company from using or selling products made by prisoners or forced labour. The company withdrew from China as a statement against human rights violations and disgust at unsafe working conditions. It also withdrew from Burma and Peru because of human rights violations (Beaver, 1995). Reebok, a corporate sponsor of Amnesty International's 'Human Rights Now', is very involved in pressing for reforms around the world. The company also gives annual human rights awards, recognising its employees who volunteer in local communities to help improve standards of living (Duerden, 1995). Another case is the Caux Group (Solomon, 1996), whose members are Chase Manhattan Bank, INSEAD, World Bank, 3M and Siemens among others. This group put forward two guidelines for corporate ethics. The first, dealing with human dignity, requires that all member companies must pledge their commitment to human dignity regardless of cultural differences. The second advances the Japanese idea of *kyosei*, that is, people live and work together for a common good to achieve mutual prosperity.

These examples highlight the development of a global consciousness of the call to reconcile the needs for economic development on the one hand and the needs of the people and protection of the environment on the other. They also illustrate the difficult balance for international managers to bring together universal standards and business interests of growth and efficiency.

Summary

This chapter discussed the different groups of stakeholders with which an international manager must interface. It presented a discussion of advertising and channels of distributions as a means of communication and reaching customers. Different models of buyer–supplier relationship typically used in Europe, Japan and the United States are presented as the firm's interface with its suppliers. The roles of host and home governments as stakeholders are discussed in relation to their power in facilitating or restricting a firm's operations. A broad discussion of the negotiation process is introduced as the means by which the firm reaches contractual agreements with customers, suppliers and host-government officials. Finally, the chapter closes with a discussion of business ethics and corporate social responsibility in the context of global business.

Discussion questions

1. A firm must make two major strategic decisions in its interface with customers. Explain these two decisions. What are the main factors affecting these two avenues of approaching foreign customers?

2. Explain the differences among the buyer–supplier models discussed in this chapter.

3. Why is it important for a business firm to be aware of its political environment? How may the home and host government affect the business firm's operations? Briefly explain.

4. Explain the different stages of negotiation and why knowledge about the cultural characteristics of the other negotiating party is as important as a solid negotiating plan.

5. Discuss the differences between business ethics and social responsibility and explain why global businesses are becoming proactive in their corporate policy of social responsibility.

Closing Case Study:
Tobacco industry and social responsibility at odds

A declining market

In the United States, due to antismoking campaigns and government regulations restricting smoking in public places and advertising, the tobacco industry has seen a decline in its customers of around 1 to 2 per cent per year over the last decade. In Europe, the industry will also be affected by the proposal of the European Commission, dated 30 May 2001, banning tobacco advertising in print media, radio and the internet and of tobacco companies sponsoring events or activities involving or taking place across member states. This proposal is an extension of the 1989 EC directive banning television advertising and sponsorship. With these developments taking place in the industrialised countries, the American and English tobacco companies are scrambling to replace these markets with markets in developing countries.

A thriving market

The tobacco industry has been aggressively pursuing markets in Africa, Asia and Latin America. In Asia, the largest English tobacco company is finalising a joint venture with the Chinese government to produce cigarettes in China. This unprecedented agreement will provide the company with a vast market of an estimated 350 million smokers, which translates into 1.7 trillion cigarettes per year, about one-third of world consumption. The tobacco industry in China is very profitable for the Chinese State Tobacco Monopoly Administration. China has import tariffs in excess of 218 per cent on the few brands it allows to be imported. Most of the cigarettes in China are government brands. The Chinese argument for this joint venture is twofold: first, the government wants to upgrade its domestic cigarettes; second it wants to counter the black market for smuggled and counterfeit foreign cigarettes.

Advertising to new customers

In Africa, Asia and Latin America, the tobacco industry is pursuing very aggressive advertising and promotion campaigns to attract new customers with no regard for the customer's age. These campaigns use a number of different methods from hosting seminars for journalists in luxury resorts to create a positive public relations image to distributing free cigarettes to teenagers. Through the usage of television, radio and print media, advertising in these continents has concentrated on creating an image of luxury and sophistication. In some African countries for example, the tobacco industry is the fourth or fifth major advertiser. In Taiwan, as a promotional campaign, free cigarettes are dispensed at video arcades for teenagers. In Malaysia a popular comicbook for children carries cigarette ads. In Malaysia, as well as other countries including eastern Europe, one of the American tobacco companies gives free cigarettes to teenagers attending rock concerts or discos.

Government intervention

Government intervention in developing countries varies from supportive to neutral to taking some stronger stance against tobacco consumption. For example, the government taking the most active position against cigarette smoking is Egypt, which in April 2001 banned tobacco television advertising under the campaign 'Together to protect the young against narcotics'.

For those countries where the tobacco industry contributes to their GNP, such as China, Brazil, India, Malaysia, Malawi, Zimbabwe and Japan, the governments are generally supportive. In the case of Malawi, half its labour force is directly employed by the tobacco industry. Zimbabwe obtains about 10 per cent of its GNP from the tobacco industry, which employs one in five people. As an exporter of tobacco leaves, this country ranks third after Brazil and the United States.

The Japanese government is neutral in its position towards smoking, arguing that decisions must be made by consensus. In Japan concensus normally means protecting the industry. For example, in 2001 the Health and Welfare Ministry proposed a programme to halve the adult smoking rate by 2010. However, it had to withdraw because of strong opposition by the tobacco retailers. Japan has no laws to regulate smoke-free areas and the warning on packets only states in small print that cigarettes 'may damage your health'. Even after the government imposed a $4,000 fine for selling cigarettes to minors, no one has been prosecuted. As a footnote, in the fiscal year ending in March 2000, the Finance Ministry realised in excess of $400 million from profits derived from the tobacco industry.

Troublesome ethical issues

The World Health Organisation (WHO) has released a report, dated 30 May 2001, about the danger of aggressively marketing and promoting cigarettes to women. The organisation estimates that 12 per cent of the worldwide female population already smokes, contrasted with 48 per cent of the male population. However WHO estimates that by the year 2025, the number of women smokers will increase to 20 per cent worldwide, mostly in the developing countries. This is particularly troublesome in those countries where women are struggling to obtain basic rights and the tobacco industry emphasises in its advertising the relationships between smoking and emancipation of women.

Cigarette smoking doesn't come cheap. In developing countries the money spent on cigarettes is taken away from food and other essentials. Frequently in these countries, the people are too poor to buy the whole pack, so they buy individual cigarettes. Even in this way, the smoker may be spending close to 20 per cent of his or her income.

In addition there has been increase of lung cancer. In Japan where 53 per cent of the men and 13 per cent of women smoke, the incidence of lung cancer overtook stomach cancer in 1993. By 1998, lung cancer became the leading cause of death. In Shanghai, according to WHO statistics, death by lung cancer has doubled in the last ten years. In Third World countries it is very difficult to keep statistical data and in most cases death is not certified by a doctor. In addition, life expectancy is only about 40 years, so the long-term effects of tobacco are hard to measure.

Corporate social responsibility reflects the duty of the organisation in pursuing its interests by conducting business in a manner that preserves society's welfare. Ultimately, the organisation is judged by its management's responsiveness to expectations placed by society. Internationally, the firm's financial welfare must be aligned with its ethical values; these in turn, are balanced with the values, customs, financial needs and regulations of the host countries.

Sources: *Financial Times, The New York Times, Financial Post, Business Week, The Economist, BBC Monitoring Services*

Closing case study questions

1. What strategies should the tobacco industry follow in facing a shrinking market?

2. What alternative recommendations can you propose for developing countries to address their financial needs and the health of their population?

3. What do you recommend for reconciling the duty of the organisation to pursue its financial interest and its social responsibility towards the welfare of the markets where the organisation has operations?

Annotated further reading

http://www.fita.org
   This is a site for international trade that has more than 3,000 links to international trade/import-export web sites, which are annotated and indexed. The site allows one to browse by category or to search by key words. Some of the topics included are the following: entering international markets; international finance; transportation and logistics; codes, standards and conversions; government and multilateral organisations; trade and economic statistics; regional resources and multilateral trading areas; international market research; business publications.

http://globaledge.msu.edu
   This site has been developed and/or compiled by MSU-CIBER. The site provides information about news and periodicals (global or regional), journals and publications, country-specific information, culture and language, statistical data resources, government resources, organisations and associations, banking and finance, trade portals, trade leads, company directories. It is very helpful for international business research.

http://www.webofculture.com
   Web of culture is another valuable site for international business research. The content includes books, currencies, definitions, links to other sites, ISO codes, measurements, shippers, time zones, articles, consulates and embassies, dictionaries, languages and other search engines.

http://www.worldskip.com
This is another very valuable site for international business research. It contains a large amount of information by specific country. The country's page provides a currency converter, language translator and the local time in the country. Among the headings for each country are the following: news, information and radio; business, economy and government; travel, people and culture; marketplace. All these headings provide links to other sites or information in the form of well-written summaries.

References

Al-Makaty, S., Van Tubergern, G., Whithlow, S. and Boyd, D. (1996) 'Attitudes toward advertising in Islam', *Journal of Advertising Research* 36(3): 16–26.

Beaver, W. (1995) 'Levi's is leaving China', *Business Horizons* March–April: 35–40.

Boatright, J. (1988) 'Ethics and the role of the manager', *Journal of Business Ethics* 7: 303–12.

Bowie, N. (1987) 'The moral obligations of multinational corporations', in G. Luper-Fay (ed.) *Problems of International Justice*. New York: Westview Press.

Carter, J. and Narasimhan, R. (1996) 'A comparison of North American and European future purchasing trends', *International Journal of Purchasing and Material Management* 32(2): 12–22.

Cateora, P. and Graham, J. (1999) *International Marketing*, 10th edn. New York: Irwin/McGraw-Hill.

Denfeld, J. and Colosi, T. (1996) 'Mastering management: the subtle art of negotiation', *Financial Times*, 5 January: 5.

Deresky, H. (2000) *International Management: Managing Across Borders and Cultures*. New Jersey: Prentice Hall.

Duerden, J. (1995) ' "Walking the walk" on global ethics', *Directors & Boards* 19(3): 42–5.

Getz, K. (1990) 'International codes of conduct: an analysis of ethical reasoning', *Journal of Business Ethics* 9: 567–77.

Graham, J. (1985) 'The influence of culture on the process of business negotiations. An exploratory study', *Journal of International Business Studies* 16(1): 81–96.

Ha, L. (1996) 'Concerns about advertising practices in a developing country: an examination of China's new advertising regulations', *International Journal of Advertising* 15(2): 91–102.

Kalwani, M. and Narayandas, N. (1995) 'Long-term manufacturer–supplier relationships: do they pay off for supplier firms?', *Journal of Marketing* 59: 1–16.

Keegan, W. and Green, M. (2000) *Global Marketing*, 2nd edn. New Jersey: Prentice Hall.

Klatsky, B. (1994) 'Work ethics', *Chief Executive* June: 28–31.

Kotabe, M. and Helsen, K. (1998) *Global Marketing Management*. New York: Wiley.

Lummus, R., Vokurka, R. and Alber, K. (1998) 'Strategic supply chain planning', *Production and Inventory Management Journal* third quarter: 49–58.

Manakkalathil, J. and Rudolf, E. (1995) 'Corporate social responsibility in a globalizing market', *SAM Advanced Management Journal* 60(1): 29–32, 47.

Martin, X., Mitchell, W. and Swaminathan, A. (1994) 'Recreating and extending Japanese automobile buyer–supplier links in North America', *Strategic Management Journal* 16: 589–619.

McCoy, C. (1991) 'Exxon Corp.'s settlement gets court approval', *Wall Street Journal* 9 October: A3, A10.

Ricks, D. (1994) *Blunders in International Business*. Oxford: Blackwell.

Sheth, J. and Parvatiyar, A. (2000) *Handbook of Relationship Marketing*. Thousand Oaks: Sage.

Solomon, C. (1996) 'Put your ethics to global test', *Personnel Journal* 75(1): 66–74.

CHAPTER 10

Communication across language boundaries

Alan Feely

Learning objectives

When you finish reading this chapter you should:

■ understand why language is an important issue for multinational businesses

■ comprehend what the language barrier is and the impact it can have on business relationships

■ gain an insight into the ways that language is likely to influence the strategy, structure and systems of international business

■ be able to evaluate the range of options available to multinational businesses to manage language more professionally

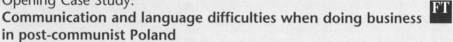

Opening Case Study:
Communication and language difficulties when doing business
in post-communist Poland

Poland's political transformation has left its stamp on the country's business life. With economic liberalisation has come growth, especially in financial services, telecoms and insurance.

In the big cities, at least, Poland has a decent transport network with good roads and up-to-date telecoms. It can also furnish essential specialists such as international lawyers, chartered accountants and secretaries with knowledge of foreign languages. In rural Poland, telecommunications are improving fast and facilities are generally available. But if you find yourself doing business outside Warsaw, Poznan or Krakow, you might need an interpreter – and country roads often leave a lot to be desired. Infrastructure can be rebuilt in a decade. Established behaviour and thought patterns are harder to change. The market economy cannot be embraced overnight – less still become second nature. Thus you will still see in Poland the remains of the old way of thinking.

In negotiations, the important question is who you are dealing with. Some younger managers have been educated in western Europe or the United States. Some have worked in subsidiaries of western companies and can communicate and negotiate in a western European or US style. It is a different matter if you are negotiating with Polish business partners who are older and have spent most of their working life within the socialist system. Such a negotiating partner will probably be well educated and possess great technical expertise. Yet, you may face difficulties in dealing with commercial and business subjects, such as accounting standards. You should spend time explaining complex commercial issues clearly, so your partner understands you.

When negotiating with Polish business partners you will usually communicate in German or English. Although their grasp of a foreign language might seem quite advanced, it is easy to overestimate someone's fluency. Even if your business partner speaks German, this does not necessarily mean he or she will understand complex issues, especially commercial implications, or be able to express problems and interests properly. This applies perhaps even more to English. As a rule, you should assume the average Polish manager will have insufficient command of the language to conduct a negotiation satisfactorily. If in doubt, you should avoid conducting the negotiations in the foreign language and seek the help of an interpreter. Because the interpreter might come to play an important role in the negotiations, it is worth finding a reputable one.

Source: 'Cultural barriers: Sergey Frank analyses the communication and language difficulties when doing business in post-communist Poland', 28 Sep. 2000 in *Financial Times* CD-ROM 2000

Introduction

Communication is essential to effective management. It underpins total quality strategies, it is the life-blood of human resource management and the vehicle for diffusing corporate culture. Yet communication relies upon a shared language, a prerequisite that in many international business situations does not exist – and that's when the problems start.

It is also important to note that the knowledge of a partner's language or use of a competent interpreter is not enough to create shared understanding between people from different cultural backgrounds. Language represents and expresses the culture, the value system behind it. Not knowing this underlying culture can cause problems. As Jankowicz (1994) points out, some people tend to underestimate the difficulties involved in the creation of shared understanding and scarcely recognise the issue of cultural differences. Ask any international manager and they will have their own cache of horror stories:

- The American CEO who wondered why his humorous and motivational speech, which had worked so well in New York, bombed when he was forced to work through an interpreter in South America.

- The French marketing director who had invented a really catchy name for his new chocolate bar only to find the word translates as 'rabbit droppings' in Portuguese.

- The Italian logistics manager who ended up inundated with material because his German supplier didn't understand that the delivery schedules written in Italian were intended to supersede earlier demand, not add to it.

- The strike caused because the Japanese management team started talking in Japanese at a delicate point in the discussion with Spanish union representatives.

- The marvellous new computer system, sitting untouched in the Chinese factory because it was only available with an English language user interface.

The book *Blunders in International Business* (Ricks, 1999) is a rich source of such anecdotes.

This chapter examines the theoretical background to problems such as these and goes on to consider the probable implications for the way that multinational business is conducted. Finally, it concludes with a review of the tools available to international businesses to manage language more effectively. However, before launching into that, it is worth summarising some general issues that help to paint the broad canvas of language in international business.

World languages

According to the *Language Industries Atlas* (Hearn and Button 1994) approximately 5,000 languages are spoken throughout the world, of which the 100 most widely employed languages are spoken by 95 per cent of the world's inhabitants. You might expect that a typical international business will at some time or another have to confront those 100 most popular languages and this seems to be corroborated by some evidence taken from two different industries. Microsoft has adopted a long-term strategy of offering their software in around 80 different languages while international pharmaceutical companies have been known to produce their labels translated in up to 150 different languages.

However, these two examples are probably atypical and most international companies will simplify the problem by working with an effective range of perhaps 15 or fewer languages. Our closing case study company Magneti Marelli, for example, managed a network of subsidiaries spanning 11 different national languages, but in South Africa where there were employees speaking a variety of African dialects it was able to adopt English as a common language of management.

Nevertheless, even this restricted language range accounts for well over half the world's population and the vast bulk of its wealth and international trade. So in planning for global management, multinational corporations cannot afford to ignore these core international languages and for anyone thinking that 5,000 languages might be unmanageable, but 15 doesn't sound too bad, it is worth remembering that 15 languages within a single company means potentially over 100 different language interfaces: English–French, English–Italian, Italian–French, etc. It is an issue to be taken seriously and managed accordingly.

The internationality of languages

In 1997 the English Company constructed a multi-dimension database called the Engco Model in order to measure the internationality of languages (Graddol, 1997). Taking into account language populations, economic factors and demographic trends, the model emerged with a composite measure termed the Global Influence Index for each language. The 12 most important ones are listed in Table 10.1. The scale is arguably not ideal for business use. For many purposes such as e-commerce applications, European languages such as Swedish and Italian would currently be far more influential than Bengali, but nevertheless the Engco Model is certainly a welcome advance in formalising and evaluating the relative importance of different languages

Languages in multinational business

From Table 10.1 you might be forgiven for thinking that English is so dominant that perhaps those fortunate individuals who inherited it as their mother tongue need never bother to learn anything else. It is true that some books already talk of English as being firmly established as the lingua franca of international business (Freudenstein *et al.*, 1981). However, this is far from the truth and the attitude that English alone will suffice is more of a myth than reality. Barnevik, the one-time CEO of ABB and one of the pioneers of the use of English as a corporate language, defined foreign language communication as his number one management problem (Barnevik and Taylor, 1991).

Looking to the future, the idea of English as a panacea to all communications problems appears even more flawed. First, the distribution of English as a second language is patchy: strong in Scandinavia, Holland, India and increasingly in Germany, but much scarcer in Mediterranean countries, South America and some parts of Central and East Asia. In some Italian companies, for example, less than

Table 10.1   Global Influence Index for languages

1. English	100
2. German	42
3. French	33
4. Japanese	32
5. Spanish	31
6. Chinese	22
7. Arabic	8
8. Portuguese	5
9. Malay	4
10. Russian	3
11. Hindi/Urdu	0.4
12. Bengali	0.09

15 per cent of managers might be able to communicate in English because until recently French and German were the dominant scholastic second languages in Italy.

Second, the dominance of English as a second language evidenced throughout the second half of the twentieth century was due in large part to technology. TV, telecommunications and computing depended on the English language and other people learned English to be able to benefit. However, those technologies have now moved on and low-cost dubbing, translation and interpretation make it more likely that people will be able to read books, watch films and surf the internet in their own language. The motivation to learn English will dry up and it is predicted that the number of people learning English as a second language will peak within the next ten years and then start to fall.

Third, the number of active languages is shrinking rapidly, with perhaps as many of 90 per cent of the world's languages dying over the next 50 years. However, this rationalisation will not benefit English, but instead will increase the global influence of regional languages, so much so that the dominant position of English will be progressively challenged by languages such as Chinese, Hindi, Arabic and Spanish – languages in which most multinational businesses have a dearth of skills.

Finally, a drift towards business nationalism is also accompanying this demographic trend. Companies and individuals in Asia, South America and the Middle East who hitherto have accepted the need to work in English have started to rebel. In particular buyers in these regions are increasingly demanding of would-be suppliers that if you want to sell to us then speak our language. Whilst this drift is most evident in sales negotiations, it can only be a matter of time before this pressure percolates down to functions such as engineering, logistics and finance, all of which need to interact on a regular basis with their international customers.

The dearth of business research on language

For the reasons given above it is essential that international businesses pay increasing attention to the impact of language on the way they operate. Yet despite this, researchers of international business and management have largely ignored the problem. Indeed the subject of management across the language barrier has been variously described as 'neglected' (Reeves and Wright, 1996), 'orphaned' (Verrept, 2000) and 'forgotten' (Marschan-Piekkari *et al.*, 1997). Table 10.2 illustrates the scale of the neglect.

Using a simple search procedure demonstrated that general fields such as communications, management, organisation and technology are well represented by contemporary research with tens of thousands of journal articles listed in recent years. However, inserting the word 'language' as a secondary search key reduced the number of articles by more than 99 per cent. When these few were individually filtered to exclude articles related to medicine, public services and computer programming languages, the original body of articles was reduced to a mere handful.

It is true that specialised language topics such as training and machine translation have been thoroughly studied and there are several journals specifically

Table 10.2 Searches conducted using the web of science database

Single search key	No. articles	No. articles after adding language as second key	No. articles after filtering non-business topics	% of articles examining language
Multinational	2,862	17	2	0.07
Globalisation	2,237	18	4	0.18
Management	100,606	1,765	31	0.03
Organisation	95,720	1,137	15	0.02
Technology	2,237	18	2	0.09
Communications	16,533	264	27	0.16
TOTAL	297,431	4,114	81	0.03

devoted to these two topics. Unfortunately even here the research rarely touches on the business impact. 'Does language training improve business performance?' 'Is machine translation more advantageous to English-speaking companies or to other-language multinationals?' The research literature offers no answers to these questions, or to numerous other questions that international business poses.

Given the rapid development of globalisation and the critical role of communication in modern management, it is hard to explain why the field of language impact has been so neglected. Perhaps the dominance of the Hofstedian dimensions of culture (Hofstede, 1991) has discouraged researchers from considering other, even more obvious, cultural issues. Perhaps the absence of operationalised language constructs has deterred would-be researchers from taking the first steps. Or perhaps the field has been left to the tender mercies of linguists who in general are more interested in syntax and semantics than in structure and strategy. But one thing is for sure. The issue of language in multinational business does matter and future research must attempt to understand its mechanisms and consequences. The next section explains the destructive patterns created whenever language becomes a problem.

Why language is a problem

We've all heard the phrase 'the language barrier' bandied around and we've probably used it ourselves from time to time, but have you ever stopped to analyse what it means? Clearly in it simplest and most predictable form you could say that language is a problem because it impairs communication and thus makes it difficult for individuals, groups and companies to achieve their goals. However, delving beyond that simple viewpoint, socio-linguistics has identified a series of effects that taken together comprise what we simplistically term the 'language barrier'. Figure 10.1 illustrates how these effects work together.

The density of the language barrier depends upon the level of language skills of the participants in the encounter. At its base where language skills of the second language users are very low, then communication is practically impossible and the

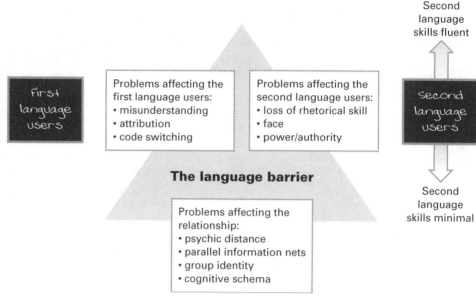

Figure 10.1 Effects of the 'language barrier'

barrier is so dense as to be impenetrable. At its summit where the second language users have native speaker capabilities, then the barrier is narrow and easily surmounted. However, neither extreme is commonplace in international business; nor is business communication generally interpersonal, more typically being an encounter between language groups. So in this explanation I've concentrated on inter-group encounters where there is a capability to communicate but imperfectly.

Figure 10.1 shows that the barrier comprises ten separate phenomena subgrouped into those that affect the relationship, those that affect the second language users and those that affect the first language users. In the paragraphs below these phenomena are briefly described.

Problems for the relationship: psychic distance

As the term suggests, psychic distance is a measure of the psychological separation of two parties from different cultures. It has been defined as 'factors preventing firms from learning about and understanding a foreign environment' (Nordstrom and Vahlne, 1992). Clearly little has such a profound effect on understanding as language. The way that psychic distance was calculated included two language factors (out of a total of five). Initially all psychic distances were calculated using Sweden as a base and predictably countries such as Norway that were educationally, economically and linguistically similar would have a low distance rating, and countries that were distinctly dissimilar in these respects such as Japan had a much higher distance rating. However, the system of measure is less important to us here than the underlying ideas that are well explained by an example adapted from the work of Hallen and Wiedersheim-Paul (1999), as shown in Figure 10.2.

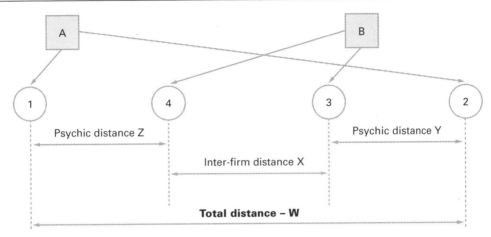

Figure 10.2 An example of measuring psychic distance between two parties

The total distance W between parties A and B is a spatial representation of the gap of understanding and knowledge that separates them. In order to achieve agreement and collaboration it is necessary to bridge this gap through communication and consensus seeking. In an intercultural relationship, the gap is made up of several components:

- the *inter-firm distance* (X) which would exist between any two parties even if they shared the same cultural provenance
- the *psychic distance* (Y) due to the failings of A's cultural and linguistic perception of B's position
- the *psychic distance* (Z) due to the failings of B's cultural and linguistic perception of A's position.

It is not difficult to appreciate that in cases where cultures are widely differing and languages may not even share a common alphabet, then the sum of Y+Z could easily exceed the inter-firm distance X. So in this circumstance the total psychic distance will make it almost impossible for one party to understand the position of the other or for the two parties to reach a mutual accommodation.

Given that the distance concept is all about cultural separation and that 'the business of international business is culture' (Hofstede, 1999), it should come as no surprise that psychic/cultural distance has been associated with very many aspects of international business.

Problems for the relationship: parallel information networks

Grapevine communications, more formally referred to as 'parallel information networks' (Marschan-Piekkari *et al.*, 1997), exist in every business and are sometimes considered advantageous, but in cross-lingual relationships their impact can be corrosive. Consider the example of an Anglo-French collaboration, as illustrated in Figure 10.3.

The UK finance manager is fluent in French, the French marketing manager is equally fluent in English, but neither of the two managing directors is fluent in

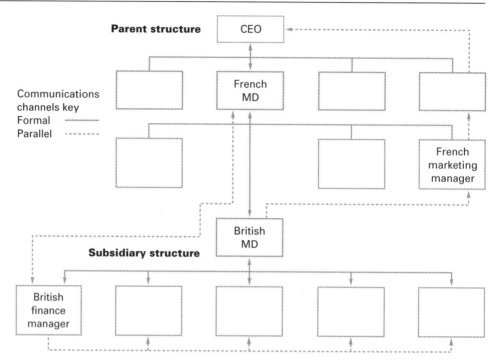

Figure 10.3 Parallel information networks

the other's language. Inevitably the communications will polarise with the French managers channelling their ideas, information and requests through the finance function in the UK and the UK managers likewise preferring to communicate through the French marketing manager. Because of their privileged positions in the information stream, the two managers develop as information gatekeepers, filtering, delaying and distorting the communications flow to their own advantage, whilst the others, particularly the two managing directors, feel that the chain of command has been undermined. Again the consequential uncertainty, suspicion, mistrust and friction serve to impose limitations on the way the relationship can develop.

Problems for the relationship: group interactions

In many international situations, meetings are not interpersonal but inter-group with all which that implies for group identity and loyalty. Socio-linguists believe that in a cross-lingual meeting of groups, language becomes the dominant factor in defining the group boundaries and composition (Gallois *et al.*, 1988). For example, a young, female French-speaking accountant is more likely to identify with other French speakers, regardless of age, gender or profession, than with a young, female English-speaking accountant. Once the group boundaries have been defined, social identity theory (Tajfel, 1982) predicts that the individual participants will take on and defend the values, interests and ideologies of that group and will 'attribute' negative intentions to the words and acts of out-group members, leading to a cooling of the relationship and a divergence of outlook between the two language groups.

There will be additional problems for the second language users for whom the degree of uncertainty will be inversely correlated with language competence and where such uncertainty will increase the tendency to overestimate the importance of group membership on behaviour (Gudykunst and Ting-Toomey, 1988).

Problems for the relationship: schema distortion

In the introduction to *Intercultural Communication* (Scollon and Scollon, 1995) the authors stress that 'language is ambiguous', that 'this ambiguity forces us to draw inferences', that 'such inferences are drawn very quickly' and that 'once drawn they rapidly mutate from tentative interpretations to fixed understanding'. A more formal statement of these ideas is called schema theory (Taylor and Crocker, 1981) in which the functionality of a schema is divided into seven sub-functions, as shown in Figure 10.4.

The first three of these functions are concerned with the processing of incoming data and it can be seen that the schema manipulates (filtering, interpreting and padding out) incoming information so that it conforms to the preconceptions

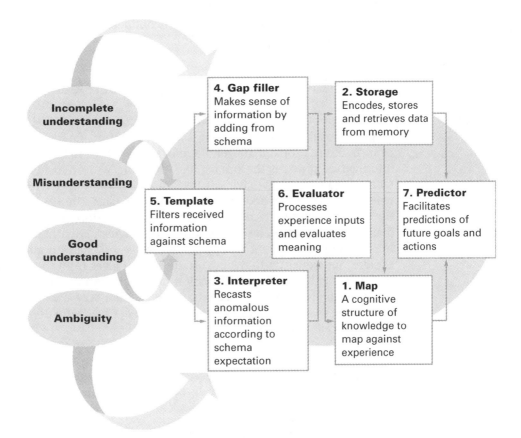

Figure 10.4 Division of functionality represented schematically

of the recipient. In the case of an inter-lingual encounter where the second language users are less than fully fluent, the risk of ambiguity, misunderstanding and imperfect comprehension are very high, leading to a polarisation of the cognitive schema of the two parties.

It is these schema which will be employed in group decision making, acting as a map to simplify complex decision criteria (Schwenk, 1988) and providing the repository of knowledge and experience upon which the key actors base their judgements (Dubin, 1978). Quite clearly therefore, where there has been cognitive polarisation, decisions taken by one group may be incomprehensible and unacceptable to the other and vice versa.

Problems for the second language user: failure of rhetorical skills

The most obvious and debilitating problem for a second language user is the loss of what are known as rhetorical skills. Certainly a competent second language user may be capable of clear communication, but robbed of the interpersonal skills of humour, symbolism, sensitivity, negotiation, persuasion and even coercion, can they really manage? The general view of authorities on power and leadership is that such skills are essential traits of effective managers and that denied them those managers will lose both self-confidence and the respect and liking of the people they manage (Allen, 1979).

Problems for the second language user: face

The concept of 'face' is much used when discussing Japanese culture, but in fact it applies to all nationalities (Ting-Toomey, 1988). In simple terms, nobody, least of all an international manager of senior status, wants to be considered stupid, ill-informed or slow on the uptake and therefore will often maintain a knowing façade even when they have lost track of a discussion. In a cross-lingual meeting where a manager is working in his second language, the risk of losing track and the need to maintain face becomes an overriding priority. As a consequence such managers can find themselves signing up to agreements they've barely comprehended and committing to objectives they've not had an adequate chance to explore. Subsequently they may distance themselves from the agreements, alleging there had been no such discussion or reneging on the commitments denying that the implications had been explained. Either way about-turns of this type undermine the credibility of the second language user who develops a reputation of being fickle, unreliable and untrustworthy.

Problems for the second language user: power/authority distortion

Scotton (1983) suggests that in a meeting between parties of two different languages, the choice of language will depend upon situational factors of which one will be the international 'vitality' of the language and another will be the relative competence of each party in the language of the other. Applying this in practice to a meeting between non-English speakers and English speakers then, unless there are other quite exceptional situational factors, English will be the language employed. This introduces a distortion into the power–authority balance. Buyers, joint venture partners and parent companies who accommodate in this way find that they have relinquished some of the control over the relationship. They may retain formal authority, but the power in the relationship will be exercised by those who are working in their preferred language for whom communications fluency becomes a tool of influence (Kim, 2001). The result of such a divergence of power and authority will be affective conflict and disputes between the two parties.

Problems for the first language user: miscommunication

By comparison to those attempting to work in their second language, the first language user has an easier problem coping with the language barrier. Nevertheless their very competence in the language may in fact lead to problems (Gass and Varonis, 1991). Often the communication they receive from non-native speakers will be confused, incomplete and inexplicit and the cognitive schema of the first language speakers will act to recast, pad out and filter these incoming messages to make them congruent with their expectations and beliefs. Such are the seeds of misunderstanding and they are not limited to encounters with novice second language users. On the contrary, some researchers have suggested that the most dangerous and severe problems of misunderstanding occur with competent second language users where their fluency is interpreted by the native speakers as evidence of a consensus and shared understanding that does not exist in reality (Takahashi and Beebe, 1987).

Problems for the first language user: attribution

When dealing with a foreign language speaker in an interpersonal encounter, i.e. not a group meeting or telephone, but face to face and one to one, there is tendency on the part of a native speaker to 'attribute' (Gudykunst and Ting-Toomey, 1988). Particularly if the non-native speaker appears relatively fluent, then the first language speaker will project his own ideas, attitudes and feelings onto that person and will tend to overestimate their linguistic fluency. In short, the first language speaker thinks that the other person is culturally more akin to them than in fact they really are. This can initially accelerate the coming together process, but later will cause problems when the second language user responds in a way that is inconsistent with the mind picture that the first language user had created of how they should react. The resultant delusion and confusion due wholly to the unrealistic expectations of the first language users can generate a sense of mistrust and even dislike between the two parties.

Problems for the first language user: code switching

The last phenomenon that often bemuses and disconcerts first language users in a group context is termed code switching (Scotton and Ury, 1977). This is where the second language users, generally at key moments in a meeting, huddle together and revert to talking between themselves in their native language. It is easy to understand the need. The second language users, aware that their comprehension may be less than 100 per cent, simply want to compare notes and realign themselves before moving on to the critical discussion issues. However, to the out-members, who probably don't speak the other group's language, such a spontaneous switching of codes just when it was getting interesting, smacks of conspiracy and double-dealing. The feelings of exclusion and suspicion caused by code switching can easily boil over into hostility, unless the two teams are sensitive to one another's problems.

How does the language barrier affect international business?

From the foregoing it should be clear that language can trigger some difficult problems for international managers and it would be ideal at this juncture to describe exactly how these problems manifest themselves in the patterns of multinational management. However, the dearth of prior research makes this impossible and so instead I shall have to conjecture. Let's begin with a general model summing up what we have previously discussed (see Figure 10.5).

Communications failures caused by miscommunication and face lead to uncertainty and anxiety. Attitudes harden and personal relationships suffer as group identities polarise and motives and actions are incorrectly and negatively attributed. The risk of affective conflict intensifies as factors such as parallel information networks and power–authority distortions compound the sense of suspicion and friction. All these negative influences then become concreted in the

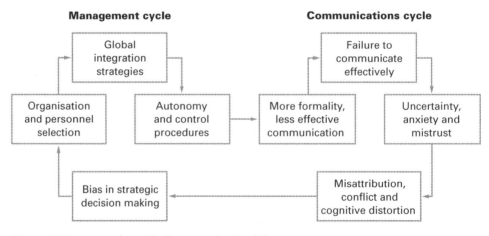

Figure 10.5 A general model of communication failure

cognitive schema of those involved. At this time we switch to the management cycle and the cognitive schema act to influence decision making and to impede the flow of accurate, objective information upon which such decisions will be based.

Typically, the first decisions to be influenced will concern future globalisation plans such as target countries, speed of globalisation programmes and methods of entry (all of which have been demonstrated to be highly susceptible to uncertainty). Following on quickly behind are likely to be organisational issues aimed at simplifying the language interfaces. To ease the problem of the language barrier, national managers may be replaced with expatriates or other personnel skilled in the parent language. Some key functions may be taken under direct parent company control, whilst others may be rationalised so that they no longer have direct contact with company headquarters.

Having reduced the uncertainty by organisational means, the head office management will be reluctant to re-expose the problems of directing subsidiaries with whom there are problems of communication. Earlier strategies aimed at maximising synergies and skills will be reviewed and watered down. Plans to integrate information systems, to enhance knowledge and technology transfer and to promote joint development of products and processes are likely to be shelved as unfeasible. The establishment of complex, multilingual supply chains is likely to be deferred as 'too risky at this time'. Even essential collaborative steps such as the development of an integrated treasury operation and the rationalisation of the combined supplier base are likely to proceed cautiously as long as language remains a barrier.

In the final step of the cycle, attention of the head office management team turns to control: 'If we can't manage our subsidiaries as we would want then at least we must ensure they are strictly controlled.' Where uncertainty is rife and communication is a problem, the typical measures adopted are centralisation of key decisions and the imposition of rigid and onerous output reporting covering not only finances but many other areas such as manufacturing, quality, purchases, stocks and service levels.

It is certainly a plausible model but is there any empirical evidence to back up these ideas? The short answer is no, there is almost no direct research that can be cited, but there is quite a lot of what might be termed circumstantial evidence and this is reviewed in the sections below.

Buyer–seller relationships

As we have seen, companies facing the prospect of globalising will sense a greater cultural distance and will be aware of greater uncertainty about markets that do not share their language. Salespersons working in their second language and thereby robbed of their rhetorical skills will appear less able, less credible and less likeable and will ultimately be less persuasive. For the same reason, buyers working in their second language will be less effective in negotiating the deals they wanted. They may get the price but the more subtle issues of tooling, prototype programmes, production transport and delivery schedules and penalty clauses will be hard to nail down without excellent communications. If these inferences are correct then there should be some evidence that:

* companies will have more success selling into countries that share their language (or where the parent country has strong skills in the language of the customer)
* companies with weak customer language skills will underperform
* buyers will see language as a major barrier to global sourcing strategies.

There is indeed evidence to support these ideas. A series of international researchers beginning with Johanson and Vahlne (1977) have identified patterns in export sales that begin close to home and only then progress to culturally and linguistically distant target countries. Specifically in the case of English-speaking companies, Marschan-Piekkari *et al.* (1997) have suggested that the priority targets for overseas sales are other English-speaking countries, even if these are geographically and logistically remote.

Other researchers (Hagen, 1999) have reversed the focus and examined the problems of companies that lack language skills. Again the conclusion is that companies who are unable to communicate effectively in the language of the customer will lose contracts and grow their export activities more slowly than those with the requisite language skills.

These inferences are also endorsed by looking at research from the perspective of the buyer. An early study of internationalisation strategy (Hakansson and Wootz, 1975) demonstrated that companies were more likely to source from countries that they felt to be psychically close. Clearly in this context language is a key component of this closeness with smooth communication a prerequisite for negotiation, persuasion and relationship building.

More recent research of North American and European companies (Peterson and Frayer, 2000) identified language skill as by far the most important factor in achieving global sourcing business capability.

The overwhelming conclusion from the above is that the language barrier presents a significant hurdle to the establishment of sound and mutually beneficial customer–supplier relationships.

Joint ventures

Bearing in mind the definition of psychic distance as factors preventing firms from learning about and understanding a foreign environment, there can be little doubt that the highest barrier to that understanding is the inability to communicate effectively in the host-country language. It is reasonable to predict therefore that the resultant uncertainty will be reflected in a cautious approach suggesting that in host countries which do not share the parent language there is a greater probability of market entry through joint venture as opposed to the higher risk option of wholly owned subsidiary.

Although these issues have not been directly researched, there is nevertheless some support for these ideas. A seminal study (Kogut and Singh, 1988) examining the choice of entry mode of overseas companies into the United States found that the United Kingdom and Canada strongly preferred acquisition to joint venture as did parent companies domiciled in linguistically strong countries such as the Netherlands, Switzerland and Germany, while France and Japan, not noted for their English language skills, adopted a preference for joint ventures.

International joint ventures have been described as contested terrain where groups compete to assert their norms and practices. Looking at this definition from the perspective of power in communication it is to be expected that joint ventures between partners, only one of whom has an international language, will end up working in that language. Subsequently the partner with that language will start to dominate the relationship. A study of an Anglo-Italian joint venture noted exactly that pattern (Salk and Shenkar, 1997). English became the default corporate language and then power, communication and decision making quickly fell under the control of the English partner.

Multinational subsidiaries

Dating back to the Uppsala Model of Internationalisation, the issue of uncertainty has been inextricably linked with the choice of where to site global subsidiaries. Numerous researchers beginning with Johanson and Wiedersheim-Paul (1975) have demonstrated that companies will initially prefer to establish subsidiaries in countries they are culturally close to. Though this research has not specifically examined language as a distinct variable, it has been suggested that companies are especially alert to language issues when selecting host countries for expansion and this is borne out by a survey carried out for the UK's Department of Trade and Industry (1995) in which one in five investors defined language as a key factor in host country selection.

The theoretical discussion on the dysfunctional effects of psychic distance and miscommunication led to an expectation that there will be mistrust and friction between parent and subsidiary managers where there is a language barrier. Moreover it is to be expected that these problems will be aggravated in situations where the subsidiary is English speaking and the parent company accommodates to manage in the language of the subsidiary. The consequential imbalance of power and authority is likely to cause resentment.

These problems have been examined and confirmed in a number of empirical studies, for example, in a Swedish–Finnish bank merger (Varra et al., 2000), in Japanese transplants in Scotland (Wright et al., 2001) and in an American subsidiary of a Japanese multinational (Wiseman and Shuter, 1994). However, probably the most thorough research was conducted by Neal (1998) who interviewed 174 foreign managers working in the UK and concluded that the majority found working with their British colleagues in English to be frustrating and irritating and compounded their sense of being outsiders. This qualitative evidence is also corroborated by evidence from the United States that post-acquisition turnover of managers is much higher where the acquiring company is foreign rather than American. Clearly there are multiple interpretations of the data but one of the most plausible is that either the new owners or the exiting managers found the working relationship unacceptable due to cultural and linguistic problems.

Companies attempting to globalise from a springboard of a minority language are likely to be disadvantaged on several fronts. Communication between the parent and its international subsidiaries will be strained, recruitment of language-skilled nationals for management positions in the subsidiary will be difficult and the problems of miscommunication will fuel suspicion and mistrust. Logically such companies will respond to the uncertainty in the relationship by employing expatriates to lubricate the information flow. This leads to an expectation that parent companies with minority languages will proportionally employ more expatriates and that conversely companies with international languages are more likely to employ expatriates in countries where language is more likely to be a barrier. Contemporary international business research endorses these expectations (Harzing, 1999). Parent countries most likely to use expatriates include Germany and Japan and those least likely include the USA and UK. The host countries most likely to attract expatriates include Mexico and Japan, while those least likely include the United Kingdom and Ireland. The United States bucks the trend by attracting a high level of expatriates too, but this could be explained by the strategic importance to most companies of the American market.

Having discussed earlier the advantage that English-speaking and linguistically skilled nations enjoy in being able to adopt global configurations, it is worth examining the same issue from the perspective of control systems. Harzing (1999) provides one of the most useful taxonomies of control. She defines four basic styles of control: centralisation, bureaucracy, socialisation and output control. Bureaucracy with its demands for global standardisation of policies, procedures, norms and systems, and socialisation with its emphasis on diffusion of corporate culture and interpersonal contact, are both communications-intensive control styles. Therefore, it is to be expected that these styles might be preferred by companies domiciled in English-speaking and linguistically skilled countries. Other countries will prefer to control through centralisation or through intensive reporting of performance measures. Harzing's findings again demonstrate that this is a plausible theory, with Swiss and Swedish corporations favouring the socialisation approach and the United States and United Kingdom favouring bureaucratic control. As might be expected, less linguistically advantaged countries favour those control styles that are not communication intensive, with Japan preferring centralisation (albeit with the aid of expatriates) and Germany output control.

Communication is the vehicle for conveying knowledge and technological know-how. Where language is a barrier it might be expected that the level of knowledge and technology transfer may be constrained. One important piece of research (Subramaniam and Venkatraman, 2000), looking at the development of new products by geographically dispersed project teams, identified the frequency of communication between project team members (in different countries) as being one of the key determinants of transnational product development capability. Another study (Gupta and Govindarajan, 2000) uses the phrase 'absorptive capacity' to describe the ability of a subsidiary of a multinational company to assimilate and apply knowledge from a parent company and goes on to demonstrate a correlation between absorptive capacity and levels of knowledge transfer. However, whilst the authors acknowledge in the text the importance of commonality of language, they do not specifically test language difference as a variable in their research. However, a third study (Davidson and McFetridge, 1985) examining technology transfers of leading American companies found that similarity of language between countries is positively associated with technology transfer.

In concluding this section, it is important to stress that these examples fall a long way short of being hard evidence. In almost all cases the research cited was not specifically looking at language as a variable and so it would be quite wrong to draw any firm conclusions. However, it does amount to a prima facie case that language has a significant influence on multinational management and the information has been presented in the hope that it will act as launch pad for a new programme of research.

Options for managing language problems

As with any other business difficulty, the key to resolving the language problem is first to understand it. To achieve this researchers have developed a methodology called linguistic auditing (Reeves and Wright, 1996). The audit system is designed to enable international companies to benchmark their foreign language communication capability and to identify areas of strength and weakness. It goes on to assess the company's language training and recruitment needs and evaluates the efficacy of these programmes. Finally it provides the means to match the organisation's foreign language capability against its strategic needs. The linguistic audit is a process structured into seven stages as illustrated in Figure 10.6.

- *Stage 1* initiates the project, establishing terms of reference, defining objectives and deliverables, agreeing resource requirements, budgets and timescales and sensitising management to the audit process and its expectations of them and their staff.

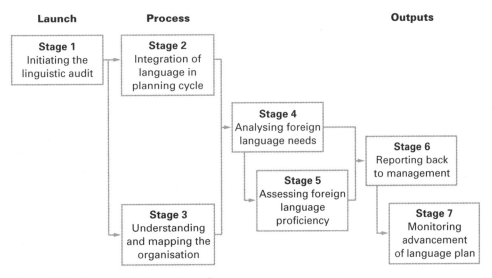

Figure 10.6 Stages of the linguistic audit

- *Stage 2* examines the language impact and language skill requirements of planned strategies, focusing on the threats and weaknesses components of the widely employed SWOT analyses.

- *Stage 3* commences with the production of process roadmaps, then defines the communication routes and concludes with top level mapping of the language interfaces.

- *Stage 4* looks at language requirements from a functional perspective and defines job-related language standards for each key post-holder.

- *Stage 5* uses observation and language proficiency testing, to assess the current post-holder's language skills against their job standards.

- *Stage 6* presents back to management the 'language resource inventory' accompanied by a prioritised and time-phased language plan.

- *Stage 7* monitors advancement against the language plan with periodic retesting and re-alignment with the evolving company strategies.

Having completed the audit, the company will be fully informed about the nature and scale of its language problems, but what are the solutions they can consider?

External language resources

An obvious response to the language barrier is to employ external resources such as translators and interpreters, and certainly there are many excellent companies specialised in these fields. However, such a response is by no means an end to the language barrier. For a start, these services can be very expensive, with a top simultaneous translator commanding daily rates as high as a partner in an international consulting company.

Also, any good translator or interpreter will insist that to be fully effective he or she must understand the context of the subject matter. This is not always possible. In some cases it is prohibited by the complexity/specialisation of the topic, sometimes by lack of preparation time, but most often the obstacle is the reluctance of the parties to explain the wider context to an 'outsider'.

Another problem is that unless there has been considerable pre-planning between the interpreter and his or her clients, it is likely that there will be ambiguity and cultural overtones in the source messages the interpreter has to work with. He or she will of course endeavour to provide a hi-fidelity translation but in this circumstance the interpreter has to use initiative and guesswork. This clearly injects a potential source of misunderstanding into the proceedings.

Finally, while a good interpreter will attempt to convey not only the meaning but also the spirit of any communication, there can be no doubt that there is a loss of rhetorical power when communications go through a third party. So in situations requiring negotiation, persuasion, humour, etc. the use of an interpreter is a poor substitute for direct communication. In view of these problems many companies seek to supplement the role of external language bureaus with specialist in-house language resources.

Training

The immediate and understandable reaction to any skills shortage in a business is to consider personnel development and certainly the language training industry is well developed and offers programmes at almost every level and in any language. However, without doubting the value of language training, no company should be deluded into believing this to be a painless or short-term remedy.

Take the Volkswagen group for example. They have developed a language strategy over many years and in many respects can be regarded as a model of how to manage language professionally. Nevertheless, the evidence from Volkswagen demonstrates that language training is a strategic rather than tactical solution. In their system, to progress from 'basics' to 'communications competence' in a language requires the completion of 6 language stages, each one demanding approximately 90 hours of classroom tuition, supported by many more hours of self-study, spread over a 6 to 9 month period. The completion of each stage is marked by a post-training achievement test, which is a prerequisite for continued training. So even this professionally managed programme expects a minimum of three years of fairly intensive study to produce an accountant, engineer, buyer or salesperson capable of working effectively in a foreign language.

Clearly companies intending to pursue this route need to do so with realistic expectations and with the intention of sustaining the programme over many years. Except in terms of 'brush-up' courses for people who were previously fluent in a foreign language, training cannot be considered a quick fix and hence other methods will have to be considered.

Corporate languages

An alternative to a customised training programme is to adopt a single corporate language. All recruitment and personnel development could then be focused upon achievement of required standards in that one chosen language. A number of major multinational companies have adopted this strategy including Siemens, Electrolux, Daimler-Chrysler and Olivetti. A corporate language can be considered to have a number of important benefits:

- facilitation of formal reporting
- ease of access and maintenance of technical literature, policy and procedure documents and though not stated, implicitly information systems
- facilitation of informal communications between operating units and within cross-national teams
- fostering a sense of belonging as an element in diffusing a corporate culture
- and of course it does focus the management of language problems.

However, in no sense is a corporate language solution without problems. Marschan-Piekkari *et al.* (1997) highlight a number of drawbacks:

1. It is a long-term strategy. One study of a major Finnish company reported that seven years after the designation of English as the corporate language, the minutes of board meetings were still taken in the parent language.

2. It is sometimes effectively impossible to adopt a single language for all

circumstances. Nestlé, for example, faced by a polarised split of personnel designated both English and French as the company's official languages.

3. A corporate language will often incur resistance if there is a large body of corporate personnel lacking competence in the chosen language. For example, Kone, the Finnish elevator company, adopted English as the corporate language, despite the fact that almost two-thirds of its employees were non-speakers of the language.

4. Although a corporate language may well enhance intra-company communications, it does nothing to ease the language barrier with external bodies such as customers, suppliers, international agencies and governments. So for these other solutions must be examined.

Language nodes

In the absence of sufficient language capability and without the time or finances to adopt a training or corporate language approach, companies become heavily dependent upon their scarce linguistically skilled personnel. These key personnel become informal 'language nodes', establishing themselves as the default communications channel between the company and the external world. Whilst it is understandable that companies leverage their scarce skills in this way, research, notably by Marschan-Piekkari *et al.*, has indicated that the approach has numerous drawbacks:

- It places an onerous burden on those acting as language nodes, impairing their ability to perform their formal organisational duties.

- It introduces an increased risk of miscommunication, as the language node personnel might be inexpert in the field of work that is the subject of the communication.

- It invests in those individuals the power to act as communication gatekeepers. This inevitably brings with it the risk that this power will be used in counter-productive ways filtering, distorting or even blocking transmission, thereby impeding rather than facilitating the flow of information from the parent company.

- Within a parent subsidiary or joint venture relationship the parallel information networks based on these nodes undermine the formal chain of reporting, weakening the positions of the senior managers who are being bypassed and hence creating potential for conflict.

So whilst it is important to leverage skills within an organisation, it is of paramount importance that language skilled personnel are not allowed to undermine the formal organisation.

Selective recruitment

As noted in the case of Nestlé, the easiest and cheapest way to approach the language problem is to hire people already possessing the required skills (Lester, 1994). However, this is clearly not a painless solution, implying as it does the redeployment and perhaps redundancy of existing post-holders lacking those skills. Moreover, there is considerable evidence to show that the right level and mix of language skills is not available in the marketplace.

So the recruitment approach to bridging the language barrier must be used very selectively and is probably advantageous only in three distinct situations: to fill critical areas of language exposure; to create a language node (see above); and to develop as expatriate managers.

Expatriate management

Continuing that theme, one immediate solution to any multinational company facing a language barrier with its subsidiaries is to assign expatriates to work within each subsidiary and to act as the 'language node' linking back to corporate headquarters. Every major global company employs expatriates, but there is considerable evidence to suggest that companies with parent operations domiciled in countries with minority languages will rely more heavily on them. As an example, the two key components of the Japanese model of globalisation have been summarised by Yoshihara (1999) as management by Japanese and management in the Japanese language.

Yoshihara's research of leading Japanese multinationals indicates that the vast majority of their subsidiaries (78 per cent) are managed by Japanese executives and more than half employ Japanese expatriates at departmental manager level. One clear explanation for this is the necessity of Japanese headquarters to continue working in the Japanese language as evidenced by an analysis of telephone and fax traffic between the Japanese headquarters and their US subsidiaries. Nearly 90 per cent of all telephone calls were either partly or wholly conducted in the Japanese language and 83 per cent of fax traffic was also drafted in Japanese. Clearly in Yoshihara's example the use of expatriates has eased the problem of the language barrier between the parent and subsidiary, but in no sense can this be considered a satisfactory solution because it is inherently costly. Nine years ago it was estimated that a typical expatriate package for a senior manager cost around US$1 million for a three-year assignment. This is clearly way in excess of comparable costs for a host-country manager of similar qualifications and experience.

In addition, it does not eliminate the language barrier, but merely shifts it down a level. Linguistically the expatriate managers have to develop a twin personality. In Yoshihara's survey, while 80 per cent plus of headquarter contact is conducted in Japanese, 99 per cent of local management is conducted in the local language. This is a serious source not only of expatriate stress but also of internal conflict within the subsidiary where several researchers have shown that language problems are often the principal barrier to team working.

Finally, but most importantly, this approach limits local managers to supporting roles in the company development, impeding knowledge transfer, blocking career opportunities and undermining the potential benefits from cultural diversity. Using a phrase now famous in international business, companies like the Japanese multinationals relying heavily on expatriation will be unable to tap their subsidiaries for global reach (Bartlett and Ghoshal, 1986).

These defects allied to the earlier problems discussed under language nodes suggest that expatriation is at best an interim solution capable of bridging the language gap only until a more complete solution is developed.

Machine translation

All the potential solutions to the language barrier discussed previously rely upon human means. However, computing does hold out the possibility of an alternative – machine translation and its sister technology machine interpretation. Machine translation has been around for over four decades. Machine interpretation is more recent, but is essentially a machine translation kernel with a speech recognition front-end (in the source language) and a post-translation speech generation module (in the target language). All of these technologies are quite mature and extensively used. One source (Haynes, 1998) suggests that machine translation is now extensively used in business (he quotes an estimate of more than 30 billion pages of text per year). So is this the definitive answer to language management? Well, at the moment the jury is out.

Reviewers of machine translation are fairly unanimous in recognising an advantage in efficiency, though the scale of the advantage varies from 4 times to 50 times depending upon the author. However, there is less of a consensus about the quality of translation possible. Although Haynes confidently predicted that there were no longer any real barriers to widespread adoption of machine translation, numerous sample tests of difficult texts have generated largely nonsensical translations. The answer for any company intending to employ machine translation seems to be:

- To select the system well considering only the better quality systems that are now on the market.
- To train well the users not only in the mechanics of the system but in how to write clear source text that avoids symbolism, idioms, ambiguity, colloquialisms and inferential knowledge.
- To invest considerable effort up-front developing company and functional specific dictionaries that provide exact translations of concepts and jargon in the sense normally used within the company.
- To manage and monitor the quality of translations, fixing standards for quality of translation that are progressively improved.
- To define and implement formal procedures such that documents of higher importance to the business are never released without a manual check of the computer translation. The European Commission, which has been using machine translation for 25 years, defines 3 levels of translation quality. The lowest level 'gisting' is wholly computerised, the middle level 'internal' uses machine translation followed by human post-editing, and the highest level 'publication' makes no use of machine translation at all relying wholly on human capabilities.

Without these prerequisites, machine translation and by extension machine interpretation must be considered clever toys rather than valid business tools.

Controlled language

The last approach used by multinational companies to bridge the language barrier is that of controlled language, which imposes limits on vocabulary and syntax rules so as to make the text produced more easily comprehended by the non-native speaker/reader and equally more amenable to machine translation. Caterpillar in 1970 was the first to launch such a system with CCE (Caterpillar Controlled English) that allowed a vocabulary of only 8,000 words including product terminology (compared to over half a million words in the full English vocabulary). General Motors then followed this lead, launching their own system called CASL (Controlled Automotive Service Language).

Clearly such systems have merit, as evidenced by Caterpillar that has successfully employed theirs for over three decades. However, as a solution to multinational communications the potential of a controlled language is clearly limited. The costs and time scale for implementation are prohibitive to all but the world's largest companies. A restricted vocabulary is advantageous only to those who share the same alphabet and its usage is effectively limited to the written form where it is possible to filter and simplify language before transmission. More importantly still, the scope for communicating in a controlled language is clearly limited to conveying operational detail. To impose this constraint on business situations demanding persuasion, negotiation or motivation would clearly rob the participants of their powers of rhetoric.

Summary

The problem of cultural and linguistic diversity is already a severe one for many international businesses. Most of the world's 7,000 or so multinationals have already extended their network of operations into 20 or more countries and this trend is likely to continue. A 1997 Delphi study (Czinkota and Ronkainen, 1997) predicted that the globalisation trend would continue apace but that the focus for twenty-first century expansion would be towards more remote and exotic locations in Asia, Latin America and South America. In these countries it will be local rather than international languages that will dominate and multinational companies undertaking such steps will be well advised to prepare for the impact of increased ethnic, cultural and linguistic diversity.

In managing this diversity multinational companies will have to be able to consider a range of solutions, but none of these strategies is without flaws. The mix of language skills coming from schools and universities does not match the requirements of industry. In-house language training, though focused and effective, is anything but short term. The use of English as a lingua franca is likely to wane and the current generation of machine translation systems is best considered an aid to manual translation rather than a substitute for it. So the message for these businesses is clear: you need to understand the nature and scale of the language problem urgently, because whatever you decide to do, it will probably take far more time than your customers will allow you. A linguistic audit is an essential first step.

Discussion questions

1. In their research on US/Canadian retail companies, O'Grady and Lane (1999) uncovered what has become known as the psychic distance paradox. They found that companies underperformed in markets that were culturally very similar to their domestic market. Why do you think this should be?

2. The linguistic audit methodology concentrates on the language skills of company personnel. If you were auditing a company's language capabilities what else would you look at?

3. From what you have learned in the chapter, produce a simple decision tree to illustrate the logic by which the language is chosen for a parent company meeting one of its international subsidiaries (one that does not share the parent language).

4. Which of the ten language barrier factors do you think are most likely to have their impact in the early stages of a relationship and which will be ongoing?

Closing Case Study:
Magneti Marelli

Magneti Marelli has now developed into a large and highly respected competitor in the global automotive components marketplace. But it was not always thus. Formed over one hundred years ago, Magneti Marelli until 1984 continued as a domestic company serving the Italian automotive industry from a variety of product-focused factories based in Italy. Then in the mid-1980s stimulated by the Fiat Group's Progetto Internazionalizzazione, Magneti Marelli launched its global initiative. The first steps were decisive and ambitious. Magneti Marelli acquired two large French companies, Solex and Jaeger, and soon afterwards they bought the lighting and small motors divisions of the UK Lucas Group.

Over the years Magneti Marelli had developed a characteristic management style with an informal, emergent approach to strategy formulation, a relaxed approach to control but balanced by a strong emphasis on shared visions, values and objectives. This style was predictable given that Fiat, despite its size, remained a family run business and that the majority of Italian employees felt privileged to work for the Agnelli extended family. To their credit the Italian management made every effort to extend the same style to their newly acquired French and British satellites. From the outset they were at pains to stress their faith in the subsidiary management teams and made no efforts to introduce Italian managers. On the contrary many local managers found themselves rewarded with increased salaries and conditions and their degree of autonomy to act locally was left intact.

Socialisation also became a key component of the relationship with very frequent, bi-directional visits that were not just business meetings but opportunities for the two management teams to get to know one another. However, the meetings were not always easy, with the Italian management struggling to convey their ideas, visions and expectations in English and French languages in which many of them had only a long-forgotten, school-level capability. Magneti Marelli also organised global get-togethers of all its managers, a chance to mingle, sup wine and to listen to Agnelli or Romiti spelling out their thanks for past performances and their expectations for the future. However, these too were of only marginal benefit with national and language groups congregating together rather than mixing. In keeping with this relaxed family approach, reporting requirements for the subsidiaries were kept at a basic financial level and were standard for all Fiat companies inside and outside Italy. Yet despite these efforts to create a team atmosphere, the relationships did not gel.

The local management teams remained suspicious of their Italian colleagues and the Italians became increasingly frustrated with what they saw as the nationalistic and uncollaborative attitudes of their French and British managers. Something had to give and by 1990 Magneti Marelli had markedly revamped its approach to managing subsidiaries.

For a start it largely abandoned acquisition as an entry method. Since 1988 it has continued a rapid pace of globalisation but after its early problems has shown a strong preference for either joint ventures or for green field sites invariably run by Italian-based expatriates.

It has also taken decisive steps to improve control by inserting expatriate managers in key positions within its French and British subsidiaries. This has been in part balanced by a concerted programme of inpatriation whereby managers from foreign operations have been progressively recruited to increase the cultural diversity of the head office management teams in Italy.

The output reporting methods that had once been characterised by their simplicity have become ever more onerous, with intricate monthly reports on all operational areas including manpower and salaries, product and process quality, manufacturing efficiency and utilisation, purchase price inflation and even computer usage and utilisation. The caring uncle had turned into big brother.

Inevitably the level and frequency of social and professional contact has receded. The weekly private jet that in the early years had shuttled an army of Italian managers from Turin and Milan to Birmingham has long since ceased and the international get-togethers at the Milan conference centre were discontinued in 1991. Even the excellent acculturation programme entitled 'Fiat Italian Briefing', designed to give foreign managers an insight into the culture, customs and language of Italy, was abandoned after only a few of the French and British managers had been through it.

Why the turnaround? It runs contrary to the conventional wisdom of internationalisation theory. So clearly we have another influence at work here, and that influence was language.

The Fiat group and in particular Magneti Marelli in the 1980s was not a linguistically skilled organisation. Statistics at the time suggested that only about 20 per cent of Fiat's management had any post-scholastic capability in a second language. In northern Italy where Fiat is mainly based, German is as likely as French or English to be that second language. Yet despite this obvious problem, the managers of Magneti Marelli were caught in a cleft stick. They could not manage in the Italian language – the Italian skills of their French and British colleagues were non-existent and in any case French and especially English were seen as the languages of international business. So the Italian managers worked invariably in their second language.

The results were predictably detrimental to the relationship. Denied the rhetorical skills of persuasion, negotiation, self-expression and humour, the Italian managers working in their much weaker second language came across as rigid, confused and lacking personality and vision. Forced to maintain 'face' they also from time to time nodded sagely even when they had lost track of the discussion. As a consequence they developed an unfair reputation for reneging on agreements, most of which they were unaware they had signed up to. At critical moments in any discussion the visiting Italian managers would code switch back to their native language, fuelling the paranoia of the watching host management team who did not understand a word. A further complication came with the emergence of a few key managers who were genuinely skilled in the other's language. Parallel information networks grew up around these 'gatekeepers', bypassing the formal chain of communications and further undermining the degree of trust and easiness between the key managers involved on both sides. The level of uncertainty and mistrust, which should have receded over time, had in fact escalated. And it was this that caused Magneti Marelli to reappraise its approach to its second and subsequent phases of internationalisation.

Closing case study questions

1. Magneti Marelli were always strong on bureaucratic controls policies, procedures and systems, but were slow to impose these on their acquired subsidiaries. Why do you think this was?

2. Magneti Marelli used both systems to aid cultural integration. Which system do you think was the more effective method of diffusing corporate culture across the language barrier, and why?

3. At the outset of the relationship Magneti Marelli tried lots of different measures to make the relationship with their new subsidiaries work well. What do you believe they might have done better?

4. In what way did the Magneti Marelli experience run contrary to the conventional wisdom of internationalisation theory?

Annotated further reading

Asante, M. and **Gudykunst, W.** (1989) *Handbook of International and Intercultural Communications*. London: Sage.
A useful text for those of you wishing to understand better some of the underlying socio-linguistic theories.

Graddol, D. (1997) *The Future of English*. London: The British Council.
A small but very interesting book explaining the trends in globalisation, population demographics and culture and the impact they will be have on the relative importance of national languages.

Harzing, A.-W. (1999) *Managing the Multinationals: An International Study of Control Mechanisms*. Cheltenham: Edward Elgar.
A thorough review of management research literature related to multinational companies and an excellent example of how such research is conducted.

Neal, M. (1998) *The Culture Factor: Cross-national Management and the Foreign Venture*. Basingstoke: Macmillan.
A fascinating insight into the problems and costs of foreign managers expatriated to the UK and required to work in the English language.

Reeves, N. and Wright, C. (1996) *Linguistic Auditing*. Clevedon, Multilingual Matters.
A useful and practical guide to how to identify, evaluate and manage the problem of language within a large international business.

References

Allen, R. (1979).'Organisational politics: tactics and characteristics of its actors', *California Management Review* 22(1): 77–83.

Barnevik, P. and Taylor, W. (1991) 'The logic of global business', *Harvard Business Review* March–April: 91–105.

Bartlett, C. and Ghoshal, S. (1986) 'Tap your subsidiaries for global reach', *Harvard Business Review* 86(6): 87–95.

Czinkota, M. and Ronkainen, I. (1997) 'International business and trade in the next decade', *Journal of International Business Studies* 4: 827–44.

Davidson, W. and McFetridge, D. (1985) 'Key characteristics in international technology transfer mode', *Journal of International Business Studies* summer: 5–22.

Department of Trade and Industry (1995) *Assessment of the Wider Effects of Foreign Direct Investment in Manufacturing in the UK*. London: Department of Trade and Industry.

Dubin, R. (1978) *Theory Building*. New York: Free Press.

Freudenstein, R., Beneke, J. and Ponisch, H. (1981) *Language Incorporated*. Oxford: Pergamon.

Gallois, C., Franklyn-Stokes, A., Giles, H. and Coupland, N. (1988) 'Communication accommodation in intercultural encounters', in Y. Kim and W. B. Gudykunst (eds) *Theories in Intercultural Communication*. Newbury Park CA: Sage. pp. 157–85.

Gass, S. M. and Varonis, E. M. (1991) 'Miscommunication in nonnative speaker discourse', in N. Coupland, H. Giles and J. M. Wiemann *Miscommunication and Problem Talk*. Newbury Park CA: Sage. pp. 121–45.

Graddol, D. (1997) *The Future of English*. London: The British Council.

Gudykunst, W. and Ting-Toomey, S. (1988) cited in W. Gudykunst and T. Nishida (1989) 'Theoretical perspectives for studying intercultural communications', in M. Asante and W. Gudykunst *Handbook of International and Intercultural Communication*. London: Sage. pp. 17–46.

Gupta, A. and Govindarajan, V. (2000) Knowledge flows within multinational coroporations', *Strategic Management Journal* 21: 473–96.

Hagen, S. (1999) *Business Communication across Borders: A Study of Language Use and Practice in European Companies*. London: Languages National Training Organisation.

Hakansson, H. and Wootz, B. (1975). 'Supplier selection in an international environment', *Journal of Marketing Research* 12: 46–51.

Hallen, L. and Wiedersheim-Paul, F. (1999) 'Psychic distance and buyer–seller interaction', in P. Buckley and P. Ghauri *The Internationalisation of the Firm*. London: International Thomson Business Press. pp. 349–60.

Harzing, A.-W. (1999) *Managing the Multinationals: An International Study of Control Mechanisms*. Cheltenham: Edward Elgar.

Haynes, C. (1998). *Breaking Down the Language Barriers, Machine Translation, the Technology that Can No Longer be Denied*. London: Aslib.

Hearn, P. and Button, D. (1994) *Language Industries Atlas*. Amsterdam: IOS Press.

Hofstede, G. (1991) *Cultures and Organizations, Software of the Mind: Intercultural Cooperation and its Importance for Survival*. New York: McGraw-Hill.

Hofstede, G. (1999) 'The business of international business is culture', in P. Buckley and P. Ghauri *The Internationalisation of the Firm*. London: International Thomson Business Press. pp. 381–93.

Jankowicz, A. D. (1994) 'The new journey to Jerusalem: mission and meaning in the managerial crusade to Eastern Europe', *Organization Studies* 15: 479–507.

Johanson, J. and Vahlne, J.-E. (1977) 'The internationalisation process of the firm. A model of knowledge development and increasing foreign market commitments', *Journal of International Business Studies* 8(1): 23–32.

Johanson, J. and Wiedersheim-Paul, F. (1975) 'The internationalisation of the firm – four Swedish cases', *Journal of Management Studies* 12: 305–22.

Kim, Y. (2001). *Becoming Intercultural: An Integrative Theory of Communication and Cross-cultural Adaption*. Thousand Oaks CA: Sage.

Kogut, B. and Singh, H. (1988) 'The effect of national culture on on the choice of entry mode', *Journal of International Business Studies* 19(3): 411–32.

Lester, T. (1994). 'Pulling down the language barrier', *International Management* July–August: 42–44.

Marschan-Piekkari, R., Welch, L. and Welch, D. (1997) 'Language the forgotten factor in multinational management', *European Management Journal* October: 591–8.

Neal, M. (1998) *The Culture Factor: Cross-national Management and the Foreign Venture*. Basingstoke: Macmillan.

Nordstrom, K. A. and Vahlne, J.-E. (1992) 'Is the globe shrinking? Psychic distance and the establishment of Swedish sales subsidiaries during the last 100 years'. Paper presented at the International Trade and Finance Associations Annual Conference, Laredo, Texas.

O'Grady, S. and Lane, H. (1999) 'The psychic distance paradox', in P. Buckley and P. Ghauri (eds) *The Internationalization of the Firm*. London: International Thomson Business Press.

Peterson, K. J. and Frayer, D. J. (2000) 'An empirical study of global sourcing strategy effectiveness', *Journal of Supply Chain Management* 36(2): 29–38.

Reeves, N. and Wright, C. (1996) *Linguistic Auditing*. Clevedon: Multilingual Matters.

Ricks, D. A. (1999) *Blunders in International Business*. Oxford: Blackwell.

Salk, J. E. and Shenkar, O. (1997) 'Cultural boundaries and cross-cultural encounters in international joint venture teams', *International Studies of Management and Organisation* 26(4): 48–72.

Schwenk, C. R. (1988).*The Essence of Strategic Decision Making*. Lexington MA: Lexington.

Scollon, R. and Scollon, S. (1995) *Intercultural Communication*. Oxford: Blackwell.

Scotton, C. (1983) 'The negotiation of identities in conversation: a theory of markedness and code choice', *International Journal of the Sociology of Language* 44: 115–36.

Scotton, C. and Ury, W. (1977) 'The social functions of code switching', *International Journal of the Sociology of Language* 13: 5–20.

Subramaniam, M. and Venkatraman, N. (2000) 'Determinants of transnational new product development capability: testing the influence of transferring and deploying tacit overseas knowledge', *Strategic Management Journal* 22: 359–78.

Tajfel, H. (1982) *Social Identity and Intergroup Relations*. Cambridge: Cambridge University Press.

Takahashi, T. and Beebe, L. (1987) 'The development of pragmatic competence by Japanese learners of English', *JALT Journal* 8: 131–55.

Taylor, S. and Crocker, J. (1981) 'Schematic bases of social information processing in social cognition', in E. T. Higgins and C. Harman *The Ontario Symposium on Social Psychology*, vol. 1. New Jersey: Hillsdale. pp. 89–134.

Ting-Toomey, S. (1988) cited in W. Gudykunst and T. Nishida (1989) 'Theoretical perspectives for studying intercultural communications', in M. Asante and W. Gudykunst *Handbook of International and Intercultural Communication*. London: Sage. pp. 17–46.

Varra, E., Tienari, J., Risto, S. and Marschan-Piekkari, R. (2000) 'Language as power in post-merger integration'. Paper presented at the European International Business Academy 26th Conference, Maastricht, The Netherlands.

Verrept, S. (2000) 'Keynote speech'. European Association of Business Communication, Antwerp.

Wiseman, R. and Shuter, R. (1994) *Communicating in Multinational Organizations*. Thousand Oaks CA: Sage.

Wright, C., Kumagai, F. and Bonney, N. (2001) 'Language and power in Japanese transplants in Scotland', *Sociological Review* 49(2): 236–53.

Yoshihara, H. (1999) 'Global operations managed by Japanese in Japanese', RIEB, Kobe Working Paper.

PART 4

Managing employees in different cultures

CHAPTER 11

International human resource management

Pawan S. Budhwar

Learning objectives

When you finish reading this chapter you should:

- be familiar with the developments in the field of western HRM

- know the five main models of HRM

- understand the key factors and variables influencing HRM in a cross-national context

- be familiar with a mechanism for examining western HRM concepts in a broader international context

- have understanding about the topic of IHRM

Opening Case Study: Assembling an empire with no instructions – B&Q in China

In the rich world, do-it-yourself has become a familiar pastime, but promoting it in China is no easy task. In spite of 30 years of Maoist education, with its rhetoric of intellectuals learning from peasants, most educated and wealthy Chinese recoil from the idea of manual work. Moreover, there are few incentives to engage in DIY when a vast pool of migrant labourers is prepared to do jobs for less than 500 renminbi (£40) a month. Undaunted by these problems, B&Q opened a warehouse store in Shanghai in June 1999, the first large British retailer to enter mainland China. To establish itself, it has had to discover when it must adapt to the local market – and when it must insist on doing things differently.

Human resources management is often hard for foreign companies in China. B&Q Shanghai has the same personnel policies as in the UK. The company encourages informality: all employees wear the same uniform – a pale grey or blue T-shirt and an orange apron with the B&Q logo. They also refer to each other by their first names – either their Chinese names or the English names they have all been given. This is a radical departure in hierarchy conscious China.

B&Q has introduced 15-minute breaks, morning and afternoon, and daily morning briefings for all employees to help foster team spirit. The company's two expatriate managers wear B&Q uniform and punch their timecards each day just like everyone else. They also take an active part in the company karaoke and go-karting after work. Local staff, used to rigid hierarchies, welcome this treatment. John Zhou, local assistant store manager, describes the company culture as 'very open, much more diplomatic and democratic than in state-owned enterprises'. One Chinese team leader characterises the approach of the expatriate Taiwanese managers at his former employer as 'management by shouting'.

Bill Kong, one of the older employees at the store, even compares the atmosphere to the early days of the communist revolution in the 1950s, when the spirit of comradeship pervaded many Chinese workplaces. It is one of contemporary China's many ironies that people who grew up learning how the Chinese were exploited by foreigners and capitalists before 1949 now prefer to work in a foreign company. Like other multinationals in China, B&Q has attracted many capable job applicants. During its first big recruitment drive in 1999, it received more than 2,000 applications. In filling its 160 vacancies, the store was able to pick the best. Many shop-floor staff have the equivalent of a college degree.

The attitude of local employees is helped by the prospect of rapid promotion and career development as B&Q expands in China. The company plans to have about 20 stores in China within 5 years. Local managers have been trained to handle the day-to-day running of the two stores. John Zhou, for instance, has been promoted to be store manager of the new store. Further, the company is about to embark on a fast-track management scheme to ensure a constant stream of well-qualified local managers. Mr Strickland says the idea is for a 'conveyor belt': employees will be trained and then moved on to new stores, where they will take on greater responsibilities and, in turn, help to train freshly recruited staff.

Source: 13 Dec. 2000, *Financial Times* CD-ROM 2000

Introduction

This chapter is divided into two broad parts. First, it discusses the developments in the field of human resource management (HRM) as reported in the western literature. Second, it highlights some of the key issues related to the topic of international HRM (IHRM) from the perspective of a multinational enterprise (MNE). The first part is divided into three sections. Section one consists of an introduction to the concept of HRM and how some writers have distinguished it from traditional personnel management (PM). In section two, five main models of HRM are analysed and their core propositions identified. Section three presents an integrative framework useful for examining the applicability of the core propositions of the five HRM models in different cross-national settings. This could be helpful in highlighting the important factors which influence HRM in different parts of the world.

The second part of the chapter attempts to cover some of the main issues relevant for HRM in MNEs. A vast majority of IHRM literature focuses only on issues related to the generic HRM functions in MNEs, but this chapter adopts a different approach. It starts with the analyses of developments in western HRM and proposes a framework to examine the applicability of western HRM concepts in a broader international and socio-cultural context. The second part then highlights the core HRM issues in MNEs. This approach is considered to be more useful as it will take the readers on a trip of developments in the fields of HRM and IHRM. As such, core aspects of IHRM are not significantly different from those of HRM, the primary difference being the latter exists in organisations within a national boundary and the former across national boundaries.

Developments in HRM

The roots of HRM go back as far as the 1950s, when writers like Peter Drucker and Douglas McGregor stressed the need of visionary, goal-directed leadership and management of integration (Armstrong, 1987). This was succeeded by the 'behavioural science movement' in the 1960s, headed by writers such as Maslow, Argyris and Herzberg. These writers emphasised the 'value' aspect of human resources (HRs) in organisations and called for better quality of work life (Sparrow and Hiltrop, 1994). The issues raised by the behavioural scientists formed the basis of the 'organisational development movement' initiated by Bennis in the 1970s, which began to focus on the importance of seeing the organisation as a whole. Such an approach emphasised a systematic analysis of the management of change process. The 'human resource accounting' (HRA) theory developed by Flamholtz (1974) was also an outcome of such sequential developments in the field of HRM.

Before the HRA theory, human resources were considered to be just a cost. Like other organisational resources their value was derived from their ability to render services which have economic value. HRA emphasised that human resources are core assets for any organisation. It was defined as a process of identifying, measuring and communicating information about human resources to decision makers, especially about their cost and value.

This view began to gain support in the 1980s, when events started to change at a rapid pace in the international economic environment. US organisations were under severe competitive threat from Japan and the existence of low levels of worker commitment in American organisations became very clear. The increased level of competition in the national and international marketplace combined with slow rates of productivity growth in the United States and western Europe indicated a strong need for major restructuring and reorganisation.

All these developments made the academics and practitioners realise the significance of human resources in combating these challenges. The need to integrate human resource strategy into business strategy was felt and academics responded to the challenges caused by the changing scenario by theorising about the models of HRM. The increased importance of the topic of HRM is evident from the fact that over a span of 20 years or so it has become the subject of fast-growing research and teaching interest. The creation of new chairs in HRM in the universities on one hand, and the alteration of the names of industrial relations and personnel departments to HRM both in universities and industry on the other, confirmed the importance of the topic (Guest, 1991). As a result of these changes, HRM initially developed in the United States in the 1980s. Academics introduced an entire new course of HRM into the first year of the MBA curriculum in 1980 and also developed important models of HRM (Walton and Lawrence, 1985). These models formed the basis for the development of further theories of HRM and also differentiated it from the personnel management by emphasising the involvement of HRM strategy in business strategy.

Personnel management and HRM

While the above developments were taking place in the field of HRM, another important and more related debate persisted in the early 1980s in the west, mainly in the United Kingdom. The debate was to distinguish HRM from traditional PM. Legge (1989) drew some distinctions between the two topics by reviewing the definitions of a variety of writers and identifying three main differences:

1. Personnel management is an activity aimed primarily at non-managers whereas HRM is less clearly focused but certainly more concerned with managerial staff.

2. HRM is much more of an integrated line management activity whereas personnel management seeks to influence line management.

3. HRM emphasises the importance of senior management's culture whereas personnel management has always been rather suspicious of organisation development and related to unitarist, social and psychologically oriented ideas.

Legge further argued that in comparison with PM, HRM is a more central, senior management driven strategic activity.

Walton (1985) argued that 'control' and 'commitment' distinguish between PM and HRM. According to him, PM is characterised by control, which stresses subdividing work into small tasks, clearly fixing job responsibilities and holding individuals accountable for specific job requirements. HRM, on the other hand, emphasises mutual goals, mutual influence, mutual respect, mutual rewards and mutual responsibility. All this elicits commitment, which in turn yields both better economic performance and greater human development (see also Guest, 1991).

Storey (1992) proposed a model involving 27 points of difference between PM, industrial relations (IR) and HRM. The model depicts the change in the nature of personnel function from prescriptive and reactive to descriptive and proactive. Through this model he presented the expected direction and destination of the HR function.

However, such debates were full of controversies. Practitioners in the field regarded HRM as 'just another set of initials' or 'old wine in new bottles' or 'old bottles with new labels' (Armstrong, 1987). It would be inaccurate to suggest that one approach has taken over from the other, just as it would be wrong to suggest that one is modern and other old fashioned, or that one is right and other wrong. Both are usually present in one organisation at the same time, sometimes even in one person.

These developments have taken place over the last 20 years or so, as a result of which the nature of HR function has changed drastically from reactive, prescriptive and administrative to proactive, descriptive and executive (Legge, 1995). At present the literature is largely concerned with how HRM contributes to the improvement in performance and overall success of organisations. But it is clear that as firms are entering into a more dynamic world of international business and as the globalisation of world markets continues apace, comparative issues will gain momentum. Both practitioners and academicians in the field of HRM are increasingly realising the need to find relevant HRM practices for different parts of the world. It can become an important training tool for expatriate managers. The increased probability of having to manage in an international situation has made this an imperative.

Academics have responded positively to meeting the challenges raised by the dynamic business environment. They have developed and proposed different models of HRM both between and within nations. Interestingly, most models of HRM have an Anglo-Saxon base. During the infancy stage of the HRM literature such an ethnocentric approach was understandable and unavoidable. However, the present dynamic international business environment demands appropriate information and guidance to develop relevant HRM policies and practices for different parts of the world. Under such conditions, the relevance of lessons learned from the Anglo-Saxon experience is questionable. The context-specific nature of HRM suggests that a number of key factors determine HRM in different national and regional settings. It is therefore important to examine the extent to which Anglo-Saxon models of HRM are applicable in other parts of the world and to highlight the factors important in determining HRM in different parts of the world. It has also now become clear that the study of HRM needs an international perspective.

Five models of HRM which have been extensively documented in the literature are chosen for analysis: the matching model; the Harvard model; the contextual model; the 5-P model; the European model. An important issue at this stage is to find a framework that can help to examine the applicability of the main models of HRM in an international/cross-national context and the core factors influencing HRM in such a context. Over the last few years, the research conducted by Budhwar and associates (Budhwar, 1996, 2000; Budhwar and Debrah, 2001a; Budhwar and Khatri, 2001; Budhwar and Sparrow, 2002) has involved, among others, an analysis of these models. They have identified the core propositions of the models and suggested an integrative framework to examine their applicability in a cross-national context. Their analysis, a summary of which is presented below, can be adopted to examine the applicability of western HRM concepts in different parts of the world.

Models of HRM

Matching model of HRM

The main contributors to the matching model of HRM come from the Michigan and New York schools. The model of Fombrun *et al.* (1984) highlights the resource aspect of HRM and emphasises the efficient utilisation of HR to meet organisational objectives. This means that, like other resources of organisation, HRs have to be obtained cheaply, used sparingly and developed and exploited as fully as possible (Sparrow and Hiltrop, 1994).

1st model

Fombrun *et al.* (1984) expanded Chandler's (1962) argument that an organisation's structure is an outcome of its strategy and developed the matching model of strategic HRM which emphasises a tight fit between organisational strategy, organisational structure and HRM system. The main aim of the matching model is therefore to develop an appropriate human resource system that will characterise those HRM strategies which contribute to the most efficient implementation of business strategies.

Further development to the matching model and its core theme of strategic fit were made by Schuler and colleagues in the late 1980s. Relating HRM practices to organisational strategies, Schuler and Jackson (1987) argued that the successful implementation of different organisational strategies requires different 'role behaviours' on the part of employees, who must exhibit different characteristics. They also argued that similar HRM practices (such as those related to recruitment, training and retirement) are used differently by organisations that differ in their organisational strategies. As a result, Schuler and Jackson note, when organisations change strategies they are likely to change HRM practices. They identified the most important HRM practices about which strategic decisions had to be made and for each practice noted the dichotomous (but logical) alternatives that could be applied. For Schuler and Jackson, HRM could then be seen as a menu of strategic choices to be made by human resource executives in order to promote the most effective role behaviours that are consistent with the organisation strategy and to ensure that they are aligned with each other.

Despite many criticisms, the matching model deserves credit for providing a framework for subsequent theory development in the field of HRM. Researchers need to adopt a comprehensive methodology in order to study the dynamic concept of human resource strategy. Do elements of the matching model exist in different cross-national settings? This can be done by examining the presence of some of the core issues of the model. The main propositions (P) emerging from the matching model are:

P1:   Do organisations show a 'tight fit' between their HRM and organisation strategy where the former is dependent on the latter? Do personnel managers believe they should develop HRM systems only for the effective implementation of their organisation strategies?

P2:   Do organisations consider their HRs as a cost and use them sparingly? Or do they devote resources to the training of their HRs to make the best use of them?

P3:   Do HRM strategies vary across different levels of employees?

The Harvard model of HRM

The Harvard model is considered as the 'soft' variant of HRM. It stresses the 'human' aspect of HRM and is more concerned with the employer–employee relationship. The model highlights the interests of different stakeholders in the organisation (such as shareholders, management, employee groups, government, community and unions) and how their interests are related to the objectives of management. This aspect of the model provides some awareness of European context and other business systems which emphasise 'co-determination' (Boxall, 1992). It also recognises the influence of situational factors (such as the market situation) on HRM policy choices.

According to this model the actual content of HRM is described in relation to four policy areas: human resource flows, reward systems, employee influence, works systems. Each of the four policy areas is characterised by a series of tasks to which managers must attend. The outcomes that these four HR policies need to achieve are commitment, competence, congruence and cost effectiveness. The aim of these outcomes is therefore to develop and sustain mutual trust and improve individual/group performance at the minimum cost so as to achieve individual well-being, organisational effectiveness and societal well-being. The model allows for analysis of these outcomes at both the organisational and societal levels. As this model acknowledges the role of societal outcomes, it can provide a useful basis for comparative analysis of HRM (Poole, 1990). However, this model has been criticised for not explaining the complex relationship between strategic management and HRM (Guest, 1991).

Both the matching model and the Harvard analytical framework represent two very different emphases: the former is closer to the strategic management literature, the latter to the human relations tradition. Based on the above analysis, the main propositions emerging from this model which can be used for examining its applicability in different cross-national contexts are:

P4: What is the influence of different stakeholders and situational and contingent factors on HRM policies?

P5: To what extent is communication with employees used as a source to maximise commitment?

P6: What level of emphasis is given to employee development through involvement, empowerment and devolution?

The contextual model of HRM

Based on the human resource policy framework provided by the Harvard model, researchers at the Centre for Corporate Strategy and Change at the Warwick Business School developed an understanding of strategy making in complex organisations and related this to the ability to transform HRM practices. They analysed empirical data, collected through in-depth case studies of over 20 leading British organisations, to examine the link between strategic change and transformations and the way in which people are managed (Hendry et al., 1988; Hendry and Pettigrew, 1992).

Hendry and associates argue that HRM should not be labelled as a single form of activity. Organisations may follow a number of different pathways in order to achieve the same results. This is mainly due to the existence of a number of linkages between the outer environmental context (socio-economic, technological, political–legal and competitive) and inner organisational context (culture, structure, leadership, task–technology and business output). These linkages directly contribute to forming the content of an organisation's HRM. To analyse this, past information related to the organisation's development and management of change is essential (Sparrow and Hiltrop, 1994). The main propositions emerging from this model are:

P7:   What is the influence of economic (competitive conditions, ownership and control, organisation size and structure, organisational growth path or stage in the life cycle and the structure of the industry), technological (type of production systems) and socio-political (national education and training set-up) factors on HRM strategies?

P8:   What are the linkages between organisational contingencies (such as size, nature, positioning of HR and HR strategies) and HRM strategies?

Debates in the early 1990s suggested the need to explore the relationship between strategic management and HRM more extensively. The next model analysed is strongly based on this premise.

The 5-P model

The literature reveals a trend in which HRM is becoming an integral part of business strategy. The emergence of the term strategic human resource management (SHRM) is an outcome of such efforts. It is largely concerned with 'integration' and 'adaptation'. Its purpose is to ensure that HRM is fully integrated with the strategy and strategic needs of the firm; HR policies are coherent both across policy areas and across hierarchies; and HR practices are adjusted, accepted and used by line managers and employees as part of their everyday work (Schuler, 1992).

SHRM therefore has many different components, including HR policies, culture, values and practices. Schuler developed a 5-P model of SHRM which melds five HR activities (philosophies, policies, programmes, practices and processes) with strategic needs. Strategic needs reflect management's overall plan for survival, growth, adaptability and profitability. The strategic HR activities form the main components of HR strategy. This model to a great extent explains the significance of these five SHRM activities in achieving the organisation's strategic needs, and shows the interrelatedness of activities that are often treated separately in the literature. This is helpful in understanding the complex interaction between organisational strategy and SHRM activities.

The model further shows the influence of internal and external characteristics on the strategic business needs of an organisation. Internal characteristics in this model consist mainly of factors such as organisational culture and the nature of the business. The external ones consist of the nature and state of economy in which the organisation operates and critical success factors, i.e. the opportunities and threats provided by the industry. This model attracts criticism for being over-prescriptive and too hypothetical in nature. In addition, although it seems very attractive, practitioners might find it difficult, if not impossible, to implement. Nevertheless, the model raises two propositions important for HRM comparisons:

P9:   What is the level of integration of HRM into the business strategy?

P10:   What is the level of responsibility for HRM devolved to line managers?

Brewster *et al.* (1997) successfully compared cross-national HRM across European nations based on the last two propositions. These propositions presently form one of the central themes of the debate in the HRM literature.

European model of HRM

Based on the growing importance of HRM and its contribution towards economic success and the drive towards Europeanisation, Brewster (1993, 1995) proposes a European model of HRM. His model is based on the premise that European organisations operate with restricted autonomy. They are constrained at international (European Union) and national levels by national culture and legislation; at the organisation level by patterns of ownership; and at the HRM level by trade union involvement and consultative arrangements. Brewster suggests there is a need to accommodate such constraints in a European model of HRM.

Further, the European model shows an interaction between HR strategies, business strategies and HR practice, and at the same time their interaction with an external environment constituting national culture, power systems, legislation, education, employee representation and other previously mentioned constraint factors. Significantly, Brewster considers factors external to the organisation as part of the HRM model, rather than as a set of external influences upon it. This helps to place organisational approaches firmly within the national context, which contributes to a better understanding of the unique situations of and differences between nations in their HRM practices, as well as how MNCs try to adopt local practices (Brewster, 1995). Such an approach helps to build a better model of European HRM and saves it from becoming too normative. It also moves beyond the traditional discussion about whether the term HRM should be accepted or rejected, towards a more positive debate about different forms and styles of HRM. More importantly, it helps to analyse HRM at a national level.

From the above analyses it can be seen that there is an element of both the contextual and 5-P models of HRM present in Brewster's European model. Apart from the emphasis on 'strategic HRM' mode, one main proposition important for cross-national HRM comparisons is emerging from Brewster's model:

P11:   What is the influence of international institutions, national factors (such as culture, legal set-up, economic environment and ownership patterns), national institutions (such as the educational and vocational set-up, labour markets and trade unions) on HRM strategies and HRM practices?

The above discussion presented an overview of some of the main theoretical developments in western HRM. It also identified and highlighted the main propositions that can be used to examine the applicability of these HRM models in different parts of the world. The question that arises then is how to carry out such an investigation. What factors and variables should be considered in examining the identified propositions in different national or comparative settings? Is there a comprehensive framework for conducting this type of evaluation? An integrative framework is found useful in this regard. This is presented in the next section.

An integrative framework for cross-national HRM evaluations

HRM evaluations can be conducted at various levels, ranging from nation state to the level of firm. A framework is now proposed for HRM investigations and comparisons at the firm level in cross-national settings. This is developed after a thorough review of literature in the fields of comparative management, HRM and IHRM. A number of frameworks for conducting HRM and IHRM research are available in the literature. The relevant contributions useful for cross-national HRM evaluations from these frameworks have been collated and more factors and variables have been added to develop the integrative framework (see Figure 11.1). It consists of three levels of factors and variables which are known to influence HRM in different national settings: national factors, contingent variables and organisational strategies and policies. The framework has been successfully adopted to examine the applicability of the 5 models (via the 11 propositions identified above) in a cross-national context – in India (Budhwar and Khatri, 2001) and Britain (Budhwar, 2000). Similarly, it could be used to examine the western HRM context in other parts of the world.

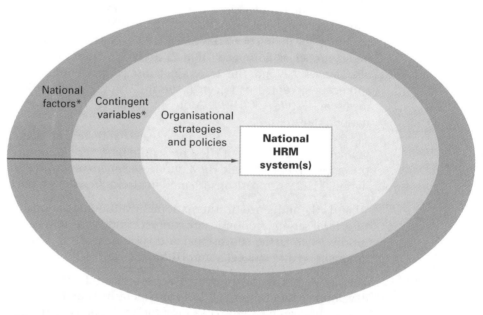

* See pp. 249–250 for a list of national factors and contingent variables

Figure 11.1 An integrative framework of HRM

Organisational strategies and policies influencing national HRM systems

Cross-national HRM researchers believe that in order to get a better understanding of the context-specific nature of HRM practices, an evaluation of the impact of organisational strategies on them (along with possible contingent variables and national factors briefed below) is important. Propositions 1, 2, 3, 5, 6, 9 and 10 suggest a similar emphasis.

Some of the most frequently cited typologies of organisational strategies are by Miles and Snow (1978, 1984) and Porter (1980, 1985). Miles and Snow classify organisations as 'prospectors', 'analysers', 'defenders' and 'reactors'. These generic strategies dictate organisations' HRM policies and practices. Similarly, Porter's competitive strategies distinguish firms that compete on the basis of 'cost leadership', 'product differentiation' and 'market focus'.

Recent research also shows that organisational policies related to recruitment (such as to emphasise the recruitment of fresh graduates), training and development (for example, to monitor training through formal evaluation after training) and communication (for example, to communicate with employees through immediate superiors) also determine HR practices and policies in a cross-national setting.

Contingent variables influencing national HRM systems

Propositions 4, 8 and parts of 7 strongly emphasise the impact of different contingent variables on HRM policies and practices. These are:

1. Size of the organisation (based on the number of employees).
2. Level of technology adopted.
3. Age of organisation.
4. Presence of a formal HRM department.
5. Type of HR strategy.
6. Representation of personnel on the board.
7. Type of ownership.
8. Existence of training units in the HR department.
9. Union status.
10. Interests of influential stakeholders.
11. Structure of organisation.
12. Lifecycle stage of the organisation.

National factors influencing national HRM systems

Propositions 11 and 7 demand the examination of the impact of national factors on HRM in a cross-national setting. Four national factors along with their different aspects are found useful in this regard: national culture; national institutions; national industrial sectors; dynamic business environment.

National culture

Research highlights the influence of national culture on HRM policies and practices. The most important processes or aspects of national culture that have been identified for comparative evaluations are:

1. The socialisation process through which managers are 'made'.
2. The basic assumptions which shape managers' behaviour.
3. Their common values, norms of behaviour and customs.
4. The influence of social elite or pressure groups unique to a country.
5. The unique ways of doing things and management logic in a particular country which are reflective of the broader national business system.

National institutions

Researchers in the field of cross-national HRM have been considering the impact of different institutions on HRM policies and practices for some time. They have identified a number of institutional systems whose influence on HRM in a cross-national context must be considered:

1. National labour laws.
2. The structure, density and role of trade unions.
3. The educational and vocational set-up.
4. The role of professional bodies.
5. International business institutions.
6. Labour market dynamics and overall preferences for internal or external markets.
7. Employers' federations and representative bodies.
8. The legitimate role of consulting organisations.

National industrial sectors

Studies of national business systems suggest that the industrial sector is best considered as a country level or national unit of analysis and is worth considering for national level HRM evaluations and comparisons. The main aspects of an industrial sector which can influence national pattern of HRM are:

1. Common strategies, business logic and goals.
2. Regulations and standards.
3. Specific requirements or needs associated with supply chain management.
4. The need for sector-specific knowledge.
5. Informal or formal benchmarking against sector competitors.
6. Cross-sector cooperative arrangements.
7. Common developments in business operations.
8. Sector-specific labour markets or skill requirements.

Dynamic business environment

HRM research has also demonstrated the impact of dynamic business environments, characterised mainly by distinctive sets of competitive pressures on HRM policies and practices at the national level. Although many of these dynamics are unique to each nation, a series of developments is pan-national and has been identified as representing the major determinants of IHRM activity. The aspects of a dynamic business environment that have been identified as influencing HRM policies and practices in a cross-national context are as follows:

1. Increased competition and pressures on productivity, quality or social costs of employment at both national and international level.

2. The resulting growth of new business alliances or forms of corporate governance.

3. Automation of information systems and their impact on international business structures and coordination systems.

4. Change in the composition and demographics of the workforce.

5. Downsizing of organisations and the transfer of work across a new international division of labour.

6. Transfer of convergent best practice, for example, through the Japanisation of production systems, emphasis on customer service, or creation of like-minded international cadres of managers.

All three sets of variables and factors (see Figure 11.1) are known to influence cross-national HRM. However, it is suggested that more meaningful cross-national HRM comparisons can be made by examining the influence of national factors on HRM. This suggestion is based on the premise that national factors such as national culture and national institutions form the very basis of HR functions in any country. Recently, this approach has been successfully adopted to analyse the national HRM systems of 13 developing countries (Budhwar and Debrah, 2001b). A similar analysis can be conducted for other countries as well.

The chapter has so far discussed the developments in HRM and how the applicability of western HRM concepts can be examined in a broader international and cross-national context. It also highlighted the significance of key national factors in determining national patterns of HRM. Next, HRM issues specific to the multinational enterprise (MNE) are analysed.

MNE and IHRM

It is widely accepted that IHRM is critical for the survival and success of an MNE. However, due to reasons such as high costs, lack of time and absence of comprehensive framework, the field of IHRM research has not received as much attention as it should considering the ever-increasing levels of globalisation of business. Schuler *et al.* (2002) have conducted a thorough review of literature of the IHRM field. They have identified three areas which need specific research attention:

1. Need of comprehensive frameworks to reflect the complex set of environmental factors that significantly influence management of human resources in an international context.

2. Need to identify and establish any pattern of international human resource activities in a way that recognises their systematic interaction.

3. Need to utilise more theoretical basis to predict and explain relationships between HRM patterns and their determining factors.

To a great extent, the integrative framework and its different components, discussed above, contributes in this regard.

Broadly speaking, IHRM is about the worldwide management of HRs. However, most of the writings in the field of IHRM tend to be conceptualised from the perspective of MNEs based on the inherent tension that exists between the need for control and coordination of foreign subsidiaries and the need to adapt to local environments. The purpose of IHRM is therefore to enable the MNE to be successful globally, achieved by implementation of the MNE's global strategy whilst creating sufficient flexibility to meet local conditions.

In this connection, Morgan (1986) argues that IHRM operations are structured around three functions: procurement, allocation and utilisation of the human resources of an organisation. These three broad functions cover six HR activities generally practised under domestic HRM: HR planning; staffing; performance appraisals; HR development; HR compensation; employee relations. Each of these is carried out for three separate categories of employees: home-country nationals (HCNs); professionals and managers relocated to the host country – parent country nationals (PCNs); employees from other countries who fill shortages of labour – third country nationals (TCNs). IHRM then is a more complex version of western domestic HRM (Dowling *et al.*, 1999). However, HR departments of most MNEs are required to develop and administer the three broad policies and practices for three categories of employees (HCNs, PNCs and TCNs) across a wide variety of nations, each with its own social, cultural, legal, economic, political and historical characteristics. These broadly fall under the four national factors discussed earlier in the chapter.

In the following sections some of the core issues related to IHRM and MNEs are briefly discussed. These are arranged under the six basic HR functions identified above.

HR planning

HR planning is by far the most important of the core HR activities and crucial for synchronising the remaining five sub-functions of staffing, appraisal, training and development, compensation and employee relations. Some of the critical HR planning issues facing MNEs include: identification of potential candidates for overseas assignment; identification of core success factors for international assignees; a comprehensive selection procedure for expatriates; continuous appraisal and development of expatriates both through different training programmes and career management; appropriate compensation packages; suitable adjustment considerations for working spouse and family and a well-structured repatriation process.

Staffing

Staffing function enables an MNE to coordinate and control its international operations. The existing literature suggests four broad approaches to international HR staffing: ethnocentric; polycentric; geocentric; regiocentric.

Ethnocentric approach

This emphasises filling managerial positions with people from headquarters, i.e. the parent country. The main advantage of this approach is that managers are familiar with company goals, policies and procedures. This approach is more suitable when there is a scarcity of skilled HRs and a need for close communication and coordination with headquarters. The main disadvantages of this approach include discouragement to local managers for not getting the opportunities to be promoted and poor performance of expatriates in foreign countries.

Polycentric approach

This emphasises hiring local managers from the host country (where the operations are started). The approach is most effective when implementing a global strategy region-wise. These managers are familiar with the local culture, language and ways of doing business and already have many contacts in that place. One major disadvantage of this approach is related to coordinating activities and goals between the subsidiary and parent company, including the potentially conflicting loyalties of the local manager.

Geocentric approach

This emphasises that the best managers are recruited within or outside the company, regardless of nationality. There are a number of advantages to placing third country nationals in subsidiaries. First, there is a greater pool of qualified and willing applicants from which to choose. Second, they bring more cultural flexibility. Third, it can be cost effective to have managers from certain countries.

Regiocentric approach

This emphasises recruitment on a regional basis. The approach is more suitable if the emphasis of international business is on specific products for specific regions; for example, software MNCs recruit within India.

The choice of staffing policy depends on factors such as strategy and organisation structure and factors related to particular subsidiary such as duration of a particular foreign operation, the types of technology used and the necessary production and marketing techniques. Factors related to the host country also play a part. These include level of economic and technological development, political stability, regulations regarding ownership and staffing and the socio-cultural setting.

Presently, MNEs recruit PCNs mainly to use them as troubleshooters, structure reproducers and general management operatives. However, research shows that with the increase in the managing of expatriates' costs, the ethnocentric approach has become less attractive for the MNEs and they have turned increasingly to third country and host-country nationals to satisfy international staffing needs. In such conditions, it is important for the policy makers to consider carefully the different aspects of the four national factors (see Figure 11.1) to develop relevant staffing and socialisation programmes.

The existing research suggests that the foreign assignment selection process should be done systematically, based upon the critical dimensions (such as suitability to foreign assignment, spouse support, different required skills, knowledge of local language, business practices, technical competence) of the foreign assignment.

Appraisals

Like the appraisal function within national settings, the individual's performance on international assignment must be appraised. So far, the research on expatriate performance appraisal has not fully addressed the relative impact of the uniquely international dimension of performance, regardless of the type of expatriate assignment (Dowling *et al.*, 1999; Peterson *et al.*, 1996).

Different approaches to performance appraisal of expatriates can be adopted depending on the nature of assignment. However, subsidiaries of a large MNE may pursue different strategic missions, face different legal conditions and encounter different competitive situations. Consequently, MNEs must account for various environmental conditions when constructing appraisal formats for international managers (Lindholm *et al.*, 1999). It can help to highlight the important factors dictating appraisal functions in different part of the world. Such information could guide managerial career development, future promotion decisions and compensation adjustments (Schuler *et al.*, 2002).

Compensation

International managers tend to have greater income security because of a number of obvious reasons such as they go away from home to a less certain environment which is more demanding, and so on. The high salaries of international managers result in a substantial disparity between the salaries of PCNs and those of HCNs or TCNs and create status distinctions in an MNE's global workforce. Similarly, there is also a disparity regarding the provision of different benefits such as fringe benefits. At the moment very little is known about international compensation and benefits administration. However, it is clear that this is an important area of IHRM considering the high rate of expatriate failures on the one hand and the increasing international compensation packages on the other.

Developing human resources

There are different aspects of development of international managers starting from pre-departure training extended to PCNs and their families to their return back home. A variety of training is provided to overseas managers such as language, interpersonal skills and culture sensitivity. However, by far the most important is the cross-cultural training. An important question is how to develop a cross-cultural training programme.

Developing cross-cultural awareness programmes (CCAPs)

A well-structured CCAP includes a number of steps.

Identifying target audiences

The initial step to develop any CCAP is to identify the target audience(s) for whom it is to be prepared. They can be expatriates of different levels and fields.

The goals of programmes

Once the target audience is identified, then the main goals of the programme are detailed. Primarily, the main goals of any CCAP are related to people's adjustment and effectiveness. It should increase their benefits and reduce stress.

Needs assessment

The success of a CCAP largely depends on the extent to which different needs of the programme are assessed. These include expectations of the receivers (for whom the programme is developed) from the programme, the amount of time required to complete the programme, budget for the programme and different methods to be adopted for needs assessment. This may look simple but in practice it might be problematic, for example, to assess the needs of receivers (it is difficult to cover and then satisfy the needs, desires, wishes and preferences of receivers). However, the adoption of a mixture of methods (to acquire information) can help to gather a comprehensive picture.

Methods of needs assessments

Needs assessments help to obtain information about the audience who will participate in the programme and about the organisation(s) in which it will be run. Such information also helps to decide about the content of a CCAP and techniques of implementing it (Mead, 1990). Four comprehensive methods highlighted in the literature are observation (both overt and covert), interviews, consultation with experts in the field and questionnaires.

Contents of programme

The content of a CCAP is mainly decided by the requirements of the receivers and much of it will involve three major aspects: (a) awareness, knowledge and information about culture, cultural differences and specific culture in which receivers will live; (b) attitudes related to cross-cultural communication such as feelings about others who are culturally different, and the emotional confrontations people experience when dealing with cultural differences in their everyday communication; (c) skills for effective interaction when living and/or working with people from other cultural backgrounds (Brislin and Yoshida, 1994).

Implementation of programme

This step consists of putting all the elements of the programme together, i.e. administering the programme. Based on the needs assessment, the programme developer/administrator gathers a good understanding about the amount of prior cross-cultural experience the receivers have had, issues that receivers would like to see addressed and the methods more appropriate for such analysis. Because of the concept of 'culture' being the focal point, generally a CCAP should start with an introduction about the awareness of culture by examining a list of its features identified by different specialists in the field (e.g. educators, psychologists, anthropologists or practitioners).

In the next phase, important knowledge about interactions and adjustment to other cultures should be discussed. Time and again the required type of behaviour which can enhance success in certain circumstances is emphasised. A number of techniques such as role playing, group tasks, etc. are organised to give a practical taste to receivers. Lastly, feedback from receivers is taken and different queries are clarified.

Evaluation of the programmes

The success of a programme is realised from its evaluation. To some extent this is achieved by the feedback from receivers (in the earlier step). From time to time an independent expert is also invited to evaluate the programme. S/he generally looks at the extent to which the programme met its goals. Generally, the evaluation report is given less importance as the programme administrator is too eager to finish the programme and start marketing for the next one. However, this could be disastrous, as the evaluation report might consist of some important suggestions which can further enhance the awareness of receivers. Hence the evaluation process should be carried out carefully and required suggestions should be incorporated.

Management development activities could be housed in corporate or global headquarters with local, regional and other HR units assisting in programme design and delivery (Dowling et al., 1999). However, the efficacy of this or other structural approaches remains to be empirically investigated.

Employee relations

As the spread of MNEs around the globe is increasing, the issue of employee relations is also becoming important. Good relations amongst the different units of the MNE are crucial for its smooth functioning. The role of key actors such as the management team of local subsidiary and its understanding with the headquarters, local/national unions and the respective governments is important in this regard. Cross-cultural training briefed above has proved useful in developing a better understanding between units of an MNE. The knowledge of the key institutions and socio-cultural environment are also equally important in developing and maintaining appropriate employee relations.

Summary

This chapter discussed some of the main developments in the fields of HRM and IHRM. The first part of the chapter analysed some of the key theoretical developments in HRM by examining five main models. The identification of the core propositions of these models is useful as they can enable the researchers to examine the applicability of these models in different parts of the world. To test this empirically, an integrative framework consisting of three sets of factors and variables known to influence HRM in different settings was presented. This framework is useful to glean the context-specific nature of HRM. It also helps to conduct comparative IHRM analysis.

The second part of the chapter discussed HRM from an MNE's perspective. Apart from the six core HR functions of planning, staffing, appraisals, compensation, development and employee relations, a number of other important HR functions need careful attention. These include HR issues during the acquisition and mergers of firms and during the repatriation of expatriates. However, the bottom line for the success of any HR programme is the careful consideration of the socio-cultural environment. The knowledge of the four national factors discussed in the chapter is therefore very useful for both HRM/IHRM academics and practitioner.

Discussion questions

1. Highlight the main theoretical developments in the field of western HRM.

2. HRM is known to be context specific. Discuss the main national factors, contingent variables and organisational strategies and policies which help to highlight the context-specific nature of HRM in different national settings.

3. What is international HRM? Discuss the main functions of IHRM.

4. To what extent is the integrative framework presented in the chapter useful for cross-national HRM evaluations? Discuss.

Closing Case Study:
HRM in Bharat Textile Mill

The roots of the personnel function in India can be traced back to the early twentieth century when the social reformer and entrepreneur J.R.D. Tata sought to legislate provisions for work hours and to ameliorate working conditions for factory workers. The Trade Union Act of 1926 gave formal recognition to workers' unions. Similarly, the recommendations of the Royal Commission on Labour gave rise to the appointment of labour officers in 1932 and the Factories Act of 1948 laid down the duties and qualifications of labour welfare officers. In the early 1950s two professional bodies were set up: the Indian Institute of Personnel Management (IIPM) formed at Calcutta and the National Institute of Labour Management (NILM) at Bombay. During the 1960s, the personnel function began to expand beyond its welfare origins with the three areas of labour welfare, industrial relations and personnel administration developing as the constituent roles for the emerging profession. In the 1970s the thrust of the personnel function shifted towards the need for greater organisational efficiency and by the 1980s personnel professionals began to talk about new concepts such HRM and human resource development (HRD). The two professional bodies of IIPM and NILM were merged in 1980 to form the National Institute of Personnel Management (NIPM) in Bombay. The status of the personnel function in India has therefore changed over the years. However, presently it is changing at a much more rapid pace than ever, mainly due to the pressures created by the liberalisation of economic policies initiated in 1991. Moreover, the state is forcing organisations to employ people from backward and reserved categories. The antagonistic role of trade unions is also on the verge of change. However, they still significantly influence HRM in Indian organisations.

Bharat Textile Mill (BTM), a privately owned firm, was set up in 1964 in an agricultural town in north India which had a below national average literacy rate. The main reason for the creation of this mill was the availability of both cheap labour and cotton. Like most Indian private sector organisations, all the managerial positions at BTM during the first two decades or so were occupied by family members or close relatives. Accordingly, most HRM practices were strongly influenced by social contacts and relationships. During the initial six years, the management did not allow the formation of any union in the mill. However, in 1970 one of the major Indian national unions managed to enter the plant. The same union still has a strong hold in the mill. Over 95 per cent of the blue-collar employees out of a total of 1,100 are members of the union. Over the last 30 years, the plant has experienced many disruptions (such as strikes and lockouts) from the union. Until 1982 the accounting department of BTM was responsible for its personnel function. In 1982 the personnel department was created which was responsible for recruitment, industrial relations, employee safety and welfare and legal requirements. Due to the lack of awareness of employees about the provisions of various pieces of Indian labour legislation (India has over 150 labour laws), at times the management was successful in exploiting the workforce. For example, there are no works committees for joint consultation in the plant. Indian legislation requires the formation of works committees in organisations having over 100 employees. On the other hand, provisions of many other labour laws are strictly adhered to such as minimum wages. Moreover, the management is forced by the union to recruit locals (irrespective of their capabilities), claiming that it is their right as 'sons of the soil'. The state government also bothers the management for different kinds of donations and in the recruitment of new employees.

A change in the managerial set-up of BTM came in 1988 when the eldest son of the owner became the new CEO. He returned from the United States after graduating from a top management school. Like many Indian managers, he had also internalised two sets of values: those drawn from the traditional moorings of the family and community, and those drawn from modern education, professional training and the imperatives of modern technology. These two sets of values coexist and at times create a conflicting situation for the person involved. Nevertheless, a number of changes have taken place at BTM regarding the personnel function. This is an outcome of both the new management and the level of competition which has increased tremendously due to the liberalisation of the Indian economy (not only from other textile mills but also from the rapid growth of other small-scale industries such as software-related and multinational companies which have established HR practices and policies).

To tackle the challenges thrown up by competitors, such as to improve quality, reduce costs and produce a variety of products, BTM has lately focused on the development of its human resources. In this regard, the name of personnel department has been changed to HRD. A number of in-house training programmes have been initiated. The line managers are being made more accountable and delegated responsibility for routine HR activities. The top HRD managers are now actively involved in the strategic planning of the firm.

Over the last decade BTM has come a long way. Still it has to make many more macro-level changes to become a fully professional firm and to survive in the present competitive environment. For example, decisions related to key HR functions such as recruitment and promotion are still made on the basis of the social relationships of those involved. The union is still playing a less supportive role towards the achievement of overall organisational objectives. The decision making is still centralised. Managers fear the loss of power if they devolve responsibility to line managers.

In the present competitive context, BTM is required to adopt a more participative approach to decision making, flexible working patterns, internal labour markets based on performance rather than social connections and a more open approach to information sharing amongst its employees.

Closing case study questions

1. Summarise the main factors which have contributed to the development of the Indian personnel/HR function over the last century.

2. Which HRM models are applicable to the case study company? Point out the key characteristics of each model and relate them to the relevant material from the case study.

3. Highlight the main factors which any foreign firm thinking of starting an

operation in India should seriously consider regarding the development of its HRM policies and practices.

4. As the HRD director of BTM, what challenges do you face regarding the management of your human resources in the new economic environment?

5. What do you propose to do to tackle them?

Further reading

Budhwar, P. and Debrah, Y. (eds) (2001) *Human Resource Management in Developing Countries*. London: Routledge.

Dowling, P. J., Welch. D. E. and Schuler, R. S. (1999) *International Dimensions of Human Resource Management*, 3rd edn. Cincinnati: South-Western College Publishing.

Schuler, R. S., Budhwar, P. and Florkowski, G. W. (2002) 'International human resources management', in O. Shenkar and B. J. Punnett (eds) *Handbook for International Management*, 2nd edn, Ann Arbor: University of Michigan Press.

References

Armstrong, M. (1987) 'A case of the emperor's new clothes', *Personnel Management* 19(8): 30–35.

Boxall, P. F. (1992) 'Strategic human resource management: beginning of a new theoretical sophistication?', *Human Resource Management Journal* 2(3): 60–79.

Brewster, C. (1993) 'Developing a "European" model of human resource management', *International Journal of Human Resource Management* 4: 765–84.

Brewster, C. (1995) 'Towards a European model of human resource management', *Journal of International Business* 26: 1–22.

Brewster, C., Larsen, H. H. and Mayrhofer, W. (1997) 'Integration and assignment: a paradox in human resource management', *Journal of International Management* 13: 1–23.

Brislin, R. and Yoshida, T. (1994) *Intercultural Communication Training: An Introduction*. London: Sage.

Budhwar, P. (1996) 'Developments in human resource management: an analytical review of the American and British Models', *Indian Journal of Industrial Relations* 31(3): 307–29.

Budhwar, P. (2000) 'A reappraisal of HRM models in Britain', *Journal of General Management* 26(2): 72–91.

Budhwar, P. and Debrah, Y. (2001a) 'Rethinking comparative and cross national human resource management research', *International Journal of Human Resource Management* 12(3): 497–515.

Budhwar, P. and **Debrah, Y.** (eds) (2001b) *HRM in Developing Countries*. London: Routledge.

Budhwar, P. and **Khatri, P.** (2001) 'HRM in context: applicability of HRM models in India', *International Journal of Cross Cultural Management* 1(3) (in press).

Budhwar, P. and **Sparrow, P.** (2002) 'An integrative framework for determining cross-national human resource management practices', *Human Resource Management Review* (forthcoming).

Chandler, A. (1962) *Strategy and Structure*. Cambridge MA: MIT Press.

Dowling, P. J., Welch. D. E. and **Schuler, R. S.** (1999) *International Dimensions of Human Resource Management*, 3rd edn. Cincinnati: South-Western College Publishing.

Flamholtz, E. (1974) 'Human resource accounting: a review of theory and research', *Journal of Management Studies* 11: 44–61.

Fombrun, C. J., Tichy, N. M. and **Devanna, M. A.** (1984) *Strategic Human Resource Management*. New York: Wiley.

Guest, D. E. (1991) 'Personnel management: the end of orthodoxy?', *British Journal of Industrial Relations* 29(2): 147–75.

Hendry, C and **Pettigrew, A. M.** (1992) 'Patterns of strategic change in the development of human resource management', *British Journal of Management* 3: 137–56.

Hendry, C., Pettigrew, A. M. and **Sparrow, P. R.** (1988) 'Changing patterns of human resource management', *Personnel Management* 20(11): 37–47.

Legge, K. (1989) 'Human resource management: a critical analysis', in J. Storey (ed.) *New Perspectives on Human Resource Management*. London: Routledge.

Legge, K. (1995) *Human Resource Management: Rhetorics and Realities*. Basingstoke: Macmillan.

Lindholm, N., Tahvanainen, M. and **Ingmar, B.** (1999) 'Performance appraisal of host country employees: western MNEs in China', in C. Brewster and H. Harris (eds) *International HR*. London: Routledge pp. 143–59.

Mead, R. (1990) *Cross-Cultural Management Communication*. Chichester: Wiley.

Miles, R. E. and **Snow, S. S.** (1978) *Organizational Strategy, Structure, and Process*. New York: McGraw-Hill.

Miles, R. E. and **Snow, S. S.** (1984) 'Designing strategic human resources systems', *Organization Dynamics* 16: 36–52.

Morgan, P. V. (1986) 'International human resource management: fact or fiction', *Personnel Administrator* 31(9): 43–7.

Peterson, R. B., Sergant, J., Napier, N. and **Shim, W. S.** (1996) 'Corporate expatriate HRM policies, internationalization, and performance in the world's largest MNCs', *Management International Review* 36(3): 215–30.

Poole, M. (1990) 'Editorial: Human resource management in an international perspective', *International Journal of Human Resource Management* 1: 1–15.

Porter, M. E. (1980) *Competitive Strategy: Techniques for Analyzing Industries and Competitors.* New York: Free Press.

Porter, M. E. (1985) *Competitive Advantage: Creating and Sustaining Superior Performance.* New York: Free Press.

Schuler, R. S. (1992) 'Linking the people with the strategic needs of the business', *Organisational Dynamics* summer: 18–32.

Schuler, R. S. and Jackson, S. E. (1987) 'Organisational strategy and organisational level as determinants of human resource management practices', *Human Resource Planning* 10(3): 125–41.

Schuler, R. S., Budhwar, P. and Florkowski, G. W. (2002) 'International human resources management', in O. Shenkar and B. J. Punnett (eds) *Handbook for International Management*, 2nd edn. Ann Arbor: University of Michigan Press.

Sparrow, P. R. and Hiltrop, J. M. (1994) *European Human Resource Management in Transition.* London: Prentice Hall.

Storey, J. (1992) *Developments in the Management of Human Resources.* Oxford: Blackwell.

Walton, R. E. (1985) 'From control to commitment in the work place', *Harvard Business Review* 85(2): 77–84.

Walton, R. E. and Lawrence, P. R. (eds) (1985) *HRM Trends and Challenges.* Cambridge MA: Harvard Business School Press.

CHAPTER 12

International industrial relations and the transfer of best practices

Jaime Bonache and Julio Cerviño

Learning objectives

When you finish reading this chapter you should:

■ understand the main reasons for governments intervention in employment relationships

■ know how national legislation can help or hinder cross-national transfer of HRM 'best practices'

■ understand other complex issues involved in the international transfer of human resource practices

Opening Case Study: European Union's information and consultation law

Employers' organisations yesterday pleaded with European Union governments to block a directive that would force companies to consult workers on redundancies and the sale of subsidiaries. They voiced concern after signs emerged that opposition by Germany and Denmark to the 'information and consultation law' was crumbling, leaving Britain and Ireland alone – not enough for a blocking minority.

The Confederation of British Industry said the French government was 'playing politics' and launching a 'destabilising campaign' over the directive. 'We are fully behind our government in stopping it,' said John Cridland, deputy director-general of the CBI. 'We hope other governments in Europe have the same steel to stand up against what would be a very bad measure for business.'

Daniela Isreal-Achwili, deputy secretary-general of Unice, the European employers' organisation, said the issue of how companies operating in one country should consult workers was for national governments and 'should not be decided at the European level'.

The directive, proposed by the European Commission two years ago, would require governments to impose sanctions on companies employing 50 or more workers if they fail to consult employees on important decisions. The government is expected to launch a diplomatic campaign to dissuade the Germans and Danes from switching sides. 'We have no reason to believe our allies have changed their stance,' the UK prime minister's office said.

The German government said it could not agree the directive in its present form, but German diplomats in Brussels said they expected Berlin to back the proposed law. One said there were no matters of substance holding back Germany from supporting the directive, though there could be 'technical reasons' for delaying agreement.

Willi Buschak, confederal secretary of the ETUC, representing European trade unions, said the German government had told unions it had no objections in principle, but wanted the EU first to agree on a European company statute, another measure involving worker participation. France, holder of the EU's rotating presidency, has scheduled a meeting of employment ministers on Wednesday to agree details of the statute after the Nice summit approved it in principle. Even if Britain succeeds in keeping the consultation directive off the agenda, it could face defeat under the Swedish presidency, starting next month.

John Monks, general secretary of the British Trade Union Congress, wrote to Prime Minister Tony Blair, urging him to stop opposing the EU proposals. General Motors' decision to end carmaking at Luton, and threatened job losses in steel, textiles and motor components, must lead to a change in employment laws to protect workers.

Neil Kinnock, European Commission vice-president, backed the directive as a 'safeguard' to ensure companies follow best practice.

Source: *Financial Times* CD-ROM 2000

Introduction

The previous chapter discussed the context-specific nature of HRM polices and practices. The present chapter focuses on some of the national contextual elements, notably government legislation and culture, which could help or hinder the successful implementation of the so-called 'best practices' which, some argue, are associated with high performance everywhere regardless of national differences.

Any professional who works internationally is aware of the wide range of employment issues in which different governments intervene. Practically every country has laws that establish minimum wages, length of the work week, conditions at the workplace, what rights employees have to collective bargaining, who can work, etc.

The variety of national employment regulations has important implications for multinationals. In the first place, it can be source of problems. For example, according to US legislation, American companies are accountable to domestic employment laws, unless complying with US law would require the firm in question to violate host-country laws. In one case, Saudi Arabian officials told a US employer that, because of security reasons, Saudis did not want any Jews in their country. This drove the company to reject Jewish applicants, but an American court found this violated the Civil Rights Act. In the second place, it can be also a barrier to replicate HR practices. What is allowed or voluntary in a country, might be forbidden or compulsory in another.

In this chapter, our aim is not to offer a comparative analysis of the different national employment laws and regulations since this would fill a multi-volume encyclopaedia, but instead to analyse the implications of the diversity of national employment regulations for multinational corporations, in particular, for the transfer or implementation of their HR management practices. Thus, our focus will be fundamentally that of management and we will analyse questions such as: What human resource practices are easily copied in an international context? Do they vary from country to country? Would it be better to duplicate exactly the practices, or had we better adapt them to the cultural context of different countries?

The chapter is structured in the following sections. First, we will present the management practices that within Anglo-Saxon environments are considered to bring about the best results. Second, we will analyse, through several examples, how governmental intervention can facilitate or hinder the implantation of these best practices. Finally, we will review the existing empirical evidence as to whether these practices truly produce good results in all countries, in other words, whether or not they are universally valid.

The chapter concludes that multinationals cannot simply transfer these so-called 'best practices', since some governments may facilitate and others hinder their implementation. But neither is it clear that even when possible, it is always desirable, since the best practices approach is a typically Anglo-Saxon management style which could be detrimental in some national contexts.

The best practices approach

An interesting question for any organisation is how to encourage employees to achieve its business objectives. Many studies have been carried out, almost exclusively in American companies, which show how a series of management practices invariably produces better economic results. In other words, if obtaining good results is what is desired, one has to carry out the implementation of these best practices, regardless of the country or type of organisation. Its application is thus universal.

What are these best practices? Different authors have their own preferred best practices but the following are some of the most often mentioned practices: job security, training, performance-based salaries, rigorous selection, participation, market-competitive salaries, teamwork or symbolic egalitarianism. We will discuss these below and take a close look at how different national contexts facilitate or hinder organisations' efforts to implement them.

Job security

In spite of the downsizing occurring in many large organisations in the last few years, many experts affirm that job security has several advantages. First, job security allows for a return on investment in employee recruiting and training costs. Second, it encourages employees to acquire knowledge which is of great value to the organisation, but not quite so useful in other companies, for example, the corporate culture, who is who within the organisation, or any particular technology not shared by other companies. If the employees are not going to remain in the company, they will have no interest in gaining this knowledge. Third, job security increases employees' loyalty and commitment, that is their identity within the organisation, their willingness to remain there and make an effort to improve it. In order for this commitment to exist it is essential that it be reciprocal; workers cannot be expected to feel committed to their company and its progress if the firm does not demonstrate similar commitment to them.

Training

The traditional benefit attributed to training is that it increases the employees' productivity. There are other advantages too. Training involves an exchange between the worker and the company. Investing in training the employees indicates that the company is concerned with and counts on them; thus, employees can be expected to respond by working harder. Moreover, investment in training enables a greater adaptation of the pool of candidates. Indeed, if the company acquires a reputation of training its staff, it will attract those employees who are interested in training, which means that it will have a workforce that is more motivated and more highly qualified. Also, training has the added value of expanding the knowledge base, since the employee who has received a training programme can share what he or she has learned with co-workers. Finally, training programmes can reinforce the corporate culture, enabling employees to gain the values and skills considered valuable and necessary to strengthen the company.

Performance-based pay

This practice is perhaps one of the most deeply engrained in traditional business management because it meets two basic objectives. First, it encourages a greater effort on the part of employees. Insufficient or lack of compensation will tend to translate into the smallest effort possible. Second, the company not only requires that employees make the maximum effort, but also that they support the company's interests. A performance-based pay system signals the type and level of effort required, that is workers must concentrate their efforts. Thus, by pursuing their own best interests (wage compensation) they will do what is best for the company.

Rigorous selection

Regardless of how good strategies and management practices are in the organisation, if it does not have the right personnel it is unlikely that the company will obtain good results. Among the initiatives which are usually considered as examples of selective hiring are the following:

1. A large number of applicants for each vacancy.
2. Hiring based more on cultural adaptation and attitude than on intelligence or easily acquired skills.
3. Conducting a series of interviews in order to create commitment as well as to send the message that this is a serious process.
4. Involvement of directors and senior personnel in order to emphasise the importance of the selection process and to facilitate the integration of new employees.

Sharing information

In traditional bureaucratic organisations, employees had to limit themselves to implementing the rules and guidelines which were dictated from the top down. The top management also had a monopoly of information about the company's objectives and workings, which formed its power base. By contrast, the best practices model maintains that participation in the decision-making process is necessary to get greater commitment from employees. In addition, sharing information with the company's employees about essential aspects of the business, such as strategies, financial and operating results, helps to establish a relationship of confidence and to motivate the employees to make decisions which help achieve the goals of the organisation.

Efficiency wages

This term is used to indicate that the company's employees have a salary level which is higher than that of competitors. This is considered positive because it promotes a more efficient workforce. The reason is that if a company chooses this policy, it will probably attract the best candidates. Moreover, it will reduce turnover costs and, in turn, those of selection and training. Finally, efficiency wages contribute towards creating an elite climate within the company because it is assumed that the best employees work for the organisation.

Teamwork

Teamwork allows employees to bring together their ideas, experiences and knowledge in order to look for better and more creative solutions to problems and, as a consequence, to achieve higher quality results. In addition, top-down control over the worker is substituted by a broader, colleague-oriented one, allowing the elimination of hierarchical tiers, with a subsequent reduction in cost. At the same time, it foments greater employee responsibility, as they now feel they have a hand in the organisation's inner workings. Finally, teamwork leaves decision making to those individuals who are more familiar with the pertinent information.

Egalitarianism

An increasingly competitive environment forces organisations to pay more attention to employees. This maximises employee input in the form of contributing progressive ideas. All the members of the organisation feel committed to improvement. This can be achieved in two ways. The first is symbolic: differences in company status are eliminated through changes in behaviour. The elimination of privileges such as 'management only' offices, parking facilities or cafeterias and the suppression of such terms as subordinate contribute to this. The second, which is more tangible, is closing salary gaps between different levels and, in particular, between the higher and lower ends of the organisational hierarchy.

Up to this point, we have analysed the best management practices which have universal application, regardless of the country or organisation. In what country is it not beneficial to provide incentives to employees or to include them in problem solving, objective setting and teamwork? Is there anywhere where careful employee selection is not efficient?

In the next three sections we focus on government initiatives and regulations which could help or hinder the transfer and implementation of best practices, followed by a fourth section in which we go beyond governments and discuss the implication of national culture for transfer of best practices across countries.

Best practices and centrally planned economies: the case of Cuba

The legal and economic environments of some countries make the implementation of the best practices approach impossible. To illustrate this point, we will look at Cuba, a communist country where government is in full control. Cuba is an important emerging market, progressively opening to investment and trade from market economies and offering good potential for foreign investors. The country has normal trading relationships with virtually every nation in the world except the United States. Since the implementation of the new investment law of 1995, many multinational companies have been attracted to invest there.

Investment is allowed in virtually every sector of the economy, excluding only health, education, armed forces and retail distribution. Although Cuba's foreign investment law permits the establishment of 100 per cent foreign-owned enterprises, most of the foreign investment is in the form of joint ventures. By December 1999, the Cuban government reported a total of 374 joint ventures. The investors are from 50 countries. Spain is the leading country in sheer numbers of joint ventures, followed by Canada, Italy, France, Germany and Mexico.

Within this framework of an emerging market, human resource management presents far-reaching problems for the foreign investor. Some of the best practices mentioned before, such as training, can be quite effective in the Cuban context, some can be effective but are difficult to implement there, while others can be highly ineffective or even counter-productive.

Best practices that work in the Cuban context

Technical training

One of Cuba's primary attractions for foreign investors has been its large, relatively well-educated human capital (the literacy rate is approximately 95 per cent and university enrolment is very high). Cuban workers are acceptably equipped from an industrial and technical point of view, especially in the area of production. However, because of the companies' obsolete production technologies, the employees need to update their knowledge through specific training programmes in order to be able to work with the new technologies implanted by the foreign investors.

Value orientation training

Furthermore, Cuban society in general and employees of the commercial and services sectors in particular, lack a market orientation. Over 40 years of planned economy, centred on achieving production plans, has created a business orientation centred on production and not on sales or commercialisation. The end result has been a bureaucratic value system, very similar to those established in the communist central and eastern European countries before the fall of the former Soviet Union. According to Prokopenko (1994), in these countries companies' main objectives were to satisfy the needs of managers themselves, employees, shareholders (government) and customers – in that order. Prokopenko contrasts this with a different order of priorities which he argues underlies the entrepreneurial value system of the west: customers, shareholders, employees, managers themselves.

In a communist country, the job of the manager is to fulfil the plan established by the relevant ministry and to request funds for input. Everything is centred on production objectives. Quality, cost and timeliness are important and customer orientation is systematically squeezed out of existence. The energy savings plan carried out by the Cuban government is a good example here. Several ministries imposed objectives on their companies in order to reduce energy consumption during the summer of 2000. The response of some companies was dramatic; they closed down for the summer. Instead of looking for formulas that would have permitted a reduction in energy consumption while maintaining a certain production efficiency, the factory managers' main goal was compliance with their ministry's request. Closing down the plants was a very efficient way to reduce energy consumption. Other considerations such as market demand, customer service, competitive advantage or profitability were not taken into account.

But the increase in foreign investment and joint venture creation is changing managerial approaches from bureaucracy to entrepreneurial value systems. From this perspective, training employees in the values of quality and service is simply vital, and training programmes play a very important role in the strategic positioning of foreign corporations in the country.

Training as an incentive scheme

Aside from the need to improve quality and service, training programmes are also a good mechanism as incentive schemes. Cubans are generally aware that things will be changing towards a market economy in post-Castro Cuba. Therefore, one of the Cuban workers' incentives for working in a mixed company is to prepare themselves for the future. Working in a foreign company allows access to new and more modern equipment, knowledge and organisational patterns of management; in general, new ways of doing things in more modern and efficient organisational systems.

The incentive dimension of training is also highlighted when it is conducted in a country like Cuba. For example, airline tickets for international trips must be paid for in dollars, beyond the reach of the average Cuban. In addition, the Cuban government has restricted the number of visas allowed for outbound trips. All of this means that it is very difficult for Cuban citizens to travel abroad. For this reason, any training programme that includes international travel is highly motivating.

Best practices that could work but are difficult or impossible to implement

Selection

Under the foreign investment law, foreign businesses cannot directly hire or pay Cuban workers. They must obtain labour services through an intermediary Cuban employer proposed by the Ministry of Foreign Investment and Economic Cooperation and authorised by the Ministry of Labour and Social Security.

Once the business is approved, the number and profile of personnel required is sent by the joint venture to the Cuban employment agency (ACOREC). The agency does the search and pre-selection process. However, candidates are often selected for political reasons. Thus, it is not surprising that the candidates sent by the agency have little resemblance to the profiles solicited. This lack of congruence between the job profile and the selection process makes it necessary to increase considerably the time and investment in personnel training, as well as control processes.

In order to minimise such problems, foreign company executives usually interview the pre-selected employees, but a representative from the Cuban partner is also present at these interviews. As a result, issues such as the candidate's ability and desire to learn western management techniques, gain greater status or enjoy better work conditions often do not come up during the interview, due to fears that the Cuban representative might be a communist party member, which is usually the case. The final decision rests with the Cuban employment entity. This process, seemingly simple, might take several months and is sometimes complicated for the worker himself. If the Cuban worker is employed by a ministry or state-run company, he must explain why he wishes to leave, thus entering into the area of his political commitment to the revolution and the state. On occasions this can be interpreted as a betrayal of revolutionary ideals.

Efficiency wages

Wages are centrally established and the same all over the country and for all corporations. The foreign investor cannot directly pay its employees. Instead, Cuban employees are paid by the state employment agency, which receives the salaries in US dollars and then converts the currency into Cuban pesos. This peso salary has a very low purchasing power, as the majority of products are only available in US dollar stores. Therefore, it is almost impossible to motivate employees through money.

Foreign investors find requirements such as these very onerous. They result in higher employment costs (compared to other emerging economies), affect the motivation of Cuban workers and limit the implementation of western-style HR compensation practices and incentive systems.

What then motivates the employees within this context? In general, Cuban workers prefer to work in a JV for a variety of reasons, all of which are of non-monetary kind. For example, as was mentioned above, they will get better prepared for the future while working in the company because they acquire a lot of knowledge which will be useful in these types of companies or in local firms if the political system changes. The joint ventures implement new work systems and advanced computer equipment which are superior to those used in the state-run companies. This means getting continuous on-the-job training which meets international standards. The working conditions, equipment and facilities, such as offices, computers, printers, photocopiers, fresh water machines, air conditioning, quality and quantity of meals, are superior to those of the state-run companies.

Best practices that can be highly inefficient or even counter-productive

Sharing information

According to the best practice approach, sharing information between management and employees is considered an efficient practice. In Cuba, however, achieving confidentiality rather than sharing information is the key to doing business, not only at the employee level, but among all managing personnel. Let us illustrate this point by an example: the Suchel Lever joint venture.

Union Suchel, which depends on the Ministry of Light Industry, is responsible for production and distribution of personal hygiene and home-care products. Suchel Lever's top management is formed by four members, two from Lever and two from Suchel. One of these Cuban managers is also a member of the management committee of other joint ventures, including one with a Spanish company (Suchel Camacho) and another with a Venezuelan company (Suchel Tropical). These two joint ventures manufacture and sell similar products to those manufactured by Suchel Lever. It is not surprising then that competitors are able to get up-to-date information about a rival's possible new product launches, new research, and advertising and marketing campaigns. Thus, when asked who his main competitor in the Cuban market was, a general manager of a joint venture answered: 'My Cuban partner.'

The sharing of information among competitors is not limited to new product launches or marketing campaigns. Even technical data are 'illegally' transferred to the ministry. For example, prior to the aforementioned joint ventures, the only toothpaste available on the Cuban market was the brand Perla, which was obtained through the ration card in Cuban pesos or in the free market in US dollars. The quality was not very good, but because it was the only one consumption was massive. Once the new brands manufactured by Suchel Lever and Suchel Camacho were established on the market, the Cuban consumer stopped buying the Perla brand on the free market. However, production managers in the joint ventures are Cubans who are familiar with the ingredients and production techniques. This know-how was transferred to Union Suchel, who began to manufacture a Perla toothpaste which was considerably improved in active ingredients, taste and packaging.

Fears about the lack of confidentiality in information are also transferred to the employee level. Indeed, once the control over employees falls on the Cuban partner and the ties between employee and the joint venture are weakened, a lot of information may be given to employees who may well end up being assigned to a direct competitor.

Egalitarianism

Cuban society is a collectivist, communist society whose main value has been egalitarianism. The unwritten social norm of 'equal pay for everybody' in the same work group still exists in most Cuban companies. In such an environment, it is doubtful that a firm insisting on symbolic egalitarianism will achieve any competitive edge. What would be essential in Cuba is that employees work differently from the way in which the country does, that is, learning that doing a good job is important, that quality is vital and that a qualified, self-motivated employee is more valuable to the firm than someone who just barely fulfils the job requirements. From this point of view, symbols granted to people who exhibit the appropriate behaviour could be very helpful.

A Spanish multinational company, manufacturer of consumer products, uses the following strategy. In order to differentiate its salesforce from that of the competition and make its salespeople feel different from others, it provides employees with high-quality suits and ties (paradoxically a symbol of white-collar capitalism) and a car. The message to clients and distributors is clear: 'Our salesmen are the best professionals, just as our products and services are superior.' This strategy of differentiation extends throughout the company, where only the 'best employees' get prizes and recognition. Here too it is considered essential to break with egalitarianism.

Government intervention in market economies

The preceding section focused on the analysis of the case of a highly regulated economy in which the government's actions make it practically impossible to implement many of the best practices. In countries with market economies there is also frequent governmental intervention in labour relations.

For some traditionally liberal executives and economists, governmental intervention is a kind of intrusion which introduces 'rigidity' and is a source of great inefficiency. If the market could act independently, its discipline would force the companies to adopt efficient management practices, because those who do not could end up producing worse results and as a consequence could be expelled. However, there are also several reasons why government intervention might sometimes be justified (Baron and Kreps, 1999).

Paternalism

Sometimes society knows what is good for an individual better than the individual himself, and therefore forbids transactions that the individual might undertake to his own detriment. Health and safety regulations can be justified, in part, by this reason.

Externalities

Transactions between firms and employees might adversely affect a third party (society). This provides a good reason for regulating these transactions. Regulations on mass layoffs (society bears the costs of unemployed people), pension funds, child labour and health and safety can be justified by citing externalities.

Redressing power imbalances

In the same way that a society has an interest in redistributing wealth and in promoting justice and equality, some also maintain that there must be an interest in balancing the power between companies and their employees. Without government intervention, power tends to be in favour of the companies. That is why regulations are introduced which give workers the right to collective negotiations with the company, or other laws that specify when and under which conditions workers can be dismissed.

Promoting social efficiency

The most reasonable individual decisions for business do not necessarily lead to the most satisfactory overall solutions. Let us, for instance, consider the case of training programmes. A company may wish to invest in training in order to increase its employees' skills and capabilities and, by implication, their productivity. But let us suppose that this company's competitors do not wish to make such investment. In this case, if our company undertook this investment in training, it would have higher employee costs compared with its competitors and would also run the risk of having its highly trained employees headhunted by them. Both these eventualities would provide the competitors with a clear competitive advantage. Faced with this possible scenario, our company may decide to reduce rather than increase its training budget. In this way, a decision which seems reasonable when examined at the individual company level, might lead to poor results for the entire general economy, because fewer people will now be trained and the economy will have a smaller pool of skilled workforce. Governmental intervention in training programmes or in minimum salaries can thus be justified based on this argument.

Protecting inalienable rights for the individual

Some rights of the individual, such as working in a safe environment or privacy, are considered by some societies as rights which cannot be renounced. In these societies, governments introduce legislation to prevent certain labour transactions which violate these inalienable rights.

Initiatives that favour the implementation of a best practice

For these and other similar reasons, governments intervene in a noticeable way in national systems of labour relations. In contrast to what the Cuban case's analysis suggested, a certain amount of government intervention is directly aimed at encouraging practices of high performance. For example, in Australia, France and Singapore companies must invest a set proportion of its payroll in training or face paying a tax to the government. Training not only leads to social efficiency, but also avoids the externalities that would be produced if the companies did not train their employees (because the society would have to bear the costs of unskilled people).

Another example of governmental action that can promote the development of a human resources practice of high performance is that of the laws of codetermination. This practice, which establishes a structure of workers' mandatory inclusion on the companies' board of directors, exists in countries like Germany, Denmark, Sweden, Austria and Luxembourg. Codetermination is not limited to Europe; indeed, in South Korea the law states that there be mandatory employee–management boards in all companies with 50 or more employees.

A final initiative that we should mention is an organisation which exists in the United Kingdom called Investors in People. This organisation, created in 1993, aims to motivate UK organisations towards reaching certain levels and enabling them to understand how investment in people can help companies to improve commercial success. The standard or established level is a set of evaluation criteria used to determine if an organisation deserves to be designated as an investor in people. In this sense, it has a similar orientation to the European Commission's European Model of Quality Management (EFQM), which establishes the regulations and principles of good management, and encourages their adoption when it presents a certificate of quality to those companies that demonstrate its correct implementation.

Beyond legislation: best practices, national culture and firm strategy

So far we have seen that varying national legislation can either facilitate or hinder the transfer of best practices. Based on the universalist approach, we should conclude that if there are no legal difficulties, all companies, regardless of their nationality, should implement this set of practices. Likewise, the role of governments should be that of favouring them or at least of not impeding their development.

Contrary to this approach, some authors argue that there is no one best way of managing organisations, so that the same HR practices are not equally effective in all locations. Different concepts of management and organisation can be equally successful. The most effective will depend, in part, on the character of the national culture involved. Different national cultures will support different recipes for managerial effectiveness and success. The different but equally successful German, Japanese and US models of managing organisations provide strong support for this type of what might be termed 'weak' relativism.

The essential logic behind what one might call 'radical' relativism (Bonache, 2000) is that, as we saw in earlier chapters, nations vary in the degree to which they hold certain work values. Moreover, the effectiveness of HR practices depends on how well they match a national culture's value system. If the national culture and a particular HR practice are congruent, i.e. if employees are asked to behave in a way that is consistent with their own values, employees' expectations will be better met and, as a result, the practice may work well. The opposite is also true. Given that culture is viewed by its members as the correct way to perceive, think and feel, then when HR practices and national culture are inconsistent, employees are likely to feel dissatisfied, distracted, uncomfortable and uncommitted. As a result, they may be less able or willing to perform well. It follows from the above premises that, even in the face of no legal or market constraints to standardise their HR systems, companies should adapt them to different cultural environments.

In support of this relativist view, Newman and Nollen (1996) examined the economic results of 176 units in 18 European and Asian countries of an American multinational company. They found that the economic results, measured by the profitability of the assets and the profitability of the sales, are best when the human resources practices of the unit are congruent with the national culture, as defined by Hofstede's dimensions (see Figure 12.1). The following results were obtained:

- The units of countries with a low power distance obtained better results if they offered a high level of participation. In contrast, the units of countries with a higher power distance obtained better results if they offered a low level of participation in decision making.

- Among individualistic cultures, the results were better when individual contributions were emphasised, while collectivist cultures got better results when this individuality was de-emphasised.

- The units within masculine cultures obtained better results if they used compensation systems based on merit, while in those with feminine cultures just the opposite occurred.

- In societies oriented towards short-term results, the units with less emphasis on job security obtained better results than those that placed greater emphasis on this variable. The opposite was found to be true in societies geared towards more long-term planning.

- Finally, in the units of cultures with high aversion to uncertainty and whose employees have a clear idea about the company's human resources policies, there are better results than those whose employees lack knowledge of HR policies.

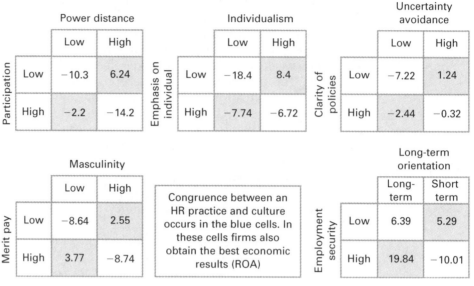

Figure 12.1 Effects of congruence between culture and HR policies on firm's profitability (ROA)

The message from this study is clear and categorical. In order to improve results, organisations have to adapt their human resource practices to the cultural context of each of their affiliates, which can be expressed by the saying: 'When in Rome, do as the Romans do.'

Yet culture is only one of several factors that affect the transferability of HR practices. In designing their HR practices, companies that operate internationally are not only subject to pressures for cultural adaptation, but also for global standardisation. If the demands for standardisation outweigh the demands for local adaptation, a subsidiary's HR practices will coincide more with those of its headquarters or a global standard than with that subsidiary's specific local conditions.

The first of these pressures for standardisation concerns the extent to which an MNC's headquarters links a particular HR practice to the firm's attaining competitive advantage. By way of example, take the transfer of Japanese HR practices to industrial subsidiaries in North America. The fundamental source of competitive advantage of firms in Japan was their capability to obtain first-rate products and zero defects. Certain HR practices, such as job flexibility, intensive on-the-job training, teamwork and cooperative relations between management and employees were essential in achieving this. As a result, work in the North American subsidiaries of these firms was organised according to these practices. In contrast, other HR practices of a more peripheral nature, such as the use of uniforms or of the same restaurant for all the organisation's members, were abandoned in some of the subsidiaries.

A second standardising pressure concerns high levels of interdependence between various MNC units. The greater the subsidiary's dependence on the resources and capabilities of the headquarters or of other units (e.g. to supply technology, raw materials, production components or management practices), the more influence the headquarters will be able to have over its practices. Similarly, the greater the headquarters' dependence on the subsidiary to supply the resources required for the corporation (e.g. profits, sales, import/exports of components or finished products to the head office or other units, or a strategic position), the greater the need to control it. In both cases, headquarters will try to implement management procedures that it is familiar with, a situation which will result in high levels of standardisation.

A third reason for standardisation relates to the MNCs' attempts to maintain consistency and internal equity in employee management. This is of particular importance to firms that make extensive use of international assignments of employees, either to control and coordinate different sub-units in the corporation or to transfer experience and know-how.

Finally, a fourth motive for standardisation is related to MNCs recognising the need to facilitate flows of information and knowledge among their different units. There is a growing consensus in the strategic literature that in today's MNCs every unit (both headquarters and overseas subsidiaries) can be a source of capabilities, expertise and innovation that can be transferred to other parts of the organisations. If they are managed with a similar logic (i.e. similar marketing, production and HR policies), the transfer of these intangible assets takes place more easily. For this reason, when a company wants to facilitate information and knowledge flow between different units, it tends to develop a global approach in management practices.

In sum, although a local adaptation strategy might be the most efficient one regarding particular practices and in certain countries, on other occasions a standardisation strategy (that is, implementing a best practice) might be the most rational option. Analyses regarding the transfer of HR practices must be carried out practice by practice and country by country. From this point of view, the saying 'When in Rome, do as the Romans do' cannot be utilised as a general prescription for firms operating in an increasingly global economy.

Summary

- The study of international industrial relations focuses on how employment relationships are regulated in different countries.

- Government intervention in multiple matters connected with employment is enormous. Almost every country has laws establishing minimum wages, length of the work week, workplace environment, employees' rights to collective bargaining, work eligibility, etc.

- The reasons for governments' intervention are diverse, including such things as paternalism, avoidance of external influences, promotion of efficiency, or protection of an individual's inalienable rights.

- The variety of national employment regulations has far-reaching implications for multinational companies. It can be a source of problems and a barrier to the duplication of HR practices.

- Legislation can play in favour of or against the implementation of high performance human resource practices. There are countries in which it is practically impossible to duplicate some of the practices which are considered by the western world to be 'best'.

- Legislation is only one aspect to keep in mind in the international transfer of human resource practices. Both culture and company strategy are also fundamental variables.

Discussion questions

1. In which main aspects does national legislation affect the implementation of high performance human resource practices?

2. To what extent should governments intervene in employment relations?

3. Cuba is a very particular case. What other countries can present similar problems and situations to those found in Cuba?

4. Within the constraints of Cuba's legislation and cultural environment, is it possible to achieve efficiency results? Why?

5. What do you think it is more important to take into consideration for the transfer of management practices: culture or legislation?

Closing Case Study:
Ford's idea suggestion system in five countries

In 1994, Ford Motor Company implemented an idea suggestion system in five electronic product units of its international network. This suggestion system is designed to solicit, evaluate and implement suggestions from teams of employees and then reward them for worthwhile ideas.

The units were located in three Latin countries (Brazil, Mexico and Portugal), and two Anglo countries (the United States and Canada). They were high-tech subsidiaries belonging to the same corporate division and manufactured car audio systems, airbags, speedometers and other sorts of electronic auto components. These components were used as inputs for other corporate-owned, regional auto-assembly plants. In 1994, the number of eligible employees (those full-time hourly and salaried employees, trainees and apprentices) were 3,700 in Brazil, 1,400 in Canada, 3,000 in Mexico, 1,200 in Portugal and 2,300 in the United States. The automobile company signed a three-year contract with a North American consulting firm, which had extensive experience in the implementation of this type of programmes, in order to design and launch the programme, promote participation, train employees, as well as to consolidate and report the programme's performance.

The corporate-wide idea suggestion programme was created in the United States, starting in mid-1991. It was designed to encourage a high level of employee involvement, with particular emphasis on team dynamics, by addressing the long processing times and low idea approval rates of the previous corporate suggestion programme. To accomplish these objectives, a decision was made to minimise administrative controls (i.e. to move idea evaluation to the lowest levels possible and to increase reliance on trust and empowerment). In September 1993, the final structure of the programme was reviewed by the corporate policy and strategy committee and launched in 1994 for worldwide application, with programme control responsibilities based in the corporate quality office.

To ensure that the company accomplished the key objectives of the programme, an integrative standard approach was developed, which included six elements: process design, administration, training, promotion and marketing, management commitment, and rewards:

- *Process design* refers to the specific rules under which the programme operates: who can submit ideas, what the approval process is, how ideas are evaluated, what points must be attributed to the submitted ideas, how ideas are awarded, how they should be implemented, etc. In order to treat employees equitably, these rules were fully standardised throughout the five subsidiaries.

- The *administration* element measured programme efficiency at each location. Information regarding ideas, decisions and cost savings was entered into the consulting operating system (COS) by each subsidiary and fed back to headquarters.

- The *training* element was designed to develop a common understanding of the programme and to institutionalise the cultural changes required for its success. Extensive training was provided at all levels of each unit and, particularly, to those employees who handle such specific programme roles as team leaders, evaluators and data coordinators.

- High levels of visibility and participation in the programme were achieved through extensive use of internal *marketing materials*, including audio-visuals, focused prints and other promotional items. These materials were designed to inform all employees of how the programme worked, the personal benefits and its impact on the company. The marketing plan also included a kick-off meeting to announce the programme to the employees, as well as ongoing communications to inform them of progress.

- Active *involvement and visible support by all levels of management* were crucial to create an environment that encouraged submission, a short evaluation time and the implementation of ideas. The corporate quality office encouraged all management levels to take the programme as an integral part of day-to-day operations and business planning. To this end, subsidiaries were compared with one another in regard to their efficiency rates and against corporate programme goals.

- A *standard rewards structure* was used to drive behaviour, since teams were rewarded for ideas that produced revenue or reduced costs by receiving points. These points were redeemable for merchandise from the programme's book of awards and selected local catalogue retailers or for worldwide travel, but they could also be applied to the purchase or lease of a new Ford vehicle. These non-cash awards were intended to serve as constant reminders of the programme's success.

Any significant change in any of these six elements had to be approved by the corporate office. However, the programme's standardisation was not total, because minor local deviations were introduced to address particular idiosyncrasies. Thus, although the same promotion and marketing materials were sent to each plant, bilingual printed materials and voice-overs for the audio-visual materials (English and the local language) were also established. Moreover, the training budget could be modified at the subsidiary level to reflect national educational and skill levels. Finally, the value of the rewards was adjusted to the purchasing power of the host country's subsidiary and the book of awards was adapted to local needs and interests.

Closing case study questions

1. Do you think that differences in national legislation across these five countries discourage the implementation of the programme?

2. Following Hofstede's cultural dimensions, to what extent do you think that cultural differences across these five countries affect the success of idea suggestions programmes?

3. What are the reasons for standardising the programme in the five units?

4. Do you think that changing management practices is the only way corporations can adapt to local business culture?

Further reading

Bamber, G. and **Lansbury**, R. **(eds)** (1993) *International and Comparative Industrial Relations*, 2nd edn. London: Routledge.

Pfeffer, J. (1998) *The Human Equation*. Cambridge MA: Harvard Business School Press.

References

Baron, J. and **Kreps**, D. (1999) *Strategic Human Resources Frameworks for General Managers*. Chichester: Wiley.

Bonache, J. (2000) 'The international transfer of an idea suggestion system: against radical relativism in IHRM', *International Studies of Management and Organization* 29: 24–45.

Newman, K. and **Nollen**, S. (1996) 'Culture and congruence: the management practices and national culture', *Journal of International Business Studies* 4: 753–79.

Prokopenko, J. (1994) 'The transition to a market economy and its implications for HRM in Eastern Europe', in P. Kirkbride (ed.) *Human Resources Management in Europe. Perspectives for the 1990s*. London: Routledge. pp. 147–63.

CHAPTER 13

Expatriates

Wes Harry

Learning objectives

When you finish reading this chapter you should:

- know who the expatriates are – of various types
- understand the head office and host-country view of expatriates
- be aware of the issues encountered by expatriates and their families
- have an understanding of some of the causes of expatriate failure
- be aware of the situation upon repatriation
- understand the role of expatriates in the process of localisation
- be able to consider the future of the expatriate role

Opening Case Study: An expatriate in Belgium – I wish I'd signed up sooner for cultural rewiring

A short while ago I found myself sitting in a large room in a gracious residence south of Brussels with about 100 American women, listening intently to a lecture called Tackling the Groceries List. After the coffee break, we all streamed back for the climactic session of the morning, the much anticipated module entitled Mastering the Cleaning Products. If only, I thought, swept up by the occasion, I had done this two years ago. I would have known exactly what to do with all those lamps I had rewired in Washington DC. I would have known where to buy videos in the right format. I would have discovered how to ask for dishwasher salt in the three official languages of Belgium, saving myself hours of prowling up and down supermarket shelves. So for those who, like me, were too cocky to admit that Belgium is a foreign country (I had lived here before) and too pushed for time to go to the Hints course, here, for what it's worth, are my top tips for living here.

Be prepared for bureaucratic challenge. Approach the process of having utilities registered in your name, getting your ID card from the *maison communale* and so on, as a test of your grit rather than an assault on your principles of fairness (no one queues) and efficiency (you will have to present yourself in person more than twice for your ID card). Make five copies of your marriage, divorce, vaccination and birth certificates.

Greet shop owners and so on with a servile '*Bonjour, madame*' when you enter a shop and do not forgo the '*Au revoir, madame*' when you leave, or their equivalents in Dutch, *Goede morgen mevrouw/Goedendag*. Remove your sunglasses when you talk to someone and never use the second person singular unless your interlocutor breaks the ice and uses it to address you. Don't try to go to the bank in your lunch hour. In fact, don't try to do anything businesslike in your lunch hour, a time of the day when you don't even need to feed parking meters.

In Brussels, *l'heure de repas* is even more sacred than the Spanish siesta. Many smaller branches of banks and post offices and some shops will close just when working people have a chance to visit them – between 1 pm and 2 pm. Trying to fit your chores into your Brussels lunch break is for wimps. Instead, have a three-course lunch with wine and a *pause-café* in your nearest brasserie. Learn French or Dutch. Though my husband, for some mysterious reason, urged me to take a cookery course, I defied him and tried to improve my French. There are any number of courses and, believe me, knowledge of at least one of the three official languages in Belgium is a first step to ingratiating oneself with neighbours and officials, who invariably suffer from foreigner fatigue (at least a third of Brussels is expatriate). The main thing to remember, though, is that living in Brussels is pretty blissful, a fact that both snooty Parisians and trendy Londoners these days have been forced to acknowledge (though American residents have been heard to complain that the little cobbled roads are 'kinda narrow', which is indeed the case if you're driving a Chevy Suburban rather than, say, a Fiat Seicento).

Source: 02 Dec. 2000, *Financial Times* CD-ROM 2000

Introduction

Chapter 11 made a number of brief references to expatriates while discussing core HRM issues from the perspective of multinational companies. The present chapter focuses specifically on these groups of employees who are significant players in companies with international and global business.

Foreign workers comprise substantial proportions of some wealthy states such as those of the Gulf Cooperation Council in the Middle East. The definition of expatriates used in this chapter will not necessarily cover all of these foreign workers but expatriates and other non-nationals are important to many economies, not just the wealthy ones. Much of the focus of academic research on expatriates has been on those seconded from North American or European companies. This chapter will, in addition to those expatriates, cover other expatriates who are either not tied to one company or who come from countries outside the industrially developed countries.

Expatriates have different motivation from their colleagues at home and host-country nationals and have to be managed differently. They have to cope with the stress or challenge of working in a foreign land where the culture is different and they may not always be welcome or well treated. However their very presence shows that they are necessary, or believed to be necessary, for the operation and development of many economies.

Who are the expatriates?

The majority of workers employed outside their home countries are skilled artisans or technicians, semiskilled or unskilled labourers. For the purpose of this chapter these workers are not considered to be expatriates. They are often known within organisations as 'third country nationals' to identify them as not belonging to the parent or host.

Definition

We will use the term expatriate to refer to professional or managerial staff employed outside their home country either on secondment from a parent organisation or directly by the host organisation. This use of the term expatriate differs slightly from that of Cohen (1977, p. 5) who defined an expatriate as a:

> voluntary temporary migrant, mostly from the affluent countries, who resides abroad for one of the following reasons – business, mission, teaching, research and culture or leisure.

The expatriates considered in this chapter are employed in some capacity and are not on research, cultural or leisure activities. They are located in the foreign country for a period of at least a year rather than being short-term visitors.

Expatriates in the past

During the period of European colonisation expatriates tended to be found in governmental roles as administrators or in senior military or police positions. The expatriates tended to come from the parent country while the less senior military or third country nationals or people from different regions from those being governed often filled police positions. This system had been used from the time of the Roman empire through to the British empire. Merchants and business people also tended to fall into these categories with usually the richer and more influential being from the parent country or a country close to the parent and the other foreign workers being from poorer countries brought in to do work which the hosts either did not want to do or were deemed not capable of doing.

After the colonial powers left, the foreign businesses usually stayed to make use of the expertise they had developed or the products they had to sell. It was rare for there to be sufficient numbers of well-educated and experienced nationals able to carry out the tasks of government or modern business so the newly independent countries and the few countries of the developing world which had not been colonised had to rely on expatriates to keep their government and businesses operating.

The number of expatriates

It might be thought that 40 years after extensive colonisation had finished that the number of expatriates would have been substantially reduced. But this does not seem to have been the case. Brewster (1991) argues that although there may be a reduction in the number of expatriates sent abroad by the large multinational companies, small and medium sized companies are sending an increasing number of expatriates abroad.

There is also a trend, identified by Brewster, to send expatriates to other developed countries rather than to developing ones. This trend for increasing use of expatriates is particularly marked in Europe where professional and managerial staff are transferred from parent to host especially in merger and acquisition situations. However, as discussed in the section on freelance expatriates, it might just be that the type of expatriate employed is more difficult to carry out research upon when compared to the expatriates seconded from a parent organisation. There is no doubt though that many organisations are trying to limit the number of expatriates they employ in order to reduce the costs of this group of expensive employees.

Head office view of expatriates

Why should organisations bear the cost of expensive expatriates rather than rely on host-country nationals? The reasons are complex and often based on prejudice as well as rational thought.

Reasons for employing expatriates

Some organisations, according to Scullion (1991), prefer to employ nationals of the parent company in sensitive posts such as regional chief executive or head of finance, to protect their own shareholders' interests. Some do not believe that host countries have staff available with the necessary managerial or professional skills. Some believe that it is necessary to have a cadre of staff who maintain the organisations culture and ways of working. There is also sometimes an expectation by customers and staff in some host countries that companies demonstrate their commitment by sending parent country nationals to fill important posts.

Expatriates as a means of control

Many international organisations attempt to control their foreign operations by putting trusted expatriate staff in key jobs, especially in the early stages of a venture. These expatriates are believed to be more willing to follow head office directives than local staff who may have competing pressures on them to favour their fellow nationals or host-government policies rather than to look after the interests of the foreign parent organisation. The expatriates are seen as owing loyalty and career advancement to the parent organisation rather than to the hosts. Their performance is assessed by head office managers who also make decisions on pay and benefits.

Difficulty of finding suitable host-country nationals

Finding suitable host-country nationals is often more difficult than finding secondees within a head office or other parent organisation location who can be sent out as expatriates. There can be language barriers between those selecting and the possible recruits because they are not fluent in each other's language. This can lead to decisions being made only on the basis of the candidate's ability to converse in the language of the recruiter.

The host-country's education system may not have produced sufficient numbers of citizens with the skills, knowledge and attitudes necessary to be successful in the particular job category. Gamble (2000) gives examples of financial management and human resource management in China, so those who are seen as having these attributes will be in high demand and often command a higher salary than an expatriate. Turnover among host-country managers and professionals can be very high, especially if the employing organisation is not responsive to their needs when these are different from the needs of expatriates or seen as threatening the status of expatriates.

Those host-country nationals who are employed in key positions are seen as being of uncertain loyalty and capability. They are not trusted in the same way as head office staff sent out to the host country. This is because they are seen as being influenced more by their duties as a citizen than as an employee, so will give greater weight to the interest of their fellow nationals than the interests of an international organisation.

Carriers of organisational culture

Some organisations prefer to have a cadre of expatriates, not necessarily from the parent country, to act as 'cultural standard bearers' for the employing organisation. These staff are considered to have been inculcated with the core cultural values of the employer and are used as the means of transferring and maintaining these values. Oil and oil service companies, banks and airlines have all built up these groups of expatriates who are regularly moved from country to country supervising the standards in the host location.

These expatriates are rarely in one country long enough to feel an affinity to the local people. They identify completely with the parent organisation and often act almost in a police role in their relationship with the host-country operation. They are employed to ensure that the interests of their parent organisation dominate over those of the host organisation and the host country.

Expatriates as a symbol of commitment

Many people in developing countries believe that the developed world fears them catching up and so will not transfer up-to-date technology and skills and apply patent and intellectual property rights to hold back their material progress. Sometimes organisations try to convince the host country that they are providing up-to-date technology and means of managing work by sending teams of expatriates to manage a facility, to provide technical training and be present on the ground to show that the parent is interested in developing the relationship with its customers. Gamble (2000) suggests that East Asian companies operating in China favour this strategy. Although the companies may argue that sending out teams of expatriates shows commitment, it might be that they are driven more by a desire to control the local operation and maintain parent company policies.

Management of expatriates

The apparent misunderstanding of the means of increasing the effectiveness of expatriates is, at least in part, due to a lack of skills in managing expatriates within the parent organisation. Brewster (1991) points out that very few organisations employ enough expatriates to be able to afford to develop the necessary expertise to manage those staff. Fewer head office staff have themselves been expatriates so are less able effectively to manage the performance of those posted away from home. Expatriates are seen as enjoying a lifestyle not within the reach of those at head office.

Pay and benefits

Head office's ignorance of the motivation and management of expatriates contributes greatly to the overpayment and occasional underpayment of expatriate staff. Harris and Brewster (1999a) draw attention to the lack of reliable performance measurement by parent organisations of their expatriates despite these being among the most expensive of their employees. The reward systems tend to be short term in their focus and reward results which suit the head office rather than the local operation.

Expatriates typically cost a multiple of two or three times as much as the equivalent post-holder in the parent country. With few exceptions they will cost a much higher multiple than a host-country national at an equivalent level in the organisation. Many employers think that expatriates need high pay with high savings potential to put up with the hardship of the overseas post. The expatriates themselves encourage this perception partly for short-term benefit but also because, as discussed below, they feel that taking an expatriate post means a loss of job security and career advancement compared with their colleagues at home.

Most employers pay more for an expatriate than they do for a home-country employee. Some employers base remuneration on a notional home-country salary with a tax equalisation formula; some base pay on the cost of living in the host country compared to the home country; others pay the going rate in the host country irrespective of the home pay market. Each approach has its advantages and disadvantages.

Beyond the cost of salary, the head office or local operation generally has to pay for housing, transport, flights home (often at a higher class and so more expensive rate than the expatriate would pay for personal travel), children's education, medical facilities, social clubs and other benefits not usually included in the home-country compensation and benefits scheme. They often pay a foreign service allowance and provide compensation for currency fluctuations.

Freelance expatriates

The lack of suitable host-country nationals and of parent organisation secondees has led to a market for expatriates who are not part of a parent organisation but who sell their skills to the employer prepared to pay for their services. The local market determines the pay and benefits of these staff. Their employer is most often a local organisation with no link to an international body. Sometimes an international company which cannot find suitable secondees within its own ranks employs them.

Being posted away from the head office can be seen as career limiting so many staff who would be good candidates for an expatriate assignment choose to refuse and prefer to stay close to the centre of organisational power.

Why be a freelance expatriate?

Many of the freelance expatriates have been with international organisations and found that their career progress had indeed been hampered by working as an expatriate, or grew to enjoy the challenge and lifestyle which could not be offered by the parent organisation. Some transferred their employment and loyalty to the local operation and others became what Banai and Harry (2002) have called transnational managers, employed for their international skills, not for their nationality or knowledge of their employer's organisation.

Neglected by researchers

This group of expatriates has been neglected by academics as they are much more difficult to track down and study than the expatriates belonging to an international organisation which may have its head office close to the academic's location. Most academic studies have focused on expatriates who were of the same nationality as the researcher or at least were easily accessible. But freelance expatriates might be from another nationality and may not share the same language as the researcher. These expatriates are also less homogeneous than those seconded from parent organisations. As an example, the author worked for one company which had over 40 different nationalities in one location. So researchers may find it more difficult to establish what differences are due to their being from different cultures.

Attractions to employers of freelance expatriates

Freelance expatriates can be hired and fired fairly easily so they have none of the problems of reassimilation back into the parent at the end of the assignment. They have few claims on the employer other than for their pay and benefits. The employment of freelance expatriates is usually governed by a short-term contract for a specific period. The laws of the host country apply to such contracts and are usually of more benefit to the employer than to the employee. The employer does not give them the same level of training and development as provided for seconded expatriates. Any training is likely to be job specific as they are expected to be ready trained before they are taken to carry out a task. If the work changes and they are no longer capable of handling a job they will be replaced by another ready trained expatriate or by a host-country national.

Like the host-country nationals, the freelance expatriates' loyalty and commitment to their employer are not certain. This can be seen as an advantage for the employer as it feels no need to give support or commitment beyond that necessary to accomplish a particular task. The employer may also view the absence of loyalty and commitment as providing neutrality and impartiality.

Freelance expatriates tend to specialise in working in a particular region or industry. They have specific knowledge and capability not always available to other expatriates or to host-country nationals. They are often more willing to work in locations not attractive to other expatriates and seem to be more willing to take risks in their career – if the immediate reward is sufficient.

Motivation of freelance expatriates

The motivation of freelance expatriates may be that they were among those who were seen as having 'gone native' and moved their loyalty to the host society. They may be motivated by the money and lifestyle which are higher than they could enjoy back home. They might enjoy the challenge and interest of the expatriate way of life, or it might be that they are not capable of getting a suitable job back home.

Host-country nationals' view of expatriates

Some host-country nationals believe that most expatriates are not capable and enjoy privileges in terms of pay and status which they would not be able to achieve at home. These nationals focus on the lack of up-to-date knowledge and drive of some expatriates. They feel that they are not receiving the highest standard of work from them and that the expatriates are only interested in saving and remitting money back home.

Resentment

In countries of the Gulf Cooperation Council (GCC) in the Middle East non-nationals are up to 95 per cent of employees in the private sector. Not all of these can be defined as expatriates but, as Harry (2001) has shown, the nationals of these countries are concerned about any foreigners taking jobs which their fellow citizens could hold and sending money out of the country which should be invested locally. This feeling is especially strong in those countries where the level of unemployment among nationals is high – it is believed to be in excess of 20 per cent in some GCC countries.

The upset about the employment of foreigners is particularly strong if the expatriates employed are not seen by non-expatriate employees as being worth the cost to the organisation. Some parent organisations have not sent their best staff abroad as expatriates. They have selected those they wish to move out to create opportunities for staff with more ability or more acceptable behaviour and attitudes; or they have selected favoured staff as a reward for loyal service rather than because they will be the best person for a job.

If the expatriates are seen as transient then resentment is muted, but if they are seen as being more permanent then their presence can be met with hostility. Some South Asians in the Middle East have been accused of attempting to impose an alien culture and to claim rights which are resented by the host-country citizens.

If the foreigners get the best jobs then this can encourage racist or nationalist attitudes between the expatriates and the host citizens. The expatriates think they have the job because they are better than the natives and the hosts think that the foreigners got the job because they have influence or privilege.

Positive view

Sometimes the racial attitudes are positive towards the expatriates, especially Caucasians from rich, developed countries. Despite of or because of the colonial experience of many developing countries, they are accorded prestige and privileges not granted to fellow nationals or people of similar racial groups to the hosts. Poor manners are forgiven and expertise assumed just because of the racial origin of the expatriates, irrespective of capability.

Many host citizens recognise that there is much to be learned from capable expatriates, who usually have much more varied and intense work experience than the host-country nationals. Because professional and academic qualifications are demanded before an employment permit is issued by the host government, the expatriates are invariably well qualified in comparison with both the hosts and those holding equivalent positions in their home country.

Those expatriates who enjoy challenging work and training others can make a very positive impression on those they work with (Harry, 1996). They are able to manage facilities and transfer skills to the hosts. They can often care more about the success of the activity than other staff because they are given greater responsibility and accountability.

It might be that the demands of a changing economy mean that there are just not the numbers of trained and capable people available within the country or the skills are only needed for a short time. In these cases it is uneconomic or too time consuming to train staff when ready trained and capable workers are available from abroad.

Host's expectations

Most host-country staff have little choice but to try and fit in with the expatriates' style of working. The expatriates usually have knowledge they want to acquire and, even if they do not have ability, they have the organisational clout to make life difficult for the locals who do not do as they wish. However the more effective expatriates try and build a sound working relationship. The most effective probably build a sound interpersonal relationship as well. Understanding how others view us is the first step towards building a relationship. Bedi (1991) considers that the Asians' perceptions of an expatriate manager include the following:

- The expatriates are fair in their dealings, liberal and patient regarding the behaviour of their staff, generous, frank and straightforward.

- They are also seen as being excessively career oriented, spend too long reporting to head office, superficially aware of the local culture, do not transfer skills and knowledge in a consistent and organised manner and form opinions based on first impressions. They also spend too much time decorating their homes and acquiring nick-nacks. They mainly socialise with their own nationality, are very sports minded and talk too much about their maids.

In the past professional and technical ability was a desired attribute of expatriates but now it is an essential basis of employment with much emphasis placed on passing on skills to others. So social skills or interpersonal skills become more important to expatriates. Host-country nationals now expect the expatriates to be paid for their contribution to long-term organisational success, not just for the passport they hold or the social contacts they have.

Expatriates' privileged position

Expatriates usually have more influence with head office than the local managers, especially if they are of the same nationality as the staff at head office. They are often treated very well within the host country just because they are representatives of important organisations or because they are citizens of powerful countries. Their employers are able to use influence with local authorities to have rules and regulations interpreted in favour of the expatriate.

The privilege granted to some can lead to the dissatisfaction of others and this ill feeling can arise in the case of the relationship between hosts and expatriates. The hosts think: 'This is my country. Why should the foreigners have status and benefits which are denied to me?'

Expatriates' view of their situation

The expatriate status is generally high within the local community. They have privileged access to embassies and social circles based on their employment status and nationality and enjoy a standard of living beyond the expectations of their colleagues at home. In return for these benefits they face disruption in their home life, have to work hard and receive little support from their colleagues in the parent organisation.

Expatriate communities

Cohen (1977) believes that expatriates' lifestyle often resembles that of a colonial official. He considers the structure of expatriate communities arises as a way of coping with being strangers in a foreign land. Thus the expatriates tend to create for themselves a 'social bubble' similar to that of tourists which shelters them from the host society. But not all expatriates take refuge in the 'bubble' to the same degree and Cohen suggests a number of adaptive strategies developed by expatriates. He also points out that although the expatriate communities may exist for prolonged periods their membership is in a state of continual flux with people arriving and leaving at regular intervals.

Parent companies often encourage staff to mix socially with their fellow expatriates and to live in expatriate compounds. Many companies, especially those that use expatriates to maintain core culture, provide their own compounds so that expatriate staff work and live together. Frequent trips back to the head office or a regional centre reinforce the links with the parent organisation.

Housing, as discussed further later, becomes an emotive issue for many expatriates. Sometimes the housing issue is important because of security concerns, sometimes because housing on an expatriate compound creates a separate world from that outside, but more often the issue appears to be driven by status and prestige. In the expatriate community the standard of housing provided by an employer clearly demonstrates their place in the organisational and social hierarchy.

The expatriate communities which become separated from the host communities can lessen the impact of culture shock, but in doing so they remove an important means of networking and understanding the host country. A feeling of superiority is often generated within these communities encouraged by 'old hands' and reinforced by national or racial stereotypes.

Some expatriate staff become sympathetic to the local requirements and mix more with the hosts than with the expatriates. For many the experience of being treated as a 'foreign friend' is part of the joy and interest of being an expatriate. Head office and other expatriates then condemn them for 'going native'. However, Mendenhall and Oddou (1995) have shown that those expatriates who develop relationships with the host-country nationals are more likely to succeed in the assignment than those who remain aloof.

Responsibility and effort

Because head office and the local management see expatriates as expensive, they are given more responsibility and expected to work harder than would be the case for home or host-country employees. Obviously this is not always the case and there must be a few expatriates sitting on verandas sipping gin instead of working, but most find that the challenges and the working hours are greater than at home.

Many managers and professional staff thrive in the environment with less direct supervision and more ambiguous rules. The levels of responsibility can be awesome but capable individuals find ways of dealing with the wide variety of issues and decision making. They can become protective of the local responsibilities and resent interference from bosses in the parent organisation or close at hand. However it is also likely that many expatriates become focused on entirely short-term objectives to be achieved during the period of the assignment, even at the cost of the organisation's longer term success.

Lack of support

While complaining about interference and lack of understanding from other parts of the organisation, many expatriates complain about the lack of support. They feel that those in the field are forgotten about and do not have access to decision-making processes which have an impact on their work. A mentor at head office and/or within the region has been shown by Feldman and Bolino (1999) to be a great help when adjusting to the new situation, providing guidance to deal with directives and policy statements and to provide a 'lifeline' to seconded staff.

Performance appraisal procedures and reward schemes seem geared to the parent or the general international environment rather than to the specific situation in the host country. Training opportunities seem to be reserved for the home country or host-country staff and not for the expatriate who is expected to 'know enough already – or else they would not have been appointed'. A significant issue that expatriates feel is neglected by their employers is the upheaval caused to their families by undertaking work abroad.

Expatriate families

Previously expatriate families were expected to pack their bags, send the children to boarding school and follow the (normally male) breadwinner to whichever part of the world his employer posted him. Recently the rise in numbers of dual career families and of female expatriates has challenged the ability of employers to disregard the expatriate family.

Adjustment

For the expatriate the work, although often more challenging and with more responsibility, is similar to that found at home. The routine of leaving home in the morning and returning in the evening having spent the day in an office or facility carrying out managerial or professional work is the same or at least similar.

For the family, however, the routine is now very different and the adjustments to be made are greater. There are no readily accessible colleagues to spend time with, often few shopkeepers fluent in the same language, different types of food-stuffs available, utilities can be less reliable than at home and the school system may be completely alien. The spouse, still usually a female, is often restricted from working by government regulations. Even if work is found, it is rarely of the same level of pay or interest as that undertaken at home. Children not only have to make new friends but might also have to attend a school teaching a different syllabus and in a different language from that at home. Schooling issues become more important for teenage children who may find that they have to follow part of one examination scheme for a few years and then another type for a few more years. In many but certainly not all locations the children are more vulnerable to illness than they would be at home. They are certainly subject to different illnesses than they would face in their home country.

Living conditions

Living conditions can become of major emotional significance to those who are surrounded by a novel environment. In pre-colonial times European traders were often confined to special areas, for example, Nagasaki in Japan, and this continued with the development of expatriate compounds which had the short-term advantage of allowing them to live in an accustomed way with little adjustment. This continues in countries such as Saudi Arabia. The segregation reduces the strain of adaptation. The compound living provides a way of coping with the environment but it cuts off the expatriates from contact with the local citizens.

Expatriate failure

Many studies of expatriates focus on the high rate of expatriate failure and the costs of this failure. Foster (2000) argues that it is in fact psychologically impossible for most people to cope with the dislocation and upheaval that regular international relocation would cause. Clearly many expatriates do in fact cope well with the dislocation and upheaval, but many fail. Yet organisations do not seem to be able to deal properly with the causes of failure.

Selection methods

As Harris and Brewster (1999b) show, despite the improvements in selection methods in recruiting staff for home assignments, the selection of expatriates, especially those seconded from the parent organisation, tends to be haphazard and unstructured. The informal criteria and selector's individual preferences seem to be given more weight than clearly defined formal criteria.

It appears that often the most capable staff refuse to be considered for an expatriate assignment if it is not certain how exactly this will help their career. They exclude themselves from the selection process at an early stage so that they can protect their career close to the organisation's centre of power. This might be a good thing because realistic enthusiasm and commitment to the expatriate assignment are likely to be the greatest contributing factors to a successful completion of the task. A reluctant expatriate is virtually certain to be a failed expatriate.

Many studies have shown how the attitudes and behaviours if not actual skills needed by expatriates are greater than those working in a home country, but the selection methods used seem to exclude judgements on attitudes and behaviour. Brewster (1991) found that expatriates tended to be selected purely on the basis of their technical competence, although (as discussed below) his later research shows that other less formal assessments can be at least as influential. He found that most organisations assume that managerial competence is universal so if a manager performs well in one location they will perform well in all locations. It is likely that those expatriates who adjust and prove themselves capable in one foreign location may have fewer problems in other locations, but this is because the expatriate has the personal qualities, attitudes and behaviours rather than because they have universal competence as a manager.

Training

It seems that although the importance of training and preparation for foreign assignments is recognised, the actual provision of pre-assignment training is minimal. Selmer et al. (1998) found that many international organisations do not provide systematic training for expatriate staff. Expatriates, in the view of Selmer and his colleagues, not only need training prior to the beginning of an assignment but also need reinforcement training to help them cope and be effective as they go through various stages of adjustment. They strongly believe that expatriates need regular training to help them be effective in their work. However, it is rare for an employer to offer such help.

Any training given tends to be focused on technical and managerial matters such as how the parent company wants accounts to be prepared or costs to be allocated. Training in how to adjust to a different way for working and how to enjoy and develop with the challenges is neglected. Most expatriates are left to sink or swim in the local organisation and its cultural environment.

Cost of failure

It was estimated by Swaak (1995) that the cost of a failed expatriate assignment was in the range of $200,000 to $1.2 million. This is a significant cost for even the largest organisations. Swaak's data were from US organisations and other US researchers have claimed that up to a third of expatriate assignments end in failure. Harzing (1995) disputes the figures for failure but there is no doubt that many expatriate assignments end prematurely.

European writers have suggested that expatriate failure is not as frequent or as costly. Perhaps this is because European employers are not as demanding or are prepared to put up with a lower quality of performance from their expatriate staff. Maybe the European expatriates (and other nationalities) are more able to succeed in different roles and different locations than the Americans.

Any failure of expatriates is more costly than a failure of a home-based employee just on the costs of expatriation and repatriation without taking into consideration management effort, time to find a replacement and the impact on the effectiveness of the local operation.

Culture shock

The term culture shock implies something harmful, to be coped with and to be overcome. It is something threatening. Previously many western international organisations such as oil companies and banks carried their culture with them to wherever they operated. There was little concern with culture shock because there was no different culture. As these organisations find it less easy to impose their own culture on workers and societies (even their own), they must learn how to become more sensitive and responsive to the expectations and needs of local societies and their cultures. The expatriates must face these issues when they operate in the host country and work with host nationals.

The expatriates are required to question their own culture, expectations and needs. Some retreat into their own culture and become ultra nationalist and contemptuous of the local people and of their fellow nationals who have remained at home. Others embrace the local culture and assimilate into it, 'going native' as mentioned earlier. Most fit somewhere between the two extremes. But even those most willing to adapt and enjoy the new culture still go through a period of adjustment which may go as far as culture shock and inability to work effectively in the new situation.

The culture shock is not all one way, as Florkowski and Fogel (1999) point out. The hosts may not be prepared to accept expatriate managers and resist their attempts to create an effective and successful local organisation. Hosts may withhold support from the expatriates to make their tasks harder or impossible to achieve. The host society may not be prepared to adjust its cultural expectations to suit the foreigners, for example, the restrictions put on females in some Muslim countries.

Negative racial stereotypes are not only found in European countries. Some host staff resent people of the same race as themselves being paid at expatriate rates or expect a person from the parent organisation to be of a particular racial group and create problems with those who are not from that race.

Family not happy

As we have seen in the section on expatriate families, they are the ones most exposed to the local culture and environment. If they are not happy they exert a substantial negative influence on the expatriate. Sometimes this leads to the failure of the family relationship and, more frequently, to the failure of the expatriate assignment.

Support from other families and friends can do much to help the newly arrived family to adjust. It seems that the more difficult the location, then the more helpful others are – either because they have gone through the adjustment themselves or because they have fewer distractions or interests to occupy their time.

As Foster (2000) suggests, the increase in dual career couples puts added strain on the expatriate family where one partner may have to give up an interesting and/or well paid job at home to follow the other. Other problems arise for the couples who are not married, either because theirs is a same sex relationship or they chose not to formally marry. Many governments will not issue a dependant's residence visa to partners who are not formally married to the holder of an employment visa.

Repatriation

As shown by Selmer (1998), the qualities which make a successful expatriate are not necessarily those which lead to a successful domestic career. Selmer found that organisational policies and practices made it very difficult for the expatriate to adjust back into the home-country operation. Often expatriates are brought back to the parent organisation with no clear idea of where they will fit and how the organisation will benefit from the period abroad. Too often the returning expatriate finds that during the period away there has been a reorganisation and jobs which were promised before the overseas assignment have disappeared. The fortunate repatriate finds the employer will try hard to find a suitable post and maybe allocate a mentor to assist with the resettlement process. Feldman and Bolino (1999) show how an effective mentor is particularly valuable. Most repatriates spend time doing 'special projects' before being fitted into a job which ignores their development while they were an expatriate, or else change employer and maybe become freelance expatriates.

The expatriate who has not been seconded from a parent organisation has to find a new job without any help from the previous employer. Potential new employers, unless they are looking for a recruit to fill an expatriate position, will assume that the repatriate will find it difficult to adjust to the home environment and its rules and rates of pay. So employers will be reluctant to consider expatriates and prefer to select others whose career path is clearer and more conventional.

Pay and benefits at home

After a time spent abroad on a higher salary and benefits than paid at home, it is difficult for the repatriate to adjust. The costs associated with a return to the home country are underestimated due to the impact of inflation whilst away or the cost of re-equipping a home (rarely paid for by the employer) and even the expense of visiting relations and friends who may not have been seen for some time.

Now all the household bills have to be met from the employee's salary and savings. There are no servants or maintenance staff ready to attend to domestic chores. The impact of tax on salary is forgotten when abroad, especially if in a low tax environment or one in which the employer meets the tax bill. Even without tax, for most expatriates the savings potential of the expatriate assignment is unlikely to continue after the return home.

Annual leave tends to be less generous in the parent organisation's location than it is overseas and the ability to reach exotic locations for holidays is much reduced, especially now that leave fares are not provided.

Inbound culture shock

Among the greatest shock for repatriates is that others are not greatly interested in what they have been doing or experiencing. This is not just at work but also among family and friends. The latest TV drama is of more importance than events abroad. The social circle which perhaps used to revolve around the club and embassy has disappeared. Acquaintances are not particularly interested in the job or employer of the repatriate.

There may be some jealousy of the image of the expatriate lifestyle involving sitting on a veranda sipping gin as the sun sets. The repatriate may have saved enough to move to a better house amongst people they do not know. If their finances were stretched to buy the property it may not be possible to maintain the lifestyle expected in the neighbourhood.

Missed opportunities

So many employers seem to miss the opportunity of a repatriate adding to the stock of knowledge of the organisation. Even if the expatriate assignment was well planned and handled, it seems rare for the repatriation to be more than an ad hoc attempt to slot the returnees back in and virtually tell them to forget about their holiday and get on with some real work.

The challenges, personal growth and individual responsibility of the expatriate are replaced by a need to operate within a closely controlled hierarchy with strict rules and policies to be followed. The adjustment is usually more traumatic than that experienced upon expatriation. There are exceptional employers who manage the repatriation well but they are very few.

Localisation

The objective of the process of localisation is to replace expatriates with local people – host-country nationals. While in the past expatriates might have possessed knowledge, skills, behaviour patterns and attitudes which were not found among the host citizens, this is unlikely to be the situation now. Nation states and their governments are not willing in the long term to allow foreigners to hold jobs crucial to the society's prosperity.

The expatriate dilemma

Expatriates are in a quandary regarding localisation; they are in a position to hinder or aid the process of localisation. By helping the nationals to develop, the expatriates may lose their job, and the income and the lifestyle which go with them. There is the fear of returning home and searching for a new job. So to resist or assist is the choice to be made. Most expatriates choose a mixture of resistance and assistance. A few blatantly resist and a few more enthusiastically assist.

Resisting

Resisting could mean being thrown out early and replaced by a more amenable expatriate. However there are a number of subtle and not so subtle ways of resistance. Favoured methods include:

- to set the standards of entry at a level that few if any citizens can meet, e.g. higher degrees or professional qualifications in countries which lack suitable educational institutions
- to set the pay and benefits of the hosts, especially during training, at levels which are not attractive
- to require excessively long periods of training
- to give undemanding tasks and then say the host citizen is lazy.

Assisting

Assisting could mean being thrown out and replaced by a local employee. For many expatriates an important part of their job and their enjoyment is passing on knowledge and helping the local people to increase their capability and progress to jobs in which they can make a more valuable contribution to their employing organisation and to the material progress of their country. These expatriates set realistic recruitment standards, encourage training and development that are necessary to succeed in a job and establish and monitor tasks and goals to stretch but not break the people being groomed to replace expatriates. Perhaps the most effective way of assisting the localisation process is for the expatriates to set a good example of the way of work.

Until recently parent organisations ignored the need to assist the localisation process so gave little help or training to the expatriates who assisted the host citizens. If localisation was undertaken it was looked upon as a cost of doing business in a location rather than something to lead to long-term benefit. This has changed due to pressure from many governments to create real employment opportunities for their own citizens and governments, placing severe restrictions on the number of employment permits which are issued to expatriates.

Capability of host-country nationals

Local subordinates (or even supervisors or peers) seeing an expatriate carry out a task may underestimate the skills and expertise being applied. This occurs especially when older, experienced but unqualified expatriates are observed by younger and more qualified local citizens. Increasing standards of education and training, along with recognition of the methods of succeeding in modern industrial or post-industrial societies, means that individual host-country nationals are at least as capable as the expatriates.

There may be a shortage in the required numbers but with investment in training and active support the host nation will be able to provide nationals capable of replacing expatriates, especially those jobs which require a local rather than a global outlook.

Advantages of employing locals

Host-country nationals are attractive to international organisations because they are usually cheaper than expatriates and do not have to adjust to a different culture. Their families are resident in the country already and do not have to consider giving up a job, changing schools or home. They could be with the employer for a long time so repay the investment in training and development. It is also expected that they have greater knowledge of the host market, better communications with the local government and employees and may be less concerned with the long-term success of the local operation. Employing host-country nationals also demonstrates a commitment to the country and its citizens.

The future of the expatriate role

The increasing drive for organisations to become more global in their outlook requires a global workforce from diverse backgrounds. Global organisations which use local labour wherever they do business face substantial changes in their work force compared to that of their home countries. They need to develop skills in handling the complexities of foreign markets and expatriates can help them to understand and manage these complexities.

Managing diversity

Matsushita's President, Yoichi Morishita, in 1994 said that 'to become a truly international company, we have to have diversity in top management'. That diversity is likely to take the form of host-country national and expatriate representation and participation in much of the management of organisations developing internationally. Where the national and foreign styles of management meet and maybe disagree, skill and sensitive handling are required. Each style has value but has to work in a complementary fashion for the organisation to be successful.

Head office and local centre will often have different expectations and priorities and rarely will the platitude 'think global, act local' be easy to implement. Hence there is a need to have expatriates who can cope with ambiguity and find ways to cope with conflicting requirements and still get things done.

Global opportunities and local responsiveness

Global organisations aim to be able to exploit knowledge on a world scale while at the same time being responsive to national needs and expectations. Expatriates can be a valuable resource in passing on the knowledge gained in the countries which have higher levels of research and development, a wider skill base and larger numbers of capable managers and professionals compared to those countries which lack these resources. They can also act as a conduit for providing information to the global organisation on the need for local responsiveness, the diverse market conditions and the social and political environment in which the local organisation has to operate.

Transnational managers

Research conducted by Banai and Harry (2002) suggests it is likely that globalisation and the need for well-educated managers and professional staff will lead to greater demands for cosmopolitan staff capable of operating effectively outside national and ethnocentric boundaries. These cosmopolitan staff will be employed to carry out specific tasks, perhaps over many years, but their long-term loyalty will be to themselves rather than to a particular organisation or country's interests unless there is a strong correlation between the individual's interests and that of the employer or state. They will be the mercenaries of the commercial world.

Some of these transnational managers will be employed to train host-country nationals but many will be employed to manage and work with the large numbers of other foreign workers who have become increasingly important to wealthy countries and global organisations.

Summary

Expatriates are an important part of international management. The management and motivation of this group is difficult because the world is becoming more complex and confusing. These staff and their families are at the front line between home and host-country expectations. They are required to bring sophisticated methods of working and apply them in less sophisticated environments. They have to deal day by day with the challenge of living and working in a country whose social culture and business expectations are quite different from that at home. The skills, attitudes and behaviours they develop are essential to the success of international organisations.

Discussion questions

1. What are the advantages, to an international organisation, of employing expatriates?

2. What challenges are an expatriate family likely to have when moving to a new location?

3. What are likely to be the issues facing the expatriate upon return to the parent country?

4. What is the role of the expatriate in localisation of the host country's workforce?

Closing Case Study:
Tradeco

Tradeco is a fictitious organisation made up of a composite of various companies. This type of international company exists in many parts of the world. Tradeco operates throughout the Gulf Cooperation Council (GCC) states. The company has a number of different activities including retailing, motor vehicle dealerships, small-scale manufacturing, agriculture and construction. The GCC operating companies have been purchased by a major international group, which has its head office in London, over the past 25 years with little synergy between activities and little strategic direction. Each operating company is intent only on maximising its own contribution to group profits. Where GCC government regulations prevent a foreign company owing 100 per cent of the shares a major regional family owned firm acts as the local partners.

Management of the companies is a mixture of host-country nationals and expatriates from Europe and South Asia. The majority of staff are foreign workers from South and South East Asia or from Egypt, Jordan, Lebanon and Sudan.

Some expatriate staff are permanent employees of Tradeco's parent. They are regularly moved from subsidiary to subsidiary, rarely spending more than three years in any one country and never more than ten years in the region. Other expatriate staff are employed on a contract basis to meet specific needs and some may have their contracts extended for a significant period of time. Eventually some are looked upon as being permanent Tradeco staff. Host-country managers are based only in one country and are permanent employees of the subsidiary in that country.

The parent company expatriate staff are paid a notional home-country salary with enhancements based on the perceived cost of living and hardship in the country to which they are posted. They enjoy certain privileges such as a pension paid in sterling at the age of 55, higher pay and status with housing in company-owned villas. They are paid in pounds sterling and have to change sufficient sterling to meet their local expenses. There are only 20 staff in this category throughout Tradeco, but there are 250 expatriates on a contract basis. These contract expatriates have no pension from the company but have an end of service benefit based on final salary, receive pay based on their country of origin (so that Indian managers receive less than Europeans but more than Sudanese). They are given a housing allowance to find their own accommodation and are paid in local currency, but have a complex currency protection scheme which pays a monthly supplement if their home-country currency fluctuates negatively in relation to the host-country currency.

The managers' different rates of pay and benefits lead to a great deal of unhappiness and jealousy which is having an adverse impact on teamworking and cooperation. The head office has instructed the human resources department to investigate the situation. The HR staff have found that local practice is to pay based on the home country of the expatriate staff and to pay host-country nationals the same as expatriate staff from Europe in some countries and the lower rate for expatriates from South Asia to the host-country nationals in other countries.

If Tradeco starts to pay all managers on the same basis they will find that if the pay and benefits are based on the parent's permanent expatriates their costs will increase substantially. If the company pays based on the contract expatriates from outside Europe and Asia they will not be able to attract and retain other expatriates or host nationals in some countries. Those expatriates who have been benefiting from the decline in their home currency will be reluctant to move to being paid in sterling which is the currency being given to the highest paid staff. The staff who have been looking forward to an end of service benefit to invest as they wish are not keen to have a sterling pension.

The company would provide housing for all managers in company owned or rented compounds. It is likely that cost savings could be made by negotiating with landlords and maintenance suppliers to provide housing and services more cheaply for many managers. That means that those who work together will live together and the staff will no longer be able to choose their own accommodation – saving some of the housing allowance if they wished.

One operating company wishes to appoint a general manager for its motor vehicle dealership. The parent company wants to have Assaf, one of their permanent expatriate staff, appointed because he had previously been the general manager of the dealerships in another GCC country. Assaf is a tough and demanding manager who succeeded in generating a 100 per cent increase in profit within one year. He did this by replacing most of his host-country managers with cheaper expatriates who were already trained and experienced in management of a motor vehicle dealership. Unfortunately the local authorities, especially the labour department, became upset as the sacked workers brought cases against the company.

The local press became full of letters and articles about the attitude of the company to local staff and its unwillingness to employ and train citizens. Foreign companies continued to buy vehicles from the dealership and so helped to maintain profits but other customers preferred not to buy. Eventually the government refused to renew Assaf's work permit and put restrictions on the employment of expatriates by the company.

Management of the present dealership is not keen to employ Assaf and has advertised for an expatriate to be employed on a contract basis. The HR department has drawn up a shortlist of candidates: Ahmed who ran a dealership in his home country for many years before being appointed head of sales of the same dealership in another GCC country; Arif who has not worked outside Europe before but is now the general manager of the largest dealership of the same vehicle manufacturer; Abdullah who is a citizen of the country and presently maintenance manager of a rival dealer.

Each candidate seems to meet the job's requirements although Mr Arif is the best fit. They are all seeking the same basic annual pay of $100,000. Mr Arif has three children aged between 8 and 16 who would move to the country with him along with his wife who would have to give up her job as a university lecturer. Although there are suitable schools in the country, the fees are $10,000 per child and the cost of business class airfares is another £3,000 each. The company pays the cost of school fees and airfares for its employees. Mr Arif has also requested a bigger house than his predecessor because of his larger family. The other candidates are married with dependent children.

The HR manager believes that the family circumstances should not be an influence on the decision about which candidate to appoint. As Mr Arif is the best of the candidates he should be appointed. The managing director is reluctant to pay over 40 per cent extra to have Arif compared with his predecessor. However the MD is quite prepared to have Assaf if he can increase profits by 50 per cent and never mind what the local authorities might think of the methods of achieving this.

Closing case study questions

1. What are the advantages and disadvantages to the expatriate of standardising the pay and benefits of the management staff?

2. Should expense of an expatriate family be considered when selecting suitable staff?

3. Should ability to work with host-country staff be a key part of the expatriate's job?

4. How could Tradeco manage the localisation process more effectively?

Annotated further reading

Bedi, H. (1991) *Understanding the Asian Manager*. London: Allen and Unwin.
This book gives considerable insights into the minds of Asian host-country nationals.

Brewster, C. (1991) *The Management of Expatriates*. London: Kogan Page.
The key text on expatriates especially the management of those seconded from a parent organisation.

Cohen, E. (1977) 'Expatriate communities', *Current Sociology* 24(3): 5–129.
This article is an important sociological text giving considerable insights into the minds of expatriates.

International Journal of Human Resource Management.
An excellent source of up-to-date articles on expatriates and their management.

References

Banai, M. and **Harry, W.** (2002) 'From the expatriate to the transnational'. Paper presented at European Institute for Advanced Studies in Management workshop on Strategic Human Resource Management, at Linz International Management Academy, Austria, 11 April.

Bedi, H. (1991) *Understanding the Asian Manager.* London: Allen and Unwin.

Brewster, C. (1991) *The Management of Expatriates.* London: Kogan Page.

Cohen, E. (1977) 'Expatriate communities', *Current Sociology* 24(3): 5–129.

Feldman, D. C. and **Bolino, M. C.** (1999) 'The impact of on-site mentoring on expatriate socialisation: a structural equation modelling approach', *International Journal of International Human Resource Management* 10(1): 54–71.

Florkowski, G. W. and **Fogel, D. S.** (1999) 'Expatriate adjustment and commitment: the role of host unit treatment', *International Journal of Human Resource Management* 10(5): 783–807.

Foster, N. (2000) 'The myth of the "international manager" ', *International Journal of Human Resource Management* 11(1): 126–42.

Gamble, J. (2000) 'Localization management in foreign invested enterprises in China: practical, cultural and strategic perspectives', *International Journal of Human Resource Management* 11(5): 883–903.

Harris, H. and **Brewster, C.** (1999a) 'The coffee machine system: how international selection really works', *International Journal of Human Resource Management* 10(3): 488–500.

Harris, H. and **Brewster, C.** (1999b) 'An integrative framework for pre-departure preparation', in C. Brewster and H. Harris (eds) *International HRM: Contemporary Issues in Europe.* London: Routledge.

Harry, W. (1996) 'High flying locals', *People Management* 11 July: 37.

Harry, W. (2001) 'Foreign workers: essential but not welcome', *Worldlink* April: 4–5.

Harzing, A.-W. (1995) 'The persistent myth of high expatriate failure rates', *International Journal of Human Resource Management* 6(2): 457–74.

Mendenhall, M. and **Oddou, G.** (1995) 'Expatriation and cultural adaptation', in T. Jackson *Cross-Cultural Management.* Oxford: Butterworth Heinemann. Chapter 9: 342–54.

Scullion, H. (1991) 'Why companies prefer to use expatriates', *Personnel Management* November: 32–5.

Selmer, J. (1998) 'Expatriation: corporate policy, personal intentions and international adjustment', *International Journal of Human Resource Management* 6(9): 996–1007.

Selmer, J., Toriorn, I. and de Leon, C. T. (1998) 'Sequential cross-cultural training for expatriate business managers: pre-departure and post-arrival', *International Journal of Human Resource Management* 9(5): 831–40.

Swaak, R. A. (1995) 'Expatriate failures', *Compensation and Benefits Review* November–December: 21–9.

PART 5

Taking stock

CHAPTER 14

Concluding case study:
The international manager's world

Wes Harry

Learning objectives

When you finish reading this chapter you should:

■ have an understanding of the complexity of the business environment in which international managers operate

■ understand that working internationally requires sensitivity to local norms and standards combined with determination to get things done

■ realise that decisions often have to be made between following head office instructions and undertaking what is going to be effective in the local situation

■ discover that successful international managers find ways of translating foreign ways of working into practical local solutions

Introduction

The case study given below is made up of a composite of typical organisational issues that an international manager will face. Although the companies and situations are fictional, all the issues are realistic and examples of those likely to be found by management in the international business environment.

The case study draws upon many of the subjects discussed in the earlier chapters. Readers are recommended to check with the relevant chapter if they wish to explore, in greater depth, the issues raised in the case study. A few questions are suggested at the end of the study but there are many situations described which could be used for other questions or to act as a focus for discussion groups.

Some of the points raised may seem controversial but these should help the reader to understand that international management can involve making decisions in difficult circumstances where there are no 'right' answers but often only a choice among 'least wrong' solutions.

Although the case study is based on countries of the Middle East, similar situations to those described arise in other parts of the world.

Tradeco

Tradeco is a trading company operating in the Gulf Cooperation Council region of the Middle East. It is active in retailing, motor vehicle dealerships, small-scale manufacturing, agriculture and construction. A major international group has purchased the GCC companies, over a period of 25 years. This international group has its head office in London. It tends to second the CEOs of the operating companies and of Tradeco itself from a cadre of British managers who can be posted anywhere within the group and who have general management skills rather than specialisms in a particular field of management or of industry.

Many of the individual companies have been in existence for a very long time and most have a well-respected image, in part due to their having been around for so long. Although the CEOs are seconded from the parent of Tradeco, most of the managers are locally employed on three-year, renewable contracts if they are expatriates and on open-ended contracts if they are host-country nationals.

There is not much synergy between the operating companies' activities and there has been little strategic direction. Each operating company aims to maximise its own contribution to group profits. At times the operating companies compete against each other, for example, the internet company competes against retail outlets in many countries. Where GCC government regulations prevent a foreign company from owning 100 per cent of the shares, Gulfco, a large regional family owned firm acts as the local partner.

Gulfco

Gulfco has been in existence almost as long as many of the Tradeco companies. It was originally established by an Arab merchant about 60 years ago. The founder still enjoys being involved in the business and makes regular visits to facilities, often arriving unannounced to make a snap inspection. Managers fear these visits because the founder is known to take quick on-the-spot decisions without necessarily considering the current business environment.

Gulfco is present in all the GCC countries. Where it is not the local partner of Tradeco, it operates its own businesses, many of which are similar to those of Tradeco. The company has close ties to senior government officials in each country in which it operates. This helps smooth the way past various regulations and rules that can often be obstacles to foreign firms. As a national company it is able to bid for contracts and win them even if its prices are higher, by up to 5 per cent, than non-national companies.

Gulfco has been undergoing significant changes in personnel and power during the past three years. The head of the family is now in his eighties and has gradually been handing over responsibility to younger members of the family. The second generation who are in their forties and fifties have been managing parts of the business in a traditional way which has not been very different from the way their father worked. However, the third generation in their twenties and thirties have very different ideas, based partly on their education which has tended to be in the United States.

Gradually the younger generation is trying to bring in professional management techniques such as appointment and promotion on merit. The older managers think that loyalty and connections or influence are of more importance than apparent ability. Long-serving employees or those with connections, known as wasta, are able to circumvent the policies of Gulfco and gain advantages over other employees and their supervisors.

One young manager has recently tried to dismiss a long-serving employee who has been turning up late for work or not coming in at all during the previous six months. The employee went to see the manager's uncle and persuaded him that he should be allowed to keep his job and that his timekeeping was not to be monitored. The employee explained that he had a teenage daughter who had to be taken to school and collected during working hours.

The older managers consider it their right to exercise power and feel that policies and rules are impersonal and often inhumane. They prefer to look at the individual's circumstances before they make a decision. So if the person has a daughter to be married or a son to be educated he will deserve a pay increase or bonus irrespective of his work performance. The younger workers who have lesser expenses should be paid less and when they later have more expenses they will deserve greater reward.

Gulfco Arab staff are all Sunnis, that is they follow the main form of Islam. But in a number of the GCC states there are sizeable numbers of followers of the Shia form of Islam. The owners refuse to employ Shias. This sometimes leads to conflict with staff of Tradeco which has a few senior managers who are Shia. The Shias tend to try to work in international firms where they consider they will be rewarded on merit and not discriminated against. The government departments of the GCC states are dominated by Sunnis and this also causes some problems to Tradeco's business activities.

Governments

The GCC governments have been introducing commercial laws and regulations that have changed the nature of the relationship between Tradeco and the states in which it operates. Previously, having a foreign parent or strong local sponsor was all that was needed to keep government officials from interfering in business activities. Now the GCC states are coming under pressure from the United States and European Union governments concerned that Tradeco's textile manufacturing plants are being used to avoid import quotas in some countries and that the retail outlets are selling pirated computer software.

In the GCC countries, regulations state that all goods must be labelled in Arabic and their country of origin; the origin of all parts must be clearly stated and accepted by the relevant government departments. These regulations are extremely onerous if they are applied rigorously so all companies try to find ways of persuading officials to be generous in their application. Wasta is a crucial way for persuading these officials, but in return they expect favours such as discounts on goods or jobs for their relations.

All the GCC governments are also concerned to create employment for their citizens so they are imposing quotas on the number of expatriates who can be employed. Some countries are forbidding foreigners to hold particular posts such as human resource manager. Gaining employment permits becomes more and more difficult. The governments are also discouraging long-term expatriates by refusing to renew employment permits for those who have been resident for more than 20 years. Labour law in most countries now says that employment must first be offered to host-country nationals, then to citizens of other GCC countries, then other Arabs, and finally to other nationalities.

Workforce

The composition of Tradeco's workforce has changed in the last decade. Prior to that time most managers were British and most supervisors and skilled workers from India with a few from Pakistan. Now there are several host-country nationals in managerial posts along with Australians and South Africans. The middle management has newer and younger Palestinians and Lebanese and long-serving Indians. The skilled technical staff are often Filipino or Sri Lankan. Although Indians and Pakistanis still dominate in the unskilled positions, there are now more Bangladeshis and Nepalese employed in these types of jobs.

Along with a diversity of workers there is also a diversity of rates of pay. The western expatriates generally receive higher pay than the nationals who in turn receive more than the Indians, with Nepalese at the bottom of the pay levels – even when they perform the same work as other nationalities.

Management takes the view that market forces in the worker's home country should determine rates of pay, not the market rate for a job within the host country. Therefore the job being done is not the basis for pay. Managers try to recruit as many workers as they can from the low wage countries and put up with poor productivity, poor morale and high rates of turnover as necessary costs of using cheaper labour. Strict rules and regulations are applied to the workers to keep them under control.

Labour grievances

In all the GCC countries except one, strikes and labour disputes, apart from those handled through the local labour office, are illegal. The workers can in theory take a complaint to the labour office but in practice they are unlikely to have a complaint upheld, especially against a local company.

Many low paid workers have to pass on a substantial percentage of their salaries to the recruitment agent who arranged a job for them. In the construction industry salaries are as low as US$5 a day so there is not much surplus to pay these agents. However, even with these low rates of pay workers compete for these jobs because they have no other means of feeding their families back home.

The less reputable employers than Tradeco mistreat their workers by providing poor living accommodation, poor food, long working hours and late payment of wages. These malpractices enable those employers to undercut Tradeco when bidding for contracts or providing services.

Tradeco is finding it difficult to compete with unscrupulous employers even with its economies of scale, technology and organisational ability. So it is seeking ways of persuading government officials to be more rigorous in applying labour law and to revise the laws to reflect higher international standards and expectations. But many of the employers who exploit their workers have strong influence with governments and their officials.

Business organisation

The head office has recently decided to organise its activities in business streams rather than by geographical area. This means that there are no longer country managers, but now each business will report to a regional business manager. These business streams are retailing, motor vehicle dealerships, manufacturing, agriculture and construction. Head office managers are convinced that this type of organisation will enable Tradeco to maximise its competitive advantage in each business activity.

The change has led to great resistance from the country managers who were used to having wide responsibility within their geographical area. Now managers report directly to a business manager in London, who has responsibility for an activity rather than to the country or regional manager.

The family members of Gulfco are convinced that the new business stream style of organisation has been developed to reduce their power and to hide profits from them. They are very suspicious, especially as some of Tradeco's activities are seen as harmful to their interests. A feeling is developing that Tradeco gains more from the relationship than does Gulfco.

Construction company

One of the business streams, construction, has entered a strategic partnership with Conco, a French construction company which has access to offset funds from a series of military supply contracts to GCC governments. Tradeco and Conco have recently bid successfully against Gulfco to build a new airport terminal building in a Gulf state in which the Gulfco family is not their partner. This has caused stress in the relationship between Tradeco and Gulfco. Rumours are now circulating that the Conco board of directors is keen to buy the construction arm of Tradeco.

Although the board of Conco is thought to see useful fits between their business and the construction business of Tradeco, there are difficulties on the ground between the French and British management. The French expect to exercise much more central control than the British are used to. The French site managers wait for direction from Paris whereas the British site staff are used to having a great deal of authority delegated to them and having their results rather than their activities monitored.

The French managers find it difficult to deal with the Indian and Arab managers and staff who tend to cover up problems and say yes to any question rather than drawing attention to problems or bad news. The French have not yet found a way to ask a question in a non-threatening way or one which does not encourage people to say yes or to put an optimistic tone into their answer. Many staff are seen as reluctant to take responsibility for their actions and seem to trust that in the end everything will work out right.

An issue which demonstrates this is in the attitude to pollution and damage to the environment. The foremen and other supervisors are content to have waste dumped in any convenient location. They appear to believe that it is not their country, they are not well treated by the government and its officials so why should they care for the countryside. It is much easier, faster and cheaper to dump in the desert rather than have to go to a municipal site and have to deal with an official who will monitor what is being deposited and make a charge for the service.

Retail business

The retail business of Tradeco is keen to expand through internet sales and has constructed a virtual mall mainly selling books, ladies' and men's fashion items, children's clothes, sports goods, CDs and jewellery. These goods are supplied from a free trade area in the northern Gulf to customers throughout the GCC.

Advertising is through onscreen internet sites arranged through browsers and newspaper adverts in the Arabic and English media with occasional television adverts on the main Arabic, Indian and English channels.

Although in theory most goods can move without customs duty within the GCC, there are different opinions among government officials and frequently duty is charged on items which customers thought they had paid for in full. There is no standardisation of censorship so severe problems have arisen when goods are sent to some countries that restrict import of material which is fully acceptable in other GCC countries. These problems have arisen with CDs as well as books.

A local newspaper has been running a series of articles on child labour and drawn attention to the fact that most of the sports goods being sold by Tradeco are produced by children in Silkot in Pakistan. The buyers in Pakistan have argued that if the children are not employed then their families will not have enough income to feed themselves. If Tradeco buys sports goods elsewhere it will have to buy more expensive products and its competitors will buy cheaply from the suppliers who use child labour.

There have been quality problems with some sports goods, fashion items and jewellery in that many customers have been refusing to accept goods or have returned them after a few days. Some of the problems appear to arise from the description of the item not being accurate (at least in the opinion of the customer). It is suspected that some customers are trying out or even using the items for a few days and then rejecting them.

Sometimes customers claim not to have received the items or to have returned them but the postal authorities are unable to confirm this. These are then treated as lost in transit. When customers find out from friends that Tradeco's internet service is unable to keep track of the goods dispatched, the number of complaints seems to rise, suggesting that many claims are spurious. Even if it seems clear that the claim is fraudulent, Tradeco has little chance of successfully pursuing the customer in another country.

The range of problems confronting the internet service is causing Tradeco to consider withdrawing from the market. Already the losses have been substantial but it is difficult to be sure who is responsible for the actions which led to the problems. The purchasing staff, the inventory control and warehousing and despatch staff all report to the director of administration in London. The marketing staff report to the regional head of marketing and the internet management report to the director of retail operations (Africa and Middle East) in London.

Performance management

Tradeco's head office HR staff have started a new initiative to have standardised performance management systems linked to performance-related pay. They see the key to success in business as making the best use of human resources. In order to identify those who are the contributors, a new individual performance appraisal system has been designed.

The system is based on individual performance and contrition. Twice a year all staff are required to agree business objectives and are then judged on their achievement of these objectives. The objectives must align with the business stream's plans and the results are coordinated within the HR department in London. The achievement of the objectives has a significant impact on the person's pay. There will now be no increases in basic pay but incentive pay can be up to 50 per cent of the staff's salary.

In the past there was no incentive pay but salary increases were based on a variety of factors, some of which have been discussed earlier. Broadly, the amount of money available for increases was based on the success of the business in generating profit. With the break-up of the country-based businesses and the move to business streams, it has become less easy to fix rates of increase for groups in a particular location. So this has aided the move to paying for individual contribution.

Included in the system is 360-degree feedback from subordinates as well as supervisors. If the subordinate does not give a high rating to the supervisor, his incentive bonus is adversely impacted. Many staff have objected to their juniors having a say in their pay. There have already been allegations of staff agreeing amongst themselves to give poor reports on successful but unpopular bosses. Some teams have become competitive between each other and try to minimise the performance of those they think might get higher than average incentive bonuses.

Despite these setbacks, Tradeco's head office is convinced that standardisation is necessary and that the managers and staff will have to work within the global system or leave the company.

Discussion questions

1. What are the main advantages and disadvantages of using wasta?

2. Should governments encourage the employment of cheap foreign labour rather than local citizens?

3. What type of problems might internet companies face when providing services across borders?

4. Is using child labour always a bad practice for a company?

5. Should pay always be determined by individual performance?

Abstracts of case studies on the website

Introduction

The book's website offers, among other things, two real-life European case studies, one concerning a cross-border alliance and the other a cross-border acquisition. The cases examine different managerial issues but have in common a multicultural, multinational settings. You will read below the abstracts of these cases. The full texts and the respective discussion questions are found at: www.booksites.net/tayeb.

Case 1: Dandy Chewing Gum
Development of the Dandy–KGFF relation

Svend Hollensen and Anna Marie Dyhr Ulrich

Abstract

The Danish chewing gum manufacturer Dandy (www.dandygroup.com) produces about 30,000 tonnes of chewing gum per year. They sell to over 80 countries with an annual turnover of DKK1.6 billion (1999). Dandy's general core competence lies in the coating process of the dragée chewing gum pieces. Dandy develops, produces and markets its own brands: STIMOROL®, V6® and DIROL®.

Cooperations and networks are one of the ways forward for Dandy. That is why they have entered partnership agreements with a series of large international companies for the production and distribution of chewing gum. Dandy's first strategic alliance was with the American-owned Kraft General Foods France (KGFF) which had an almost monopolistic position in France. KGFF's chewing gum brand, Hollywood, represented 80 per cent of the market whereas Dandy's Stimorol represented a market share of 7 per cent. KGFF was in a strong position for sticks (the 'oblong' chewing gum), but for dragées it had a rather old-fashioned production technology. Dandy's dilemma was that their market share increased only a little because the big chains in France would demand large amounts for the listing of Stimorol; i.e. you have to pay money (besides the usual price) in order to continue to be favourably represented on the retail chains' shelves. The consequence was that Dandy's subsidiary company in France could barely make any profits.

In September 1986 Dandy was contacted by KGFF's parent company via a company agent. Kraft General Foods had noticed Dandy's special core competence in dragées and wished to discuss the possibilities of cooperation. When the representatives from Dandy heard that, things started to develop. Six months and a number of meetings with KGFF later, the headings of the contract between the two companies had been defined and were ready to be discussed. In 1988 the ultimate contract between Dandy and KGFF was ready to be signed. Of course the cooperation with KGFF was not unproblematic. If you consider the different sizes of the two companies, Dandy's essential interest was to maintain and develop the alliance. (Economically, the agreement meant relatively a great deal for Dandy.) Therefore, Dandy made much of pointing out how KGFF would benefit from the cooperation.

The relation with KGFF being a reality, apart from KGFF's 2,000 tons per year of the Hollywood brand, Dandy sold approximately 900 tons of Stimorol per year to the French market through KGFF's distribution facilities. Stimorol's market share in France developed positively, though the Dandy sales subsidiary in France was closed down. Further, the relation with KGFF was the beginning of Dandy entering into new relations with other chewing gum producers around the world.

Case 2: Fenix – European management revisited

Cordula Barzantny

Abstract

This case study deals with the influence of national culture on a cross-cultural management setting in Europe. It is based on a real-life case of cross-border acquisition with the aim of 'Europeanising' a manufacturing business. It therefore illustrates many of the problems faced by multinational corporations (MNCs) in the international, cross-cultural field of global management. The acquisition by an originally German MNC concerned a French high-technology manufacturing plant with exposure to competitive international markets. The initial question for the French subsidiary was how to deal with the new shareholders, the German headquarters, in order to find a balance between necessary independence and useful integration. For the acquiring headquarters, the question was one of integrating the new French subsidiary into the global corporation.

One aim of the case is to show how unnecessary upheaval with negative effects on business and performance can be avoided. It also aims to reveal some key factors of success in European cross-cultural management. Furthermore, the case seeks to develop skills in adapting to different cultural environments, managing effectively in an intercultural context and raising awareness of possible problems in cross-cultural merger and acquisition integration, notably in the field of organisational behaviour (OB) and human resources management (HRM). The case attempts to build an understanding of how national culture influences management styles, communication patterns and organisational structures.

The case is conceived in a modular way: parts of it can be used separately and therefore it is adaptable to various audiences (MBA to executive) and different time constraints.

Coventry University

Index